LIGHT FROM JEWISH LAMPS

BOOKS BY RABBI SIDNEY GREENBERG

Inspirational Essays

Adding Life to Our Years
Finding Ourselves
Hidden Hungers
Say Yes to Life
Lessons for Living

Anthologies

A Treasury of Comfort
The Bar Mitzvah Companion (Co-editor)
A Modern Treasury of Jewish Thoughts
A Treasury of the Art of Living
Teaching and Preaching: High Holiday Bible Themes
   Volume 1: Rosh Hashanah
   Volume 2: Yom Kippur

Youth Prayer Books

Siddurenu (Co-editor)
High Holiday Services for Children
Sabbath and Festival Services for Children
A Contemporary High Holiday Service (Co-editor)
The New Model Seder (Co-editor)
Junior Contemporary Prayer Book for the High Holidays (Co-editor)

Prayer Books

Contemporary Prayers and Readings
   for the High Holidays, Sabbaths, and Special Occasions

Likrat Shabbat: Worship, Study, and Song
   for Sabbath and Festival Evenings (Co-editor)

The New Mahzor for Rosh Hashanah and Yom Kippur (Co-editor)

LIGHT FROM JEWISH LAMPS

A Modern Treasury
of Jewish Thoughts

Compiled and Edited by
SIDNEY GREENBERG

Introduction by
CHARLES ANGOFF

JASON ARONSON INC.
Northvale, New Jersey
London

In memory of my parents,
Sadie and Morris Greenberg.
They kept the lamps burning
and transmitted the light.

ISBN 0-87668-918-7

Library of Congress Catalog Number 86-71270

Acknowledgements

The editor wishes to convey, first, his profound appreciation to Mrs. Albert Wanicur. It was she who graciously offered her typing services both for the manuscript and for the voluminous correspondence necessary to obtain the permissions listed below. Her availability for this huge assignment provided the editor with the encouragement needed to begin the anthology. Her competence and loyalty enabled him to see it through.

Mrs. Herman Leff, the editor's secretary while the book was in preparation, also earned his warm gratitude for her helpfulness in many important ways.

The editor's good friend, Dr. Melvin A. Bernstein of Alfred University, made many valuable suggestions and criticisms. The book is a better one for his kindness.

Finally, the editor wishes to acknowledge with sincere gratitude the permission granted him by the following publishers and authors to quote from their publications :

Abelard-Schuman, Ltd., for quotations from *The Earth Is the Lord's* by Abraham J. Heschel.

Rabbi Morris Adler, for passages from his writings.

Rabbi Jacob B. Agus, for passages by Abraham Isaac Kuk from *The Banner of Jerusalem*, Bloch Publishing Co., Inc.

The *American Mercury*, for quotations from " The Education of a Jew " by Michael Blankfort.

Rabbi David Aronson, for quotations from *The Jewish Way of Life*, National Academy for Adult Jewish Studies ; for a passage from "Occasional Talks " delivered before the Rabbinical Assembly of America.

Dr. Max Arzt, for a passage from an address delivered before the Rabbinical Assembly of America.

The *Atlantic Monthly*, for a quotation from " I Kept My Name " by David L. Cohn.

Beacon Press, Inc., for a quotation from *A Dreamer's Journey* by Morris Raphael Cohen.

Rabbi Leonard I. Beerman, for " Religion : Something to Be Discovered."

Behrman House, Inc., for passages from *Anthology of Modern Jewish Poetry* edited by Philip M. Raskin ; for quotations from *Rebirth* edited by Ludwig Lewisohn ; for quotations from *Some Aspects of Rabbinic Thought* by Solomon Schechter ; for a passage from *Sabbath Queen* by A. A. Steinbach.

Bloch Publishing Co., Inc., for quotations from *Authorized Daily Prayer Book* edited by Joseph H. Hertz ; for a passage from *Justice to the Jew* by Madison C. Peters ; for quotations from *A Book of Jewish Thoughts* edited by Joseph H. Hertz.

B'nai B'rith, for a quotation from " Jewish Contributions to Civilization " by James W. Parkes in *Jewish Heritage*.

The Bobbs-Merrill Co., Inc., for a quotation from *Going Home* by Ernest Harthern.

Central Conference of American Rabbis, for quotations from *Blessings and Praise* ; for a passage from *Report of Commission on Social Justice*.

Rabbi Beryl D. Cohon, for a quotation from *Water Spilt on the Ground* ; for a quotation from *Conference Sermon*.

Columbia University Press, for a passage from *Social and Religious History of the Jews* by Salo W. Baron.

Commentary, for a quotation from " Can We Moderns Keep the Sabbath ? " by Emanuel Rackman.

Contemporary Jewish Record, for a quotation from " The Way to Avoid Jewish Self-Hatred " by Kurt Lewin.

Congress Weekly, for a quotation from " Notes on Jewish Survival " by Menachem Boraisha ; for a quotation from " These Days of Holiness " by Jacob S. Minkin ; for a quotation from " Why Study Hebrew ? " by Samuel M. Blumenfield ; for a quotation from " Reflections on the Tercentenary " by Abraham Duker.

Crown Publishers, Inc., for passages from *A Treasury of Comfort* edited by Sidney Greenberg ; for passages by Meir b. Isaac Nehorai, Arthur Schnitzler, and Hayyim Zhitlovsky from *A Treasury of Jewish Quotations* edited by Joseph L. Baron.

The Devin-Adair Co., for a passage from *The Religions of Democracy* by Louis Finkelstein, J. Elliot Ross, and William Adams.

Rabbi Samuel H. Dresner, for " What Is Compassion ? "

Ambassador Abba Eban, for excerpts from his addresses.

Wm. B. Eerdmans Publishing Co., for a passage from *Knight's Master Book of New Illustrations* by Walter B. Knight.

Farrar, Straus and Cudahy, Inc., for a quotation from *Tiger Beneath the Skin* by Zvi Kolitz ; for quotations from *The Sabbath* by Abraham J. Heschel ; for quotations from *Judaism and Modern Man* by Will Herberg ; for quotations from *The American Jew* by Ludwig Lewisohn ; for quotations from *God in Search of Man* by Abraham J. Heschel.

Rabbi Solomon B. Freehof, for a passage from his " Tercentenary Address " on the program *Message of Israel*.

Louis Golding, for quotations from *The Jewish Problem*, Penguin Books, Ltd.

Rabbi Israel M. Goldman, for an excerpt from an address delivered before the Rabbinical Assembly of America.

Rabbi Albert S. Goldstein, for selections from his Temple Bulletin.

Rabbi Herbert S. Goldstein, for a quotation from *Letter on Prayer*.

Dr. Israel Goldstein, for " An Affirmation. "

Dr. Robert Gordis, for passages from *The Jew Faces a New World*, Behrman House, Inc. ; for passages from *Judaism for the Modern Age*, Farrar, Straus and Cudahy, Inc. ; for a passage from *The Ladder of Prayer*, National Academy for Adult Jewish Studies ; for " Ways to Destroy Judaism " from his Synagogue Bulletin.

Dr. Simon Greenberg, for quotations from *Living as a Jew Today*, Behrman House, Inc. ; for a quotation from an address delivered before the United Synagogue of America.

Rabbi Harry Halpern, for " What Is Faith ? "

Harcourt, Brace & Co., Inc., for a quotation from *The Conduct of Life* by Lewis Mumford.

Harper and Brothers, for quotations from *Crisis and Decision* and *A Rabbi Takes Stock* by Solomon Goldman.

Harvard University Press, for a passage from *Judaism, in the First Centuries of the Christian Era, Volume I*, by George Foote Moore.

Hebrew Publishing Co., for quotations from *A Treasury of Judaism* edited by Philip Birnbaum.

Rabbi James Heller, for " To Be a Jew."

Rev. John Haynes Holmes, for a slightly condensed version of his lecture " Christianity's Debt to Judaism — Why Not Acknowledge It ? "

Hutchinson and Co., for a quotation from *Anti-Semitism Through the Ages* edited by Count Richard Coudenhove-Kalergi, translated by A. S. Rappaport.

The *Jewish Frontier*, for quotations from " To the Young Jewish Intellectuals " by Ludwig Lewisohn and " Jewish Culture and Education in the Diaspora " by Hayim Greenberg.

Jewish Publication Society of America, for a quotation from *Blessed Is the Match* by Marie Syrkin ; for a quotation from *Germany's Step-Children* by Sol Liptzen ; for quotations from *Jewish Contributions to Civilization* by Joseph Jacobs ; for a quotation from *Songs of a Wanderer* by Philip M. Raskin ; for quotations from *Stars and Sand* by Joseph L. Baron.

The Jewish Reconstructionist Foundation, for a quotation from *Why We Should Survive* by the Reconstructionist Editors ; for passages by

Robert Gordis and Mordecai M. Kaplan in *The Reconstructionist;* for "Where God Is Found," "The Majesty of God," and "The Pious Man" by Abraham J. Heschel and "What We Want from Judaism" from the *Reconstructionist Prayer Book for Sabbaths and Festivals.*

Judaism, for a passage from "Religious Trends in American Jewry" by Will Herberg.

Dr. Leo Jung, for quotations from *The Jewish Library — Third Series* edited by Leo Jung; for "The Kaddish."

Horace M. Kallen, for quotations from *Judaism at Bay,* Bloch Publishing Co., Inc.

Dr. Mordecai M. Kaplan, for quotations from *Judaism as a Civilization,* Thomas Yoseloff, Inc.; for quotations from *The Meaning of God in Modern Jewish Religion,* Behrman House, Inc.; for quotations from *The Future of the American Jew,* The Macmillan Co.; for quotations from *Questions Jews Ask,* The Reconstructionist Press; for a quotation from *Education for Democracy,* Bureau of Publications, Teachers College, Columbia University.

Rufus Learsi, for a quotation from "Two Tercentennial Orations" in *Congress Weekly.*

Dr. Israel H. Levinthal, for quotations from *Judaism,* Funk and Wagnalls Co.

The Macmillan Co., for a quotation from *Jews in a Gentile World* edited by Isacque Graeber and Stewart Anderson Britt; for a quotation from *A History of the Inquisition in Spain,* Volume I, by Henry Charles Lea; for a quotation from *Judaism and the Modern Mind* by Maurice H. Farbridge.

Message of Israel, for quotations from a sermon by Joshua Loth Liebman.

Joseph Miller, for his paraphrase of Lincoln's "Gettysburg Address."

National Women's League of the United Synagogue of America, for a quotation from *The Jewish Home Beautiful* by Betty D. Greenberg and Althea O. Silverman.

Abraham A. Neuman, for quotations from *Landmarks and Goals,* Dropsie College Press.

Dr. Louis I. Newman, for passages from *The Hasidic Anthology* edited by Louis I. Newman in collaboration with Samuel Spitz, Bloch Publishing Co., Inc.

The New York Times, for an editorial "Abraham Krotoshinsky," April 19, 1919.

Pierre van Paassen, for a quotation from *Days of Our Years,* Hillman-Curl.

G. P. Putnam's Sons, for quotations from *Toward a Solution* by Israel Goldstein.

Random House, for passages by Cecil Roth and Salo W. Baron in *Great Ages and Ideas of the Jewish People* edited by Leo W. Schwarz.

Rabbi Samuel Ruderman, for " Cheated. "

St. Martin's Press, Inc., for a quotation from *Peace and War* by Guglielmo Fererro, translated by B. Pritchard.

Maurice Samuel, for quotations from *The Professor and The Fossil*, Alfred A. Knopf, Inc. ; for a quotation from *Jews on Approval*, Liveright Publishing Corp. ; for a quotation from an article in *Jewish Digest* ; for his translation of " If Thou Wouldst Know " by Chaim Nachman Bialik.

Schocken Books, Inc., for quotations from *The Essence of Judaism* by Leo Baeck ; for quotations from *In Time and Eternity* edited by Nahum H. Glatzer ; for a quotation from *Tales of the Hasidim* by Martin Buber ; for quotations from *Israel and the World* by Martin Buber.

Charles Scribner's Sons, for quotations from *Man's Quest for God* by Abraham J. Heschel.

Dr. Abba Hillel Silver, for quotations from *The World Crisis and Jewish Survival*, Richard R. Smith, Inc. ; for quotations from *Religion in a Changing World*, Richard R. Smith, Inc. ; for quotations from *Where Judaism Differed*, The Macmillan Co. ; for an address delivered before the Central Conference of American Rabbis.

Rabbi Morris Silverman, for " God Is King," " The Old Prayerbook," and " Kol Nidre " in *High Holiday Prayer Book* edited by Rabbi Morris Silverman, Prayer Book Press ; for passages by Robert Gordis, Abraham J. Heschel, Louis Finkelstein, Simon Greenberg, David Aronson, Waldemar Haffkine, Max Arzt, Moses Gaster, Israel H. Levinthal, and Abraham Isaac Kuk in *Sabbath and Festival Prayer Book* edited by Rabbi Morris Silverman, The United Synagogue of America and the Rabbinical Assembly.

Rabbi William B. Silverman, for three selections from his Temple Bulletin.

Simon and Schuster, Inc., for a quotation from *The Story of Philosophy* by Will Durant ; for quotations from *Peace of Mind* by Joshua Loth Liebman.

Rabbi Elias L. Solomon, for a quotation from *The Message of Judaism*.

Soncino Press, for quotations from *The Pentateuch and Haftorahs* edited by Joseph H. Hertz ; for quotations from *Speeches, Articles and Letters of Israel Zangwill* edited by Maurice Simon.

Shalom Spiegel, for a quotation from *Hebrew Reborn*, The Macmillan Co.

Edith Steinberg, for permission to quote from the following works by

Milton Steinberg : *The Making of the Modern Jew*, The Bobbs-Merrill Co., Inc. ; *Basic Judaism*, Harcourt, Brace and Co., Inc. ; *A Believing Jew*, Harcourt, Brace and Co., Inc.

Union of American Hebrew Congregations, for quotations from *The Small Sanctuary* by Solomon B. Freehof ; for a quotation from *Judaism : A Way of Life* by Samuel S. Cohon ; for a quotation from *Humanitarianism of the Laws of Israel* by Jacob S. Raisin ; for quotations from *Jewish Ethics* by Samuel Schulman ; for a quotation from *The Jewish Idea of God* by Samuel S. Cohon ; for quotations from *Judaism and Democracy* by Louis Witt ; for a quotation from *Judaism and International Peace* by Joseph S. Kornfeld ; for a quotation from *Post-Biblical Judaism, Its Spiritual Note* by Israel Bettan.

United Nations Educational, Scientific and Cultural Organization, for a quotation from *Jewish Thought as a Factor in Civilization* by Leon Roth.

The United Synagogue of America, for a quotation from " A Sprinkling of Saints " by Louis Finkelstein in *The United Synagogue Review*.

The Viking Press, Inc., for a quotation from *Anti-Semitism* by Hugo Valentin.

Henry H. Villard, for a quotation from *Fighting Year and Memoirs of a Liberal Editor* by O. G. Villard.

Meyer Waxman, for poems by Zalman Schneour and Zevi Maneh in *A History of Jewish Literature*, Volume IV, Bloch Publishing Co., Inc.

Rabbi Jacob J. Weinstein, for " Are Prayers Repetitious ? "

Trude Weiss-Rosmarin, for quotations from *Jewish Survival*, Philosophical Library, Inc.

Rabbi Joseph I. Weiss, for a quotation from *Strength in Grief*.

The World Publishing Company, for quotations from *What Is a Jew ?* by Morris N. Kertzer.

Zionist Organisation of America, for a quotation from *Brandeis on Zionism* ; for a quotation from *Hebrew : The Story of a Living Language* ; for quotations from the following articles which appeared in the *American Zionist* : " Hebrew Revival and Redemption " by Menachem Ribalow and " Troubled Intellectuals " by Charles Angoff.

Introduction

Something historic in the annals of American Jewry has taken place within the last generation. Well into the fat and fabulous twenties, it was the height of fashion among certain sections of young American Jewish intellectuals to look down upon Jewish culture both here and abroad as parochial, laden with obscurantism, far removed from the concerns of modern life. More than a decade before, Louis D. Brandeis and, somewhat later, Ludwig Lewisohn had startled these same intellectuals with their return to the Jewish fold and their proclamation, in effect, that Judaism and Americanism were closely related, and that Judaism was one of the glories of human history, ever vital and ever timely. But the civilized minority (a phrase coined by the master sneerer of them all, H. L. Mencken) persisted in keeping aloof from Jewish affairs. Dr. Morris R. Cohen of the College of the City of New York, one of the way-showers of these emancipated ones, gave them his blessing from his professorial chair and in the pages of the more advanced liberal weeklies.

Those, indeed, were bleak days for American Judaism. And they continued bleak into the Depression thirties. Yiddish and Anglo-Jewish publications, including newspapers and magazines, were, in the main, barely managing to exist. Their readers were chiefly older folks who were "still living in the past." Hebrew was the language of a minute and fanatical coterie. The membership of synagogues and temples was either stationary or declining. Jewish young men and women with literary talent seldom thought of drawing upon the Jewish experience here for their stories or novels or plays or poems. When they did it was either to lampoon Jewish people and customs, with almost no qualifications, as in *Haunch, Paunch and Jowl* and *I Can Get It for You Wholesale,* or to show them up as little better than proletarian slaves, as in *Jews Without Money.* Zionism continued to be, in the main, the obsession of a little band of impractical idealists, even when the Hitler madness rolled across Germany and then across the rest of Europe. Maurice Samuel, lay missionary of Judaism and Zionism to the intellectuals, was looked upon as something of a throwback to the days of the *maggidim.*

But then, for reasons that are not yet fully known and perhaps, as is usually the case with historical events, never will be — American participation in World War II and the establishment of the Republic of Israel could not have been the only causes — there was a complete reversal of thinking and orientation among intellectuals. The reversal was dramatic in intensity and on a scale so vast as to challenge comparison with any other similar event in our annals. This Grand Return of American Jewish intellectuals is still going on — and will continue for years. Undoubtedly it will affect our life on every plane in many profound ways. It may well place the Jewish community here in the very forefront of Jewish history for the next half century, second only to Israel. We may be entering a new epoch in Jewish history. For the first time Babylonia and Jerusalem (America and Israel) will be coequal centers of Jewish civilization. The Diaspora will, at long last, achieve full status.

Not only are the intellectuals coming back, the so-called common people are, too. They are finding spiritual refreshment in the whole complex of Jewish activities which had been alien to them for so long: synagogue attendance, participation in sisterhoods and brotherhoods and in community center and lodge affairs. And the children, influenced by the climate of emotion in the whole Jewish-American world, are displaying a pride in Jewishness that must be surprising (and satisfying) to their elders. Both young and old are reading more Jewish books and showing greater interest in the arts that rely for their inspiration or content on Jewish history, religion, or folklore. This interest is still far from being as widespread as it should be, but compared to what it was two decades ago, it is phenomenal.

Does all this represent a genuine revival of Judaism in America — using the word *Judaism* strictly as a word denoting a body of religious observances? Probably not. Years of immersion in non-Jewish "worldliness" do not vanish from the mind quickly. Are we then witnessing a genuine revival of Jewishness — using the word *Jewishness* in the broadest cultural sense? The evidence that we are is plentiful and mounting.

Alas, the leaders of the Jewish-American world are not fully alert to what is going on in their midst. It is not enough merely to be pleased with bulging congregations and with the increasing number of temples and synagogues and centers. The many new eager faces are looking for something that they are not always getting. They are seeking information about the essence of Judaism, they want to read about the world Jewish history and American Jewish history. They want to know the background of our customs. They want to know the significance of the various objects on and around the Torah, and what is behind the *aliyahs*. They want to know why Spinoza was excommunicated, and why Dr. Mordecai M. Kaplan, founder and leader of the Reconstructionist Movement, is considered by some a modern Maimonides, by others as little more than a follower of Dr. Isaac Mayer Wise, founder of American Reform Judaism, and by still others as a rank *apikores*. They want to know the basic ideas of the various factions of Zionism. They want to know whether the spreading day-school movement really makes sense in our democracy, or whether it isn't an unnecessary divisive force. They want to know even more fundamental things: What is a Jew? Precisely Who or What is the Jewish God? Can an intelligent man engage in prayer? Exactly what takes place in an act of prayer, and what does Jewish tradition say about it? What about *kashrut?* Should a modern man adhere to it? If so, how can the meaning and necessity of it be imparted to one's children?

There are many books that deal with one or another of these questions, but few of them are satisfactory from the point of view of writing or content. Many of the questions are dealt with largely in rabbinical journals. The rabbis, laden as they are with their institutional work, can hardly be expected to be full-time teachers as well. Clearly, what is needed now is a series of one-volume encyclopedias and anthologies, of varying depths and comprehensiveness, dealing with Jewish life on every important level. Some have already been published. One of the best is *Light from Jewish Lamps.* It answers many of the aforementioned questions, and it does so brilliantly. It seems to be especially addressed to those who have found life cold outside the Jewish fold, yet are still bewildered by their new Jewish environment. Rabbi Greenberg rightly assumes that his readers are troubled most by the abiding philosophical and religious questions: To Be or Not to Be a Jew, Judaism and the Jew, The Quest for God, Prayer: the Bridge Between Man and God. There are also sections defining the contours of our heritage and indicating what distinguishes it from other major faiths. There is a chapter entitled "Comfort in Sorrow" that should prove truly meaningful. There is a chapter entitled "Judaism and Democracy" that should give pride to all Jews who read it, and enlightenment to non-Jewish readers. There is a chapter boldly entitled "The Destiny of the Jew" that ambles pleasantly through the realms of prophecy and mysticism.

Rabbi Greenberg has arranged his anthology under proper and significant rubrics. He has had "the impoverished returning Jew in mind," and he has a fine insight into the precise areas of this Jew's intellectual impoverishment. He has not assumed too much or too little knowledge on the part of his reader, but always his aim has been to reveal "Judaism as an exalted way of life." One of the many pleasant things about *Light from Jewish Lamps* is that it is made up almost entirely of writings by modern Jewish thinkers, a very large number of them American. This adds an intimacy to the volume that it might otherwise lack. It also points up the wealth and depth of modern Jewish intellectual life. The past seventy-five or one hundred years may not have produced another Spinoza or Maimonides or Vilner Gaon, but they have produced men and women of considerable stature. And it is good that through Rabbi Greenberg's anthology, common Jewish readers, to borrow a phrase from the tradition of English literature, will become acquainted with the thinking of Hayim Greenberg, Milton Steinberg, Leo Baeck, Israel Friedlander, Trude Weiss-Rosmarin, Franz Rosenzweig, Simon Dubnow, Solomon Shechter, Ludwig Lewisohn, Harry A. Wolfson, Abba Hillel Silver, Maurice Samuel, Mordecai M. Kaplan, and dozens of others.

Rabbi Greenberg has not hesitated to include some selections from the work of such non-Jews as James W. Parkes, John Haynes Holmes, Ellsworth Huntingdon, and Leo Tolstoy. The forces of assimilationism are still powerful. One of its most celebrated proponents is Boris Pasternak, who says in *Doctor Zhivago* that he sees no sense in Jews holding on to their "outworn" traditions and suggests that they join Christianity. Boris Pasternak and his father knew Leo Tolstoy. There is no record that the father felt quite the same way as does his son. It is true that for a long stretch of his life he was something of a non-Jewish Jew, but toward the end he was on terms of friendship with several distinguished Jews, among them Chaim Weizmann. The son appears to persist in his assimilationist ideas. He (along with other assimilationists) might therefore be interested in reading what Leo Tolstoy, who was a non-Jew, had to say about Jews. Rabbi Greenberg quotes him as follows:

The Jew is that sacred being who has brought down from heaven the everlasting fire, and has illumined with it the entire world. He is the religious source, spring, and fountain out of which all the rest of the peoples have drawn their beliefs and their religions.

The Jew is the pioneer of liberty. Even in those olden days, when the people were divided into but two distinct classes, slaves and masters — even so long ago had the law of Moses prohibited the practice of keeping a person in bondage for more than six years.

The Jew is the pioneer of civilization. Ignorance was condemned in olden Palestine more even than it is today in civilized Europe. . . . The Jew is the emblem of eternity. He whom neither slaughter nor torture of thousands of years could destroy, he whom neither fire nor sword nor inquisition was able to wipe off from the face of the earth, he who was the first to produce the oracles of God, he who has been for so long the guardian of prophecy, and who transmitted it to the rest of the world — such a nation cannot be destroyed. The Jew is everlasting as is eternity itself.

CHARLES ANGOFF

Contents

Editor's Preface to the New Edition

Before I reread the lengthy preface I wrote for the first edition, I fully expected that I would be prompted to either update the original or discard it in favor of a new one. To my pleasant surprise, I found no justification for either. The quarter century that has elapsed since this book originally appeared has demonstrated that the motivations for its initial publication are still operative, and that the need for this volume is undiminished. Indeed, in many respects the intervening years have served to deepen the need for *Light from Jewish Lamps*.

I am therefore grateful to the publisher, Jason Aronson, who has made this book available once again to the reading public. A new generation of readers — Jewish and non-Jewish — deserves the opportunity to acquaint itself with the essence of the Jewish identity, the saga of Jewish destiny, and the content of the Jewish heritage. A deeper understanding of these dimensions of the Jewish experience can only be a source of enrichment and blessing.

It is in this hope that this book is offered to the reader.

SIDNEY GREENBERG
Temple Sinai
Dresher, Pennsylvania

Editor's Preface

In recent years, a revolution of impressive dimensions has taken place within the American Jewish community. The flight from Judaism has been arrested, and, to an appreciable extent, the process has been reversed. Parents who had consciously discarded much of their spiritual and cultural baggage in an effort to facilitate their exodus from Jewish life have lived to see their children return to rebuild the ramparts they had forsaken. The amazing mushrooming of imposing synagogues, the constantly expanding enrollment in religious schools, the flourishing memberships in a host of fraternal, philanthropic, cultural, and Zionist-oriented organizations — these are only the most conspicuous indications that we are witnessing a phenomenon undreamed of a short generation ago. This dramatic turn of events has prompted one perceptive observer to remark that what the children of Jewish immigrants to America wished to forget, their grandchildren wish to remember.

Despite this heartening development, those who are vitally concerned with the spiritual health of the American Jew are quick to discern distressing symptoms that engender deep anxiety. Too often the reaffirmation of the Jewish identity has been accompanied by only the most nebulous understanding of the nature of that identity. What does it mean to be a Jew? What is the character of the heritage which is his? What duties does it spell out? What blessings does it offer? Why persist in perpetuating for oneself and one's children this Jewish label which bigots and madmen periodically convert into a target? These crucial questions have not been asked with the earnestness and the insistence they warrant. Small wonder, and a great pity, that the American Jew is largely innocent of the answers. Hermann Steinthal, a modern Jewish philosopher, delivered an indictment that contains a disquieting amount of truth when he said: "Judaism is rich, but the individual Jew is a beggar." This book was prepared with this impoverished returning Jew in mind.

Then there is the American Jew who in a Jewish sense never left home. He simply drifted away or outgrew his childhood training. Too frequently, his early religious education was ineffectively administered and prematurely terminated. While his intellectual, cultural, and emotional development proceeded apace, his spiritual growth remained stunted. When in maturity he attempts to draw upon his spiritual resources, is it to be marveled that he finds them hopelessly inadequate to fill his needs? A man might just as soon expect to be comfortable at forty in the suit he wore to his elementary school graduation, as expect his spiritual equipment of those years to serve his expanded questing and groping. Yet it is this unreasonable demand which all too often prompts the hasty judgment that Judaism is found wanting. A more informed acquaintance with our heritage will yield the awareness that it is abundantly rich in values, beliefs, and disciplines to make life a rewarding adventure for those who turn to it for guidance. A more intimate understanding of the accumulated wisdom and the penetrating insights of our constantly developing religious civilization will lend substance to the words of caution our sages sounded to those who are tempted to proclaim the bankruptcy of our heritage. "If it appears empty to you," they counseled, "the emptiness is but a reflection of your inner self." To help bridge the gap between Judaism as a child's religion and Judaism as an exalted way of life for the contemporary Jewish adult was another purpose that prompted the preparation of this book.

The editor's concern was also directed at large numbers of alienated and unaffiliated Jews who have yet to take the first faltering step homeward. The section entitled "To Be or Not to Be a Jew" is aimed most pointedly at them. This accounts for the priority given to this chapter in the arrangement of the book. For unless the Jew is first stimulated to join himself to his people, to share in their destiny and to participate actively in their corporate life, he will have scant motivation for reading on. Indeed, the balance of the book, with its recurrent reminders of the glory and the grandeur of his people's tradition and travail, may only serve to underscore the folly of his defection. He will continue reading at his own peril. Let him be forewarned. The magnetic appeal of the unfolding story of Judaism may prove well-nigh irresistible.

The editor anticipates that his largest reading audience will come from the ranks of the positive and committed Jews who are keenly aware of their need to know more intimately the saga of their people and their faith. It is they who are most alive to Judaism's capacity to buttress their morale, bolster their pride, and immunize them against the slanders and distortions of their detractors. They already have strong intimations of Judaism's ability to invest their lives, as it did their ancestors', with a quiet dignity and a sense of supreme worth. If they sincerely desire to know more fully the sources of their being and to tap immense reservoirs for creative and meaningful living, this book can help them in their quest.

It is also the earnest hope of the editor that this book will find its way into the hands of our non-Jewish fellow Americans who would like to have a better understanding of their Jewish neighbors and the creed that sets them apart. The many articles on Judaism which have appeared in the popular magazines in recent years are eloquent testimony to the growing curiosity of the general community about the faith of the Jewish minority in their midst. The non-Jewish reader will note that the authors who speak in this anthology do not assume the cringing posture of a suppliant, begging for the moldy crumbs of tolerance. Such demeanor is neither becoming to the bearers of a rich legacy nor flattering to the mentality of those they would influence. Tolerance is a grudging concession to our inferiors. True brotherhood emerges at the point of recognition that those who differ from us are our brothers withal. Should this book awaken within non-Jewish readers the inevitable realization that, despite the areas of appreciable difference in doctrine and practice, there exists an immense domain of kinship between the followers of Judaism and themselves, this awareness may help to raze the walls of prejudice, which too often make a mockery of our professions of democracy. At the very least, it may help to clear away some of the accumulated misconceptions and popular superstitions that have gained uncritical acceptance in the absence of genuine knowledge of the character of the Jew and his faith.

Now for a word about the nature of *Light from Jewish Lamps.* It differs from all existing Jewish anthologies in one vital respect. It consists almost exclusively of selections from modern writers. The editor studiously avoided the classic Jewish texts as such, resorting to them only infrequently when a quotation was needed to fortify a theme. Needless to say, this does not imply any lack of regard for the Bible, the Talmud, the Midrash — the truly imperishable fruits of the Jewish soul. But these have already been anthologized. More significantly, the editor's attention was deliberately focused on the modern period because he wished to bring to the reader those writers who have responded to the very conditions that confront him, who have spoken of the problems that engage his attention, and who have set down their thoughts in language that rings familiar. It is to be expected that in the selections from these writers, the reader will repeatedly encounter references to and quotations from the classic sources. But when he meets them, they will have been clothed in the contemporary idiom and woven into a pattern of modern thought.

An incidental, but by no means insignificant, advantage of concentrating on the modern spirits is the opportunity it offers to introduce to a wider reading public some of the most gifted writers and creative thinkers of the present day. Such authors as Maurice Samuel, Mordecai M. Kaplan, Hayim Greenberg, Milton Steinberg, Leo Baeck, Abba Hillel Silver, Trude Weiss-Rosmarin, Abraham J. Heschel, and Robert Gordis are anthologized in these pages. After the initial meeting with them it is hoped that the reader will be stimulated to seek the more intimate acquaintance that can only be cultivated by reading their works in the original.

Like many anthologies and more so than most, *Light from Jewish Lamps* is a reflection of the anthologist. Of necessity, it was his own sense of discrimination that ultimately prevailed. It was his conception of what is "positive" and "relevant" that guided his choices. He would be less than candid if he did not confess that others surveying the identical literary realm might very well have selected passages that more closely conform to their personal perspectives. If they are prompted by this effort to do so, Judaism can only be the richer for it.

The reader will note that certain writings of non-Jews are also considered here as "lights from Jewish lamps." Light from whatever source is welcome if it serves to illumine the pathways we follow.

The nervous times during which we live confer special urgency upon the Jew's task to rediscover his heritage and to relate himself to it with a sense of personal involvement. Ours are indeed dangerous days. The threat of total annihilation hovers above us. Within ourselves there is mounting evidence of lost mooring and uncertain anchorage. There is a growing recognition that, if we are to avoid the threatened atomization of man and his world, we will have to muster a spiritual power greater than the destructive forces we have unleashed. Where else will the Jew find that power if he seeks it not in his ancestral legacy?

Ours is a tradition ripe with the wisdom of years and strengthened by a thousand anvils. Judaism was a venerable faith before other powerful religions were born. For it, millions were innocently martyred. By it, millions more have nobly and compassionately lived. Despite its antiquity, it evidences none of the infirmities of age. It remains throbbing and dynamic, capable of sustaining its adherents and enriching with its unique genius the larger family of humanity. The Jew who will strive to possess that which he rightfully owns will come into an abundant inheritance which his fathers painstakingly stored up for him to enjoy. He may then exclaim in the words of Tennyson:

> We are the Ancients of the earth
> And in the morning of the times.

If *Light from Jewish Lamps* can spur him on in this vital venture, it will have extravagantly compensated its editor for the labor of love that went into its creation.

SIDNEY GREENBERG

1

To Be or Not to Be a Jew

The past of his (the Jew's) people is his personal
memory ; the future of his people is his personal task ;
the way of his people teaches him to will and
understand his true self.

MARTIN BUBER
Reden ueber das Judentum

The greatest happiness is to be that which one is.

THEODOR HERZL

To counteract fear and make the individual strong to
face whatever the future holds, there is nothing so
important as a clear and fully accepted belonging to
a group whose fate has a positive meaning.

KURT Z. LEWIN
Resolving Social Conflicts

The Pain And Indignity Of Jewish Dying

" Why do Jews insist on survival in the face of tremendous obstacles. and refuse to take the easier way out? "

The answer can be briefly stated, for it is simple. The Jewish people refuses to die, simply because it is alive. The instinct of self - preservation is the universal trait of all living beings. The tiniest microscopic animal struggles and claws after life, uninterested in such " philosophic " issues as whether the world wishes it to live or whether it " deserves " to survive. Nor is such indifference to philosophy limited to lower animals. No normal human being or group ever considers why it should continue. When the question is raised, it is a sign that the normal reaction is lacking and that we stand on the brink of suicide.

Actually, the question is meaningless, because life is the ultimate end, for which no additional justification is either necessary or possible. Every normal organism regards life, even under pain, as a good and annihilation as the greatest evil. In Spinoza's words, " No virtue can be conceived as prior to this virtue of endeavouring to preserve oneself."

The consciousness of millions of Jews the world over demonstrates that the Jewish group wishes to survive as such, no less than the Czechs or the English, the Catholics or the Mohammedans, without defense and without apology. The right of the Jewish people to survive into the future is rooted in its life in the present. It requires no other charter.

Strictly speaking, that should be sufficient and the rationale of Jewish survival could end here, but it is reinforced by several other momentous considerations. The most striking is the disastrous effect of Jewish escapism on the spirit of the modern Jew. Contemporary life is crowded with Jews of all types and schools of thought, in whom the process of group amnesia has progressed to various stages. For all their differences, most of these Jews, by accident of birth only, have one element in common. They are almost all pathetic figures, with heavy overtones of farce . . . .

Most assimilationist Jews are no more at home after the process is completed than before . . . . Their plight has been pictured by Robert Nathan in his novel, *There is Another Heaven,* which describes a group of Protestant pilgrims on their way to Paradise. Among them is a convert named Levy, whose generous assistance to foreign missions and all other church causes has won for him a deserved place in Heaven. Before the journey to the celestial abode is half complete, Levy realises that he is *in* the company, but not *of* it, and he voices his complaint, " It is not being kept out that hurts. It is being let in and made to feel out ! "

In fine, modern Jewry tends increasingly to oppose assimilation because there are too many examples of maladjustment in the lives of escapist J e w s. They are human beings without roots in any tradition, having no home for their souls, only temporary quarters, so long as they are on good behaviour. They find no strength or comfort in their religion, no intuition of victory in their people's history, no sense of solidarity with their brothers . . . .

Twenty-six hundred years ago, the prophet Hosea denounced the same tendency in the inhabitants of the Kingdom of Israel, whom he compared to an unturned cake, burnt to a cinder on one side and raw on the other. The simile is equally apt today. Assimilation means the loss of the only i d e n t i t y the Jew possesses, his own, and leaves him without any other individuality to take its place. He suffers the degradation and persecution which is the lot of his people, but he finds no compensation in the glory of the Jewish heritage. His life is tragic, but lacks the character and dignity of tragedy. He is comic, without the cheer and healing of comedy. It becomes increasingly clear that spiritual extinction is evil for the individual Jew. The evil lies not only in the fact that he would be Jewishly dead, but that there is so much pain and indignity in Jewish dying.

ROBERT GORDIS,
The Jew Faces the World

To continue to be whatever we happen to be makes in the long run for the greatest human happiness.

HARRY A. WOLFSON,
Escaping Judaism

The Tragedy Of Assimilation

What I understand by assimilation is loss of identity. It is this kind of assimilation, with the terrible consequences indicated, that I dread most —even more than pogroms.

It *is* a t r a g e d y to see a great, ancient p e o p l e, distinguished for its loyalty to its religion, and its devotion to its sacred Law, losing thousands every day by the mere process of attrition. It *is* a tragedy to see a language held sacred by all the world, in which Holy Writ was composed, which served as the depository of Israel's greatest and best thoughts, doomed to oblivion. It *is* a tragedy to see the descendants of those who revealed religion to the world, and who developed the greatest religious literature in existence, so little f a m i l i a r with real Jewish thought that they have no other interpretation to offer of Israel's Scriptures, Israel's religion, and Israel's ideals and aspirations and hopes, than those suggested by their natural opponents, slavishly following their o p i n i o n s, copying their phrases, and repeating their catchwords. I am not accusing anybody. I am only stating facts. We are helpless spectators of the Jewish soul wasting away before our very eyes.

Now, the rebirth of Israel's national consciousness and the revival of Judaism are inseparable. When Israel found itself, it found God. When Israel lost itself, or began to work at its self-effacement, it was sure to deny its God. The selection of Israel, the indestructability of God's covenant with Israel, the immortality of Israel as a nation, and the final restoration of Israel to Palestine, where the nation will live a holy life, on holy ground, with all the wide-reaching consequences of the conversion of humanity, and the establishment of the Kingdom of God on earth—all these are the common ideals and the common ideas that permeate the whole of J e w i s h literature extending over nearly four thousand years.

SOLOMON SCHECHTER,
Seminary Addresses

Man is made by history. It is history that causes the men of historic nations to be more civilized than the savage. The Jew recognizes that he is made what he is by the history of his fathers, and he feels he is losing his better self so far as he loses his hold on his past history.

JOSEPH JACOBS
Jewish Contributions to Civilization.

The Sin And Danger Of Assimilation

The immigrants (to A m e r i c a) arrived during the period of America's gigantic industrial development, its unparalleled growth in wealth and power. Cultural pressures had never been very potent in America. Now they almost disappeared. Often, indeed, an odd inverted pressure set in, which had been operative for long on the diminishing frontier. Books, values, ideas, the arts, grace of speech or manners were discredited as unpractical, effeminate. There arose the symbolic figure of the two-fisted American with hairs on his chest, ranging in shadings from the rough frontiersman with a heart of gold to the go-getting Babbit. And a thing arose, a phenomenon came into view, so hilarious and melancholy, so degraded and sickly, so grotesque and unnatural, that the long ages of human civilization have not seen its detestable like. Jews, members of the *Am - ha - Sefer*, the people of the Book, Jews who had sustained s c h o o l s for their children and academies for their youth in the long illiterate ages of Europe when a priest who could half read his missal was considered a great scholar, Jews who had made of a book a living substitute for their lost fatherland, Jews who in every other corner of the diaspora had sought to excel in the cultures of their adopted countries and had indeed done so, Jews eagerly aped this decay of the humanities and this contempt for humanistic values. Proudly Jewish merchants and manufacturers and professional men aver that they have no " time " to read literature. They cannot go to synagogue because they are tired and must play golf or bridge. They cannot sustain the serious theater because they need amusement. They endow, when they can, football stadiums and athletic fields. Plain people, proud of their " plainness " — another incredibly grotesque phenomenon among Jews —and pseudo-intellectuals of Jewish birth actually fell so low as to co-operate with that contempt for values and ideas which fills the minds of authentic Americans with horror and dismay. They yielded and yield to that notion destructive of a free and democratic society which has never been better diagnosed than by Professor R. B. Heilman in a presidential address before the American Association of University Professors. " One of the most disquieting of the phenomena of democracy is a suspicion of various kinds of superiority, a desire to ignore it, or at worst to ridicule and undermine it ; the converse of this is the misuse of democracy to glorify the commonplace or even the meretricious . . . . The worst blow that can be struck against

a democracy is for standards of excellence to be identified with exclusiveness, and therefore to be considered ' undemocratic '."

What was the result of the process here described ? To say that it was an assimilation too rapid and too eager is not to say enough. Assimilation is no simple problem. Co-operation with the society and culture in which they live is both the right and duty of Jews. What took place in America, for the first time in all history, was assimilation on the lowest possible plain— assimilation *not* on the level of Emerson and Thoreau and Henry James, but on the level of baseball, gin-rummy, the average Hollywood film and the comic strip. The representative folk-heroes of great masses of American Jews—not all, thank God, not all—are Eddie Cantor (a truly good and righteous man in his private character) and the Marx brothers. Nowhere and at no time in all history have Jews fallen so low. *Total* assimilation is a great sin and a terrible danger. But assimilation to Pascal and Racine or to Goethe and Beethoven left the assimilationists the bearers of high and eternal though alien values. American assimilation on the " folksy " level is destructive of every value by which Jews must live, if they would survive in any guise except the guise of apes and fools, of objects of contempt to those Americans who are seeking to guide the Republic to better things, of no less hatred and suspicion from that rabble with whom they have made common cause. Unless J e w s reintegrate themselves with their Judaism, its traditions, its values, its standards, and co-operate as such, as integrated Jews, on highest levels of American culture and on these alone, there is no future for the American Jewish community except one of shame and disaster.

LUDWIG LEWISOHN,
The American Jew

Death and suicide are the most radical reliefs from disease. Similarly, assimilation is the most radical solution of the Jewish problem.

BER BOROCHOV,
Nationalism and the Class Struggle

Individuals, Not Imitators

We recognize with each child the aim of education should be to develop his own individuality, not to make him an imitator, not to assimilate him to others. Shall we fail to recognize this truth when applied to whole peoples? And what people in the world has shown greater individuality than the Jews? Has any a nobler past? Does any possess common ideas better worth expressing? Has any marked traits worthier of development? Of all the peoples in the world those of two tiny states stand preeminent as contributors to our present civilization—the Greeks and the Jews. The Jews gave to the world its three greatest religions, reverence for law, and the highest conceptions of morality . . . . Our teaching of brotherhood and righteousness has, under the name of democracy and social justice, become the twentieth-century striving of America and of western Europe. Our conception of law is embodied in the American Constitution which proclaims this to be a "government of laws and not of men." And for the triumph of our other great teaching—the doctrine of peace—this cruel war is paving the way.

While every other people is striving for development by asserting its nationality, and a great war is making clear the value of small nations, shall we voluntarily yield to anti-Semitism, and instead of solving our "problem" end it by ignoble suicide? Surely this is no time for Jews to despair. Let us make clear to the world that we, too, are a nationality striving for equal rights, to life and to self-expression.

LOUIS D. BRANDEIS,
The Jewish Problem
(written during World War I)

To be a Jew is the least difficult way of being truly human. It is for this reason that the Jew must remain a Jew.

BERNARD LAZARE,
quoted in *Rebirth*

The Ethical Courage To Be A Jew

It would often appear that this is the task of Judaism, which it has also to fulfil even by its mere existence, namely, to give expression in the history of the world to the idea of the *community*, of standing alone, the *ethical principle of the minority*. Judaism bears witness to the power of the idea as against the power of mere numbers and of outward success; it stands for the enduring protest of those who seek to be true to their own selves, of those who claim to be different, as against the crushing pressure of the victor and the leveller, who want all to think alike. This attitude is itself a constant preaching to the peoples of the world, to all who have ears to hear. Judaism, by its mere existence, is a never silent protest against the assumption that the multitude can be greater than right, that force may be the ruler over truth, that in the battle between spirit and the utilities, profit may have the last word. As long as Judaism continues, nobody will be able to say that the soul of man has allowed itself to be subjugated. Its existence through the centuries is by itself proof that conviction cannot be mastered by numbers. The mere fact of Judaism's existence shows that it is impossible to conquer the spirit, that the spirit can make men invincible, and that though spirit and mind may sometimes assume the appearance of an extinct volcano — Judaism has often been depicted thus — power yet dwells in them, power which quietly renews itself, and breaks out afresh, and causes movement. The few, who are the few for the sake of God and for the sake of the spirit, are they who abide, and it is from them that the great and decisive effects, the fresh directions in history, emanate. In respect of this fact alone one is often tempted to use a well-known phrase, and to say : " If Judaism did not exist, one would have to invent it." Without minorities there can be no world-historic goal.

Because it has been a minority, Judaism has become a measuring test for the height to which morality has risen upon earth. What the Jewish community has experienced from the nations among which it lived, has always been a measure of the extent of right and justice among the nations. For all justice is justice for the few. What Israel, which gave of its faith to mankind, *receives* back from mankind in religion and religious justice, always reveals clearly the change and development of religion. From Israel's lot men could judge how far they have yet to go until the days of the Messiah. When Israel can live securely among the nations, then the promised times will have arrived, for then and thereby it will be proved that faith in God has become a living reality. The significance of Judaism is not only contained in its character and in its ideas, but equally in its history among the nations. Thus this history is itself a deed.

Until this Messianic time arrives, many days will come and go, and with them the many demanding and testing hours, asking and answering. It requires religious courage, courage to think and to await, to belong to a minority, which J u d a i s m always has been and always will be, especially among majorities which so often allow might to triumph over right. It requires ethical courage to be a Jew, when worldly comforts, honours, and prizes often lure the Jew over to the other side. Jews have very frequently had to fight a battle between ideas and interests, a battle between belief and un-belief. It is the peculiarity of the Jewish spirit to be rooted in conscience and in the fear of God, not

merely to know, but to know the good. Therefore it possesses the capacity of not allowing itself to be conquered by time ; it has the strength of resistance against all powers and multitudes, against all which seeks only to rule and to oppress. It is, therefore, its peculiarity to keep on seeking, never thinking that it has reached the end and the conclusion ; it is always demanding, without rest or easy contentedness. It implies a persistent quest for knowledge for the sake of the commandment, a never tiring will for the ideal, a demand to sacrifice itself constantly and never to give up. LEO BAECK,
The Essence of Judaism

We are never more modern, never more progressive, than when we are ourselves. MAX NORDAU,
Address, 1907

I've Kept My Name

I find that keeping my name, far from complicating my life, simplifies it. I was born an American and a Jew, as you were born an American and a Gentile. I am what I am, as you are what you are. " Jews," wrote Mark Twain, " are members of the human race. Worse than that I cannot say of them." But it would not be wholly admirable if I should, by changing my name, reject the fifty centuries' history and tradition of my people in order to gain a hotel room at Newport.

Nor is this all. Bearing an unmistakable Jewish name, I am spared the crude comments of virulent anti-Semites, for even they retain a modicum of manners in my presence ; and, there being no possibility of mistake, I am not asked to join groups that do not " take " Jews. I am accepted by my fellows as a human being, or I am rejected as a Jew, and while I have no apparatus for measuring hatred and love as they move the hearts of millions of non-Jews, I do know this: that

Gentiles, knowing me to be a Jew, have all my life taken me into their hearts and homes, with no self-consciousness on their part or mine, with no abrogation of dignity on either side, without condescension by them and without obsequiousness by me.

The fact that I have been free of most of the blatant prejudices that often run against so many of my co-religionists does not make me insensitive to their plight, nor do I detach from them as though I lived upon a private planet of my own. The war between good and evil never ceases. It was once suggested to Luigi Luzzatti, a Prime Minister of Italy and a Jew, that he change his faith. " I do not think of myself as a Jew or a Gentile," he replied, " but only as an Italian. But when Jews are attacked, then the voice of Isaiah rises in my soul." Here it would seem meet to do battle under true colors rather than false.

If I should resort to the plastic surgery of the courts, it would be only because I should like to pass myself off on the community as a synthetic Plantagenet. This, conceivably, could bring me certain dubious " advantages" such as eligibility for clubs that reject me because I am a Jew, or admission to hotels in " restricted" resorts that refuse me for the same reason. With a new name—preferably one suggesting kinship with a high-church bishop—I might even be asked to dine with some newly minted family that, having gouged the government during the First World War, is now almost as pedigreed as a grand champion bull. These considerations leave me cold.

We already have an overproduction of social climbers in this country, folks who, in the telling and contemptuous rural N e g r o phrase, have " got above their raisin '." There is no real reason why I should add to their number; I can derive a sufficient knowledge of their obscene antics, without closer relationship, by reading the considerable American literature that deals with them.

I have, for all these reasons, kept my name. The United States is, I repeat, the kindliest of countries; how kindly only those can know whose history is nearly all somber tragedy. But if, unhappily, the United States should ever change, my course would remain unchanged. It is not only that I can do no other. It is also that the upright posture of man, though it is a biological disadvantage, is a great psychological triumph. Speaking for myself alone, it would be too high a price for survival to abdicate that posture which raised man toward the rising sun.

DAVID L. COHN,
Atlantic Monthly

Help and respect can come to a people only through self-help and self-respect.

STEPHEN S. WISE,
Sermons and Addresses

The Way To Avoid Jewish Self-Hatred

Those individuals who would like to leave a group do not have . . . loyalty. In an underprivileged group, many of these individuals are, nevertheless, forced to stay within the group. As a result, we find in every underprivileged group a number of persons ashamed of their membership. In the case of the Jews, such a Jew will try to move away as far as possible from things Jewish. On his scale of values, he will place these habits, appearances, or attitudes which he considers to be particularly Jewish not particularly high ; he will rank them low.

This situation is much aggravated by the following fact : A person for whom the balance is negative will move as far away from the center of Jewish life as the outside majority permits. He will stay on this barrier and be in a constant state of frustration. Actually, he will be more frustrated than those members of the minority who keep psychologically well inside the group. We know from experimental psychology and psychopathology that such frustration leads to an all-around state of high tension with a generalized tendency to aggression. The aggression should, logically, be directed against the majority, which is what hinders the minority member from leaving his group. However, the majority has, in the eyes of those persons, higher status. And besides, the majority is much too powerful to be attacked. Experiments have shown that, under these conditions, aggression is likely to be turned against one's own group or against one's self . . . .

It is recognized in sociology that the members of the lower social strata tend to accept the fashions, values, and ideals of the higher strata. In the case of the underprivileged group it means that their opinions about themselves are greatly influenced by the low esteem the majority has for them. This infiltration of the views and values of what Maurice Pekarsky has called the " gate-keeper " necessarily heightens the tendency of the Jew with a negative balance to cut himself loose from things Jewish. The more typically Jewish people are, or the more typically Jewish a cultural symbol or behavior pattern is, the more distasteful they will appear to this person. Being unable to cut himself loose from his Jewish connections and his Jewish past, the hatred turns upon himself . . . .

The only way to avoid Jewish self-hatred in its various forms is a change of the negative balance between the forces toward and away from the Jewish group, into a positive balance, the creation of loyalty to the Jewish group instead of negative chauvinism. We are unable to safeguard our fellow Jews or our growing children today against those handicaps which are the result of their being Jewish. However, we can try to build up a Jewish education both on the children's level and on the adult level to counteract the feeling of inferiority and the feeling of fear which are the most important sources of the negative balance.

The feeling of inferiority of the Jew is but an indication of the fact that he sees things Jewish with the eyes of the unfriendly majority.

KURT LEWIN,
Contemporary Jewish Record

We Serve Humanity By Being What We Are

Mankind does not have the choice of religion and neutrality. Irreligion is not opiate but poison. Our energies are too abundant for living indifferently. We are in need of an endless purpose to absorb our immense power if our souls are not to run amok. We are either the ministers of the sacred or slaves of evil. To be a Jew is to hold one's soul clean and open the stream of endless striving so that God may not be ashamed of His creation. Judaism is not a quality of the soul but spiritual life. With souls we are born; spirit we must acquire.

Judaism is the track of God in the wilderness of oblivion. By being what we are, namely Jews; by attuning our own yearning to the lonely holiness in this world, we will aid humanity more than by any particular service we may render.

We are Jews as we are men. The alternative to our Jewish existence is spiritual suicide, disappearance, not conversion into something else. Judaism has allies, partners, but no substitute. It is not a handmaiden of civilization but its touchstone.

ABRAHAM J. HESCHEL,
The Earth Is the Lord's

There is something higher than modernity, and that is eternity.

SOLOMON SCHECHTER

It Is Glorious To Live

I believe that the assimilation of the Jew is undesirable. Because he constitutes a minority he is compelled to think more and harder than his neighbor; he must be a liberal; his outlook must be international, his perspective universal. Assimilation would mean the absorp-tion of such valuable assets in large crowds and majorities in no way superior. The Jew, too, is in many ways an indispensable factor in European civilization; he is an antidote for Western paganism; he is a force for universal peace. His continued existence is also a tremendous spiritual asset and means for cultural enrichment of our civilization.

But above all, it has a profound esthetic appeal to the Jew himself and to the world. It is glorious to live, to roll up years, decades, centuries, millennia. It is thrilling to look back on vistas of time; there I was — then I was. Age, mere age, evokes interest, admiration and respect. A diamond wedding anniversary gets a headline in the newspaper. The celebration of the hundredth birthday of almost anyone arouses comment. Medicine is deeply concerned with the prolongation of life; it is making every effort to procure longevity for the individual. An American need not go beyond his own country for natural beauty, but he travels to Rome, Jerusalem, Cairo to worship the old. Napoleon, standing in the shadow of the pyramids, begins to poetize and pays reverential homage to the age of Egypt's civilization. How pained we all are to see an old landmark, an age-hoary shrine disappear. Gibraltar is huge, massive, picturesque; some even declare it ugly, but there it stands. Suggest to anyone that it be reduced to the level of the sea and build with its stone magnificent cathedrals. No! We love to venerate the merely old.

Here is the Jew — roll back the book of history; you are almost at its very beginning. Abraham was there to exchange compliments with Hammurabi. Turn a leaf; here is

Rameses, well, he had his difficulties with the God of the Hebrews. Rameses, as we now know, was the scion of a great people, but he is, after all, only a mummy. But even as a mummy, because it is so very old and has so admirably defied time, Rameses has attained a commendable reputation; but Moses, mind you, is no mummy and his burning bush is not yet consumed.

Continue to turn the pages; new names, new cultures, new countries, new habits, customs. The Jew, the Jew, he is yet there. You are at the end of ancient times. The whole world is at the feet of mighty Rome. The Jew, amongst many other, is battling for his life; Rome scores a victory.

Some three years ago a collector of coins brought to my study a number of coins of Jewish interest. One of them brought tears to my eyes. It was a coin that was minted between 69 and 70 C.E. at the request of Titus. There was stamped on it a crouching Jew, symbolizing Judea, and it bore the inscription, " Judea Capta, Judea Devicta."

I held the coin in my hand and mused with a pain at my heart. Suddenly I recalled that the firebrand which set the Temple on fire and reduced it to ashes 1,859 years ago, was hurled by one of Titus' soldiers from Mount Scopus. At the very same moment it occurred to me that the University of Jerusalem was being built on the very mountain and that the world's greatest intellect, "The Tip Topper" of our age, as Bertrand Russell put it to me, Albert Einstein, emerged from his laboratory to campaign for funds in order to assure its existence and growth. I turned to the other face of the coin; there was Titus with his helmet and all his imperial R o m a n dignity. "Perhaps you are best remembered," I reflected, "because of your accursed deed, because you linked your name with an undying people."

"In social as in biological problems, time is the sole real creator and the sole great destroyer. It is time that has made mountains with grains of sand and raised the obscure cell of geological eras to human dignity." Time has made the Jew. Time has thought him thus far desirable. Time alone will have to prove him undesirable.

SOLOMON GOLDMAN,
A Rabbi Takes Stock

Our emancipation will not be complete until we are free of the fear of being Jews.   MORDECAI M. KAPLAN,
The Future of the American Jew

Indifference Is Not Tolerance

The one universal God does not require one universal church in which to be worshipped, but one universal devotion. In the realms of ascertainable facts, uniformity can be looked for. In the realms of art and philosophy there can be only sincerity of quest and expression — only dedication. Religion is the supreme art of humanity.

Judaism developed through the ages its own characteristic style, as it were, its own view of life, its code and forms of worship. It possesses its own traditions based on Torah and covenant. Its adherents today find inspiration and spiritual contentment in it, as did their fathers before them, and wish to continue its historic identity within the configuration of other religious cultures.

Other religions, too, developed their characteristic ways based on their unique traditions and experiences. There is much which all religions have in common and much which differentiates them. Their common purpose in the world will not be advanced by merger or amalgamation. Were all arts, philosophies, and religions cast into one mold, mankind would be the poorer for it. Unwillingness to recognize differences in religions is no evidence of broadmindedness. To ignore these differences is to overlook the deep cleavages which existed in the past and to assume a similarity of doctrine and outlook which does not exist in the present. The attempt to gloss over these differences as a gesture of goodwill is a superficial act which serves neither the purposes of scholarship nor the realities of the situation. It is far better and more practical to look for ways of working together on the basis of a forthright recognition of dissimilarities rather than on a fictitious assumption of identity. Indifference to one's own faith is no proof of tolerance. Loyalty to one's own is part of a larger loyalty to faith generally.

There are great areas of common interests in which all religions can cooperate in mutual helpfulness and respect, influencing one another and learning from one another.

Judaism, which differed and continues to differ from other religions in significant matters of belief and practice, has sought and seeks opportunities of friendly cooperation with them in all things which may contribute to the building of the good society, firm in its own convictions, reverent of theirs, hoping for the great day of universal reconciliation of all peoples, when " they shall not hurt nor destroy in all My holy mountain, and the earth shall be full of the knowledge of God as the waters cover the sea."

ABBA HILLEL SILVER,
Where Judaism Differed

By vulgarity I mean that vice of civilization which makes man ashamed of himself and his next of kin, and pretend to be somebody else. SOLOMON SCHECHTER,
Abraham Lincoln

Why We Should Survive

We should survive, I say. First, because of our heritage. We have given to the world the concepts of moral law and of the One God. We gave the world its supreme Book. That was while we were still a nation. When we ceased to be a nation in the sense that we had one land to be our hearthstone and one language to give expression to our dreams, we still continued to create and to interpret. I believe that there is a great deal of fine literature and art and music for us to create, fine philosophy for us to expound, which would never be created or expounded if we allowed ourselves to be absorbed among the peoples where we live. We should survive because we have shown for two thousand years that it is a stronger thing to have no armies and navies than to possess armies and navies . . . .

Secondly, I believe the Jew should survive precisely for the same reason that I want the Red Indian and the Basque to survive, the Welshman and the Cornishman, the New Englander and the New Mexican. From day to day the world tends to become more and more monotone and monochrome. The forces of standardization, mechanization, mass production, hang heavily over us, flattening like lead-coloured clouds our world's brilliant diversity. We listen to the same music on the air, whether we are Eskimos or Hottentot. We read the same syndicated articles in the newspapers. Giant liners and aircraft obliterate all our frontiers. We must hang on to what separates us, our traditions, our folk-song and dance, lest we bore each other and ourselves to extinction. For God's sake, as D. H. Lawrence once cried out : Let us hang on to the Sacred Differences !

There is a third reason why we should survive. It is less magnanimous than the two others I have brought forward. It is this. It is merely a matter of the devil in us, or the small boy in us. What ? Did Titus, did Torquemada, want to finish us off ? Does Hitler want to finish us off ? To the devil with them ! We shall go on !

If it wanted any arguing, these are the arguments why we should survive. But the fact is, whether we should or should not, whether we want to or do not, we will survive. We cannot help it. Whatever our friends or enemies do to us, whatever we do to ourselves, we go on

. . . . .

In any given generation, some Jews are destined to carry on the torch, the tradition, the destiny. I think it is not a common sense of race, of religion, of colossal tradition, of moral impulse, that makes Jews of them, though each or all of these may function. It is a sense of decency, it is a sense of loyalty. When I meet a Jew and he meets me, we salute in each other without knowing it the conqueror of Titus and Torquemada and Hitler. I know that he will need my help, and I will need his, five hundred years from now. We cannot fail each other. We will go on.

There is another knowledge we bear with us, some of us obscurely, too deep for words, some of us clearly ; and we render it in word or sound or stone. It is not only that we need each other, but that the world needs us. We have stood since our beginnings for certain values, which the world would cherish without us, but with us cherishes more bravely and continuously. We have stood for the idea of One God, for Peace throughout the Lands, for Love to All Men. The treatment of us is a touchstone of a land's chivalry. Where things are well with us, there the newer values flourish, Religious Liberty, Democracy, the Right of Free Speech. Where things go ill, these values sicken, and soon after, those older values follow.

The world needs us. We cannot fail each other. We will go on.

LOUIS GOLDING,
The Jewish Problem

Only When We Respect Ourselves . . . .

Before we can effectively combat anti-Semitism, we must first of all educate ourselves out of it, and out of the slave-mentality which it betokens. Only when we respect ourselves, can we win the respect of others; or rather, the respect of others will then come of itself.

ALBERT EINSTEIN,
The World as I See It

To Stand Erect . . .

Too many of us Jews have no God and no Torah, no Jewish knowledge and no Jewish practices — only the penalties of being Jews. We never enjoy Judaism — we only suffer for it and even that not heroically. The Jew who knows Judaism has his head and heart too full of positive healthful values ever to be invaded by self-contempt. But the Jew who is a hollow shell, a Jewish zero, a Hebraic cipher, a vacuum, is flooded inevitably with hostile notions about Jews. The anti-Semite convinces him. He comes to doubt his work and to despise Judaism, Jews, and even himself.

When libels about Jews come to his ears, his reaction is not anger; he assumes that they are true, not of him, of course, but of other Jews. Cursed with a sense of inferiority, convinced that everything Gentile is better than anything Jewish, sick to death with that dread disease, Goyitis, he is incapable of being offended by anything a Gentile does no matter who the Gentile or how unjust the act.

There are many advantages which Jews may derive from a knowledge and love of Judaism. It can give them a high, clear religious faith. It can supply them with a system of ethical values, personal and social, idealistic and practical at the same time. It can grace their lives with poetic observances and with the treasures of an ancient tradition. It can make them, in sum, nobler, stronger, better human beings and more valuable citizens.

But one service Judaism performs for Jews which is often overlooked: it is the first function of a human being to respect himself, to stand erect and foursquare before the world, to injure none, to help all, but to allow none to injure him — to be in sum, a man.

This is the last and climactic contribution of a living Judaism to the Jew — it delivers him from being a worm; it guarantees that he will be a man.

MILTON STEINBERG,
A Believing Jew

Unfinished Business

There is still a long road ahead of us, to finish what we have begun to do. We began to speak a great word, among ourselves and in the ears of the entire world, and we have not yet completed it. We stand in the midst of our speech. We cannot stop it. Nor do we want to stop it . . . . The truth within us is sufficiently powerful, but it is so rich and overflowing that we are not yet capable of expressing it in clear language. But we shall not retreat because of this failure. We shall speak and explain as much as our power of speech will allow us. In our inwardness, we understand our thoughts, and, in the course of time, our speech too will be liberated from the stultifying cobwebs of exile in which it is presently caught, so that we shall be able to speak, portray and explain in clear concepts that which we seek with our whole being. But, until the advent of this Golden Age, we shall not cease our spiritual and practical labors ; only a nation that had completed what it began can afford to go off the stage of history.

ABRAHAM ISAAC KUK,
quoted in *Banner of Jerusalem*

The Jew's Need To Rediscover His True Self

We are living in an age in which Jewish souls have been so intolerably anguished by the vastness of Jewish martyrdom, by the cold indifference of the world to that martyrdom and then briefly and strangely and not without an echoing pang have been elated by the establishment of the M e d i n a t h Y i s r a e l. These have been the experiences of the contemporary Jew. And to these should be added too, the war in Israel, the war which would have been lost, had not naked hands been able for a space to hold off tanks — had not, as a sagacious journalist wrote, the *koach ha-ish*, the power of man, of moral heroism, been stronger than the *koach ha-esh*, the power of fire, of ammunition. Jews who have witnessed this, Jews who are deeply troubled by their being and the future of that being, why should they not descend to the depth of their souls, of their psyches, and rediscover their oneness with the sources of their people's life ? The Jew who succeeds in doing that will find, to use the unrivaled formulation of Buber, that " his people is to him a community of men and women who were, who are, who will be, a community of the dead, the living and the unborn who together represent a oneness — the precise oneness which he perceives to be the groundwork of his ' I,' of that ' I ' which was destined from all eternity to be *this* necessary link in the long chain of being . . . . The past of his people is his personal memory ; the future of his people is his personal task ; the way of his people teaches him to will and to understand his true self."

LUDWIG LEWISOHN,
The American Jew

Ways Of Being A Jew

There are various ways of being a Jew.

He who is content to be a Jew by the pressure of the world and because he cannot well do otherwise, such a one will not be very fruitful or useful either to Judaism or to humanity. For his attitude is wholly negative. Many such have remained Jews because under the onslaught of anti-Semitism they felt it beneath their human dignity to desert their people. There were such even in the Russia of the Tsars.

There are also those who have become J e w s again because the world has cast them back into that Judaism from which they were in flight. That is the case of certain recent fugitives from Germany.

Lastly there are those who say : " I become a Jew when one attacks the Jews." It is well enough, but it is very little. These might be called the Yom Kippur Jews. Israel has need of another spirit . . . .

A man must be a Jew not through resignation, but by a voluntary act of loyalty. He must enter upon a second *brith* or covenant by the instincts of his soul and the operations of his reason.

Like our ancestors at the foot of Horeb, he who returns to us must once more freely accept the yoke. He has returned to the bosom of Israel which proclaims at morn and eve the Unity of the Name and which must, if need be, die for it . . . .

He who returns knows how hard it is to maintain himself upon that peak of being. But he soon discovers that Israel sanctifies and blesses life at every instant, operates within life with all its difficulties, that it seeks and supplies life's fulness through the harmonious accord of all the faculties of being, since it causes the divine to manifest itself in the concreteness of human living.

It is that love of life that is characteristic of Israel. The merit of the individual consists in his striving after perfection which works for and within the collectivity. But Jewish purity is not renunciation nor is Jewish chastity a mortification of the flesh. The Law is the direction of the good life by the sanctification of all human action in joy. This ancient and living idea has been too often obscured.

Judaism is a yoke to take upon

oneself. But it is a yoke that can be born in freedom and serenity and a just pride.

The sanctified life of Judaism is a life of joy and Israel can be reborn out of itself.

MAXIME PIHA,
quoted in *Rebirth*

The World's Need For The Jew

No people in the world has presented such a vivid example of unwavering perseverance and unflinching devotion to faith as the Jewish people. No nation has exerted so mighty a religious influence on humanity as Israel. Their Bible is by far the greatest book among the holy books of nations, and it makes the Jews " God's People " . . . . The disappearance of the Jewish faith would be the more grievous today, precisely because the conception of God has been weakened almost to the vanishing point, at least for the present, among very many people who regard themselves as enlightened and educated. The human conscience is in need of Israel's eternally vital protest, and of the firm support which it may find therein against the w e a k n e s s and doubt that threaten Christendom.

JULES BARTHELEMY SAINT-HILAIRE,
quoted in *Stars and Sand* who quoted from *Briefe berühmter Zeitgenussen über die Judenfrage* by I. Singer

Make A Virtue Of Necessity

Every so often a rabbi will preach a sermon, a publicist write an article, entitled, " Why I am a Jew " — an abstract defense of a choice that was never made. It is a pity that Jews cannot reconcile themselves to the simple truth : they are Jews because they were born Jews, and they remain Jews because in the mass they can become nothing else. That is to say, they are born into a certain group, trained in a certain consciousness, and kept there by the force of circumstances.

The whole of this book is dedicated to the proposition that Jews must make a virtue of necessity ; and if this sounds like a dissatisfied admission, the tenor of my arguments has been misunderstood. Whatever beauty or dignity there is in life is born of a necessity transformed into a virtue. We are born by a necessity outside of ourselves, but, being born, nothing remains — nothing human and reasonable and livable — but to turn this compulsion to fine account by an affirmative attitude. We must work for bread, and we must repress many instincts lest the world tumble about our ears, which are circumstances not of our choosing. But since they are there they must be accepted as the framework of our creative will. Finally, we must die, and even this hateful necessity is transformed into good by proud acceptance and by contemplation of the relative immortality of our influence. So to live that we forget the compulsion, and come to derive joy from living and from working, is the aim of all practical philosophy and ethics. " The pursuit of truth is a form of courage, and a philosopher may well love truth for its own sake, in that he is disposed to confront destiny, whatever it may be, with zest when possible, with resignation when necessary, and not seldom with amusement." (Santayana) . . . .

The Jewish tradition has become, for Jews, a necessity of morale ; its function is no longer (as it never consciously was) that of a direct preparation for the economic struggle, but that of a creative escape from an intolerable situation into the basis of a decent and creative life. To live together at all, Jews must live together in a tradition.

My people is my instrument for cooperating with mankind, my channel to humanity. It organizes my affections and hatreds and brings them to effective focus. The ugliness I hate in Jewry is hateful everywhere, the good in it good for everyone. Love of humanity, when not implemented by the love of a people, is usually gushy and diffused sentimentalism. Depend upon it that the man who works for the world as a whole, not through the most immediate, most natural and most accessible passions, will forget the Eskimos one day, the Chinese the next.

Through ourselves we Jews, like every other people, can reach the world. But we must remember that the affirmative powers in us and their interplay with the world situation, call for the acceptance of a heavy discipline. Only the terrific illusion that we can be Jews on easy terms, that we can take life as it comes, tacitly — as others do — can be fatal to us. In childhood and manhood we must carry the yoke which our forebears carried, and we must carry it gladly, because the only alternative is an intellectual and moral leprosy from which there is no escape unto death.

MAURICE SAMUEL,
Jews on Approval

Israel Is The Tree

Why is my belonging to the Jewish people the most sacred relation to me, second only to my relation to God ? Israel is spiritual order in which the human and the ultimate, the natural and the holy enter a lasting covenant, in which kinship with God is not an aspiration but a reality of destiny. For us Jews there can be no fellowship with God without the fellowship with Israel. Abandoning Israel, we desert God.

Judaism is not only the adherence to particular doctrines and observances, but primarily the living in the spiritual order of the Jewish people, the living in the Jews of the past and with the Jews of the present. Judaism is not only a certain quality in the souls of the individuals, but primarily the existence of the community of Israel. Judaism is neither an experience nor a creed, neither the possession of psychic traits nor the acceptance of a theological doctrine, but the living in a holy dimension, in a spiritual sphere. Our share in holiness we acquire by living in the Jewish community. What we do as individuals is a trivial episode, what we attain as Israel causes us to grow into the infinite.

Israel is the tree, we are the leaves. It is the clinging to the stem that keeps us alive.

ABRAHAM J. HESCHEL,
God in Search of Man

We Will Be Preserved

In the early days of the Zionist movement Achad Ha-Am declared it to be a principle that the redemption of man, of the people, the *ge-ulath ha-am*, would have to precede the redemption of the land of Israel, the *ge-ulath ha-aretz*. He was eternally right. Those young men and women who laid the perilous foundations of the re-colonization, who shook with malaria and endured the rigors of labor and half-starvation and the additional rigor of speaking a language they did but half know — these were all souls self-redeemed from the emancipatory *galuth* of Europe. Only a perfect vision, only an unalterable faith could have caused them to accomplish what they did accomplish. So it must be here ; only so can any help or healing come to us now. The redemption, the liberation, of the individual American Jew from the thousandfold lie of *galuth* must precede the acts which can assure Jewish survival. He must be free of the lie that the idols of wood and stone can ever be his gods except at the expense of his very life ; he must be free of the lie that uniformity is a virtue and that it is well for him to feign to be what he is not ; he must be free of the lie that in this mimicry there is any measure *even* of security ; he must be free of the lie of lies, the desperate and dastardly lie at the core of a materialized society, that any good thing can be won without suffering, without martyrdom, if need be, or that new devices will be different if employed by the same unredeemed and unilluminated souls. A Jewish community in A m e r i c a can be preserved from dwindling, from corruption and decay, only by Jews, by individual Jewish men and women who, having descended to the depths of their souls, have recovered themselves and with those selves have recovered and regained the history - willing, the history-creating, the self-determining power of the Jewish people.

LUDWIG LEWISOHN,
The American Jew

The Danger Of A Great Common Monotone

I am afraid that the Jews as a whole scarcely appreciate how much of this long tradition of education and religion which has been theirs peculiarly has become a common cultural heritage of all people in the world.

You know this idea, for instance, that there is a purpose running through the world, that the whole movement of history is strung on a golden chain which threads all events and reaches out towards a far-off perfect goal — where did that come from ? You cannot find that in the Oriental cultures. That was a contribution of Judaism. And Judaism impressed it so upon our Western culture that Christianity and Islam simply took it over as a matter of course. Most people who have not become too sophisticated still would say that it is basic. They would still say that there is at the end of man's endeavour a glorious era to come . . . .

Their tradition, their long past, call therefore to the modern Jew to be loyal to this historic heritage — a heritage which is worth preserving. However, it is important not only to be proud of what has been, but to make sure that those who represent the living embodiment of a cultural heritage shall represent it worthily . . . .

It would be too bad if in the great union of humanity which is coming, when the Jew who has advocated justice, righteousness, love and brotherhood, joins hands with the Christian who has advocated justice, righteousness, love and brotherhood, and the great human family emerge, if we were then all lost in a great common monotone. It should really be a mosaic, a unity of culture, of mind, of ideal, of program, but each of us with his individuality and each group with its own distinctive cultural quality. And the only way you can accomplish that is by maintaining the educational program which will preserve not only the pride, but also the learning, the understanding, the appreciation of what Judaism has been and of what the Jew has contributed in philosophy, in literature, in language, in social idealism.

A. EUSTACE HAYDON,
Address, 1940

I Wish To Be Myself

I cannot think of a religion in a vacuum. I cannot conceive of my own religious life in a vacuum. I do not derive my life-determining ideas from my neuro-cerebral system exclusively but from the close social life about me. If I think of my religion I think of it in terms of my people's religion. I share the faith-life of my group. I like to pray as my fathers prayed. I like the ancient rhythm and the ancient psalm. I like my people's festivals. Their mood, their atmosphere and their associations are congenial to deep and joyous religious sentiments. I like the ceremonies of my faith into which ages have poured their rich color. They bring beauty into my life and inspiration. They are mighty streams of religious idealism. Why should I surrender them ? . . . .

Our age needs a form of good will which will not only tolerate differences but which will gladly use them for the enrichment of life.

There are people who would like to acquire good will through assimilation. They know that intolerance, in the last analysis, is due to the existence of differences — religious differences, racial differences, cultural differences. They would therefore do away with intolerance by obliterating these differences.

But that is paying too high a price ! The thing gained is less than the thing surrendered. To use Benjamin Franklin's phrase, " That is paying dear, very dear, for the whistle."

I like to be on the best of terms with my neighbor. I invite his friendship even as I proffer mine — but only on one condition : that he respect my individuality even as I respect his. He must take me for what I am even as I take him for what he is, not for what each of us would like the other one to be. I am what I am. I have been molded by centuries of distinctive cultural experiences. I am a unique racial precipitate. I wish to remain what I am. I am ready to acknowledge that my neighbor has the same right to retain his individuality and his racial and cultural distinctiveness. It is on the basis of such contrasts which are not conflicts that I would build a real comradeship of free men and good works.

I am Hebrew and not Anglo-Saxon. I am Hebrew and not Teuton, Gaul or Slav. I never will be anything else. I do not wish to take on, as protective coloration, the manners, attitudes and points of view of the Anglo-Saxon, Teuton, Gaul or Slav. I do not wish to take on the livery of any man in order to enjoy the privilege of being in his retinue. I wish to be myself. Any other basis for good will is spurious. Any movement for good will which demands of me self-abnegation, is a hostile attack. The man who would be my friend only if he can convert me to his way of living and thinking and believing, is not my friend. He is my enemy. He does not like me for what I am. He would like to see his own reflection in me.

The Jew who casts aside his distinctiveness for the sake of fellowship with other groups will bring nothing to that ultimate communion of minds which alone makes up human fellowship. He will bring to that hoped-for fraternity nothing but a masquerading self, a spurious and washed-out personality. He will have nothing to give. He has destroyed his uniqueness. It is only an integrated, vibrant and affirmative personality which has something to contribute to a community of personalities.

There is a type of good will which is based on indifference. "I am a Jew but I do not care very much about my religion. You are a Christian and you do not care very much about yours. Why, then, let us be broad-minded about it." This is not good will. It is unconcern. For an unbelieving Jew and an unbelieving non-Jew to be tolerant of each other's non-belief is no achievement. It is when a believing Jew, who is profoundly moved by his faith, and a believing Christian, who is profoundly moved by his, discover a common basis for good will, that a significant event is consummated.

ABBA HILLEL SILVER,
Religion in a Changing World

The Four Sons Of The Haggadah

THE WISE SON, WHAT DOES
HE SAY?

How shall we meet the challenge of the contemporary world? The wise son has taken to heart the lessons of Jewish history. He glories in his people's past and knows that our fortunes are linked to those of a hundred generations preceding us. He has watched the new waves of attack against the position of the Jew and recognizes them as part of the familiar anti-Jewish pressure which he must prepare to meet through fortifying himself in Jewish culture and in labor toward the upbuilding of Palestine. He will also

bring up his children in loyalty to their people and in intelligent understanding. This wise son is welcome in our midst to share in the celebration of the Passover.

THE WICKED SON, WHAT DOES
HE SAY?

Why don't we assimilate and lose our national identity? The Jews bring all their troubles upon themselves through their own clannishness and unwillingness to mix with their neighbors. The Jews should think less of their own affairs and devote themselves more thoroughly to becoming better South Africans.

Jewish nationalism especially, is an attempt to drag the Jew back to the Ghetto which we must oppose with all our vigour. All the ancient ceremonies are so much superstition, which as modern persons we should shake off.

Then you answer him: Undoubtedly in ancient Egypt, too, there were those who kissed the task-master's whip and patriotically refused to seek freedom under Moses. May your share be with them and we shall celebrate the Passover without you.

THE SIMPLE SON, WHAT DOES
HE SAY?

What is happening to the Jews?

Indeed, he says very little. For him earning a living and then finding his little recreation is the end-all of his life. Occasionally an exceptionally vigorous blast from the hostile anti-Semitic world may evoke the question, "What is happening?" It is our duty to stimulate the indifferent Jew and to encourage his questioning in order to bring him into the orbit of Jewish life.

AND HE WHO DOES NOT EVEN ASK!

Too many Jews are so far removed from Jewish life and problems as to be unable even to talk about them intelligently. We must awaken these Jews to a sense of their future. A new world is dawning; new forces are regrouping the peoples of the earth. New loyalties are being forged. The Jew, as a Jew, will have to readjust himself to this new world actively, whether he is now conscious of the problem or not.

Exchange

Thou Shalt Choose Life

It is possible to give three reasons why Jews should seek to survive as a group.

1. The Jew owes it to his fathers to keep Judaism alive. Our life did not really begin with our birth but had a pre-existence in the past before we were born. We cannot, therefore, be indifferent to the aspirations and unfulfilled purposes of our ancestors. They suffered that they might bequeath life to us, a life enriched and enhanced by their efforts and sacrifices. It is impossible for us to stifle our awareness of our spiritual heritage and the obligations that it imposes on us without causing a trauma or psychic wound in our personality. The Jew that tries to forget his parentage and all that it implies is seeking a sort of deliberate amnesia or loss of memory. If he succeeds in this deliberate effort to forget, he is left bewildered, restless, distraught, unreliant and unreliable. It is always better to remember than to forget. In this we see the operation of a

divine law that bids all men to honor their fathers and their mothers, and we cannot honor them by throwing away the life they imparted to us by their living and, often, by their dying, and frustrating their interest in the survival of the civilization to which they were devoted.

2. The Jew owes it to his children to keep Judaism alive. Every human child is born feeble and helpless in body and mind. No child grows to manhood without being conditioned by the cultural traditions of the group to which he belongs. If the Jewish child is not surrounded with Jewish influences, this does not mean that he will grow up to be identified as a member of the majority group and accepted by them. The American who has not been conditioned as a Jew has been conditioned as a Christian. Merely seeking not to prejudice our children in favor of Judaism would still leave them identifiable as different from other Americans in lacking the background of an affirmative Christian tradition in the home such as no Jewish parent is qualified to give. Can we afford to raise our children as spiritually *staatenlos* or without status ? Have we a right to make them feel like cultural parvenus when they are legitimate heirs of a three thousand year old tradition of culture ? Shall the whole content of their Jewish life be the experience of being excluded from fellowship in the Gentile community ? Shall they be denied the spiritual exaltation of loyalty to a people that is interested in them because they are of it and it looks to them to carry on its historic life ? True, the Jewish community may not actually do all this for its children. But without the Jewish community, our children would be utterly and inevitably bereft of these advantages ; with the survival of the Jewish community there is always the opportunity for affording them these advantages.

3. Finally, the Jew owes it to God to keep the Jewish people alive. This is not said with a view to drawing an imaginary and unreal distinction between duties to God and duties to our fellowmen. It is said with a view to stressing the thought that the religious attitude to life is one that must consistently express itself in the assertion of the will of the group to live. For the religious attitude to life is constituted of the intuition that life involves transcendent purposes far beyond the capacity of the individual to realize but to which he must nevertheless contribute the best that is in him. This is what we mean by the Sovereignty of God, the feeling that we must consecrate all of our powers to realizing the ideals that give life meaning — ideals of justice, love and peace. Obviously, if we act merely as individuals, our lives would be too short and the extent of our influence too small to effect much toward the establishment of God's kingdom of righteousness on earth. But act-

ing cooperatively, through historic groups that have a longer life and a wider range of activity than any individual, we can each of us render our personal service to God. We can not do it through a group to which we do not belong and in which we are not accepted. We can do it as Jews only through the Jewish people. It is not important that we prove that our people has a message to the world without which the world cannot get along. But it is important that we use all the elements of our Jewish culture, the fruit of our long historic experience as means to realizing that social order which bears testimony to there being a God in the world. We cannot be a " holy people," if we cease to be a people.

In our own day, the great issue is the struggle for democracy, for the right of the individual to the opportunity of the fullest freedom of self-realization in a cooperative society. But, as has been shown, the rights of the individual tend to become meaningless unless they include his right to be loyal to his ancestry and his progeny, and the historic group that embraces both. The will of dictators to power and domination feeds on the pusillanimity of those who surrender their liberties because of the feebleness of their will to live as free, creative, responsible human beings. We render a disservice to the cause of freedom and democracy whenever we fail to exercise our rights to be ourselves and to carry out our legitimate purposes. Jewish history is one long protest against the attempt of the world to regiment the Jew. In making this protest, the Jew was living up to his deepest intuition that the ultimate destiny of Man is the achievement of a social order in which all men and nations can find self-realization through cooperation and not domination. The Jew dare not surrender to the enemy in the present crisis of civilization. He must today, as in all critical ages in the past, obey what he has always felt to be a divine mandate : *uvaharta vahayim*, " And thou shalt choose life."

The Reconstructionist

2

Judaism and the Jew

Judaism is rooted forever in the soil, blood, life-experience and memory of a particular folk — the Jewish people.

SOLOMON GOLDMAN,
Crisis and Decision

Judaism is something more than a badge, something more than a birth-mark ; it is a life.

MORRIS JOSEPH,
Judaism as Creed and Life

Our people is a people only by virtue of its Torah.

SAADIA,
Emunot Videot

Can The Jewish People Survive Without Judaism?

The Jewish religion is the crowning achievement of our people and our supreme gift to civilization. It possesses such vast reservoirs of spiritual truth that it has been able to sustain and inspire generations upon generations of our people and to retain their sacrificial loyalty under all circumstances and upon all levels of culture. It thus became the strongest factor in the survival of our people, the *kesher shel kayama*, the enduring tie. It is doubtful whether the Jewish people can long survive in the Diaspora without it . . . . Those religious leaders, therefore, who are today teaching the religion of Israel to their people are not only leading them to fountains of living truth which can sweeten and refresh their individual lives, but are also conserving the most potent force which, throughout the ages, has preserved the Jewish people.

ABBA HILLEL SILVER,
The World Crisis and Jewish Survival

Interdependence Of Jews And Judaism

The contrast between Jews and Judaism, is apparent rather than real ; and not only in the obvious sense that Judaism cannot exist, for any length of time, without Jews, nor Jews without Judaism. Besides this inherent correlation which obtains between every creed and its believers, every culture and its bearers, there is a certain specific, and even more significant connection between Judaism as a creed and as a culture. To Judaism the existence of the Jewish people is essential and indispensable, not only for its realization in life, but for its very idea ; not only for its actuality, but for its potentiality. The Jewish religion without the "chosen people" is unthinkable. Neither could it, like the other religions, be transplanted from the Jewish to another people. No matter how many adherents it might gain in the outside world, the physical extinction of the Jewish people would sound the death knell of Judaism . . . .

Next to the blood ties of common descent, it is primarily their religio-cultural heritage that makes Jews Jewish ; more Jewish, indeed, when they affirm Judaism with their conscious and voluntary allegiance, than when they accept it as a sheer accident of birth. The unity of Jews and Judaism thus has a deep meaning and the interrelation between the two, the interplay of the social and religious forces throughout the entire course of Jewish history, appears to be of controlling significance.

SALO W. BARON,
A Social and Religious History of
the Jews

Israel could dispense with its State and its Temple, but not with its storehouse of divine truth, from which it constantly derives new life and new youth. KAUFMANN KOHLER, *Jewish Theology*

Judaism Encompasses Life As A Totality

Many definitions of " Judaism " have been advanced. " Judaism as a religion," "Judaism as a nationality," "Judaism as a civilization," "Judaism as ethical monotheism " are just a few of the catch phrases denoting varieties of Jewish introspection. As a matter of fact, J u d a i s m warrants all of these and some additional definitions: It is "religion," " nationality," " civilization " and " ethics." Above all, however, it is a way of life and its constitution.

Judaism encompasses life as a totality. It supplies an all-comprehensive regimen and philosophy. It orders the most trivial as well as the most important events. It blends religion, national devotion, cultural aspirations, and the hope for a better future into an inseparable union of purposeful holiness. Judaism is a system of religious culture and cultural religion which most closely approximates the highest ideal of " humanism." It infuses its followers with the assurance of the meaningfulness of life by answering the questions " whence ?" — " whither?" — " why ?" Like philosophy on the highest plane, Judaism answers these eternal questions of mankind in a manner which stresses the " whither," the goal and the purpose — thus identifying and aligning itself with the future. Through all the great books of Judaism there runs the conviction that the problems of the origin of the world, even of God, are less important than the challenges presented by the purpose of the world and the meaning of life.   TRUDE WEISS-ROSMARIN, *Jewish Survival*

Jews As A Religious Community In America

America recognizes no permanent national or cultural minorities; what E u r o p e knows under this head are in this country regarded as " foreign language " or " foreign culture " groups, whose separateness is merely temporary, the consequence of recent immigration, destined to be overcome with increasing integration into American life. America does indeed know and acknowledge the separateness of so-called minority " races," but such separateness has always involved some degree of segregation and consequent relegation to an inferior status in the social hierarchy. The only kind of separateness or diversity that America recognizes as permanent and yet also as involving no

status of inferiority is the diversity or separateness of religious communities. In short, while America knows no national or cultural minorities except as temporary, transitional phenomena, it does know a free variety and plurality of religions, and it is as a member of a religious group that the great mass of Americans understand the status of the Jew in this country and that the American Jew understands himself. This is particularly true of the younger generation of Jews. When they are moved to affirm their Jewishness, and they must do so if only to identify themselves to themselves and to others, they can conceive of no way of doing so except in religious terms. The many substitutes for Jewish religious identification which were open to earlier generations are no longer viable to them. It is simply a fact that the average American Jew — I mean the Jew who is acculturated to America — if he thinks of himself as a Jew at all, tends almost automatically to think of himself as belonging to a religious community, even if he himself does not have personal faith. In the Vilna of the 1920's, it was possible for a militantly anti-religious Jewish doctor to assert himself as a Jew by sending his children to a secular Yiddish school, and for a time this pattern was familiar among Jewish immigrants in this country. For some time too, one could "be a Jew" simply by being a Zionist or by identifying oneself with some Jewish philanthropic cause. All this is becoming increasingly untenable. Today, if the American Jew is to regard himself as a Jew, and if he is to be so regarded by his non-Jewish neighbors and friends, some religious association, however vague, is necessary. The only way in which the Jew can integrate himself into American society is in terms of a religious community.   WILL HERBERG,
Religious Trends in American Jewry

Judaism As A Culture

If Judaism is to be preserved amidst the new conditions, if, lacking as it does, all outward support, it is still to withstand the pressure of the surrounding influences, it must again break the narrow frame of a creed and resume its original function as a culture, as the expression of the Jewish spirit and the whole life of the Jews. It will not confine itself to a few metaphysical doctrines, which affect the head and not the heart, and a few official ceremonies which affect neither the head nor the heart, but will encircle the whole life of the Jew and give content and color to its highest functions and activities.

ISRAEL FRIEDLANDER,
Past and Present

A Dangerous Delusion

The American Jewish community will be centered in Judaism or it will not survive. It will be as an ethnic-religious community that it will carry on on the American scene, or it will disintegrate in the course of time. The term ethnic-religious is broad enough to include all that we mean when we speak of the Jewish way of life — Jewish philanthropy, Jewish social service, Jewish culture — but it is not so broad as to give to these derivative activities priority over the synagogue and religious education. Our concentration in the last generation upon philanthropy, foreign relief and civil defense has persuaded many Jews, I am afraid, not alone that these represent the essence and totality of Judaism, but that they are also the true means of our survival. This is a dangerous delusion. These activities are commendable, necessary and worthy manifestations of wholesome Jewish life. But they are not its roots and its nourishing strength. Jewish life in America will wither and dry-rot will set in unless the tree sends its roots deep down into the rich soil of Jewish faith and Jewish learning. It should also be borne in mind that the state is steadily moving in on all fields of social and welfare services, pensions, socialized medicine, and all forms of social security, and the importance of the private or denominational agency in these fields will progressively diminish. There will remain little which will be specifically Jewish in the field of organized social service. Likewise, campaigns for foreign relief will not continue indefinitely, and they cannot be counted upon to keep Jewish life permanently alerted and mobilized. Without a vital religion and a replenishing Jewish education and scholarship, the American Jewish community will linger on as a waning and decaying residuum of the past in a twilight zone of drift until some unforeseen storm breaks over it, attacks its weakened frame, and shatters it beyond repair.

ABBA HILLEL SILVER,
Address before the Central Conference
of American Rabbis, 1950

Duties For The Jew

To be a Jew means more than the mere question of birth. It carries with it a duty to the moral law. No matter how many wildernesses we shall have to cross in life, we must ever remember that the Torah is our pillar of cloud by day and our pillar of fire by night. To be a Jew means to be active in spreading acts of justice and purity and goodness wherever we go. It means to work for a happier world. A good Jew must be ready to take an active part in the movement to do away with war, to work for equal rights among men, to help the oppressed, the orphan, the widow, the sick, and the unfortunate. To be a Jew means to be loyal to the Commandments which were intended not only for Israel but also for all men. We are very proud that our forefathers, without questioning, took up the task that made them a " Kingdom of Priests." But we will be more proud if we, too, give ourselves anew to this task. We must prove that we have strength enough and wisdom enough to hearken unto the Torah and to do as it commands us.

ALEXANDER ALAN STEINBACH,
Sabbath Queen

The Scope Of Judaism

Judaism is inseparable from people, land, language and Torah. Its emphasis is conduct ; its institutions are the family, the school, the synagogue, and primarily society ; its m a j o r problems are national continuity and perfection, social justice and world peace. Its signal promise is a better world order.

SOLOMON GOLDMAN,
Crisis and Decision

Judaism — The Soul Of Jewish Civilization

Jewish religion is nothing less than the soul of Judaism, or of Jewish civilization. Through the Jewish conception of God and the various practices connected with it, the contents of Jewish living have always assumed meaning. Through the teachings about God and the observances with which they were associated, the Jews have been able to interpret their experiences, their hopes and their sufferings in a way that enhanced their lives. It was undoubtedly the conviction that those religious teachings constituted religion at its truest and its best that instilled in the Jew the courage to face stoically a hostile world.

MORDECAI M. KAPLAN,
The Reconstructionist

Judaism — The Unique Culture Of The Jewish People

The only name which adequately describes the Jewish heritage is civilization or culture. Judaism is, then . . . to be defined as the unique culture of the Jewish people. Like any civilization, it represents an organic complex of a literature, language, religious outlook, folk-ways, group hopes, aspirations, ethical values and esthetic judgments. In this living whole, religion is at once the driving motif and the most ideal expression, but it is by no means the whole nor the largest part.

MILTON STEINBERG,
The Making of the Modern Jew

What It Means To Be A Jew

Being a Jew in the broadest definition means first, the accident of birth; secondly, the act of choice, choosing to remain Jewish despite the difficulties; thirdly, the act of cognition, learning to know the history and literature of his people so as to understand its soul and appreciate its place in the world; and finally, the act of transmission, transmitting to the next generation his heritage and the will to carry it on so that the Jewish people may not perish from the earth.

ISRAEL GOLDSTEIN,
Toward a Solution

Our Only " Mission "

Judaism was never meant to be a church. The church is a place for worship. It is a place where believers gather on certain days to witness and partake in some religious rites and offer their prayers. The role of the church in the life of the individual ends the moment he closes its doors behind him. The synagogue, or to be more exact, the Beth Hamedrash, was never meant to be exclusively a place of worship or a prayer house for Saturdays and holidays only. It was open every day and night of the week for worshippers, for wayfarers, for itinerant preachers, for students. What we call religion did not end for the layman in the synagogue. The same *mezzuzah* which was attached to the portals of the synagogue door was also on the portals of the home. The books that filled the synagogue shelves were also to be found in the home, and the commandments and teachings in those books guided and regulated every action and deed of the individual, whether in the home or in the street, whether at work or at his dinner table or in his personal life. There was no division between one's home, the school of one's children and one's prayer house; they were all integrated into one way of life.

Judaism thus was not "religion." It was a culture, the fullest manifestation of which was the Jewish individual. It was not the Book that was the culture. Not the Bible and the Talmud and the later commentaries. Not the myriad of commandments, interpretations, legends, prayers and tales contained in the Book, but the individual who was formed by this vast accumulation of historic memories, ideas, moral concepts, hopes and visions. To the outside world Judaism represents chiefly a library. To ourselves we are the product of the truths and ideas contained in that library. These were carried in the cells of our brains, in the marrow of our bones, in the expression of our eyes, in our aggressiveness and fears, in our laughter and sadness, in the thousand and one ways in which we adapted ourselves to all circumstances. Memories of four thousand years, from the serfdom in Egypt to the slaughterhouses in Poland, are alive in us. Whether a " race " or a " nation " or a " people," we are a human type, an individuality. In that we are and must be different, as is every individual who insists on being himself. More so, we are different with the memories of thousands of years of being different.

What then does Jewish continuity mean ? It means the preservation of the " differentness." As a specific human type, as a historic individuality, we have a particular place in mankind and in its eternal process of cultivating higher types of the human species. If we preserve the accumulation of wisdom, morals and ideas impregnated in us in the course of four thousand years of struggle with brute power, with prejudices and hatred, we have a contribution to make to mankind. And again, this contribution is not in the library we have accumulated. We are no longer the sole proprietors of the Bible, and the enormous post-biblical literature is gradually becoming the property of every non-Jewish student who wants to make his way through it. We have no specific " mission " in the world. The Book that contains our message is open to everybody. What is exclusively ours and cannot be duplicated by any other people is the personality of the Jew, that mysterious, adored and despised personality which is the creation of the experience of but one people and no other. The only " mission " we have is to preserve the essence to ourselves.

MENAHEM BORAISHA,
Notes on Jewish Survival

The Nature Of Judaism

Judaism has survived through the ages because it has been a dynamic tradition. It always knew how to adapt itself to new thought and new conditions. Moses, the Prophets, Johanen ben Zakkai, Maimonides — each saved Judaism in an hour of crisis by adjusting it to the times. The entire Talmud is essentially a reinterpretation of the earlier Judaism of the Bible to meet the problems of a new age. Even post-Talmudic Judaism continued this process of growth and development.

Judaism is the complete culture or civilization of the Jewish people. It possesses all the varied attributes of language and literature, art, music, customs and law, institutions and history. We pray in Hebrew not because God understands no other language, but because it is our language, and therefore both the form and content of our thought. Our holiest sentiments must be expressed in the tongue that links us with our ancestors and our brothers everywhere. The practices and customs of Jewish life, our history and our traditions, are precious to us, because their contents reflect the noblest aspirations of which man has yet shown himself capable, and because their forms, growing out of our own group experience, are closest to us.

Our loyalty to Jewish life is therefore entirely free from a scorn or dislike for other religions and cultures. On the contrary, Judaism makes possible our appreciation of other civilizations. In Bernard Lazare's words, " Being a Jew is the least difficult way of being truly human."

Of all the aspects of Judaism, it is religion that is primary. The recognition of God in the world and the drive for ethical perfection are the two great contributions of the Jew to the world — two that are really one. Perhaps other civilizations can survive without religion, but not Judaism. Our history, our customs, our law, our literature, even our music and art, are intimately connected with the religious and ethical ideals of Judaism.

Jewish nationalism and religion are the body and soul of the living organism which is the Jewish people. Whenever Jewish religion without nationalism has been tried, it has failed. When Jewish nationalism without religion has been attempted it has been unable to maintain itself after the momentum of the religious dynamic was exhausted.

A vital Judaism in America includes a positive attitude toward Jewish tradition and an equally clear awareness of the necessity for growth and development. It does not deny the patent fact of the peoplehood of Israel, but places the emphasis properly upon the fundamentally religious character of its civilization. It is genuinely American, yet retains its bond of attachment to Israel and its zeal for the rebuilding of Eretz Yisrael.

It offers both hope and direction to all who are seeking to build a living American Judaism that will play its part in fulfilling Israel's Messianic faith in the inevitable victory of universal justice, freedom and peace, which our prophets and sages envisioned as the Kingdom of God on earth.

ROBERT GORDIS,
Sabbath and Festival Prayer Book

The early Hebrews had created the Bible out of their lives ; their descendants created their lives out of the Bible.

ABRAHAM LEON SACHAR,
A History of The Jews

The Uniqueness Of Israel

The Jewish group plainly cannot be fitted into any known scheme. It resists all historical categories and general concepts ; it is unique. This uniqueness of Israel necessarily thwarts the nations' very natural desire for an explanation, and explanation always implies arrangement in categories. The existence of whatever cannot be cubbyholed and hence understood is alarming. This state of affairs provides a basis of truth for the observation that anti-Semitism is a kind of fear of ghosts. The wandering, roving, defenseless group which is different from any other and comparable to none seems to the nations among which it lives to have something spectral about it, because it does not fit into any other given group. It could not be otherwise. The Jewish people was, indeed, always a " sinister " homeless specter. This people, which resisted inclusion in any category, a resistance which the other peoples could never become quite accustomed to, was always the first victim of fanatical mass movements (the Crusades of the eleventh century for instance). It was branded as the cause of mass misfortunes ("the Jew is responsible for the 'Black Death' "). No matter how hard it tried, it never quite succeeded in adjusting to its environment. (The Inquisition followed upon Marranism.)

When I say that the nations regard us as a specter—and this myth is symbolized in the form of the wandering Jew — we must distinguish between being and appearance. We ourselves know very well that we are not specters, but a living community and so we must ask ourselves what our nonclassifiability really signifies. Is it due merely to a lack of vision and insight on the part of the nations ? Is it that we can be fitted into a system, only they are not able to do it ? Is this resistance of ours to classification merely a negative phenomenon, one that is temporary ? Does it simply mean that we cannot be classified until — at some future time — we are ?

We have only one way to apprehend the positive meaning of this negative phenomenon : the way of aith. From any viewpoint other than faith, our inability to fit into a category would be intolerable, as something counter to history and counter to nature. But from the viewpoint of faith, our inability to fit into a category is the foundation and meaning of our living avowal of the uniqueness of Israel. We would differentiate this uniqueness from the general uniqueness we attribute to every group and each individual. The uniqueness of Israel signifies something which in its nature, its history, and its vocation is so individual that it cannot be classified.

MARTIN BUBER,
Israel and the World

The Source Of Our Strength

Jews are the people of the spirit, and whenever they return to the spirit, they are great and splendid and put to shame and overcome their knavish oppressors. Rosenkranz profoundly compared them to the giant Antaeus, except that the giant was strengthened whenever he touched earth, while the Jews gain new strength whenever they touch heaven.   HEINRICH HEINE,
Ludwig Boerne

The Bond Between People And Religion

This people, one of the smallest and oldest historic nations — now scattered over the globe — out of the depth of its own experience, attained to a lofty and unique vision of God, man, and the universe, and translated that vision into a program of living. That vision and that way of life constitute the philosophy and the precepts of Judaism.

The relationship between the people and the religion is unique in Judaism ; for the religion is inconceivable without a continuous, living Jewish people. By the normal process of religious conversion Judaism can absorb and assimilate individuals and even nations within its fold, and it has indeed done so. But were the Jews of the world to disappear, their religion would inevitably disappear with them. Other peoples who had no historic connection with the Jewish past could under such circumstances become heir to the universal teachings of Judaism ; but the precepts, ceremonials, and observances in which these principles are incorporated and which make up the body of Judaism would have no relevancy for those whose ancestors did not " go out of the land of Egypt," and who were not born to the tradition that their fathers stood at the foot of Sinai and that they and their descendants were forever to be a kingdom of priests and a holy nation.

The indissoluble bond between the people and religion is a basic part of Judaism. Judaism was not given full grown to the Jewish people as was Christianity to the pagan nations. To its adherents, the Jewish religion in essence is not the distillation of the tears and sorrows of others, freely given them by an act of divine grace or acquired through the mysteries of faith. Slowly and painfully over the course of many centuries it was beaten out of the historic experiences of the nation, illumined by the vision of its prophets and sages. The prophets of Israel, profound mystics, who envisaged God the Infinite, who perceived that His Spirit filled the universe, and who spoke in His Name with the warmth, intimacy, and conviction of personal revelation, were not detached individualists or universalists. They were essentially national heroes of the Jewish religious genius. The problems, sins, failures, and sorrows of their people were the starting-point of their spiritual brooding. However universal and far-reaching the resulting prophetic vision may have been, its light was focused upon Israel and, through Israel, its rays were diffused round the world.

ABRAHAM A. NEUMAN,
Landmarks and Goals

It is in and through the Torah that we are teachers of the nations, that we exist today, and are saved for an eternal salvation.

NACHMAN KROCHMAL,
Moreh Nebuhay Haz'man

No Jews Without Judaism—No Judaism Without Jews

I beg to submit to your readers the following passage taken from *The Letters of Robert Louis Stevenson:*

"What a strange idea to think me a Jew-hater! Isaiah and David and Heine are good enough for me, and I leave more unsaid . . . . The ascendant hand is what I feel most strongly; I am bound in and with my forbears; were he one of mine I should not be struck at all by Mr. Moss, of Bevis Marks, I should still see behind him Moses of the Mount and the Tables, and the shining face. We are nobly born; fortunate those who know it; blessed those who remember."

I quote Stevenson as an author familiar to your readers. The same sentiment, however, is expressed, if less forcibly, by hundreds of Jewish writers in ancient and modern times, all of which goes to show that the now fashionable cry (among the Little-Israelites) of our being Anglo-Saxons, or Englishmen of the Jewish persuasion, is but a sickly platitude.

Those familiar with Judaica know that the cry was raised in Germany some generations ago, many Rabbis and many more laymen shouting it with the whole power of their lungs; "We are Germanen of the Mosaic persuasion!" The theory now is exploded in Germany; and our repeating such platitudes after the terrible experience of the last decades can only be explained on the principle of Martineau, who remarks somewhere that in matters intellectual the English are sometimes apt to act as the younger brothers of the Germans, putting on the trousers which their elder brothers left off wearing years ago.

The doctrine professed now by those who are not carried away by the new-fangled "yellow" theology is, there is no Judaism without Jews, and there are no Jews without Judaism. We can thus only be Jews of the Jewish persuasion. "Blessed are those who remember!"

SOLOMON SCHECHTER,
Epistles to the Jews of England

When Jews Say " We "

Jews, speaking among themselves, Jews of authentic feeling speaking to their Gentile Neighbors, instinctively use the pronoun *we*. And in that *we* they include instinctively, as the slightest analysis will demonstrate, all the Jews in the world, the living and the dead, the martyrs of Europe and the heroes of Israel. They include in that act of speech the innumer-able generations that have gone before ; they include all the children of Abraham, and at high moments of festival or memorial, of grief or of triumph, they are aware of spiritual presences according to their range of knowledge, from Moshe *Rabbenu* to some sage or *Zaddick* of yesterday.   LUDWIG LEWISOHN, *The American Jew*

Basic Qualifications For Being A Jew

The basic qualifications for being a Jew are (1) the identification of oneself as a Jew, i.e., the acceptance of the Jewish People with its past, its present and its future as one's own People ; (2) belief in the spiritual values of the Jewish tradition, i.e., the conviction that the Jewish spiritual heritage affords inspiration for living, and constitutes a worthy contribution to the totality of man's spiritual wisdom ; and (3) participation in Jewish life, i.e., sharing in those activities which help to insure the perpetuation of the Jewish People and the advancement of its civilization.

These qualifications, and not Jewish parentage, have been stressed in the bulk of our tradition. Jews were enjoined to qualify themselves for the study of Torah (i.e., Judaism) "because it is not subject to inheritance." Converts, on the other hand, were told to address God in worship, in the same terms as born Jews, as "our God and God of our fathers, God of Abraham, God of Isaac, and God of Jacob," because converts are regarded as authentic Jews *(na-asu ikkar k'yisrael)*.

MORDECAI M. KAPLAN, *Questions Jews Ask*

The Indefinable Essence

In this human being there is something that makes him a Jewish human being, something imponderably small and yet immeasurably great, his most inaccessible secret which yet breaks forth from every gesture and from every word and most of all from the most casual . . . . The thing is not even experienced. It is simply lived. It is what one IS.   FRANZ ROSENZWEIG, *Zur Juedischen Erzienhung*

Knowledge And Self-Identification

Judaism is an outlook on life which is associated and interwoven ideologically with the history of a people. Let me put it in a simple way. If somewhere in China today an individual were to work out for himself all the ethical and theological principles of Judaism, and live up to them, would that make him a Jew ? My answer is no. He would be as good a person as any Jew, and better than most Jews ; but he would not be a Jew until he had associated himself with the fellowship, and had accepted the responsibilities and instrumentalities of that fellowship.

By the instrumentalities I mean not only a ritual ; and, as to the ritual, we must remember that the Jewish ritual is the expression of the history of a people that, when faithful to Judaism, sees history as a manifestation of God's will. Judaism cannot be separated from the Jewish Bible, the Mishnah, the Talmud, the commentators, the Kabbalah, Chassidism, the exile, the Restoration, the total fact of the Jewish experience : it cannot be separated from

these and restated in the form of a series of ethical and theological theorems. From time to time in the popular press there appear articles on the beliefs of Jews, most of them written by Jews. These efforts to transpose the key of Judaism into the key of a religion of a different order are usually a testimony to the amiability of the editors who encourage them and to the good-will-mindedness of the writers who make them. Certainly there are things that the Jews believe ; but before these can be understood, one must establish the character of the Jewish people in its peoplehood. When that has been done one may proceed to inquire : " What do Jews *know* and believe ? " For in the case of the Jew, to accept certain tenets of faith as abstractions, without a knowledge of the Jewish people and an informed self-identification with it, does not constitute true and reliable membership in it.

MAURICE SAMUEL,
The Professor and the Fossil

There Can Be No Judaism Without Torah

What then is Torah ? It is a coat of many colors, a spiritual garb of infinite variety. Torah is the embodiment of Jewish thought and vision ; the repository of Israel's historic experiences ; the vehicle of its

communion with the Infinite ; the medium of divine speech and human love ; the authoritarian voice : Thou Shalt, Thou Shalt Not ; the alternating currents of divine, thunderous wrath and the warmth of Messianic hopes and dreams for Israel and mankind. Torah is the distillation of the soul of Israel into the written word of its classic literature, in the institutions in which it has taken shelter. But the Torah in the ideal cannot be chained to the written word nor contained wholly in the institutions designed for human beings. It is the indwelling of the divine spirit in living souls as expressed in the genius of Israel.

Torah is the quintessence of Judaism. There can be no Judaism worthy of the name without Torah. A Torah-less Judaism would be pulseless, nerveless: a corpse, without life or potency.

ABRAHAM A. NEUMAN,
Landmarks and Goals

Judaism Is A Life

Judaism is something more than a badge, something more than a birthmark; it is a life. To be born a Jew does not declare any of us to be of the elect; it only designates us for enrolment among the elect. God signs the covenant, but we have to seal it — to seal it by a life of service. " What makes a man a Jew ? " is a question that is often asked. The answer is, two things: membership in the Jewish brotherhood, and loyal fulfilment of the obligations which that membership imposes. To be of the Jewish people but to trample upon Jewish duty is to be faithless to Israel.   MORRIS JOSEPH,
Judaism as Creed and Life

Is not Jewish nationalism an empty phrase if we do not connect with it Jewish religion and Jewish ethics, Jewish culture and the Jewish mode of life which gave it its individuality?

LOUIS GINZBERG,
Students, Scholars and Saints

3

The Quest for God

It is hard to live in partnership with God. To attempt to live without Him is to court spiritual bankruptcy.

ALEXANDER A. STEINBACH

God is not alone when discarded by man. But man is alone.

ABRAHAM J. HESCHEL

I believe in the sun even when it is not shining. I believe in love even when not feeling it. I believe in God even when He is silent.

Inscription on the walls of a cellar in Cologne where Jews hid from the Nazis. Quoted by ZVI KOLITZ in *Tiger Beneath The Skin*.

One Man's Spiritual Odyssey

One man's spiritual Odyssey may be of interest to others seeking peace of mind, because it may reflect something of the alternating turbulence and tranquillity of our modern age. I offer my experience — in no way exceptional — for whatever help it may give to my perplexed contemporaries.

To begin with, I have gone through a number of stages in my own thoughts on God. I shared in my childhood the usual picture of Divinity — a daguerreotype, as it were, of my grandfather — a heavenly replica of an old, bearded, patriarchal figure. Later, as a theological student, I lived through anguished years when nothing in the external world could stifle the question, "Where is God? What is his nature?" I realize now that my adolescent sufferings were a disguise for a deeper distrust of life, a sense of personal uncertainty. Yet I know that those adolescent years of searching for God were invaluable for my own spiritual maturation. No religious teacher who has not himself tasted of the bitter cup of rejection, agnosticism, and fear can be of help to other men and women.

During all these years there came a time when I thought that man was enough and that humanism was the answer. Traditionally, emphasis upon man and humanistic values is one of the fundamental Jewish concepts; yet I have come to see that humanism is not enough to explain man. Neither his mind nor his creative powers can be truly understood except as the offspring of some universal parent. I have come to feel that the whole human story, with all its tragedy and its triumph, is like a page torn from the middle of a book without beginning or end — an undecipherable page when cut out of its context. The context of man is the Power greater than man. The human adventure is part of a universal sonnet — one line in a deathless poem. Without faith that our human intelligence and haunting human conscience are a reflection of a greater intelligence and a vaster creative power, the key to the cipher is lost and the episode of mankind on earth becomes a hidden code — a meaningless jumble of vowels and consonants . . . .

Only within recent years have I begun to discover a pathway to God that is intellectually satisfying to my own wrestling spirit. I found the first hints in the pages of Hebrew wisdom. I came to understand that the prophets in Palestine were also wrestling with the same problem. They, too, held the conviction that God was all-good, but that He did not abrogate the moral laws of life for any favorites. Those ancient prophets, in effect, said to the people of Israel, "God has established natural laws in the universe, and He expects them to operate. He has also given you consciences and minds, and He expects you to use them. If you abuse them He will not set His world topsy-turvy in order to rescue you from the consequences of your deeds."

I began to see a deep wisdom in that message — the wisdom of maturity — which does not expect God to be a father cajoled and wheedled into violating the necessary principles of human life. I understood why Jeremiah told the people of Jerusalem (who were so confident that they were God's favorites) not to believe presumptuously that He would be partial to them and to their beloved city. There is no partiality in a moral universe. Gradually I came to understand how my ancestors were able to find the greatness of God and to discern His truth not in the eras of luxury and security but in the catastrophe of exile, when their world was shaken to its foundation.

The unthinking man might say that during this whirlwind of national tragedy the Jews should have lost faith in God. Is there not something startling and profound in this neglected truth that the giants of the Bible found the handwriting of God not in the sunlit hours of triumph, but on the slate of tragedy? It seems like a paradox that evil and suffering should have been the birthplace of the moral God.

The very experience that now seems to make so many people atheistic is what made the prophets of Israel maturely religious. Why? Because they had gone beyond a childish view of Divinity. At a time when thousands of Jews must have been saying with their emotions, "There is no God," it was then that the prophets — Titans of the spirit — taught their new message: "God cannot do anything that will mock his moral law. He is not an Oriental monarch, to be bribed into overlooking violations of the principles upon which the earth and human society must rest." . . . .

When I think with my mind rather than feel with my heart, I cannot conceive of a world where God would interfere capriciously with personal and social destiny, making all human effort and human striving worthless. We cannot look to God to save us from man-made evil, whether it be a civic catastrophe born out of negligence or greed or whether it be a dictatorship that mankind long knew would slay the innocent if it were not stopped in time. We dare not run to God to wipe away by a miracle the effects of our human misdeeds. We cannot have only the blessings that come with mind and conscience and that distinguish us from the lifeless rock and expect God to be our heavy insurance policy against all of the dangers and the failures of life.

God must indeed be filled with sorrow as He sees how the human race has misused its freedom of choice and how it has violated His moral laws. "Men, men," He could cry, " I gave you an earth ribbed with veins of diamonds and gold and black with frozen heat. I gave you strong and dynamic waters to drive your windmills and make your turbines hum with power. I gave you rich loam upon which you could grow waving wheat. What have you done ? My coal often you have stolen, leaving only the slag for the poor. My diamonds, my gold, my living waters, you have imprisoned behind the walls of your selfish greed. Because you refused to use my gifts in order to build a just earth, you have been forced to spend gold like water for ships blown up in the twinkling of an eye. You have seen your cities ruined and your precious sons annihilated on a thousand battlefields. Now, at last, the intelligence which I have implanted in you, O race of man, has fashioned the key to unlock my treasure house of energy. Within the secret heart of my atoms is the power of life and death for all of you. O men, will you this time choose weapons of death or tools of life, unconditional destruction or unconditional survival ? " . . .

It is true that we can never actually define God, since we human beings are so limited and our language is always inexact, and we shall probably always have to use metaphor and analogy in order to interpret Divine reality. What many people do not understand is that our scientific description of the universe is just as metaphorical as the religious description. Men thought that they were being very exact and scientific when they called the world a great machine. Is that not an analogy, a metaphor ? Whenever we speak of reality as a machine or as purely material, we are reading something into the world. Why should we continue to interpret the universe in terms of the lowest that we know rather than in terms of the highest that we experience ? Intelligence, purpose, and personality, the will to live, the need to love, the yearning to be related — these are just as important clues to reality as atoms and electrons. It sometimes seems to me that our habit of looking at the universe in terms of matter rather than in terms of purpose and of conscience is a reflection of our inferiority complex — as though we human beings were not worthy to be regarded as mirrors of the Divine. Perhaps this is part of that spiritual self-deprecation which is always fashionable in certain theological circles. There is no logical reason, however, why we should explain reality always by reducing the complex to the simple. Why exalt the atom as the clue to truth and ignore the mind of man ? Why should we not believe that that which is highest in ourselves is a reflection of that which is deepest in the universe — that we are children of a Power who makes possible the growing achievement of relatedness, fulfilment, goodness ?

We may not ever come to know

God's essence, but His attributes of activity — namely, the universal laws of social, mental, and moral health — these we can possess. God, as Hocking insists, is not the Healing Fiction but the Healing Fact, and we come upon Him at work in the majesty of nature and the fruitfulness of mind, in the laws of atoms and the goals of men.

JOSHUA LOTH LIEBMAN,
Peace of Mind

Israel's Monotheism Absolute

When Jerusalem fell, Rome was quite prepared to give the God of Israel a place in her Pantheon. Israel absolutely refused such religious annexation : the one, unique and universal God of Israel alone was a living God ; Jupiter and his like were things of naught, figments of the imagination. And the same reasons that would not permit the Jews to bend the knee to the gods of pagan Rome, prevented them in later generations from allowing themselves to be absorbed by the two great Religions that issued from Israel's bosom. Here too they found, both in dogma and morality, novelties and concessions that were repugnant to the austere simplicity of their absolute monotheism.

THEODORE S. REINACH

Salvation is attained not by subscription to metaphysical dogmas, but solely by love of God that fulfils itself in action. This is a cardinal truth in Judaism.

CHASDAI CRESCAS,
Or Adonai

Advocates Of God — Champions Of Justice

The profoundly religious men of all times were the mightiest spokesmen of social justice and its uncompromising champions. It was from the lips of men touched with the burning coal of divine faith, from the lips of the prophet, the seer, the man of God, that the first great cry for justice leaped out upon the world. They who sought God most zealously spoke of human rights most fearlessly. It was in the name of God, the stern and righteous Judge, that those spiritual men of valor wielded the scorpion whip of their fury upon those who ground the faces of the poor and turned aside the way of the humble. It was in the name of God, the compassionate and the merciful Friend, that they pleaded the cause of the orphan and the widow, the beaten and the broken of life. It was in the name of God, the Father of all men, that they espoused the cause of a human brotherhood which, over-leaping the dread boundaries of ancient enmities erected by fear and greed, leads men to turn their swords into plowshares and their spears into pruning hooks.

ABBA HILLEL SILVER,
Religion in a Changing World

Where God Is Found

God, where shall I find Thee,
Whose glory fills the universe?
Behold I find Thee
Wherever the mind is free to follow
its own bent,
Wherever words come out from the
depth of truth,
Wherever tireless striving stretches
its arms toward perfection,
Wherever men struggle for freedom
and right,
Wherever the scientist toils to
unbare the secrets of nature,
Wherever the poet strings pearls of
beauty in lyric lines,
Wherever glorious deeds are done.

Reconstructionist Prayer Book

Man is always in the presence of God, and God must always be present to man.

MARTIN BUBER

Judaism Disdains Hollow Victories

There are enough individualistic elements in Judaism to satisfy all the longings of the religionist whose bent lies towards mysticism. And just as every Israelite " could always pour out his private griefs and joys before him who fashioneth the hearts," so was he able to satisfy his longing for perfect communion with his God (who is "nigh to all them who call upon him ") by means of simple love, without the aid of any forcible means.

It must, however, be remarked that this satisfying the needs of anybody and everybody is not the highest aim which Judaism set before itself. Altogether, one might venture to express the opinion that the now fashionable test of determining the worth of a religion by its capability to supply the various demands of the great market of the believers has something low and mercenary about it. Nothing less than a good old honest heathen pantheon would satisfy the crazes and cravings of our present pampered humanity, with its pagan reminiscences, its metaphysical confusion of languages and theological idiosyncrasies. True religion is above these demands. It is not a Jack-of-all-trades, meaning monotheism to the philosopher, pluralism to the crowd, some mysterious Nothing to the agnostic, Pantheism to the poet, service of man to the hero-worshipper. Its mission is just as much to teach the world that there *are* false gods as to bring it nearer to the true one. Abraham, the friend of God, who was destined to become the first winner of souls, began his career, according to the legend, with breaking idols, and it is his particular glory to have been in opposition to the whole world. Judaism means to convert the world, not to convert itself. It will not die in order *not* to live. It disdains a victory by defeating itself in giving up its essential doctrines and its most vital teaching. It has confidence in the world ; it hopes, it prays, and waits patiently for the great day when the world will be ripe for its acceptance.

SOLOMON SCHECHTER,
Some Aspects of Rabbinic Theology

God In Need Of Man

Judaism teaches us that just as man needs God, so God needs man for the fulfilment of His divine plan. Does this sound blasphemous and irreverent ? Without man, God, who is rooted in the timeless, will persist from everlasting to everlasting, but the paradox of divinity is that mortal man gives the most sacred meaning to the reality of immortal God. According to the Rabbis, God created the universe in the state of its beginning, leaving it to man to continue the processes of creation. God needs man as a co-partner in the building of His kingdom on earth.

What greater evidence is there for the exalted concept of man in the theology of Judaism ? This speck of dust has been fused with infinite divinity. This creature of matter whose life-span is but a tick of the clock of history, has been merged with eternal timelessness. Man is not, as we are told in current existentialist philosophy, miserable and wretched, sinful and worthless refuse to be cast upon a cosmic manure-heap. Man is not doomed by his nature to be evil and guilt-ridden, without hope, without purpose, without meaning. Judaism not only beholds man as a child of God created in the divine image — but Judaism motivates the startling and humbling conviction that God needs man for the fulfilment of His divine purpose, the growth and development of a moral civilization from Sinai to the messianic kingdom of universal justice, truth and peace on earth.

WILLIAM B. SILVERMAN,
Temple Bulletin

The Majesty Of God

God is the oneness
That spans the fathomless deeps of
    space
And the measureless eons of time,
Binding them together in act,
As we do in thought.

He is the sameness
In the elemental substance of stars
    and planets,
Of this our earthly abode
And of all that it holds.
He is the unity
Of all that is,
The uniformity of all that moves,
The rhythm of all things
And the nature of their interaction.

> He binds up the Pleiades in a
>   cluster
> And loosens the chains of Orion ;
> He directs the signs of the Zodiac
> And guides the constellations of
>   the Bear.

God is the mystery of life,
Enkindling inert matter
With inner drive and purpose.

He is the creative flame
That transfigures lifeless substance,
Leaping into ever higher realms of
    being,
Brightening into the radiant glow of
    feeling
Till it turn into the white fire of
    thought.

And though no sign of living thing
Break the eternal silence of the
    spheres,
We cannot deem this earth,
This tiny speck in the infinitude,
Alone instinct with God.

By that token
Which unites the worlds in bonds
    of matter
Are all the worlds bound
In the bond of Life.

> It is He who forms the mountains
> And creates the wind,   [man ;
> And reveals His inner mind to
> He who makes the dawn and
>   darkness,
> Who marches over the heights of
>   earth ;
> The Lord, the God of hosts, is
>   His name.

God is in the faith
By which we overcome
The fear of loneliness, of helpless-
    ness,
Of failure and of death.

God is in the hope
Which, like a shaft of light,
Cleaves the dark abysms
Of sin, of suffering, and of despair.

God is in the love
Which creates, protects, forgives,
His is the spirit
Which broods upon the chaos men
    have wrought,
Disturbing its static wrongs,
And stirring into life the formless
    beginnings
Of the new and better world.

> Thou art my portion,
> O Eternal ;
> Thou art my share.

Thou wilt show me the path of life ;
Fulness of joy is in Thy presence ;
Everlasting happiness dost Thou pro-
vide.

Reconstructionist Prayer Book

The Kobriner Rabbi turned to his
Hasidim and said : "Do you know
where God is ?" He took a piece of
bread, showed it to them all, and
continued : "God is in this piece of
bread. Without the Lord's manifestation of His power in all nature,
this piece of bread would have no
existence."

The Hasidic Anthology

A father complained to the Baal
Shem that his son had forsaken God.
"What, Rabbi, shall I do ?"

"Love him more than ever," was
the Baal Shem's reply.

The Hasidic Anthology

No one is entitled to excuse his lack
of service to the Lord by affirming
that he is engaged in business and
must associate with vulgar folk. God
is everywhere. He is among the most
common of men ; he is to be found
in the lowliest occupation. Delve
deeper and you will find a way to
serve God in everything and in every
work and place.

THE BRATZLAVER RABBI,
The Hasidic Anthology

The Imitation Of God

Ye shall be holy : for I the Lord
your God am holy. (Leviticus 19 : 2).
Man is not only to worship God, but
to imitate Him. By his deeds he must
reveal the Divine that is implanted
in him ; and make manifest, by
the purity and righteousness of his
actions, that he is of God. Mortal
man cannot imitate God's infinite
majesty or His eternity ; but he
can strive towards a purity that
is Divine, by keeping aloof from
everything loathsome and defiling ;
and especially can he imitate God's
merciful qualities. This "imitation
of God" is held forth by the Rabbis
as the highest human ideal. "Be like
God ; as He is merciful and gracious.
Scripture commands, *Walk ye after*

the Lord your God. But the Lord is
a consuming fire ; how can men
walk after Him ? But the meaning is,
by being as He is — merciful, loving,
long-suffering. Mark how, on the
first page of the Torah, God clothed
the naked — Adam ; and on the last,
He buried the dead — Moses. He heals
the sick, frees the captives, does
good even to His enemies, and is
merciful both to the living and
the dead" (Talmud). These merciful
qualities, therefore, are real links
between God and man ; and man is
never nearer the Divine than in his
compassionate moments.

JOSEPH H. HERTZ,
The Pentateuch and Haftorahs

We know of some very religious people who came to doubt God when a great misfortune befell them, even though they themselves were to blame for it ; but we have never yet seen anyone who lost his faith because an undeserved fortune fell to his lot.

ARTHUR SCHNITZLER,
Buch der Sprüche und Bedenken

The Testimony Of The Universe

To think of God as a strict unity is, then, the only rational way of conceiving of Him. And this essentially Jewish conception is in close harmony with the message of the world around us. Every advance of physical science more firmly establishes the fact that the universe is marked by unity of purpose and design, that it has been planned and is controlled by one mind, and not by many minds. Phenomena, like light and darkness, sunshine and storm, growth and decay, which seemed to the men of ancient times the work of different and contending deities, are now seen to be but manifestations of one uniform law, one self-consistent Mind.

Night falls on one hemisphere only that a new day may dawn upon another ; the rain and the wind are the handmaids of the sun in his life-giving work ; the plant and the animal die in order that others may live. Despite its seeming discords, Nature is marked by a harmony of purpose throughout. All its various parts fit into each other, work with each other, as do the sections of a machine. The bee steals its sweetness from the flower, but at the same time fertilizes it with the pollen she has unconsciously carried away on her body from some other flower. Nature moves through a cycle of changes ; once complete, the cycle begins again. The seed falls upon the earth ; it germinates ; it yields the blossom, which casts the seed in its turn ; and so on for ever. The sun draws up the water from the ocean in the form of vapor ; the vapor becomes a cloud ; the cloud empties itself as rain ; the rain replenishes the river, which returns it to the sea. The universe is ruled, moreover, by a firm hand ; it is governed by fixed laws, not by caprice. The seasons follow each other in unbroken sequence. The heavenly bodies travel their appointed course with such regularity that astronomers can calculate their orbit with mathematical precision. The changes in the little life of the meanest insect are uniform ; order reigns supreme in the most insignificant part of Nature's kingdom. And if there is one truth which science has established most clearly, it is that the force or energy which works in the universe is one and persistent. Showing itself in diverse forms, it is still essentially ever the same. It is never spent ; it fails not, nor grows weary ; it is unchangeable, deathless . . . .

What a flood of light do all these facts throw upon the Divine Nature ! If unity marks the universe, the Power that made and controls it must needs be One. " One God, one law, one element " — such is the teaching of science. It is also the teaching of Judaism. Moreover it was the teaching of Judaism before it was the doctrine of science. The majestic conception of the universe implied in the dogma of the Divine Unity paved the way for the modern physicist, with his affirmation of the unity and the orderliness of the cosmos.

The doctrine of the Divine Unity is the cornerstone of the Jewish religion. It is set forth in the Pentateuch with notable clearness and force. " Hear, O Israel," so runs the impressive adjuration, " the Lord is our God ; the Lord is One."

MORRIS JOSEPH,
Judaism as Creed and Life

Hard as the world is to explain *with* God, it is harder yet without Him.

CLAUDE G. MONTEFIORE,
Liberal Judaism

The Believer Does Not Fight Alone

A confident hope, an assurance of a final victory over evil, are the last consequences of the God faith to those who hold it fast. In the heart of the agnostic or atheist there lurks forever a haunting, grisly fear : since all is chance, our ideals too are chance. The same fortuity which called them into existence may wipe them away. In the end the whole contest may end in a stalemate, or wrong may even emerge triumphant. Not so with the believer. He does not fight alone, or in human company only, nor with his heart torn by doubts over the outcome. Behind him, beside him and before, works that Power that drives the universe, which is also a Power that makes for righteousness. So much, then, can religious faith achieve against the experience of evil. It can open our eyes until, like Elisha's lad, we see " the chariots of fire " which hitherto were invisible to us ; it can cause us to hear the cheering, emboldening words :

" Fear not, for they that are with us are more than they that are with them."

MILTON STEINBERG,
A Believing Jew

The love of people is at the same time a love for God. For when we love one, we necessarily love one's handiwork.

JUDAH LÖW

Serving The Lord With Joy

Is it not a paradox that the word *simcha* — joy — should stubbornly pervade the liturgy and ceremonies and ideas of a people who have been consistently battered and bruised ? Yet the Jew believes in serving the Lord with joy — be it in misfortune when he stands erect to say the *kaddish* in praise of God, or be it to give a toast, *l'chayim — unto life —* on happier occasions. Judaism has generally shunned asceticism. It believes that the true service of God is incomplete without the joy that comes from the heart. When a Rabbi said in the Talmud that Man will be called to account for depriving himself of the good things which the world lawfully allows, surely this was his way of saying that the world is full of God. It is full of the beautiful and the good in which joy abounds. When we partake of that joy, we partake of God. And to reject that joy is to reject God.

HERBERT RICHER

When man is at one, God is One.

THE ZOHAR

The Omnipotence Of God

The entire universe, as I see it, is the outward manifestation of Mind-Energy, of spirit, or to use the older and better word, of God. God is then the essential Being of all beings, though all beings in their totality do not exhaust Him. It is His reason which expresses itself in the rationality of nature, in the fact that all things behave in conformity with intelligible forms, in the fact, in brief, that the world is cosmos not chaos. His power moves in the dynamisms of physical reality. His will is the impulse behind the upsurge of life on this planet. Individualized, He is the soul of man whose thought processes are infinitesimal sparks of His infinite fire, whose moral aspirations are fragments of His vast purpose, whose yearning to create is but an echo of His cosmic creativity. And He is an ethical being, not so much in the sense that He enters into relations with His own expressions, as in the deeper sense that He is the fountain-head, source, and sanction of man's moral life. The human quest after freedom, truth, goodness, and beauty is but the splintered spearhead of the divine drive. So to me, the whole panorama of earth and sky, the tempestuous progress of living things, the tortuous career of humanity are the external shell of a process wherein God realizes His character.

Such is my faith . . . . I shall assert that my God belief is a hypothesis, interpreting the universe as a whole.

But if it is only a faith or hypothesis, it is not one which I have adopted wantonly. Rather have I been driven to it by compelling considerations. I affirm it, first, because this seems to me to be the only theory which accounts for reality as I know it in personal experience and as science describes it. Here before me unfolds a universe which is dynamic, creative, and rational in the sense that everything in it conforms to the law of its own being, a world that has produced in living things what seems to be purposiveness and in man the phenomenon of consciousness. No other theory except that which posits a Thought-Will as the essence of things fits such a scene.

I believe as I do, furthermore, because of the practical necessities of human existence. To live well men need joy and hope concerning their destiny and courage in facing it. They require, moreover, a sense of their own worth and of the significance of the lives of their fellows. Without such convictions, the ethical life is bankrupt at its source. There will exist justification neither for self-sacrifice. Against the requirements of man's morale and morality, only the theistic outlook is adequate, for it alone assures him that life adds up to sense rather than nonsense, that it is design rather than a succession of chance syllables in a cosmic idiot's tale.

And of all possible interpretations of reality, this is the simplest. Given the one God concept, the whole universe bursts into lucidity. The rationality of nature, the emergence of life, the phenomena of conscience and consciousness become intelligible. Deny it and the whole becomes inexplicable. There is then a kind of esthetic neatness about the religious position. It is marked by that economy of idea which is one of the goals of all inquiry.

Superior plausibility, practicality, and simplicity — these are the grounds on which my God postulate rests.

MILTON STEINBERG,
A Believing Jew

God Is King

The Lord was King.
  The world about us did not spring
  From forces uncontrolled and free,

  And man is not caprice or whim
  Created without thought or form.

  Before the mountains were brought forth,

Before the sun and moon and stars,

Before the waters in the deep,
Before wild beasts or birds on wing,
       The Lord was King.
The Lord is King.
  His spirit ever hovering
  Above His world, above mankind,

To guide the destiny of man
Against a blind and helpless fate.
'Not will o'wisp nor beast to prey,
Not slave to passion, greed or
    power,
Endowed with reason, man obeys
A higher law of governing.
                    The Lord is King.

The Lord forever will be King.
    His moral rule awakening
Man's conscience 'gainst debasing
    vice
That breeds disease and blinds the
    eye,

And keeps men bowed in servi-
    tude.
When man will take his brother's
    hand,
When hate will cease and peace
    hold sway,
When nations join to walk His
    way
And all to righteous precepts
    cling,
    The Lord forever will be King.

MORRIS SILVERMAN,
High Holiday Prayer Book

Ethical Monotheism — The Heart Of Judaism

Ethical monotheism is not merely one of the numerous articles of Jewish belief, but the very heart of the Jewish religion. It gives character to all of its doctrines, its ethics and worship. Through historic experience, as interpreted by the genius of the prophets and through the reflection of the sages, the Jewish people grew aware of the reality of God and that underneath all existence are His everlasting arms. The Lord of the universe is also the God of the spirits of all flesh. He reveals Himself in the majestic sweep of the evolutionary process, in the history of races and nations and in the minds and consciences of the pure in heart who seek to commune with Him, in humility and in faith, as with a Father and King, Redeemer and Friend. We look for His revelation and purpose not only in cosmic law but also in human love and justice, in goodness and in truth, in beauty and in holiness. Through these He speaks to the hearts of all who would hear and shows them the way of life. To cherish them and to live supremely and self-sacrificingly by them is to have an experience of God and to know what He means to the soul. The idea of God has distinguished Israel as a people of destiny and of religious mission to the rest of the families of the earth. It transforms and irradiates the lives of all men. It brings sanctity and moral content and meaning into human existence. Belief in God ever has served as a dynamic of personal and social well-being and regeneration. It has inspired men with patience and with courage to face obstacles seemingly insurmountable. In the darkest night of sorrow and of raging tempest, it has shone forth as the star of hope and pointed to a brighter and better tomorrow.

SAMUEL S. COHON,
The Jewish Idea of God

God is of no importance unless He is of supreme importance.

ABRAHAM J. HESCHEL,
Man Is Not Alone

One God—One Morality

Only faith in the one God, the living consciousness of belonging to the One, were able to demand the moral decision of man ; here for the first time the one and only necessary thing was placed before him, the one thing all important and essential. As there are no other gods but the one God, this is no other commandment but His commandment. "Thou shalt be whole with the Lord, thy God." To the Jew the unity of God finds its determining expression in the unity of the ethical. He who realizes and fulfils the Moral Law, which is One, acknowledges God as the One ; here is found the demanding and final significance of Monotheism, here is found the full human sincerity of its acceptance. As monotheism means the One God, so also it means the one command, the one righteousness, the one path, and the one morality. It means the rejection of all indifference, all neutrality and unconcern, of all that which was so often considered in antiquity as the ideal of the philosopher. It also constitutes a protest against all the double morality, which was preached and obeyed in previous, and also in more recent centuries, with one special moral code for rulers and another for the ruled, one for the great and one for the small, one for the strong and one for the weak, be they weak in power or the weak in spirit. That sentence of the Psalmist, "Teach me Thy way, O Lord ; I will walk in Thy truth : unite my heart to fear Thy name," acquired in Jewish thought throughout the centuries— not only for its mysticism and its philosophy, but equally for the meditation and prayer of the people — an ever richer meaning. It spoke of the one heart which found its way to the One God and to the one command. If man attains the unity of the heart, and if with it he follows the one way, he possesses the true reverence for the One God and brings Monotheism to its realization. Thus does he make of God the One — as the ancient Hebrew morning prayer says, he "unifies God" through his love for Him. The creative element in man found its powerful note in this desire "to unify God." Through his moral action man creates the unity of God upon earth. The divine Unity becomes, as it were, the task of man.

LEO BAECK,
The Essence of Judaism

Before you can find God, you must lose yourself.

THE BAAL SHEM

The Kingship Of God

The affirmation of God as Creator is associated with the affirmation of the divine sovereignty. No appellation for God is more common in biblical-rabbinical literature or in Jewish liturgy than the term King ; no concept is more characteristic of the Hebraic outlook than the Kingdom — that is, the kingship — of God. David's prayer, as recorded in Chronicles, communicates something of the intensity and exaltation of spirit behind these phrases : " Thine, O Lord, is the greatness and the power and the glory and the victory and the majesty ; for all that is in the heaven and in the earth is Thine ; Thine is the kingdom, O Lord, and Thou art exalted as head above all " (I Chron. 29 : 11). The formula introducing virtually every prayer in the liturgy is : " Blessed art Thou, O Lord our God, King of the Universe . . . ."

What does the kingship of God mean in the context of Hebraic religion ? Its implications are in-

exhaustible, but above everything else it means that the God who created the universe is the absolute Lord over nature, life and history. No aspect of existence escapes his sovereign rule : " *All* men must bring *all* their lives under the whole will of God." Life cannot be departmentalized into secular and sacred, material and spiritual, with the latter alone falling under divine jurisdiction. No such distinction is recognized in Hebraic religion ; the attempt to withdraw anything, no matter how seemingly insignificant, from divine rule is branded as an attempt to set up a rival, an idolatrous, claim against the sovereignty of God : " I am the Lord thy God . . . thou shalt have no other gods before me " (Exod. 20 : 2-3). All life, all existence, is governed by one ultimate principle and that principle is the will of the Living God.

WILL HERBERG,
Judaism and Modern Man

The God The Jews Worship

In a corner of the world I see a singular people. All others follow idols, all others worship blindly a frightful multitude of vicious and contemptible deities. This people, called Jews, worships only one God, the creator of heaven and earth. Its fundamental law, to which its whole cult refers, obligates men to love God with all their heart, with all their soul, and with all their mind and might. This people provides in its law for a circumcision of the heart, of which that of the body is merely a symbol; and this circumcision of the heart means the suppression of every affection which does not stem from the principles of the love of God . . . .

All the philosophers esteemed reason, justice, virtue and truth in themselves. They believed that the gods gave health, riches, fame; but they claimed to have found within their own innermost depths the virtue and wisdom which distinguished them from other men. They never developed the thought of the goodness of creation, or of the power of the Creator, or of the selfless love due to Him. Hence, as I review all the nations of antiquity, I find the Jewish people alone worshipping the true God and in possession of the religion of love.

FRANCOIS DE SALIGNAC
DELAMOTTE FENELON,
Oeuvres Complètes

The Omnipresence Of God

The Burning Bush:
> And the angel of the Lord appeared unto him in a flame of fire out of the midst of a bush.

A heathen asked Rabbi Joshua ben Karhah:
" Why did the Holy One, blessed be He, choose to speak to Moses out of the midst of a thornbush?"

The rabbi answered him:
" Had it been out of the midst of a carob tree or out of the midst of a sycamore, you would have asked the same question.

Still, I cannot send you away empty-handed.

Well then: Why out of the midst of a thornbush?

To teach you that there is no place void of the Presence of God, not even a thornbush!"

Midrash,
adapted by NAHUM M. GLATZER,
In Time and Eternity

The Institutions Of Moses

No heathen ever conceived an idea of so great an object as that of the institutions of Moses, which appears to be nothing less than the instruction of all mankind in the great doctrine of the unity and universal government of God as the Maker of the world and the common parent of all the human race, in opposition to the polytheism and idolatry which then prevailed, which, besides being grossly absurd in its principles and leading to endless superstitions, threatened the world with a deluge of vice and misery. For this purpose the Hebrew nation was placed in the most conspicuous situation among all the civilised nations of the world, which were universally addicted to idolatry of the grossest kind . . . . As all mankind imagined that their outward prosperity depended upon the observance of their respective religions, that of the Hebrew nation was made to do so in the most conspicuous manner, as a visible lesson to all the world. They were to prosper beyond all other nations while they adhered to their religion ; and to suffer in a manner equally exemplary and conspicuous in consequence of their departure from it. Of this all mankind might easily judge. These great ideas occur in the sacred books of the Hebrews and nowhere else. They are all distinctly advanced by Moses and more fully unfolded in the writings of the later prophets. But certainly nothing so great and sublime could have been suggested to Moses from anything that he saw in Egypt, or could have heard of in other countries.

JOSEPH PRIESTLEY,
A Comparison of The Institutions of Moses With Those of the Hindus and Other Ancient Nations

Faith And Reason

The Bible never commands us to believe, though it commends belief. Such a command would be useless. Belief cannot be coerced. I may order another person to do an act he dislikes, and if I have sufficient authority over him he will obey ; but I can never, by simply commanding him, make him believe something to be true which he thinks untrue. Belief is a matter of mental persuasion. We believe in a statement only because our minds are satisfied as to its truth. Real belief is an intellectual condition. Reason is its ultimate foundation. We say real belief, because to accept a statement as true in spite of the protests of reason, to believe in a doctrine, as some one said he did, because it is impossible, is not belief, but credulity. Judaism asks us not for credulity but for true faith—faith based on reason . . . .

Thus it is that the Bible, the great text-book of Judaism, though never *commanding* us to believe in the Supreme, *persuades* us to believe in Him. It supplies us with proofs of the Divine Existence. It bids us turn, now to the great wonders of Nature, now to the story of the Past, and cries "Behold your God!" "The heavens declare the glory of God: and the firmament showeth His handiwork," so the Psalmist reminds us. "Lift up your eyes on high, and behold who hath created these things," so says the Prophet. From Nature the Bible leads us to Nature's God. We are asked to believe that there is a Power behind the universe, not on the mere assertion of the Bible, but on the most convincing of all testimony — the testimony of the universe itself. But this is only part of the truth. There is the life-story of Israel — his wondrous preservation, his equally marvellous chastisement, his manifest selection for the performances of a great work in the world ; and there is, more-over, the fate of the nations—of Egypt, Assyria, Babylonia. All this bears witness to the Supreme and His overruling Providence. It is to such evidence that the Bible appeals, and on which it rests its assertion that God lives and reigns . . . .

Let us not forget, however, that while the subject is huge, our powers are very limited. We are finite minds dealing with the Infinite. Just as we can see even with the most powerful telescope only a fragment of the physical universe, so we can see only a part of the workings of the stupendous Power behind it. There must always be a region into which we cannot penetrate, a mystery we cannot solve. When the intellect has done its utmost, we must still have recourse to faith. Where we cannot know we must be content to trust. Nor is it only in the domain of Religion that this exercise of faith is demanded. It is an essential element in the conduct of everyday life. Without faith in human nature, in its honesty, its veracity, its trust-worthiness, there could be no such thing as commerce. It is the very breath of life for the great world of business. And it is equally indis-pensable for the social life. Society could not hold together for a single day if men did not trust and believe in one another.

Moreover, faith is the necessary equipment even of the scientific investigator, himself being witness. Religion postulates a Divine Mind as the explanation of the universe. But the demand which it thus makes upon our faith is no greater than that put forth by physical science, with its assumption of a substance filling all space, to which it has given the name of the Ether. It is a substance not merely imperceptible by the senses, not merely imponder-able, but in its nature entirely different from all other forms of matter . . . . "We are compelled to make use of faith," Haeckel admits, " even in science itself . . . ."

Faith, then, is indispensable to physical science no less than to religion. And if it is admissible in the one domain of thought, it cannot be inadmissible in the other . . . .

The truth is, that even in the exercise of faith there is no real abdication of the reason. It is because reason discloses God to us in so large a portion of the world and of life, that it justifies us in inferring that He is everywhere in that great domain. The " great leap in the dark " of Faith has Mind for its impulse. We see God with the eye of the mind in certain phenomena, and this warrants our trust in that vision of Him which the soul's second-sight discerns " behind the veil." For let it be remembered that for the apprehension of the Divine we are not thrust back upon reason alone. We know God by way of the intellect, but by way of the soul as well. Spiritual experience is no less real and trustworthy than the evidence of the mind. God reveals Himself to us as surely in the ecstasy of prayer as in the awe that is aroused within us by the majesty of the physical universe. Even the per-

ception of that majesty is as much spiritual as intellectual. The glory of nature evokes an answering glow within us distinct from the cold light of reasoned knowledge. The splendor of a sunset, the grandeur of the sea, the silence of the everlasting hills, will arouse a mystic sense of the Divine, that at once transcends and reinforces their appeal to the intellect. Their wondrousness proclaims a Divine Power, but some nameless influence of theirs touches strange chords within us ; " deep calls unto deep " ; we become conscious of a larger life than this, of a world about us in which earth and sea and sky have no part. In Bachya's words : " We see, yet not with the eye ; we hear, yet not with the ear ; we speak, yet not with the tongue."

MORRIS JOSEPH,
Judaism as Creed and Life

Nothing is better than to search for the true God, even if the discovery of Him eludes human capacity, since the very wish to learn, if earnestly entertained, produces untold joys and pleasures.

PHILO,
Special Laws

What Judaism Says About God

One assertion the Jewish religion makes concerning God, which, by the testimony of the Tradition itself, is the very cornerstone of Jewish theology :

IT SAYS OF GOD THAT HE IS ONE.

This seemingly simple statement cuts deeper and runs richer than first appears. Its meanings are many and important. Of these, furthermore, each successive epoch called one or another into prominence, thus investing the single self - same affirmation with different primary significances for different generations. Yet each of these is no more than an aspect of the rounded and continuing Jewish God — faith ; taken in succession they epitomize Jewish theology. On both scores they are worth reviewing.

These are the significances which history from time to time has extracted from God's oneness.

GOD IS ONE, AND NOT MANY.

The ancient world was polytheistic both as to nature and as to society.

Heathendom assumed a deity in and for each object : the river, the tree, the sun ; in and for each faculty and function : fertility, memory, the artisan's skill. So it tore reality to shreds, and then, to confound confusion, assumed that each spirit had no other role except to look after its own. Under this construction there was no order, either logical or moral, to things.

In the same fashion paganism, positing a separate deity for each people, territory, and economic class, tore mankind also to shreds. For, just as a subject and his king owed political loyalty to each other and no one else, so with the relationship between a national god and his worshippers : each was expected to look out for his own exclusively, without regard for anyone else. Thus ancient religion rationalized the lawlessness of ancient society, legitima-

tizing the exploitation of all who stood outside the pale of protection of the local deity and lending supernatural sanctions to any attempt by the god-favored nation against its neighbors.

In proclaiming the oneness of God, therefore, the prophets intended more than a repudiation of idol worship. They were bent on establishing the principles that reality is an order, not an anarchy ; that mankind is a unity, not a hodgepodge ; and the one universal law of righteousness holds sway over men, transcending borders, surmounting all class lines.

At the same time and with even greater practical i m p o r t their monotheism constituted a declaration of war against spiritual idolatry in all its forms : the worship to which man is addicted of the self and its desires, or of caste and group interest, or of the state and the autarch in whom it may take on symbolic embodiment. Having proclaimed the Lord alone to be God, they asserted in effect that to Him only and to His law of righteousness supremacy is to be ascribed and unreserved loyalty to be accorded.

GOD IS ONE, NOT TWO.

Some time in the sixth century before the Common Era, Judaism met Zoroastrianism, encountering for the first time a religion rivaling itself in maturity, spirituality, and earnestness. Distinctive of this faith was its doctrine of dualism. Behind the world it discerned not one but two creative beings, the first a force of light and goodness, the other a power of darkness and evil. These twin genii wrestle ceaselessly for the world and man's soul, a struggle in which each human being, willy-nilly, takes sides. Religion's purpose, as Zoroastrianism conceived it, is to make certain that men choose the right side.

This theology has its attractions. It is dramatic in its picture of a world conflict, heroic in the demands it makes of man, and metaphysically alluring, since it offers — or seems to offer — a quick solution to the enigma of evil.

Despite all this, Judaism rejected it. Whatever its advantages, the disabilities of dualism proved greater.

Dualism makes an absolute of evil ; Judaism regards evil as contingent to a prior and more basic good.

Dualism despairs in advance of half of reality and half of human nature. Judaism holds that there is nothing which cannot be retrieved for the good. The most sinful impulses in man, as the rabbis point out, are the very forces which, properly directed, motivate the virtues.

Dualism p l a c e s the ultimate triumph of the good in jeopardy. If the dark be correlative to the light, what assurance is there that the latter will prevail ?

Judaism's repudiation of Zoroastrianism was not achieved in a moment. For centuries the possibility of " two powers " continued to tempt the Jewish imagination. But the first reaction of the prophet when he insisted that one and the same God " fashions light and creates darkness, makes peace and creates evil " — that remained in the end the Tradition's last word.

GOD IS ONE, NOT THREE.

During the Middle Ages the Jewish assertion of God's unity became an explicit denial of the Christian dogma of the Trinity, a total disavowal of the thesis that God, though one, is somehow at the same time three persons, " coeternal and coequal."

In rejecting this doctrine Jews were concerned primarily with warding off what they regarded as a misrepresentation of the Divine nature. But they were no less zealous to indicate their dissent from the notion, integral to the Trinity, of a God-man : Deity embodied in the flesh and blood of some particular individual. To them all men reflect God's nature and are His children. The suggestion that any single human being might be God Himself they spurned as blasphemy.

GOD IS ONE, NOT NONE.

So in our day Judaism declares its unyielding opposition to contemporary atheism and the materialism that attends it ; to the new, yet old, misreading of reality as the blind interplay of matter and energy ; to the error that man and his values are children of cosmic chance, destined to perish as pointlessly as they came to be.

So also the Tradition protests against another and scarcely less dangerous modern f a l l a c y. The evasive proposition that God *is* but does not *exist*, that He is only a human conception or a useful fiction, or that His name may properly be assigned to the highest value a man cherishes. Against all such slippery counsels Judaism affirms that God's existence is independent of man and that He is not only actual and real but the most actual actuality and realest reality of all.

In the end then, the Tradition at the latest stage in its career takes its stand again on the same verity which first gave it life and character.

MILTON STEINBERG,
Basic Judaism

There is no room for God in him who is full of himself.

THE BAAL SHEM

The Search For God

The sacred history of Judaism has been characterized by the search for God. Pursuing this divine quest, we have learned the lesson of humility. We have learned to doubt categorical absolutes, dogmatic certainties and theological truisms. We have been conditioned by a critical religious tradition to look with suspicion upon simple religious answers that enable fallible mortal man to comprehend the infallible, immortal God . . . . With Job, we question : " Canst thou by searching find God ? Canst thou find out the purpose of the Almighty ? . . . What canst thou know ? "

What *can* we know ? What can mortal man bound by the finitude of his being comprehend about the infinite ? We cannot know ! We cannot understand ! We cannot through searching find God ! Through searching, however, we identify ourselves with values and ideals that are holy. Through searching we sensitize our vision to behold God's presence in every aspect of life — in the wonder and beauty of the universe, the miracle of love, the chemistry of a tear — and above all in the surpassing grandeur of man struggling to imitate the divine attributes of justice and compassion. It is through service to man that Judaism has indicated a pathway that leads to God. Our Rabbis have taught us that to search for God, one must first love God — and to love God truly, one must first love man. In searching we may not find God, but through our efforts to serve and elevate man, we find pathways that lead us to truth, justice, mercy and love.

As Jews, we have no choice. We are committed to a divine quest. We are summoned to go forth in search of divinity — a divinity we will never completely understand — a divinity we will never completely find — but the quest itself will sanctify our lives with holiness, elevate our vision to the most high, and turn us — our thoughts, our aspirations, our future — beyond the edge of mystery, in the direction of God.

WILLIAM B. SILVERMAN,
Temple Bulletin

Judaism makes man find God where he finds himself.   S. R. HIRSCH,
Gesamelte Schriften

The Struggle Toward Monotheism

Not in the "discovery" of God lies the meaning of the Jews, but in what they did with that discovery. For whereas many individuals in moments of brilliant insight made the discovery before and after them, the Jews alone as a people sweated out (the Yiddish word *oisgekrenkt* is better than "sweated out") their monotheism over the millenia; they alone made it their obsession as a people and somehow or other hung on to it with unbelievable doggedness from its first emergence four thousand years ago until this day; and the record of the first half of this multimillennial torment is that collection of books known as the Jewish Bible. One may properly say that Judaism is meaningless without the Jewish Bible, not because it tells of the discovery of God, but because it mirrors the struggle of recalcitrant man with the consequences of his discovery.

Thus we are dealing not with a discovery, but with a process. The Biblical record is a continuing drama. It is fragmentary, a sacred anthology of excerpts in which there is frequent reference to other records, now lost. And yet, with all its incompleteness, it is magnificently consistent and instructive. The theme is struggle, inspiration, defection, return, near - obliteration, re - emergence against all probability, the picture of a people possessed by a divine destiny reluctantly assumed, everlastingly repudiated, everlastingly reclaimed . . . .

One is tempted to say that the Israelites and God could neither get along together nor let ·go of each other.   MAURICE SAMUEL,
The Professor and the Fossil

Yossel Rakover's Appeal To God

In the ruins of the ghetto of Warsaw, among heaps of charred rubbish, there was found, packed tightly into a small bottle, the following testament, written during the ghetto's last hours by a Jew named Yossel Rakover.
Warsaw, April 28, 1943.

" I, Yossel, son of David Rakover of Tarnopol, a Hassid of the Rabbi of Ger and a descendant of the great, pious, and righteous families of Rakover and Meisel, inscribe these lines as the houses of the Warsaw ghetto go up in flames. The house I am in is one of the last unburnt houses remaining. For several hours an unusually heavy artillery barrage has been crashing down on us, and the walls around are disintegrating under the fire. It will not be long before the house I am in is transformed, like almost every other house of the ghetto, into a grave for its defenders.

" When my wife, my children and I — six in all — hid in the forest, it was the night and the night alone that concealed us in its bosom. The day turned us over to our persecutors and murderers. I remember with the most painful clarity the day when the Germans raked with a hail of fire the thousands of refugees on the highway from Grodno to Warsaw. As the sun rose, the airplanes zoomed over us. The whole day long they murdered us. In this massacre, my wife with our seven-months-old child in her arms perished. And two others of my five remaining children also disappeared that day without a trace. Their names were David and Yehuda, one was four years old, the other six.

" At sunset, the handful of survivors continued their journey in the direction of Warsaw, and I, with my three remaining children, started out to comb the fields and forests at the site of the massacre in search of the children. The entire night we called for them. Only echoes replied. I never saw my two children again, and later in a dream was told that they were in God's hands.

" My other three children died within the space of a single year in the Warsaw ghetto. Rachel, my daughter of ten, heard that it was possible to find scraps of bread in the public dump outside the ghetto walls. The ghetto was starving at the time, and the people who died of starvation lay in the streets like heaps of rags. The people in the ghetto were prepared to face any death but the death of hunger.

" Rachel told me nothing of her plan to steal out of the ghetto, which was punishable by death. She and a girl friend of the same age started out on the perilous journey. She left home under cover of darkness, and at sunrise she and her friend were caught outside the ghetto walls. Nazi ghetto guards, together with dozens of their Polish underlings, at once started in pursuit of these two Jewish children who had dared to venture out to hunt for a piece of bread in a garbage can. People witnessing the chase could not believe their eyes. One might think that it was a pursuit of dangerous criminals, that horde of fiends running amok in pursuit of a pair of starved ten-year-old children. They did not endure very long in the unequal match. One of them, my child, running with her last ounce of strength, fell exhausted to the ground, and the Nazis then put a bullet through her head. The other child saved herself, but, driven out of her mind, died two weeks later.

"The fifth child, Yacob, a boy of thirteen, died on his Bar Mitzvah day of tuberculosis. The last child, my fifteen-year-old daughter, Chaya, perished during a Kinderaktion — children's operation — that began at sunrise last Rosh Hashano and ended at sundown. That day, before sunset, hundreds of Jewish families lost their children.

"Now my time has come. And like Job, I can say of myself, nor am I the only one that can say it, that I return to the soil naked, as naked as the day of my birth.

"I am forty-three years old, and when I look back on the past I can assert confidently, as confident as a man can be of himself, that I have lived a respectable, upstanding life, my heart full of love for God. I was once blessed with success, but never boasted of it. My possessions were extensive. My house was open to the needy. I served God enthusiastically, and my single request to Him was that He should allow me to worship Him with all my heart, and all my soul, and all my strength.

"I cannot say that my relationship to God has remained unchanged after everything I have lived through, but I can say with absolute certainty that my belief in Him has not changed whatsoever. Previously, when I was well off, my relation to God was as to one who granted me a favor for nothing, and I was eternally obliged to Him for it. Now my relations to God are as to one who owes me something, owes me much, and since I feel so, I believe that I have the right to demand it of Him. But I do not say like Job that God should point out my sin with His finger so that I may know why I deserve this; for greater and saintlier men than I are now firmly convinced that it is not a question of punishing sinners: something entirely different is taking place in the world. More exactly, it is a time when God has veiled His countenance from the world, sacrificing mankind to its wild instincts.

"In a situation like this, I naturally expect no miracles, nor do I ask Him, my Lord, to show me any mercy. May He treat me with the same indifference with which He treated millions of His people. I am no exception, and I expect no special treatment. I will no longer attempt to save myself, nor flee any more. I will facilitate the work of the fire by moistening my clothing with gasoline.

"I have three more bottles of gasoline. They are as precious to me as wine to a drunkard. After pouring one over my clothes, I will place the paper on which I write these lines in the empty bottle and hide it among the bricks filling the window of this room. If anyone ever finds it and reads it, he will, perhaps, understand the emotions of a Jew, one of millions, who died forsaken by the God in whom he believed unshakeably. I will let the two other bottles explode on the heads of the murderers when my last moment comes.

" There were twelve of us in this room at the outbreak of the rebellion. For nine days we battled against the enemy. All eleven of my comrades have fallen, dying silently in battle, including the small boy of about five — who came here only God knows how and who now lies dead near me, with his face wearing the kind of smile that appears on children's faces when dreaming peacefully — even this child died with the same epic calm as his older comrades. It happened early this morning. Most of us were dead already. The boy scaled the heap of corpses to catch a glimpse of the outside world through the window. He stood beside me in that position for several minutes. Suddenly he fell backwards, rolling down the pile of corpses, and lay like a stone. On his small, pale forehead, between the locks of black hair, there was a spattering of blood.

" I write these lines lying on the floor. Around me lie my dead comrades. I look into their faces, and it seems to me that a quiet but mocking, irony animates them, as if they were saying to me, ' A little patience, you foolish man, another few minutes and everything will become clear to you too.' This irony is particularly noticeable on the face of the small boy lying near my right hand as if he were asleep. His small mouth is drawn into a smile exactly as if he were laughing, and I, who still live and feel and think — it seems to me that he is laughing at me.

" 'Unless my face is eaten by the flames, a similar smile may also rest on it after my death. Meanwhile, I still live, and before my death I wish to speak to my Lord as a living man, a simple, living person who had the great but tragic honor of being a Jew.

" I am proud that I am a Jew not in spite of the world's treatment of us, but precisely because of this treatment, I should be ashamed to belong to the people who spawned and raised the criminals who are responsible for the deeds that have been perpetuated against us.

" I am proud to be a Jew because it is an art to be a Jew, because it is difficult to be a Jew. It is no art to be an Englishman, an American, or a Frenchman. It may be easier, more comfortable, to be one of them, but not more honorable. Yes, it is an honor to be a Jew.

" I believe that to be a Jew means to be a fighter, an everlasting swimmer against the turbulent, criminal human current. The Jew is a hero, a martyr, a saint. You, our enemies, declare that we are bad ? I believe that we are better and finer than you, but even if we were worse — I should like to see how you would look in our place !

" I am happy to belong to the unhappiest peoples of the world, whose precepts represent the loftiest and most beautiful of all morality and laws.

"I believe that to be a Jew is an inborn trait. One is born a Jew exactly as one is born an artist. It is impossible to be released from being a Jew. That is our godly attribute that has made us a chosen people. Those who do not understand will never understand the higher meaning of our martyrdom. If I ever doubted that God once designated us as the chosen people, I would believe now that our tribulations have made us the chosen one.

"I believe in You, God of Israel, even though You have done everything to stop me from believing in You. I believe in Your laws even if I cannot excuse Your actions. My relationship to You is not the relationship of a slave to his master but rather that of a pupil to his teacher. I bow my head before Your greatness, but will not kiss the lash with which You strike me.

"You say, perhaps, that we have sinned, O Lord? It must surely be true. And therefore we are punished? I can understand that too. But I should like You to tell me — *Is there any sin in the world deserving of such punishment as the punishment we have received?*

"You assert that You will yet repay our enemies? I am convinced of it. Repay them without mercy? I have no doubt of that either. I should like You to tell me, however — *Is there any punishment in the world capable of compensating for the crimes that have been committed against us?*

"You say, I know, that it is no longer a question of sin and punishment, but rather a situation in which Your countenance is veiled, in which humanity is abandoned to its evil instincts. I should like to ask You, O Lord — and this question burns in me like a consuming fire — *What more, O, what more must transpire before You unveil Your countenance again to the world?*

"I want to say to You that now, more than in any previous period of our eternal path of agony, we, we the tortured, humiliated, buried alive, and burned alive, we the insulted, the object of mockery, we who have been murdered by the millions, we have the right to know: *What are the limits of Your forebearance?*

"I should like to say something more: Do not put the rope under too much strain, lest, alas, it may snap. The test to which You have put us is so severe, so unbearably severe, that You should — You must — forgive those members of Your people who, in their misery, have turned from You.

"Forgive those who have turned from You in their misery, but also those who have turned from You in their happiness. You have transformed our life into such a frightful, perpetual struggle that the cowards among us have been forced to flee from it; and what is happiness but a place of refuge for cowards ? Do not chastise them for it. One does not strike cowards, but has mercy on them. Have mercy on them, rather than us, O Lord.

"Forgive those who have desecrated Your name, who have gone over to the service of other gods, who have become indifferent to You. You have castigated them so severely that they no longer believe that You are their Father, that they have any Father at all.

"I tell You this because I do believe in You, believe in You more strongly than ever, because now I know that You are my Lord, because after all You are now, You cannot be the God of those whose deeds are the most horrible expression of ungodliness.

"If You are not my Lord, then whose Lord are You ? The Lord of the murderers ?

"If those that hate me and murder me are so benighted, so evil, what then am I if not the person who reflects something of Your light, of Your goodness ?

"I cannot extol You for the deeds that You tolerate. I bless You and extol You, however, for the very fact of Your existence, for Your awesome mightiness.

"The murderers themselves have already passed sentence on themselves and will never escape it ; but may You carry out a doubly severe sentence on those who are condoning the murder.

"But those who are silent in the face of murder, those who have no fear of You, but fear what people might say (fools ! they are unaware that the people will say nothing ;) those who express their sympathy with the drowning man but refuse to rescue him — punish them, O Lord, punish them, I implore You, like the thief, with a doubly-severe sentence !

"Death can wait no longer. From the floors above me, the firing becomes weaker by the minute. The last defenders of this stronghold are now falling, and with them falls and perishes the great, beautiful, and God-fearing Jewish part of Warsaw. The sun is about to set, and I thank God that I will never see it again. Fire lights the small window, and the bit of sky that I can see is flooded with red like a waterfall of blood. In about an hour at the most I will be with the rest of my family and with the millions of other stricken members of my people in that better world where there are no more doubts.

"I die peacefully, but not complacently ; persecuted, but not enslaved ; embittered, but not cynical; a believer, but not a supplicant; a lover of God, but no blind amen-sayer of His.

"I have followed Him even when He repulsed me. I have followed His commandments even when He castigated me for it ; I have loved Him and I love Him even when He has hurled me to the earth, tortured me to death, made me an object of shame and ridicule.

" And these are my last words to You, my wrathful God : nothing will avail You in the least. You have done everything to make me lose my faith in You, but I die exactly as I have lived, crying :

" Hear, O Israel, the Lord our God the Lord is One.

" Into your hands, O Lord, I consign my soul."

ZVI KOLITZ,
The Tiger Beneath The Skin

God's Love

Could we with ink the ocean fill,
Were every blade of grass a quill,
Were the world of parchment made,
And every man a scribe by trade,
    To write the love
    of God above

Would drain the ocean dry ;
    Nor would the scroll
    Contain the whole,
Though stretched from sky to sky.

MEIR B. ISAAC NEHORAI,

God Cares

The old Pagan idea which pictures the gods as reclining at their ease in heaven while, all unheeded by them, mortals drag out their lives in care and misery here below, finds no place in Judaism. God has not made the world and left it to its fate. Exalted above the heavens, He yet takes a deep and loving interest in human joys and sorrows. It is impossible to think otherwise. The Supreme is bound by His own nature to care for His handiwork. An unsympathizing God is no God.

Nor are we thrown back upon cold argument alone. The Divine love is before our eyes. Its tokens are sown thick in the world and in human life. It stands revealed in the nobility of man himself, in the tender affection that binds parent to child, and child to parent, in the self-denying fidelity that makes husband and wife one flesh, in the single-hearted devotion of a man to his friend. God has created these beautiful qualities, and therefore they must mirror His nature. He must know the love with which He has filled His creatures ; He must be at least as good and tender as the souls He has made. " Behold," said God to Moses, " I will stand before thee there upon the rock in Horeb " ; " wherever " — so, according to the Rabbis, God declares — " thou findest the footprints of men, there I stand before thee." For man is the greatest revelation of the Divine.

MORRIS JOSEPH,
Judaism as Creed and Life

4

Prayer—The Bridge
Between Man and God

It is a good thing to give thanks unto the Lord
And to sing praises unto Thy name O Most High.

Psalm 92 : 2

In proper devotion a man has his eyes downward and
his heart upward.

Talmud (Yevamot 105 B)

Prayer is the bridge that carries man to God.

Quoted by LOUIS I. NEWMAN

Jewish Prayer

The Greek word for prayer means " to wish for." The German word for prayer means " to beg." The English word means " to entreat, implore, ask earnestly or, supplicate, beg." The Hebrew word is *t'phila*. Its root is *pallal* which means " to judge." The act of praying in Hebrew is *hitpallel*, the reflexive form of the verb ; it means " to judge oneself." It signifies self - examination, an inquiry into the state of one's soul, to make it ready for communication with God.

With reference to prayer, primitive minds regard themselves as serfs, and God as "the Lord of the manor," to whom one must constantly go begging for favors; flattering, cajoling, wheedling, obsequiously fawning — this is pagan prayer.

Jews look upon God as their Father and friend, in whose presence it is a delight to sit, with whom it is glorious and wonderful to converse. Whether as Father or as friend it were unseemly only to come into His presence to ask for something, begging.

Shneur Zalman of Ladi expressed the Jewish view when he interrupted his recitation of the set prayers in his Siddur to say to God : " I do not want your paradise. I do not want your coming world. I want you and you only." This ecstatic exclamation is not written in any Jewish prayer book, but it is the inevitable response of a soul sensitized by constant reading of this prayer book, a reading that is not only of the eyes and the lips and vocal cords, but of the heart, of the soul itself.

Whenever Levi Yitzhak of Berditchev came to a certain passage of the liturgy he paused to talk with God thus : " Lord of the universe. I do not beg you to reveal to me the secret of your ways. I could not bear it : the burden of this knowledge. But show me one thing, show it to me more clearly and more deeply, show me what this which is happening to me at this very moment means to me, what it demands of me. What you, O Lord of the world, are telling me by way of it. Ah, it is not why I suffer that I wish to know, but only whether I suffer for your sake."

It was the frequent, almost constant use of his prayer book and the inspiration he not only got from it, but the inspiration he brought to it, that gave Levi Yitzhok and the host of pious Jews that enjoyed this same spiritual exercise in days that were less fortunate and materially less prosperous than ours — gave them this sense of a world drenched in divine light, shimmering and holy with the grace and the beauty of the Lord.   ALBERT S. GOLDSTEIN,
Temple Bulletin

If you are not at peace with the world, your prayer will not be heard.
NAHMAN BRATZLAVER,
Reflections

Through Prayer We Are Uplifted

Prayer is an absolute necessity for us and for the whole world; it is also the most sacred kind of joy. The waves of our soul beat ceaselessly on the shores of consciousness. We desire of ourselves and of the whole world the kind of perfection that the limitation of existence renders impossible. In our despair and frustration we are likely to turn against our better judgment and against our Creator. But before this cancer of the spirit has had time enough to grow in our midst, we come to pray. We give utterance to our thoughts and are uplifted to a world of perfect existence. Thus our inner world is rendered perfect in truth, and restful joy fills our consciousness.

Every plant and bush, every grain of sand and clod of earth, everything in which life is revealed or hidden, the smallest and the biggest in creation—all longs and yearns and reaches out toward its celestial source. And at every moment, all these cravings are gathered up and absorbed by man, who is himself lifted up by the longing for holiness within him. It is during prayer that all these pent-up desires and yearnings are released. Through his prayer man unites in himself all being, and lifts all creation up to the fountainhead of blessing and life.

ABRAHAM ISAAC KUK,
Jewish Thought

If I recite my wants, it is not to remind Thee of them, but only that I may be conscious of my dependence upon Thee.

BAHYA IBN PAKUDA,
Hobot Halebabot

Prayer—An Invitation To God

Worship is a way of living, a way of seeing the world in the light of God. To worship is to rise to a higher level of existence, to see the world from the point of view of God. In worship we discover that the ultimate way is not to have a symbol but *to be a symbol*, to stand for the divine. The ultimate way is to sanctify thoughts, to sanctify time, to consecrate words, to hallow deeds. The study of the word of God is an example of the sanctification of thought; the Seventh Day is an example of the sanctification of time; prayer is an example of the consecration of words; observance is an example of the hallowing of deeds . . . .

To pray is to take notice of the wonder, to regain a sense of the mystery that animates all beings, the divine margin in all attainments. Prayer is our humble answer to the inconceivable surprise of living . . . .

Prayer is our attachment to the

utmost. Without God in sight, we are like the scattered rungs of a broken ladder. To pray is to become a ladder on which thoughts mount to God to join the movement toward Him which surges unnoticed throughout the entire universe. We do not step out of the world when we pray ; we merely see the world in a different setting. The self is not the hub, but the spoke of the revolving wheel. In prayer we shift the center of living from self-consciousness to self-surrender. God is the center toward which all forces tend. He is the source, and we are the flowing of His force, the ebb and flow of His tides . . . .

Prayer takes the mind out of the narrowness of self-interest, and enables us to see the world in the mirror of the holy.

The focus of prayer is not the self. Prayer comes to pass in a complete turning of the heart toward God, toward His goodness and power. It is the momentary disregard of our personal concerns, the absence of self-centered thoughts, which constitute the art of prayer. Feeling becomes prayer in the moment in which we forget ourselves and become aware of God . . . .

Prayer is an invitation to God to intervene in our lives, to let His will prevail in our affairs ; it is the opening of a window to Him in our will, an effort to make Him the Lord of our soul . . . .

In crisis, in moments of despair, a word of prayer is like a strap we take hold of when tottering in a rushing street car which seems to be turning over.   ABRAHAM J. HESCHEL,
Man's Quest for God

It is not permissible to petition God by prayer to change natural laws for your own sake.
MOSHE LEIB SASSOVER,
The Hasidic Anthology

Gold and silver become purified through fire. If you feel no sense of improvement after your prayer, you are either made of base metal, or your prayer was cold.
THE KORETZER RABBI,
The Hasidic Anthology

The Tzanzer Rabbi was asked by a Hasid : " What does the Rabbi do before praying ? "

" I pray," was the reply, " that I may be able to pray properly."
The Hasidic Anthology

The Language Of Prayer

The significance of the prayers consists not alone in their content but also in their traditional forms, in the verbiage in which they have been bequeathed to us, hence, also in the Hebrew language. This must remain, therefore, with few exceptions, the language of prayer.
ABRAHAM GEIGER,
Israelitisches Gebetbuch

Prayer Molds Community Conscience

Prayer is the most intensely personal expression of the human soul. But just as in the Psalms, so in the general prayers of the Synagogue, the individual worshiper immerses his individuality in the collective soul of Israel. No mediator is permitted to stand between the worshipper and Him to whom worship is directed. But granting some exceptions of prayers of an individual character, the chief prayers are designed for the individual as a member of a human brotherhood, or the household of Israel.

As the Jew bows in prayer before the Lord God, King of the universe, and pours out his heart before " the God of our Fathers, the God of Abraham, Isaac, and Jacob " he no longer stands before his Maker as a naked soul but as a social personality with hallowed memories. The contents of the prayers are cast in the collective plural. The worshiper in the Synagogue prays not for himself alone but for the common welfare. Petition, in general, is but a small part of the Synagogue prayers. Adoration, praise, and thanksgiving form the major theme of the Hebrew prayers and all living creatures are invoked to raise their voice in songs and hymns of glory. Although prayers may be recited in the home and when " thou walkest by the way " it is believed that they find greater merit when uttered in unison with other worshipers. Some themes, such as the *Kaddish*, the exalted prayer for the coming of the kingdom of God, are to be recited only when there is a quorum of at least ten male worshipers assembled. Through these and other subtle psychological suggestions, the Synagogue utilized the mystic power of prayer to foster the feeling of social responsibility and community conscience.

ABRAHAM A. NEUMAN,
Landmarks and Goals

The purpose of prayer is to leave us alone with God.   LEO BAECK,
Essence of Judaism

There Is Much Comfort In High Hills

By setting aside a place in which to worship, by repairing there frequently to replenish his spiritual powers, by learning there what his faith has to teach about life and its meaning, and by meeting there with like-minded fellows to encourage him and to strengthen him in his resolves, the Jew "ascends the mount of the Lord." He comes into contact with a world of elevated values and though he may soon come down to earth again he is the better for having been on the heights.

There is much comfort in high hills,
And a great easing of the heart.
We look upon them, and our nature
   fills
With loftier images from their life
   apart.
They set our feet on paths of free-
   dom, bent
To snap the circles of our discon-
tent.

The synagogue can do this for the modern Jew who learns, as his ancestors did, to revere it and make its ideal his own.

LOUIS JACOBS,
Jewish Prayer

The Need For Communion With God

Homesick For The Universal Parent

Judaism demands of each of us: study and action, Ma'aseh and Talmud, regarding both of them as means for communion with God. We regard this demand for Study and Practice not as one to be fulfilled only by a small professional group, who may be Jews for the rest of us. Each one of us must devote part of his day to Jewish thought and the Jewish mode of communion with God.

There may be those who feel that they can live quite happily without either religious discipline or communion with God. But they are in grave error. The restlessness which characterizes us, the confusion which has come on our times, the increasing percentage of neuroses among us, and the general unhappiness of all of us in the midst of the greatest affluence the world has yet seen, has come upon us primarily because of the lack of that sense of communion with God which made our forefathers happy in spite of their poverty and their physical

suffering. We resemble most closely those little children who, not having yet learned to interpret the symptoms of weariness and hunger, cry when bedtime or mealtime comes, and yet refuse either to go to bed or take their food. Living in a gilded palace, as it were, we are still miserable, for we are essentially orphans, having lost that most precious of all values in life, the sense of the Fatherhood of God.

The feeling of deprivation grows sharper and more poignant, instead of less severe, as we grow older. The time comes to each of us when the burdens of life seem far too heavy to carry, when the brightness of youth begins to fade, and we notice the lengthening shadows which presage our end.

More than ever then do we become homesick; homesick, not for our houses or for our countries, but homesick for the universal Parent of all of us, for that deep affection which is the heart of the universe itself, for the mercy of God; yet a wall of iron has been placed between us and Him, and we cannot find Him. What greater good can a man achieve, either for himself or for the world, than to contribute his effort to piercing this wall, and bring the Father and the children once more into loving communion with one another!   LOUIS FINKELSTEIN, *Sabbath and Festival Prayer Book*

Let your prayer be a window to Heaven.   THE BAAL SHEM

What It Means To Pray

Prayer, our Rabbis taught, is the Service of the Heart. Nothing is further from the truth than the widespread notion that to pray is synonymous with to beg, to request, or to supplicate. To be sure, to pray means to call upon God to help us. But we need Him not only when we are physically in danger. We need Him also when we are spiritually in danger.

To pray means to seek God's help, " to keep our tongue from evil," " to purify our hearts," " to put into our hearts to understand, to learn and to fulfill in love, the words of the Torah," and thus to keep us unswervingly loyal to truth, goodness, and beauty.

To pray is to feel and to give expression to a deep sense of gratitude. No intelligent, healthy, normal human being should take for granted, or accept without conscious, grateful acknowledgment the innumerable blessings which God in His infinite love bestows upon him daily — the blessings of parents and loved ones, of friends and country, of health and understanding.

To pray is to express renewed allegiance to the moral and ethical principles which we accept as the guides of our personal lives, and which we recognize as the indispensable foundation stones for a decent human society.

To pray is to meditate on events of the past which testify to God's guiding spirit in the affairs of men, and which give us courage to fight for justice and freedom, and to look confidently and hopefully to the future.

To pray is to try to experience the reality of God, to feel the purity and exaltation that comes from being near Him, and to give to our souls that serenity and peace which neither worldly success nor worldly failure, which neither the love of life, nor the fear of death, can disturb.

SIMON GREENBERG, *Sabbath and Festival Prayer Book*

One sigh uttered in prayer is of more avail than all the choirs and singers.

SAMUEL J. AGNON, *Israel Argosy No. 3*

We Cannot Help Praying

Prayer is a universal phenomenon in the soul-life of man. It is the soul's reaction to the terrors and joys, the uncertainties and dreams of life. " The reason why we pray," says William James, " is simply that we cannot help praying." It is an instinct that springs eternally from man's unquenchable faith in a living God, almighty and merciful, Who heareth prayer, and answereth those who call upon Him in truth ; and it ranges from half-articulate petition for help in distress to highest adoration, from confession of sin to jubilant expression of joyful fellowship with God, from thanksgiving to the solemn resolve to do His will as if it were our will. Prayer is a Jacob's ladder joining earth to heaven ; and, as nothing else, wakens in the children of men the sense of kinship with their Father on High. It is " an ascent of the mind to God " ; and, in ecstasies of devotion, man is raised above all earthly cares and fears. The Jewish Mystics compare the action of prayer upon the human spirit to that of the flame on the coal. " As the flame clothes the black, sooty clod in a garment of fire, and releases the heat imprisoned therein, even so does prayer clothe a man in a garment of holiness, evoke the light and fire implanted within him by his Maker, illumine his whole being, and unite the Lower and the Higher World " (Zohar).

Daily Prayer Book
JOSEPH H. HERTZ,

When wood burns it is the smoke alone that rises upwards, leaving the grosser elements below. So it is with prayer. The sincere intention alone ascends to heaven.

THE BAAL SHEM

Are Prayers Repetitious ?

You object that prayers are repetitious. So are birth and pain and joy and death. The basic emotions are not many. Every great symphony repeats a limited number of musical ideas. But they set off great surges of feeling in the listeners.

It is not what is in the prayer book that is alone important. What you bring to it is equally important. The more you experience, the more meaning and satisfaction you find in these expressions of universal human sentiments.

Nor need you sacrifice your intelligence, your freedom of inquiry or judgment to gain this faith. You need only sacrifice your smugness, your brittle sensualism, your all-pervasive, all-absorbing materialism, your nose-to-the-grind absorption in the trivia of life.

Open yourselves to the radiance of our Sabbath Service, to the blessed insights of our Torah, to the security that comes from the silence of the Sanctuary during moments of medi-tation — and you will find the faith which made our fathers sing unto the Lord.

JACOB WEINSTEIN

Sincerity Of Heart

There was a herdsman who was in the habit of saying every day : " Lord of the world, you know well that if you had cattle and gave them to me to tend, I would take no wages from you because I love you."

Once a learned man, who chanced to hear this prayer, said : " Fool, do not pray in this manner ! " When the herdsman asked : " How, then, should I pray ? " The learned man taught him the traditional blessings, the reading of the *Shema* and the *Amidah*. But, when the learned man had left, the herdsman forgot all that he had been taught and did not pray at all. He was afraid to say his old prayer because the saintly man had warned him against it.

In a dream by night, the learned man heard a voice saying : " If you do not tell him to say what he was accustomed to say before you met him, misfortune shall befall you, since you have deprived God of one who belongs to the future world."

The learned man at once went to the herdsman and told him what he had dreamed, adding : " Continue to say what you used to say." The Merciful One desires sincerity of heart.

JUDAH HE-HASID,
Sefer Hasidim

Prayer—The Food Of The Soul

What bread is to the body, prayer is to the soul. Prayer is the food of the soul. The spiritual glow of one prayer lasts until the utterance of the next, even as the strength derived from one meal lasts until the next one.

Prayer is the wireless message between man and God.

Religion brings the soul back to God, and prayer is the means which it employs to do this. Every day we send the wireless message of prayer to God, renewing thereby our con-stant friendship with Him. Those who make prayer a rare practice are only acquaintances but not friends of God.

Prayer serves not only as a petition to God, but as an influence upon ourselves. Our sages, centuries ago, voiced the thought echoed by the great poet, George Meredith, who declared, " He who rises from his worship a better man, his prayer is answered." Prayer has the double charm of bringing God down to man, and lifting man upward to God.

Prayer distinguishes man from the brute. The cattle get up in the morning, are fed, and sent out to the green pastures. In the evening they are brought back to the barn, given some food, ruminate and have their bed of straw made and then go to sleep. Are there not many of us today who, like the cattle, rise in the morning, swallow our food quickly, hurry downtown, the pasture for the day, back home in the evening, ruminate in some movie house, then home again to bed, just as the beast without a word of prayer, of thanks-giving for the life God daily renews within us ?

The conviction of all believers in prayer is that they are speaking to one who hears and cares for them. This is one of the strongest evidences that the quest for God is real. When one prays to God, it is, as the Rabbis put it, " Like a man who talks into the ear of his friend."

At times we get discouraged and seem to think that God is angry, and does not answer our prayers. We have asked for money, for success, for strength, and yet we have not been blessed with any of these things. God may show His kindness to us, my friends, in denying us some of the things for which we prayed and longed. But just as the parent does not and should not fulfill every wish of the child, so does the All-wise God deny us for our own good some of our petitions. The poet put it, " Not what we wish, but what we need, Oh, let Thy grace supply ; the good unasked, in mercy grant ; the ill, though asked, deny."

It may be that we seldom say a word of prayer. We have lost the habit, or perhaps were never taught it. We are like a home with a beautiful piano in the parlor, which is never played. We who do not pray are like that piano. We do not give forth the fine, clear notes of the spirit, that lies mute and dormant in our souls.

The Reverend Doctor H. Pereira Mendes had this to say on prayer :

God gives us much.
Should we not give Him some time?
Let no day pass without one prayer.
Better one prayer than no prayer at all.
Prayer should be the key to the morning and the bolt at night.

HERBERT S. GOLDSTEIN,
A Letter On Prayer

Prayer—The Heart Of Significant Living

Prayer is at the heart not only of great religion, but of significant living. Without prayer we cannot scale the heights of compassion, or attain the peaks of love of our fellowman of which we are capable. Prayer has been an enduring and universal phenomenon of human life, not because a priesthood ordained it, nor because tradition hallowed it, but because man is ever seeking to probe into his own depths and bring to light his hidden yearnings . . . .

Prayer requires no consecrated edifice and no appointed hour. Indeed, it needs no words. Prayer is a step on which we rise from the self we are to the self we wish to be. Prayer affirms the hope that no reality can crush; the aspiration that can never acknowledge defeat . . . .

Prayer reveals truths about ourselves and the world that neither scalpel nor microscope can uncover. But prayer, to be a vital and transforming force in our life, cannot be an occasional mood, a moment's thought, a passing response, or a fugitive insight. It must be given permanence in our normal outlook and in our habitual behavior. Its rewards will be great, for it will not only ring us about with large horizons but will evoke from us the greatness to live in their presence. Wherever we go, we shall carry a Sanctuary with us . . . .

Prayer is not an escape from duty. It is no substitute for the deed. Prayer seeks the power to do wisely, to act generously, to live helpfully. It helps to re-enforce the act rather than to replace it . . . .

Prayer is the search for silence midst noise. Life is so filled with tumult that we do not hear ourselves. Failing to hear the voice of our spirit, can we hear the voice of God ? . . .

There are those who are fearful to be alone with themselves. They run with the crowd not out of love for others but out of fear to remain alone with themselves, terrified lest they hear the voice of their own spirit, or fearful of remaining alone with their own void . . . .

Prayer takes us beyond the self. Joining our little self to the selfhood of humanity, it gives our wishes the freedom to grow large and broad and inclusive. Our prayers are answered not when we are given what we ask, but when we are challenged to be what we can be.

MORRIS ADLER,
The National Jewish Monthly

The Influence Of The Prayerbook

The idea of ethical responsibility is as old as man. As far as we can go in the human story we find not only " I want " but " I ought." Yet this ethical responsibility was always narrow, incumbent only upon members of the tribe or the clan in relation to one another. The old *mores* and *ethoi*, as the very words imply, mean the customary mutual obligations of the restricted group. But limited as it was, it was nevertheless the ethical impulse, precious and waiting like a seed to be planted in fertile soil. Judaism took the seed of tribal ethics and brought it to its greatest fruition. It connected the ethical impulse with the universal spiritual God. It visualized Him as just, merciful, and holy. It gave men the ideal of rising above the limits of their habitual group comradeship, their old tribal decencies, and bade them strive to imitate an Infinite Nobility. " Holy shall ye be, for I the Lord your God am holy." By making monotheism ethical it made morality dynamic and universal.

These great religious and ethical influences were exercised by Judaism over the world through the Bible. But through the Prayerbook, also, it exercised an influence perhaps equally important. Whereas, through the Bible Judaism taught the world an ideal of religion nobler than any known before, through the Prayerbook and the Synagogue, it taught the world a mode of communion with God which made this noble religion liveable, intimate, and effective in daily life. The Bible is the meaning of Judaism ; the Prayerbook, its method. The Bible is doctrine. The Prayerbook is spiritual training.

SOLOMON B. FREEHOF,
The Small Sanctuary

Private Prayer

A Synagogue service cannot evoke that which does not exist. A congregation composed of people who do not follow discipline of prayer in their personal lives cannot expect to generate an atmosphere congenial to worship and communion with God. Our public services can only move individuals who pray at home or when alone. We shall not make public worship more inspiring and elevating by devising additional aids or introducing new melodies. We will have spiritually enriching and emotionally satisfying services when the men and women who come to worship are not unacquainted with prayer in their private lives.

Do you really wish to have Synagogue services become more meaningful ? Begin praying at home. Recite a blessing at the beginning of your family meal and a short prayer at the end. Start the day with a prayer, however brief, and retire at night only after an expression of gratitude to God for the gifts of life, love, health and freedom. After a time, you will find, that when next you attend a service, you will experience religious devotion and interest in praying with the Congregation.

MORRIS ADLER,
Shaarey Zedek Recorder

The Old Prayer Book

The old tear-stained prayer book will
I take in my hand
And call upon the God of my fathers
In my distress.
To the God of my fathers who was
their Rock and Refuge
In ages past,
I will pour out my woe
In ancient words, seared with the
pain
Of generations.
May these words that know the
heavenly paths
Bring my plaint to the God above,
And tell Him that which is hidden
in my heart—
What my tongue is incapable of
expressing.
These words, faithful and true, will
speak for me
Before God.
They will ask His pity.

And God in heaven who has heard
the prayers
Of my fathers,
The God who gave them power and
strength—
Perchance He will hear my prayer
too,
And my distress,
And will be a Shield unto me as He
was unto them.
For, like them, I am left a spoil unto
others,
Degraded and despised,
A wanderer over the face of the
earth.
And there is none who can help and
sustain me
Except God in heaven.

YAAKOV COHEN,
High Holiday Prayer Book
(translated by Morris Silverman)

Sincerity In Prayer

Prayer, if it is to have any value, must be sincere. There is a vast difference between saying prayers and praying. To repeat the mere words thoughtlessly, in a manner as mechanical as the revolutions of the Buddhist's prayer-wheel, is to deceive ourselves and to dishonor God. It is to grasp the shadow instead of the substance, to degrade an act which should be eloquent of religious feeling into a manifestation of gross impiety. It is possible to say many prayers, and yet not to pray; it is possible to say nothing, and yet to be lifted by the soul's emotion into the nearer presence of God. "When ye make many prayers," God warns all insincere supplicants, "I will not hear." On the other hand, Hannah's lips gave forth no sound; they only trembled. But God heard her, for her plaint went up from her heart.

MORRIS JOSEPH,
Judaism as Creed and Life

A Creative Enterprise

The Talmud reflects its concern with meaningful worship in a discussion as to what is perfunctory prayer. A variety of answers is given: " Rabbi Jacob Bad Iddi said: ' Whoever finds his praying a burden.' The Sages say : ' Whoever does not offer it in a spirit of entreaty.' Rab Joseph said : ' Whoever cannot add any element of novelty to it.' Abba bar Abin and Hanina bar Abin said : ' Whoever does not pray as the sun is setting' (Berachot 29b)." In these utterances of the sages, the truth is emphasized that true prayer should bring us a sense of relief from burden, an easing of the spirit, an exaltation of the mind. It must be the result of a constant striving for close contact with the Source of our being. It must be a creative enterprise, marked by a perpetual search after new forms of expression. It must be accessible to us, as the shadows fall.

When we succeed in mastering the act of prayer, we can face the twilight of life, its tragedy and trials, and yet look hopefully for the dawn. As we ascend the ladder of prayer, we shall feel the ecstasy of the youthful Jacob at Beth-El : " Indeed, the Lord is in this place, though I did not know it."

ROBERT GORDIS,
The Ladder of Prayer

Our prayers are not exercises in reading aloud. They express Jewish devotion, Jewish hope, a reaching out for God. So too our singing. Sour notes, poor voices — these God forgives. The whole-hearted response of His people — this is His delight.

JOSEPH H. HERZOG

Praying On Regular Occasions

Why should worship be bound to regular occasions ? Why impose a calendar on the soul ? Is not regularity of observance a menace to the freedom of the heart ?

Strict observance of a way of life at fixed times and in identical forms tends to become a matter of routine, of outward compliance. How to prevent observance from becoming stereotyped, mechanical, was, indeed, a perennial worry in the history of Judaism. The cry of the prophet, " Their heart is far from me," was a signal of alarm.

Should I reject the regularity of prayer and rely on the inspiration of the heart and only worship when I am touched by the spirit ? Should I resolve : unless the spirit comes, I shall abstain from praying ? The deeper truth is that routine breeds attention, calling forth a response where the soul would otherwise remain dormant. One is committed to being affected by the holy, if he abides at the threshold of its realm. Should it be left to every individual to find his own forms of worship whenever the spirit would move him ? Yet who is able to extemporise a prayer without falling into the trap of clichés ? Moreover, spiritual substance grows in clinging to a source of spirit richer than one's own.

Inspirations are brief, sporadic and rare. In the long interims the mind is often dull, bare and vapid. There is hardly a soul that can radiate more light than it receives. To perform a *mitzvah* is to meet the spirit. But the spirit is not something we can acquire once and for all but something we must constantly live with and pray for. For this reason the Jewish way of life is to reiterate the ritual, to meet the spirit again and again, the spirit in oneself and the spirit that hovers over all beings.

ABRAHAM J. HESCHEL,
Man's Quest for God

The Noblest Liturgy

When we come to view the half-dozen or so great Liturgies of the world purely as religious documents, and to weigh their values as devotional classics, the incomparable superiority of the Jewish convincingly appears. The Jewish Liturgy occupies its pages with the One Eternal Lord ; holds ever true, confident, and direct speech with Him ; exhausts the resources of language in songs of praise, in utterances of loving gratitude, in rejoicing at His nearness, in natural outpourings of grief for sin ; never so much as a dream of intercessors or of hidings from His blessed punishments ; and, withal, such a sweet sense of the divine accessibility every moment to each sinful, suffering child of earth. Certainly the Jew has cause to thank God, and the fathers before him, for the noblest Liturgy the annals of faith can show.

GEORGE E. BIDDLE,
Jewish Quarterly Review

Prayer—A Conversation Between Souls

The institution of prayer is founded on man's conscious need of communion with God. The deep longing of the heart for God finds in prayer an appropriate vehicle for self-expression and an adequate measure of spiritual satisfaction. But God, too, say the rabbis, delights in the prayers of the righteous. They are the crown of His glory. He wants man to seek Him, that he may find Him. Prayer is thus the soul of man holding converse with the Soul of the universe. According to the rabbis, therefore, prayer, when not a mere gesture but an actual heart-experience, enables us to break through the iron wall of materiality and reach the immediate presence of God's spirit. For prayer is not an external form, like sacrifice; nor is it a mark of virtuous living, like the practice of good deeds. It is a direct approach to the throbbing heart of the universe. When with bowed head and uplifted heart we voice our deepest spiritual needs in prayer, a larger measure of the divine somehow flows into our souls. We stand face to face with the *Shekinah*. Whether we use speech for utterance or the soul wings itself aloft in purest meditation, we are, in either case, in close communion with the Spirit that is so much akin to our own, so near us in all our yearnings and strivings, so eager to receive and answer the worthy petitions of our hearts.

ISRAEL BETTAN,
Post-Biblical Judaism: Its Spiritual Note

We Need Prayer

God surely knows our thoughts and desires. What need is there therefore to give expression to them? This is quite true; and still the human soul yearns to give articulate expression to what is uppermost in its consciousness at any one time. Prayer does not affect God, but ourselves. In prayer, the divine within us asserts itself, seeks its union with the divine in the universe and through that becomes ennobled and glorified. God needs none of our praises and supplications, but we feel impelled to pour out our hearts to Him and by doing this we come to be in greater harmony with our spiritual selves, and with God, the spiritual element in the universe.

JULIUS H. GREENSTONE,
Jewish Feasts and Fasts

Prayer And Gratitude

The fact that even the petitions are also praises of God and, therefore, not exclusively or even predominantly petitional in mood, clearly reveals a significant attitude toward prayer itself as a spiritual exercise. This attitude has been specifically stated in the following rabbinic statement. "A man should always utter the praises of God before he offers his petitions" (b. B'rochos 32a). Judging by this mood in the *T'filo*, prayer is primarily the achievement of an affirmative relationship to God, a sense of gratitude and appreciation for the blessings we have received. If our faith can succeed in curing us of the mood of constant discontent and can teach us to find joyous gratitude in whatever happiness we already have, however small it may be, then it will engender a healthy-mindedness within us that makes for a happy life, itself the answer to most of our prayers. This habit of praising God rather than begging from Him has become, through centuries of this type of prayer, a prevalent state of mind which enabled our fathers to find joy even in minor blessings and thus played its part in preserving Israel through the vicissitudes of history. A poverty-stricken, forlorn, exiled Jew, raising his last crust of bread to his mouth, might perhaps be justified in cursing his lot and denouncing God, but instead it would not enter his mind to partake of this bit of bread without first saying, " Praised be Thou O Lord Who bringest forth food from the earth." The rabbis speak even of a higher state of heroism, a more triumphant conquest of bitterness when they say, " A man should praise God even for misfortunes as much as he praises Him for happiness " (m. B'rochos IX, 5). Whether this lofty courage is attainable by the average Jew or not, he learns to feel and to express, or perhaps to express and thus to feel, a constant sense of gratitude to the Master of the Universe. Prayer in Israel teaches man to overcome bitterness and self-pity ; to think not of what the world owes *him*, but what he owes the world and God. It is not primarily piteous pleading but is essentially grateful communion with the Infinite.

SOLOMON B. FREEHOF,
The Small Sanctuary

Waiting For The Spirit To Move Us

A musician must practice by pre-arranged schedule, regardless of his inclination at the moment. So with the devout soul. It may not rely on caprice or put its hope in chance. It must work. The man on the other hand who folds his hands, waiting for the spirit to move him to think of God — who postpones worship for the right mood and the perfect setting, a forest or mountain peak, for example — will do little of meditating or praying. After all, how often does one find himself in a " cathedral of nature," and when he does who shall say that he will be in a worshipful temper ?

MILTON STEINBERG,
Basic Judaism

5

Rites and Rituals

The *Mitzvoth* were given to purify man.

TANHUMA SH'MINI, 8

The ideas and ideals of a people may give it significance but its group habits give it life.

MILTON STEINBERG

Our ceremonialism is a training in self-conquest while it links the generations . . . and unifies our atoms dispersed to the four corners of the earth as nothing else could.

ISRAEL ZANGWILL,
Children of the Ghetto

In Order That I Might Be I

The rituals and disciplines that surrounded my childhood sensitized my spirit, made it permanently susceptible to the messages behind them; the names of the Patriarchs and the Kings and holy places were permanently lodged in me, and at a later period in my life reverberated again with those overtones which accompany and distinguish the essential nature of tradition. I know that it has been otherwise with many Jews who have had a Jewish upbringing; they have either "repressed" their early responses or repudiated them by an effort of will —though not always, in either case, with complete success. But thus it was with me and with many others; and thus it has been since the Destruction. I think of the persistence of the message, and I am awed by the procession of the generations of simple folk—let us leave the scholars and the self-consciously dedicated to one side— who have been its carriers. The mosque in the village of Macin symbolizes for me the variety of worlds through which the message has been carried — European and Asiatic, Christian and Moslem, Roman and Byzantine. And all of it in order that I might be I, and not someone else.

MAURICE SAMUEL,
The Professor and The Fossil

Tradition And Life

It can be said that the six days of toil are concerned with the means of life and the Sabbath with its ends. The six days of toil represent the temporal and transitory—the Sabbath represents the eternal and the enduring. That is why the Hebrew language has no names for the days of the week—they are all the first day, or the second day, or the third day, "to the Sabbath"—the Sabbath is the goal toward which time itself moves . . . .

"Happiness," said Justice Holmes to a class of graduating lawyers, " . . . cannot be won simply by being counsel for great corporations and having an income of fifty thousand dollars. An intellect great enough to win the prize needs other food beside success. The remoter and more general aspects of the law are those which give it universal interest. It is through them that you not only become a great master in your calling, but connect your subject with the universe and catch an echo of the infinite, a glimpse of its unfathomable process, a hint of the universal." One can hardly offer a better explanation of why Jews have dedicated themselves to the study of Torah. Torah was the revealed will of the Infinite and a reflection of

His universal law for the lives of men. The ultimate goal of its study was not only guidance and direction : it was also to help one catch a glimpse of God. That is why Jews who never owned an ox spent many a night and day mastering the intricate rules of torts committed by animals, and why Jews who, as aliens in the countries of their birth, could never acquire land, intoned page after page of Talmud on the manner of taking title to real property. They did this to catch " the echo of the infinite."

It is such an echo that we are to seek on the Sabbath. As the world and its needs change, certainly the problem of the Sabbath becomes more complicated ; no one has the right to turn away from the voices of those Jews who find themselves troubled and disturbed in their Sabbath observance. It is not enough to say " the Law is the Law." We must understand the Law and its ultimate purposes as best we can, and we must be prepared to interpret and develop the Law as the Rabbis did in the past. It is our privilege and our responsibility to do this. We need the Sabbath perhaps more than ever, and we must save it. However, just as its salvation does not lie in an arid fundamentalism, so its salvation cannot lie in the encouragement of the typical pastimes of American Jews. Jews must live in their tradition. But it would be fatal to forget that the tradition itself must also live.

EMANUEL RACKMAN,
Commentary

The Joy Of The Sabbath

To the Jews the Sabbath is a day of happiness. The synagogue liturgy of the Sabbath is full of the joyous note. It is marked by gay dress, sumptuous meals, and a general sense of exhilaration. The Puritans knew little or nothing of synagogue worship or of Jewish homes. They had no experience of " the joy of the commandment " — a phrase often on Jewish lips and in Jewish hearts.

WILLIAM B. SELBIE,
The Influence of The Old Testament
on Puritanism

The Sabbath — A Pause In The Brush-Work

An artist cannot be continually wielding his brush. He must stop at times in his painting to freshen his vision of the object, the meaning of which he wishes to express on his canvas. Living is also an art. We dare not became absorbed in its technical processes and lose our consciousness of its general plan. Our ideal of the personality we would become is the object we are trying to paint; the Sabbath represents those moments when we pause in our brush-work to renew our vision of this object. Having done so we take ourselves to our painting with clarified vision and renewed energy. This applies alike to the individual and to the community. For the individual the Sabbath becomes thereby an instrument of personal salvation; for the community an instrument of social salvation.

MORDECAI M. KAPLAN,
The Meaning of God in Modern Jewish Religion

Rejoice so much in a *Mitzvah* that you will desire no other reward than the opportunity to perform another *Mitzvah*.   THE BRATZLAVER RABBI,
The Hasidic Anthology

The Prayers Of My Parents

Like vivid illustrations in the book of my life are the prayers of my parents, the services at their graves, the memory of an old man chanting funeral songs at the *Yahrzeit* of my dear friend Dr. Himwich, the unveiling of the monument to the beloved comrades of my life's journeys, and the celebration of the continuity of the generations in the Passover services in the home of my parents and in the homes of my children. And though I have never gone back to theological supernaturalism, I have come to appreciate, more than I once did, the symbolism in which is celebrated the human need of trusting to the larger vision, according to which calamities come and go but the continuity of life and faith in its better possibilities survive.

MORRIS RAPHAEL COHEN,
A Dreamer's Journey

The Dietary Laws

Dietary laws are bound up for us, with the survival of the group; with the cultivation of an environment in which Jewish values may more effectively be fostered; with the strengthening of Jewish consciousness and loyalty by regular and definite acts of a Jewish nature and association. They are for us the visible outer signs of the Jewish way of life that help fortify inner attachment to and involvement with the preservation of Jewish substance and ideal. They help us spiritualize even so physical an act as eating. Such disciplines unite us with the historic past of our faith and link us with fellow-Jews the world over. Milton

Steinberg once wrote : " The ideas and ideals of a people may give it significance, but its group habits give it life. For naked ideals are frail things that often die . . . . The mortality risk of an idea clothed in a habit is much lower . . . . A people bound by a common law, ritual and habitual practices might conceivably save its law, its ideas and even itself."

MORRIS ADLER,
Shaarey Zedek Recorder

The Seventh Coin

The Chinese relate a very striking parable. They say : " It came to pass that a man went to market, having on his shoulder a string of seven large copper coins. (Chinese coins are strung on strings and carried on the shoulders.) Meeting a beggar who was pleading for alms, the man gave the beggar six of his seven coins. Then the beggar, instead of showing gratitude, slipped up behind the man and stole the seventh coin."

" That is a strange parable," you say, but not so. Are there not many people who accept from God the gift of six days to do their labor and then, instead of being grateful, they steal from Him the seventh — the Sabbath — also ?

ANONYMOUS

Spiritual Values Of Kashrut

The significance of a religious institution does not depend on what it meant when it first came into being. It depends rather on the meaning that it has acquired, or that can be assigned to it, by virtue of its answering certain human needs. In all likelihood, *kashrut* goes back to pre-Torah times. Originally, it may have been, like the dietary restrictions of other peoples, the outcome of primitive religious beliefs. But already in the Torah itself the meaning assigned to *kashrut* is highly spiritual. Its purpose is conceived as that of making the people of Israel aware of its dedication to God as priestly or holy people.

In the course of centuries *kashrut* has taken on an important additional function ; it has served as a means of Jewish identification and distinctiveness. *Kashrut* has contributed to the perpetuation of the Jewish People and the retention of its way of life. The urgency for strengthening whatever factors in Jewish life make for survival is even greater now than in the past. It is particularly effective in lending Jewish atmosphere to the home, which, in the Diaspora, is our last ditch defense against the inroads of assimilation.

Kashrut is capable of becoming a means of generating spiritual values, in that it can habituate the Jew in the practice of viewing a commonplace physical need as a source of spiritual meaning. To enable it to serve that end, the benedictions and prayers before and after the meal will have to spell out specifically the idea that "we eat to live, rather than live to eat."

MORDECAI M. KAPLAN,
The Reconstructionist

The Sabbath Insures Our Survival

If I were asked to single out one of the great historical institutions more essential for our preservation than all others, I would not hesitate to declare that it is the observance of the Sabbath. Without this, the home and the Synagogue, the Festivals and the Holy days, the language and the history of our people, would gradually disappear. If the Sabbath will be maintained by those who have observed it, and will be restored to those who have abandoned it, then the permanence of Judaism is assured. To all who are prosperous, the question of the observance of the Sabbath involves the sacrifice of a luxury, nothing more . . . . Every Jew who has it within his power should aid in the effort to restore the Sabbath to the man from whom it has been taken away. No deeds of charity or philanthropy, no sacrifices of time or fortune made by any Jew, at all equals in beneficent result the expenditure of time and money looking towards the re-establishment of the Jewish Sabbath among the Jewish people. No amount of prating about morals will ever take the place of rooted habits ruthlessly plucked out.

CYRUS ADLER,
quoted in *Book of Jewish Thoughts*

Shabbat

This is it
To come from the blazing sunlight
Into the dim quiet of the synagogue.
To sit with my grandfather, his thin shoulders
Sharp against his white silk *Talit*.
To hear the murmur of old

And the rising melancholy song of the cantor ;
The crying song of God and of prayer.
This is the great warmth, the great at-homeness ;
This is the knowledge of belonging ;

The loneness merging into a strong oneness.
One lost drop of water finding its way into the sea.
The Torah gleams white and silver, and we stand
Singing and praying,
Our hearts warm with peace,
Our spirits quiet in the quietness of Shabbat.
This is the end of the week and its beginning.
This is the moment of pause,
The refilling of the empty vessel,
The renewing of the empty spirit,
This is the remembering :
The shared memory of two thousand years
And the shared embarking upon two thousand more.
This is the hearth, the gathering together ;
The pain and the joy,
The tears and the gentle laughter.
This is the benign wisdom in an old man's eyes
And the hope in a boy's fresh voice,

The roots into the past
And the arms stretched forward into the future.
We shall live forever and ever.
We shall wander from land to land,
From nation to nation,
Sometimes driven, sometimes tormented ;
We shall suffer sharp blows and many deep-hurting wounds.
But this place will be with us
And this warmth
And this rejoicing . . .
For this is the great, the many-faceted, the bottomless *Shalom*.

E. GRINDELL,
The Reconstructionist

Each Jewish custom has something in it which may be interpreted poetically and thus acquire a genuinely modern form, with perhaps a wholly new and important spiritual content.

HAYYIM ZHITLOVSKY,
Gezamelte Shriften

Sanctifying Life

Torah as the preservative form of Jewish life has a very special and a very precise content and this content molded the form from within outward. What is that content ? The single traditional word defines it, the word *kadusha*, sanctification. Life and its various manifestations are not to be rejected, as Pauline Christianity does. It is to be sancti-fied. It is to be rendered significant. We are bidden to love the Eternal with *all* our hearts. With *all*. And the sages interpret : " With both impulses, with the impulse toward good and the impulse toward evil." This view of life is unique — as unique as the total uniqueness of the Jewish people. Man has accepted nature unqualifiedly ; man has rejected nature equally grossly. Jews alone have sought to sanctify nature — eating and drinking and labor and rest and procreation and fellowship and study and sowing and harvesting and the relations of masters and servants and homeborn and strangers and man and woman and parent and child and even the animals which are to be fed first because they are helpless. The whole of human life is to be sanctified and redeemed and rendered meaningful by that *way*, that *halakha*, that interpretative regulation. And deep, fathomlessly deep within the *halakha*, that way of life we discern an ultimate purpose : the avoidance of cruelty — the sin of sins, the unforgivable sin of the idolators. So the Law, His Law, creates significance and goodness for the Jew ; it creates both righteousness and joy and the power to endure. The *halakha*, one of the most gifted of Jewish scholars writes, " is an attempt to give form and configuration to the hour of each individual, to the year of the congregation, to the life of the people." And it is form and configuration, as has been said, which alone can give beauty and endurance in both life and art.

No matter in Jewish life has been more misunderstood in America among people supposedly intelligent than this matter. People have said : But *kashruth*, the sanctification of food, had sanitary motivation. Why should we bother ? This is an anachronism. What did our people three thousand years ago know of trichinosis ? And, granting that they saw the idolators die of eating rotting swine's flesh, they were in no position to connect this cause with this effect. Such motivations were unknown. The ritual steam bath on the eve of the Sabbath doubtless kept our people cleaner than the surrounding population. But the bath had the purpose of spiritual lustration. It was a symbolic act. It is the " modern " anthropologist who has addled people's minds. All men have founded their customs as ritual, symbol, rite, invocation, propitiation. All physical uses and consequences are secondary and by-products. The very tools of the primitive plowman have symbolic form. The *mitzvoth*, the commanded deeds, belong to the realm of art and faith, not to the realm of nature. They do not seek to change nature but to sanctify nature for the uses of man. The *mezuzah* at your door serves no " practical " purpose. It does not keep thieves out. It keeps the spirit in. It says : this is the house of a Jew, servant of the Eternal, friend of man who seeks to sanctify his life by obedience to God's Law. All men can enter at this door in peace. Our living tradition is quite aware of the symbolic character of the *halakha*, the Jewish way. " The prescriptions," our sages declare, " are given only to purify (or ennoble) man, for what matters it to God whether the animal be slaughtered by incision of the throat or the back of the neck?" The Jewish way of life is a pattern, akin to the structure and pattern of a work of art, which is to sanctify and render meaningful the hour and day and year of the Jewish people and to preserve that people by differentiating its existence in every phase and at every moment from the idolatrous life. If our form were shattered we would not be. Whenever our form is shattered we tend to die. Unless we preserve our form we cannot survive. Unless we survive we cannot perform our function in the economy of history.

LUDWIG LEWISOHN,
The American Jew

The Sanctified Phrases

Men cling to sanctified phrases not only because of the insights they contain but even more because, through ritual and repetition, they have become redolent with the wine of human experience . . . . The ritual may be diluted by English and by modernisms, but the Hebraic God is still a potent symbol of the continuous life of which we individuals are waves.

MORRIS R. COHEN,
A Dreamer's Journey

The Mistake Of " Heart-Religion "

Those persons who think it a sign of intellectual or spiritual superiority to decry ceremonial, and who are content with what they style "heart-religion," make a great mistake. None of us can dispense with outward helps to religious feeling. And if Religion is really rooted in the heart it can never be the worse, but will certainly be the better, for finding expression in ceremonial acts . . . .

But these ceremonial constituents, though they are important elements of Judaism, are important not in themselves, but by reason of what they signify and what they may effect. They are but means to an end, and that end is the religious life. If they fail to achieve that end, they are useless . . . . No religious rite has done its work unless it has sown some high thought in the mind or stirred the heart with some noble resolve.

MORRIS JOSEPH,
Judaism as Creed and Life

Judaism without ceremonial is an absurdity, a ragged garb which protects not, adorns not.

ISRAEL DEUTSCH

The Sublimity Of Ritual

Behind all the tangled network of ceremony and ritual, the larger mind of the man who has lived and loved sees the outlines of a creed grand in its simplicity, sublime in its persistence. The spirit has clothed itself with flesh, as it must do for human eyes to gaze on it and live with it; and if, in addition, it has swaddled itself with fold on fold of garment, even so the music has not gone out of its voice, nor the love out of its eyes.

ISRAEL ZANGWILL,
Ghetto Tragedies

The Commandments—A Divine Poem

The Torah and all its commandments in their minutest details, as expressed in thought and deed, form a great and mighty Divine poem, a poem of confident trust and love. Every commandment and law has a unique musical quality that the congregation of Israel perceives and appreciates. It evokes the blossoms of reverent joy and song within us. It is for us to remove the warts from the ears of our sons, "the thorns and thistles that surround the noble flower," so that the waves of song will echo in their hearts as well, uplifting their souls with the same natural exaltation that is common to all in whom the spirit of Judaism is properly developed.

ABRAHAM ISAAC KUK,
quoted in *Banner of Jerusalem*

The Sabbath—One Of Our Glories

There are higher objects in life than success. The Sabbath, with its exhortation to the worship of God and the doing of kindly deeds, reminds us week by week of these higher objects. It prevents us reducing our life to the level of a machine. The gathered experience of mankind that the break in the routine of work one day in seven will heighten the value of the very work itself is not lightly to be put aside. The Sabbath is one of the glories of our humanity. For if to labor is noble, of our own free will to pause in that labor which may lead to success, to money, or to fame, may be nobler still. To dedicate one day a week to rest and to God, this is the prerogative and privilege of man alone. It is an ordinance which we may rightly call Divine. Let every boy and every young man, let every girl and every young woman, get out of the habit of ceasing from their work on the Sabbath day at their own peril.

CLAUDE G. MONTEFIORE,
The Bible for Home Reading

The Dietary Laws—Daily Rededication

It may appear a minute matter to pronounce the Hebrew blessing over bread, and to accustom one's children to do so. Yet if a Jew, at the time of partaking of food, remembers the identical words used by his fellow Jews since time immemorial and the world over, he revives in himself, wherever he be at the moment, communion with his imperishable people. In contrast to not a few of our co-religionists who have no occasion for weeks and months together to bestow a thought on their Creed or their People, the Jew who keeps *Kashrus* has to think of his religious and communal allegiance on the occasion of every meal; and, on every such occasion, the observance of those laws constitutes a renewal of acquiescence in the fact that he is a Jew, and a deliberate acknowledgment of that fact.

WALDEMAR HAFFKINE

The Keeping Of The Sabbath

When dire necessity compels a Jew to break the Sabbath, let him not think that the Sabbath is lost to him, or he to Judaism. So long as Jewish conscientiousness is alive within him, let him endeavour to keep as much of the Sabbath as he is able. He must not say, " I have broken the Sabbath. How can I join my brethren in the Sabbath Service!" Whatever he does conscientiously will be acceptable before God, and he will thus find himself exhorted to watch carefully, and to seize the first opportunity of returning to the full observance of Sabbath. The same principle applies to all the Divine precepts.

M. FRIEDLANDER

The Role Of The Mitzvah

You have heard that in Egypt the waters of the Nile, overflowing its banks, take the place of rain; and that these fructifying waters are led by various channels into the remote fields to irrigate them. Now, the Nile with its precious floods would be of no benefit to the fields without these channels. Thus it is with the Torah and the *mitzvoth*. The Torah is the mighty stream of spirituality, flowing since ancient times through Israel. It would have caused no useful fruits to grow, and would have produced no spiritual progress, no moral advancement, had the *mitzvah* not been there to lead its Divine floods into the homes, the hearts, and the minds of the individual members of the people, by connecting practical life in all its variety and its activities with the spiritual truths of religion.

It is the greatest mistake, based on an entire misunderstanding of human nature, to assume that men are capable of living in a world of ideas only, and can dispense with symbols that should embody these ideas and give them tangibility and visible form. Only the *mitzvah* is the ladder connecting heaven and earth. The *tefillin*, containing among others the commandment: "Thou shalt love the Lord thy God with all thine heart, with all thy soul, and with all thy might," are laid on the head, the seat of thought, and on the arm, the instrument of action, opposite to the heart, the seat of feeling ; thus teaching that all our thoughts, feelings, and actions must conform to the will of God. This *mitzvah*, performed daily, has contributed more effectively to preserve and to further the morality of our people than have all the learned books on ethics written by our religious philosophers.

MOSES JUNG

The Sabbath — A Day Of Armistice

The world has our hands, but our soul belongs to Someone Else. Six days a week we seek to dominate the world, on the seventh day we try to dominate the self . . . .

To set apart one day a week for freedom, a day on which we would not use the instruments which have been so easily turned into weapons of destruction, a day for being with ourselves, a day of detachment from the vulgar, of independence of external obligations, a day on which we stop worshipping the idols of technical civilization, a day on which we use no money, a day of armistice in the economic struggle with our fellow men and the forces of nature — is there any institution that holds out a greater hope for man's progress than the Sabbath ? . . .

In the tempestuous ocean of time and toil there are islands of stillness where man may enter a harbor and reclaim his dignity. The island is the seventh day, the Sabbath, a day of detachment from things, instruments and practical affairs as well as of attachment to the spirit.

ABRAHAM J. HESCHEL, *The Sabbath*

Religion Needs Symbols

There is no religion which can live by its ideas, teachings and commandments alone : in order to embrace and penetrate man's life religion needs to embody itself in symbols and observances. These are not and must never be taken to be ends in themselves. They only serve to bring us nearer to the end of all religion : to confront man with God.

Our religion needs these means of bringing God into our everyday life all the more because we are forbidden to make images of God and because we reject all sacraments. Indeed, in the very richness of observances, which Judaism preserves, there lies great strength. Thus, the Sabbath has been given as a "sign" of the covenant between God and Israel, and this is no less true of the other festivals. Just as the fringes upon the corners of man's garments are to remind him of "all the commandments of God to do them," so are the phylacteries and the *mezuzoth*. Every prayer, every rite, as long as it does not degenerate so that it becomes merely an empty and thoughtless "ceremony" but instead is observed in the right frame of mind, with *kawana*, makes straight our souls towards God. Whether we hear the *shofar* or taste the *matza*, whether we wave the *lulav* or kindle the Chanukkah lights — they all reveal to us the rule and will of a holy God, a God who manifests Himself in history and particularly in the history of our people, and to whose presence every one of us is bound to bear witness by his personal conduct.

GEORGE SALZBERGER

The Sabbath Preserved Israel

He who feels in his heart a genuine tie with the life of his people cannot possibly conceive of the existence of the Jewish people apart from "Queen Sabbath." We can say without exaggeration that more than Israel preserved the Sabbath, the Sabbath preserved Israel.

ACHAD HA'AM,
Al Prashat Derahim

The Sabbath is the hub of the Jew's Universe ; to protect it is a virtue ; to love it is a liberal education.

ISRAEL ZANGWILL

The Need For Religious Customs

Religion, they say, is only custom. I might agree with this if the "only" were left out. Customs are the flowers of civilization. You can tell a man's education, yea, even much of his character, by his habits.

Morality, ethics, are words derived from roots denoting that which is acknowledged and adopted by the people as right and proper. Manners and usages are the silent compact, the unwritten laws which preserve the proprieties of civilized society.

Religion will not come to our aid the moment we call for her; she must be loved and cherished at all times if she is to prove our true friend in need. Much of the present indifference of our young people is directly traceable to the absence of all religious observances in their homes. Piety is the fruit of religious customs.

G. GOTHEIL,
quoted in *A Book of Jewish Thoughts*

Blessed Is The Match

Blessed Is The Match
that kindles the Sabbath lights.
Blessed Is The Home
that reflects the glow of the Sabbath Candles.

Blessed Is The Heart
that radiates the warmth of the Sabbath peace.

UNITED SYNAGOGUE BROCHURE

Ceremonies And Mitzvoth

Let us beware lest we reduce Bible to literature, Jewish observance to good manners, the Talmud to Emily Post.

There are spiritual reasons which compel me to feel alarmed when hearing the terms *customs* and *ceremonies*. What is the worth of celebrating the *Seder* on Passover eve, if it is nothing but a ceremony? An annual re-enactment of quaint antiquities? Ceremonies end in routine, and routine is the great enemy of the spirit.

A religious act is something in which the soul must be able to participate; out of which inner devotion, *kavanah*, must evolve. But what *kavanah* should I entertain if entering the *sukkah* is a mere ceremony?

Let us be frank. Too often a ceremony is the homage which disbelief pays to faith. Do we want such homage?

Judaism does not stand on ceremonies. . . . Jewish piety is an answer to God, expressed in the language of *mitzvoth* rather than in the language of *ceremonies*. The *mitzvah* rather than the ceremony is our fundamental category. What is the difference between the two categories?

Ceremonies whether in the form of things or in the form of actions are required by custom and convention; *mitzvoth* are required by Torah. Ceremonies are relevant to man; *mitzvoth* are relevant to God. Ceremonies are folkways; *mitzvoth* are ways to God. Ceremonies are expressions of the human mind; what they express and their power to express depend on a mental act of man; their significance is gone when man ceases to be responsive to them. Ceremonies are like the moon, they have no light of their own. *Mitzvoth*, on the other hand, are expressions or interpretations of the will of God. While they are meaningful to man, the source of their meaning is not in the understanding of man but in the love of God. Ceremonies are created for the purpose of signifying: *mitzvoth* were given for the purpose of sanctifying. This is their function: to refine, to ennoble, to sanctify man. They confer holiness upon us, whether or not we know exactly what they signify.

A *mitzvah* is more than *man's reference to God*; it is also *God's reference to man*. In carrying out a *mitzvah* we acknowledge the fact of God being concerned with our fulfillment of His will.

ABRAHAM J. HESCHEL,
Man's Quest for God

What The Sabbath Has Meant To The Jew

To the Jew the Sabbath became far more than the recurrent extrication of the soul from the degradations of workaday worldliness. It was also a release from the degradations he suffered at the hands of the outside world. For him the world faded away with the lighting of the candles on Friday evening, and he was confirmed in both his relationship to God and in his hope of that time when all days would be Sabbaths. It could be said of the Jew that he lived the first three days of the week in the memory of the past Sabbath, and the last three days in anticipation of the next. He understood as no one else the frequency with which the desecration of the Sabbath is denounced by the Prophets as part of the falling away of the people from God's purposes; the Sabbath is stressed more insistently than any other sacred institution, and it occupies the central place among the rituals that are bound up with Jewish morality. A saying of Achad Ha'am's has become a Jewish folkword: "More than the Jewish people has done to keep the Sabbath alive, the Sabbath has done to keep it alive."

The Sabbath also stands apart in that it has the power to repress all fasts in the Jewish calendar save the Day of Atonement. The Black Fast of the Ninth of Ab for the Destructions may not be observed or remembered on the Sabbath. The private mourner, too, must forget his loss on that day ; for it is a day of serenity and wholeness. A vast literature of legend and commentary has sprung up about its origin and efficacy. It was created before the physical universe ; the stormy river Sambattyon rests on that day ; the sinners in hell obtain a twenty-four-hour reprieve ; and on that day the poorest Jew is elevated to the rank of a king, his wife to that of a queen.

The oncoming of the Sabbath is attended by an uplifting of the heart, its departure by a gnawing melancholy. Farewell to the glimpse of paradise ! Its hours are treasured for prayer, for sacred study, for purity of conversation and thought, for the complete deletion, of course, of worldly calculations (it is even forbidden to have money in one's pocket on the Sabbath !), for rest, for gratitude, and for the impotence of the outside world to inflict suffering. Thus it was ; the exile itself was forgotten on the Sabbath.

This and more is the word *Shabbos* in Yiddish. How is it to be " translated " ?

MAURICE SAMUEL,
The Professor and The Fossil

Judaism—A Way Of Life

Judaism is a way of life which endeavours to transform virtually every human action into a means of communion with God. Through this communion with God, the Jew is enabled to make his contribution to the establishment of the Kingdom of God and the brotherhood of men on earth. So far as its adherents are concerned, Judaism seeks to extend the concept of right and wrong to every aspect of their behavior. Jewish rules of conduct apply not merely to worship, ceremonial, and justice between man and man, but also to such matters as philanthropy, personal friendships and kindnesses, intellectual pursuits, artistic creation, courtesy, the preservation of health, and the care of diet.

So rigorous is this discipline, as ideally conceived in Jewish writings, that it may be compared to those specified for members of religious orders in other faiths. A casual conversation or a thoughtless remark may, for instance, be considered a violation of Jewish Law. It is forbidden, not merely as a matter of good form, but of religious law, to use obscene language, to rouse a person to anger, or to display unusual ability in the presence of the handicapped. The ceremonial observances are equally detailed.

LOUIS FINKELSTEIN,
Religions of Democracy

These Days Of Holiness

What in the swift flow of time is the coming and passing of a year that so much thought and attention should be given to it ? What, indeed, is a year in the life and history of an ancient and eternal people like the Jews ? Yet what Jew does not feel the beauty and warmth of Rosh Hashanah and the spiritual depth and meaning of Yom Kippur ? On those holy days, casting aside for the nonce his worldly cares and thoughts, the Jew repairs to the house of God with infinite yearning in his heart to meditate and refresh his soul in song and prayer.

There is an atmosphere of holiness about Rosh Hashanah and Yom Kippur which is unique in the religious life of the Jewish people. They are the most superbly dramatized holidays of the year, captivating the imagination with their haunting beauty and magic influence. They are among the best known and universally honored holidays in the Jewish calendar. Our hearts long for the joy and comfort they supply. On those days, the Jew keenly feels a heightened sense of awareness. He becomes aware of himself, of his God, and of the ties that bind him to his faith and people.

The Jews, with their utter faith in God, are not essentially a metaphysical people. But on Rosh Hashanah and Yom Kippur all Jews direct their minds to the contemplation of their life, seeking to understand the springs of their actions, as they unashamedly lay bare before God and the full congregation their innermost thoughts and feelings. They search for the meaning of their existence and destiny. What philosopher has stated more tersely, vividly and truthfully man's role in the scheme of things than what the most ordinary Jew reads in his holyday prayerbook : " Man is like a fragile potsherd, as the grass that withereth, as the flower that faileth, as a fleeting shadow, as a passing cloud, as the wind that bloweth, as the floating dust, yes, as a dream that vanisheth."

In this mood of philosophic humility the Jew appears before his God on Rosh Hashanah and Yom Kippur . . . .

A few hours in the house of God, a few prayers recited more or less devoutly, one or two sermons listened to more or less attentively — how can these fleeting hours be so replete with pious meaning and riches ? To fathom this experience is to glimpse the human heart and mind which is outside of mere temporal reckoning. Within the dim depths of every human being there stirs a vague feeling for God, a reaching out of the spirit for something more lasting and secure than mere material and temporary joys. On Rosh Hashanah and Yom Kippur we tap the sacred fount within us and loose the stream bringing peace and balm to our souls.

Jacob S. Minkin, *Congress Weekly*

6

The Synagogue and the Home

"How goodly are thy tents, O Jacob, thy dwelling places O Israel!"

NUMBERS 24: 5

The Jew's home has rarely been his "castle"; throughout the ages it has been something far higher — his sanctuary.

JOSEPH H. HERTZ

The alchemy of home life went far to turn the dross of the Ghetto ino gold.

KATIE MAGNUS,
Jewish Portraits

The Synagogue Is Basic

The synagogue must be recognized as the primary institution of Jewish life and affiliation. It, rather than any other type of corporate Jewish fellowship, fits into the American scene and it offers the only opportunity for making Judaism an enduring, living influence in American civilization. All other forms of activity and affiliation are helpful in that they advance one or another aspect of our collective being. But the synagogue is basic and fundamental. The synagogue is the most logical, the most American and the most all-embracing form of Jewish community expression. Remove the synagogue from the center of Jewish communal life and you reduce Jewishness, in the eyes of the Jewish community, to the lowest common denominator of racialism and lead our neighbors of other faiths to believe that we practice segregation to no purpose. Accentuate any secular type of Jewish fellowship as the essence of Jewishness and you inevitably court the inexorable fate of the American melting pot which fuses all secular groups into one. Make the synagogue the dynamic center of our collective being and the embassy of our spiritual life and you have a basis for permanent survival and for self-respecting relations with our fellow Americans. What other type of organization can offer such advantages and more fully guarantee our continued and unchallenged survival as American Jews ?

MAX ARZT,
Address before the Rabbinical
Assembly of America, 1947

The Synagogue—A Unique Creation

A unique creation of Judaism is the Synagogue, which started it on its world-mission and made the Torah the common property of the entire people. Devised in the Exile as a substitute for the Temple, it soon eclipsed it as a religious force and a rallying point for the whole people, appealing through the prayers and Scriptural lessons to the congregation as a whole. The Synagogue was limited to no one locality, like the Temple, but raised its banner wherever Jews settled throughout the globe. It was thus able to spread the truths of Judaism to the remotest parts of the earth, and to invest the Sabbath and Festivals with deeper meaning by utilizing them for the instruction and elevation of the people. What did it matter, if the Temple fell a prey to the flames for a second time, or if the whole sacrificial cult of the priesthood with all its pomp were to cease forever ? The soul of Judaism lived indestructibly in the House of Prayer and Learning.

KAUFMANN KOHLER,
Jewish Theology

Judaism's Great Contribution

Judaism's greatest contribution to humanity is in the domain of public worship, where alone man develops the wings and the capacity to soar into an invisible world. This it made through the *synagogue*. The synagogue represents something without precedent in antiquity ; and its establishment forms one of the most important landmarks in the history of Religion. It meant the introduction of a mode of public worship conducted in a manner hitherto quite unknown, but destined to become the mode of worship of civilized humanity.

JOSEPH H. HERTZ,
Daily Prayer Book

The Dynamo Of The Jewish Community

The historic synagogue is not only a *bet ha-t'filah*, " a house of prayer." It is also a *bet ha-k'neset*, " a house of assembly." Not only was it the gathering place for all Jewish communal discussions, but it also reflected the joys and sorrows of every Jew in the neighbourhood. When a male child was born, candles were lit in the synagogue on the eighth day when the boy was admitted to the " Covenant of Abraham." A baby girl was named when the father was called up to the reading of the Torah. A wedding took place near or in the synagogue, and special prayers were offered in the synagogue for the bride and groom on the Sabbath before the wedding. To this day mourners are welcomed with words of comfort on their entry into the synagogue at the inauguration of the Sabbath during the week of mourning. The wandering poor often ate and slept in the synagogue. When necessary, the synagogue became a people's court.

A Jew who felt that he had a just grievance against another had the right to stop the reading of the Torah at the service until he gained a public promise of redress. And justly so ! What value is there, otherwise, in reading the Law if the congregation will tolerate an injustice !

Besides serving as a house of prayer and a house of assembly, the historic synagogue had a third function. It was a *bet ha-midrash*, a " house of study." Where necessary it housed the local Talmud Torah, the elementary religious school. In all cases, the public opinion of the synagogue brought pressure upon every parent to arrange for the religious teaching of his children. The synagogue was the library and reading room of the community— institutions which were popular in Israel many centuries before modern communities realized their public value. But what was most important, men came daily to the synagogue to study individually and in groups. Rare, indeed, was a synagogue where the sound of Talmudic discussion was not heard and where there were no groups of men studying regularly the books of the Bible and of the rabbis, the thoughts of the prophets and the sages.

Thus the synagogue was the spiritual, the social, and the cultural reservoir and dynamo of the Jewish community. It was there that the Jewish will, head, and heart developed. There too the Jew developed the ideals and the strength of character which enabled him to survive on a high moral and cultural plane.

DAVID ARONSON,
The Jewish Way of Life

Why Go To Synagogue ?

I come to the Synagogue to probe my weakness and my strength, and to fill the gap between my profession and my practice. I come to lift myself by my bootstraps. I come to quiet the turbulence of my heart, restrain its mad impulsiveness and check the itching eagerness of my every muscle to outsmart and outdistance my neighbor. I come for self-renewal and regeneration. I come into the sadness and compassion permeating the Synagogue to contemplate and be instructed by the heaving panorama of Jewish martyrdom and human misery. I come to be strengthened in my determination to be free, never to compromise with idolatry or bow to dictatorship, cringe before autocracy or succumb to force. I come to orient myself to the whole of Reality, to the thrusts of power beyond the comprehension of my compounded dust. I come to behold the beauty of the Lord, to find Him who put an upward reach in the heart of man.

SOLOMON GOLDMAN

The Role Of The Synagogue

Because of its unique characteristics the synagogue is the only institution that has the power within it to transform a community of Jews into a Jewish community. That is true not only for Jews residing in America or England or anywhere else in the diaspora, but even for those residing in Israel proper. For we differentiated ourselves from the rest of mankind in the very beginnings of our history, and not primarily in language nor in land nor in political or economic institutions, but in our sanctuary. It was around the altar that the patriarchs cemented the earliest Jewish loyalty. It was around the *Mishkan* that Moses welded the emancipated slaves into a people. It was around the

Ark and the Covenant of Shiloh that the tribes during the period of the Judges experienced their profoundest kinship. It was the Temple in Jerusalem that gave to the Kingdom of Judea its spiritual unity. It was the synagogue that since its appearance on the scene of our history has, in the words of Salo Baron, "focalized in itself the whole communal life of Jewry."

Without the synagogue we may temporarily create a community of Jews, but they can never constitute themselves into a Jewish community, for the synagogue alone speaks of the common striving of a group of Jews to establish a conscious relationship between themselves and God.

That striving has been throughout all of Jewish history the main preoccupation of our people as a group. It is that preoccupation which above all else turned us into a distinct and distinguished people.

SIMON GREENBERG,
Address to United Synagogue
Convention, 1950

Praying With The Congregation

One of the most effective instruments for preserving the Jewish consciousness is public worship . . . . The service of the Synagogue is something more than an expression of the needs and emotions of the individual worshippers who take part in it. It is an expression of the joys and sorrows, a proclamation of the hopes and ideals of Israel . . . . For the Synagogue is the one unfailing well-spring of Jewish feeling. There we pray together with our brethren, and in the act become participators in the common sentiment, the collective conscience, of Israel. There we pray with a mightier company still, with the whole house of Israel. We become members of a far greater congregation than that of which we form a physical part. We join our brethren in spirit all over the world in their homage to the God of our people. Under its influence our worship acquires a deeper fervor, a heightened dignity; our attachment to Israel is strengthened.

MORRIS JOSEPH,
Judaism as Creed and Life

If Thou Wouldst Know

If thou wouldst know the mystic
    fount from whence
Thy wretched brethren facing
    slaughter, drew

In evil days the strength and forti-
    tude
To meet grim death with joy, and
    bare the neck

To ev'ry sharpened blade and lifted
ax ;
Or, pyres ascending, leap into the
flame
And saintlike die with *ehad* on their
lips ;

If thou wouldst know the mystic
fount from whence
Thy wretched brethren drew (while
crushed betwixt
Bleak hellish steeps and scourging
scorpions fierce)
Divine condolence, patience, fealty,
And iron strength to bear relentless
toil ;
With shoulders stooped to bear a
loathsome life,
And endlessly to suffer and endure ;

If thou wouldst know the bosom
whither streamed
Thy nation's tears, its heart and soul
and gall ;
Whither like water flowed its gush-
ing moans,
The moans that moved the nether-
most abyss,
And plaints that even Satan terrified —
Rock splitting plaints though vain
to crush the foes,
Steeled heart, more adamant than
rock and Satan.

If thou wouldst know the fortress
whither bore
Thy sires to havens safe their Torah
scrolls,
The sacred treasure of their yearning souls.

If thou wouldst know the shelter
where preserved,
Immaculate, thy nation's spirit was,
Whose hoary age, though safe with
shameful life,
Did not disgrace its lovely youth ;

If thou wouldst know the mother
merciful,
The aged, loyal mother love-abound-
ing,
Who gather'd her lost son's tears
with tenderness,
And steadied lovingly his falt'ring
steps ;
And when fatigued and shamed he
would return
'Neath her roof's umbrage, she
would wipe his tears
And on her lap lull him to sweet
sleep ;

If thou wouldst know, O humble
brother mine,
Go to the house of prayer grown old,
decayed,
In the long Teveth nights, desolate,
Or in the scorching blazing Tamuz
days,
In noonday heat, at morn, at even-
tide.

If God has left there still a remnant
small,
Thine eyes shall even to this day
behold
Through sombre shadows cast by
darkened walls,
In isolated nooks or by the stove,
Stray lonely Jews, like shades from
eras past,

Dark mournful Jews with faces lean
and wan ;
Yes, Jews who bear the weighty
galut yoke,
Forgetting their toil in the Talmud
pages worn,
And their poverty in the tales of
bygone days ;
Who rout their cares with blessed
psalmody —
(Alas how mean and trivial the sight
To alien eyes !) Thy heart will tell
thee then
That thy feet tread the marge of our
life's fount,
That thine eyes view the treasures
of our soul.

If with God's spirit thou art still
imbued,
If still His solace whispers in thy
heart,

And if a spark of hope for halcyon
days
Illumines yet thy darkness great and
deep,
Mark well and hearken, humbled
brother mine :
This house is but a small spark
fugitive
That escaped by miracle the mighty
blaze,
Lit by thy fathers in their sacred
flame.
Who knows, perchance the torrents
of their tears
Ferried us safely, bringing us hither ?
Perchance with their prayers they
asked us of the Lord.
And in their deaths bequeathed to
us life,
Eternal life that will endure for aye !
CHAIM NACHMAN BIALIK,
(translated by Maurice Samuel)

The Synagogue's Contribution To Mankind

With the synagogue there began a new type of worship in the history of humanity, the type of congregational worship without priest or ritual, still maintained substantially in its ancient form in the modern synagogue ; and still to be traced in the forms of Christian worship, though overlaid and distorted by many non-Jewish elements. In all their long history, the Jewish people have done scarcely anything more wonderful than to create the synagogue. No human institution has a longer continuous history, and none has done more for the uplifting of the human race.

ROBERT T. HERFORD

Cheated

He sat by himself in the Synagogue on Friday night. We have seen him often ; sometimes he came with other boys his age and sometimes alone. But never with his parents.

If we did not know the facts, a not unfair inference would be that he had no parents.

He was a handsome lad in his early teens, with a sensitive face and a good mind. We know that he has parents — fine parents, who dote on him and are prepared to give him everything within reason. They can afford to give their son the finest opportunities ; the best schools, the best summer vacations ; the best of everything that money can buy. Except one thing — the warmth and security and vitality of a vibrant religious faith.

Of course they encourage the lad to go to services. But they have never once come with him. Why ? Who can tell ? Perhaps they share that sadly belated and mistaken notion that they can be " good Jews " without ever identifying themselves actively with the Synagogue or ever performing a Jewish act. Perhaps they are among those who, during their early years, grew up in a Jewish vacuum, and have never taken the pains to fill that vacuum with the stuff of positive Jewish living. Or perhaps they have become identified in their own eyes, and especially in the eyes of their friends, as " non-Templegoers " and have not the courage to break out of the rut.

We are always happy to see that young lad in the Synagogue. But his presence also fills us with poignant sadness. His parents are giving him everything — except the most precious commodity of life ; a living faith. We cannot suppress a sigh, " Alas, dear boy, how you are being cheated."

SAMUEL RUDERMAN,
The Bulletin of Temple Beth-El

The Influence Of The Synagogue

To the Jews . . . the synagogue was a place for instruction in the truths and duties of revealed religion ; and in imparting and receiving this divine instruction no less than in praise or prayer they were doing honor to God — it was an act of worship. The consequence of the establishment of such a rational worship for the whole subsequent history of Judaism was immeasurable. Its persistent character, and, it is not too much to say, the very preservation of its existence through all the vicissitudes of its fortunes, it owes more than anything else to the synagogue. Nor is it for Judaism alone that it had this importance. It determined the type of Christian worship, which in the Greek and Roman world of the day might otherwise easily have taken the form of a mere mystery ; and, in part directly, in part through the church, it furnished the model to Mohammed. Thus Judaism gave to the world not only the fundamental ideas of these great monotheistic religions but the institutional forms in which they have perpetuated and propagated themselves.

GEORGE FOOT MOORE,
Judaism in the First Centuries of the Christian Era

The Synagogue Kept Judaism Alive

Since the Middle Ages, the synagogue has been the visible expression of Judaism ; it has kept the Jew in life, and enabled him to survive to the present day. With a truer application than that made by Macaulay in his day, we may declare that the synagogue, like the Ark in Genesis, carried the Jew through the deluges of history, and that within it are the seeds of a nobler and holier human life, of a better and higher civilization.

JOSEPH A. HERTZ,
Daily Prayer Book

The Synagogue Nurtures The Eternal Vision

It is the synagogue which in every community stands as the witness to God, as the testimony of our faith that the world is not a meaningless accident, that there is a Power making for justice and mercy in the world, and that we live well only as we permit that Power to enter into our hearts, and to form our thoughts and deeds. The synagogue is the visible embodiment of the soul's irrepressible cry, "Oh Lord, our God, how glorious is Thy name in all the earth." It is in the synagogue that man is constantly admonished to meditate on the high purposes of his life. It is from the synagogue, yea, even from its mute walls, that there emanates daily into the thoughts and life of the body politic the admonition, "It is not by human might, and not by human power, but by the Divine spirit within us that man ultimately prevails. Thine, Oh Lord, is the greatness, the power, Thine are riches and honor and Thou art Sovereign over all." The synagogue nurtures within us the eternal vision of Father Jacob's dream, the vision of an earth joined to heaven, of a human society distinguished by its divine attributes, the vision of an earth in which no one shall have to flee from the wrath of his brother, for it shall be full of the knowledge of the Lord " as the waters cover the sea." That service the synagogue must be prepared to perform for us today as human beings, as Jews, and as citizens of America.

SIMON GREENBERG,
Address to United Synagogue
Convention, 1950

Judaism Begins At Home

Judaism begins at home. It doesn't begin at a meeting or a conference or at a philanthropic campaign. It begins in homes where Judaism lives in the atmosphere and is integrated in the normal pattern of daily life. It begins in homes where the Jewish words re-echo, where the Jewish book is honored and the Jewish song is heard. It begins in homes where the child sees and participates in symbols and rites that link him to a people and a culture. It begins in homes where the Jewish ceremonial object is visible. It begins in the home where into the deepest layers of a child's developing personality are woven strands of love for and devotion to the life of the Jewish community.

MORRIS ADLER,
Shaarey Zedek Recorder

The Jewish Home

Whenever we think of the Jewish home and its marvelous preservation throughout the millennia, we think of it as a little Holland, wrested from the waters of materialism, paganism, and animalism; and safeguarded against their deadly onslaught by certain dikes, constructed under divine guidance by Israel's inspired engineers in the days of old. I would mention but a few of these dikes — *kashrut*, and the moral discipline of the Jewish home; *kiddush*, and home-religion; and *kaddish*, and all those beautiful symbols that sanctify birth and death, and link the generations in filial piety. If, whether through folly or disloyalty, any home or community levels these dikes, it is only a question of years before the waters of assimilation sweep over that home or that community, and it is no longer reckoned among the homes or communities of Israel. In a word, without a home-religion there is neither religion nor a true Jewish home for the Jew. "Except the Lord build the home, they toil in vain that build it."

JOSEPH H. HERTZ,
Affirmations of Judaism

The Priestess Of The Home

How simply the *Shema* sums up the whole duty of man. In the opening sentence it defines our belief: The Lord is our God, and He is One. We must love Him and we must serve Him. How are we to do this? By learning from our parents what are our duties as laid down in the Torah, "these words which I command thee." Parents are to teach them diligently to their children at all times. This injunction is addressed to mothers equally with fathers. It is the mother who is with the child when he lies down and when he rises up; it is the mother who sits with him in the house and shows him, as well as tells him, how his life must be guided by fixed rules and principles. It is the mother who walks with him and shows him the beauties of nature by the way. Bringing a child to a love of nature quickly leads him to a greater love of nature's God, the Creator of heaven and earth. All this and much more is contained in the *Shema*. So with every prayer, there are meanings we all can find if we seek them.

The carrying out of the laws of *kashrut*, of Sabbath holiness, and Holyday observance are duties that fall naturally and almost exclusively into woman's sphere. Her systematic observance of these will make them a part of her very being. But she must be ready at all times to explain her reasons for carrying them out, for on her satisfactory answers to questions put by her children may depend their future adherence to these traditions. The curiosity and sentiment of childhood should be completely satisfied by the mother's explanation of the domestic symbols and ceremonies of Judaism. She it is who can show them the beauty and the reasons behind customs which to the ignorant or the uninitiated may seem but meaningless forms. She it is who can weave into the children's nature such a love and reverence for Judaism that it will permeate their whole life, never to be lost. Gone is the age when children were content to ask no questions about religious observances, or were satisfied with the reply. "I do this because my mother did it before me and her mother before her and we must carry on our customs without question." Happily, Judaism stands as a pillar of enlightenment. It will withstand the onslaughts of doubt and questioning and rear its head above them all; the more we know of our religion the more we can revere it, for it appeals to the might of our reason as well as to our heart and to our soul.

Stress of circumstances in a Gentile world, unfortunately, often make it appear imperative for the wage-earner to work on the Sabbath day; in such cases, all the greater is the responsibility that rests on the woman of preserving the Sabbath spirit. There is no reason for the intrusion of worldly cares into the home on the Sabbath. Above all, Friday evening should be kept sacred, thus making for tranquillity and happiness. The eve of the Sabbath is essentially a home evening, an evening devoted to family reunion; neither commercial interests nor social engagements nor frivolous amusements may interfere with its sanctity. The candles lighted by a loving mother, the priestess of the home; the parents' blessing of the children; the white tablecloth gleaming with the best dishes and savory food—what can replace the memory of these through life? What more precious moments are remembered from childhood than the candles of Hanukah, the festivity of Purim, and the Seder table at Pesach? The man or woman who can look back upon such truly Jewish memories will have a bond with Judaism too strong to be broken by any passing influence or temptation. . . .

A woman's deepest concern, the center of her affection, is her home.

She should, however, have some outside work to which she gives attention. . . . Well-advised is she who joins some study group or some charitable organization. There are so many ways in which a woman may find an outlet! The interest aroused in her children by her accounts of her activities may lead to an awakening also of an interest in communal affairs, for they may begin to feel their duty to the whole family of Israel . . . .

But, primarily, the essential work of the Jewish woman, especially of the Jewish mother, will be performed within the home. The solution for much of the present domestic unrest is not to take woman out of the home, but to enlarge the concept of home, so as to bring into the home a widened interest. Extensively, this interest may be as broad as life itself, but, intensively, the essential work of the Jewish woman is to create and maintain that institution of unique purity and loveliness — the Jewish home.

IRENE R. WOLFF,
The Jewish Library (Third Series)

The Primary Locus Of Jewish Life

What native soil is to a plant, territory is to a civilization. Yet a tropical plant may be enabled to thrive in a northern climate by means of an enclosure within which the necessary conditions of temperature and sunshine are provided. Likewise, if Jewish life is to be cultivated outside its national homeland, it must be provided with a milieu congenial to its aims and modes of self-expression. The primary and indispensable locus of Jewish life is undoubtedly the home, where the child receives his first impressions, and where he obtains the basic layer of his cultural and spiritual life. It is there that the principal Jewish habits and Jewish values should be transmitted from one generation to the other. Therefore, whatever touches upon Judaism as a way of life has a bearing upon the Jewish home.

Since Judaism is more than a religion or a religious philosophy, it cannot even begin to function in the individual as such. The family is the smallest social unit through which it can articulate itself. A philosophy, whether religious or secular, presupposes a high degree of individualization and detachment from the heat and turmoil of life; but it is only some form of associated life with all its accompanying vicissitudes that gives rise to a civilization. The minimum unit of a civilization consists of man, wife and child, for no person by himself can be a carrier of a civilization, which depends upon social interaction as well as upon transmission of cultural content from one generation to the next.

MORDECAI M. KAPLAN,
Judaism as a Civilization

Teach These Commandments To Thy Children . . .

To all too many parents, " Jewish Education " means sending their young child for religious instruction, for a few hours a week, for one or more years, until adolescence.

What it should mean is daily participation in the Jewish life of a Jewish home, from infancy to old age.

When religious training is left exclusively to the school room, Judaism becomes, not a way of living, but merely a course of subjects — not too unlike arithmetic and spelling. And how enchanted were you with multiplication exercises and word drills ?

Where there is no adult and parental participation in Jewish education — which means multiplication of examples of Jewish teaching within the bosom of the family, spelling out of the ethical and ceremonial practices of Judaism in the home — religion remains something associated only with childhood textbooks, exams and report cards.

Parents pay, one way or another, for being innocent bystanders in the Jewish education of their child — innocent of knowledge or participation in the Jewish way of life.

We pay in heart-break when our off-spring ask, candidly : "What does it matter if I do date gentile fellows? If I do marry a non-Jewish girl ? "

If Judaism consists only in what happens several hours a week for a few years before adolescence, what difference can it make with what other wellbred person one shares the rest of life ?

It isn't what happens in the religious school - room, but what happens in our homes that determines Jewish loyalty and love.

ALBERT S. GOLDSTEIN,
Temple Bulletin

The Jewish Family

The Family as the Western world knows it is the creation of the Jews, who laid the foundations of family living — reciprocal love and respect between husband and wife and parents and children — in the remote past. While government agencies and church groups began to focus attention upon the family only recently, Judaism has always emphasized it as the basis of civilization and a powerful prop of Jewish survival.

Jewish ceremonial practice is inseparably bound up with the home and the family. The Sabbath and Jewish festivals are essentially family holidays. The *kiddush*, on the Sabbath and the holidays, the *zemiroth*, which grace the Sabbath meal with charm and festiveness, the *seder*, the *sukkah* and the Purim *seudah*, and many more ceremonies and rites require the setting of the traditional Jewish home, which thus becomes invested with sanctity and dignity.

The religious importance of the home has contributed much to developing and strengthening the family instinct of the Jew. To be sure, the pressure from the outside contributed to it as well. But the Jewish family instinct is more than a mere defense mechanism; it is, first and last, the proud fruit of the importance and value Judaism assigns to the family.

The traditional Jewish home is altogether different from the typically modern home, a combination refueling station and dormitory. It fills not merely the physical wants of those under its roof, but also their religious, spiritual, intellectual, esthetic and emotional needs. The Benedictions before and after the meals, the study of the weekly Pentateuchal and Prophetic Portions in the family circle, the discussion of worthwhile themes at the table (according to a talmudic dictum, the table at which matters of the Torah are not discussed resembles an idolatrous altar), and the efforts of the parents to stimulate their children intellectually and guide them ethically and religiously, make the traditional Jewish home a shrine of sacred devotion and high spirituality.

"Modernism" and prevalent discarding of traditional patterns have also had a deleterious effect upon the Jewish family. Still, it has weathered the storm more successfully than the Christian family. "Friday night" remains even in families that have drifted from Jewish traditions and religious observances an "occasion."

The home has always been the sanctuary where the Jew found rest and succor from the harshness of a hostile world. Despised and shunted about in the street, his human dignity was restored to him when he crossed the threshold of his home. The affection within the family circle has been a very important ingredient of the magic potion which has strengthened the Jew to survive.

TRUDE WEISS-ROSMARIN,
Jewish Survival

Anyone who has had the opportunity of knowing the inner life of present-day Jewish families that observe the Law of the fathers with sincere piety and in all strictness, will have been astonished at the wealth of joyfulness, gratitude and sunshine, undreamt of by the outsider, which the Law animates in the Jewish home.

RUDOLPH KITTEL,
Religion of the People of Israel

The Jewish Mother

Living as a Jewess is more than a matter of faith, knowledge or observance. To live as a Jewess, a woman must have something of the artist in her. She must have an appreciation for things beautiful and a desire to create those beautiful things herself. The widely - held opinion that our ancestors were not artistically inclined is now being rapidly revised. Examples of impressive Jewish art are being discovered in increasing numbers. But the finest artistic achievements of our people were not intended for museums ; they were created to beautify the Jewish home and ennoble every Jewish life.

The beauty of the Jewish home resembles the ever-changing beauties of nature. God did not paint one sunset and hang it permanently in the sky. He paints a new sunset daily. Thus too do the beauties of the Jewish home pass through an endless cycle of repetition but not of exact duplication. Our mothers evolved new and beautiful settings and culinary masterpieces for the various days and seasons of the Jewish year. And just as today does not automatically inherit the brilliant array of yesterday's sunset, so the Jewish home of today does not and cannot automatically inherit the beauties of the Jewish home of yesterday. The Jewish woman today, guided by the memories and traditions of yesterday, must herself create new glory and new beauty for the Jewish home of today. . . .

We urge every mother in Israel to assume her role as artist, and on every festival sabbath and holiday. to make her home and her family table a thing of beauty as precious and as elevating as anything painted on canvas or chiseled in stone.

Nothing less than the best of our effort and of our possessions should satisfy us. A little skill and love and understanding can transform the humblest surroundings into a sanctuary more holy and beautiful than the house decorated elaborately, but without love and intelligence and religious warmth.

It is well for every mother to remember that the ethical and historical lessons associated with the holidays have been as deeply impressed upon many a youthful mind by memories of unique foods and symbolic ceremonies round the family table, as by books and teachers.

It lies within the power of every Jewish woman, with the expenditure of just a little effort, to transform whatever habitation she may occupy into a Jewish Home Beautiful.

BETTY D. GREENBERG and
ALTHEA O. SILVERMAN,
The Jewish Home Beautiful

The Poetry Of Family Life

If Israel, with stiff-necked obstinacy, has survived so many nations and peoples, it has been by virtue not only of the cunning inevitably developed in the struggle of the weak with the strong, but by indomitable cheerfulness and humour, a faith in God and the future, and the cultivation of the domestic affections. A French writer has just been enviously attributing Anglo-Saxon superiority to the home life. In home and family life the Jews have had no superiors: religion threw its cheerful sanctification over every meal and made every home a temple, and therefore it is that the Ghetto was no such dungeon to the Jew as has been pictured by sensational writers.

> Stone walls do not a prison make,
> Nor iron bars a cage.

I have already indicated the great movements of thought and literature which kept the Jewish mind alive — the Battle of the Books — but, even at its deadest, the Ghetto was a realm of Poetry, almost a dream-world, in which the faith that Israel was the chosen people expressed itself in a wealth of ceremony and imagination, as well as by an all-embracing piety and penitential fervour, while the great historic traditions of the race were linked to daily life by feasts and fast.

ISRAEL ZANGWILL,
Speeches, Articles and Letters

The Role Of The Jewish Mother

There is something peculiar to the Jewish woman which distinguishes her from the rest of womankind. The Jewish woman has not only to live, but to live Jewishly ; not only to carry her own life, but also that of her people. The blending of her life with that of the Jewish vision constitutes the highest form of Jewish womanhood. Her immediate flow of being carries with it the past with all its memories, and the future with all its hopes and problems. She is born with a destiny, and with a consciousness of it . . . .

The same vital force which created and maintained Jewish existence has also given character and color to Jewish womanhood. It is this impetus which has kept Judaism from being destroyed either through persecution or assimilation . . . .

There is sufficient ground for asserting that woman's natural craving for beauty and romance can find satisfaction in the essence of Jewish being. For there is beauty in a life with a vision of beyond the horizon, there is poetry in the moral striving to transform the physical into the ideal, there is loftiness in the passion to draw near to the perfection of God, and there is vitality in the joy of living. The Jewish *élan vital* flows from this very romance which has constituted itself the Jewish being. A romance woven out of God, land, and people, fused together into an organic spiritual life, carries with it its own regenerating strength. It is romantic for the Jewish woman to be part of a history which is self-creative and more romantic than any of our epic poems. It is a poem wrought in deeds ; it is the story of human imagination welded with action, of dreams and visions knitted with life, of ideals brought to bear upon that life and not divorced from it. Life, constantly moved by the vision of the ideal, is the greatest epic poem of human creation . . . .

The twentieth - century Jewish woman seems to be faced with the hardest task in Jewish history. It is incumbent upon her to reconstruct the Jewish home so that the values of old may interpenetrate the life of today and transform it into an harmonious whole. Life in the ghetto was integral and harmonious ; the island within was unsplashed by the outside currents. Nowadays, how-

ever, to be born a Jew means to be born into a conflicting world, into a world which is one's own and yet not one's own. The Jewish mother can bring meaning and continuity into the life of the modern Jewish child by connecting his outer life with the living fountains of the Jewish past and present which are inseparable links in one continuous chain — the past appearing as the retrospective present, and the present as an enlarged and richer past.

In this way the Jewish woman, who draws her strength from the impetus which gave momentum to the Jewish people, can revitalize that very source and help to make it a continuous stream.

NINA H. ALDERBLUM,
The Jewish Library

The Light In The Home

In the Greek legend the world and man were left for long ages in darkness. Light was too divine for mere mortals. It was the exclusive, jealously guarded possession of the gods. Then Prometheus stole some fire from Olympus and brought it down to earth. For this offense he was condemned by Zeus to perpetual torment.

The Hebrew tradition is that " In the beginning . . . God said : Let there be light ! And there was light . . . ." before man or even the sun existed.

From a flaming bush the voice of God issued sending Moses forth on

his liberating mission. A luminous pillar of fiery cloud led Israel through the wilderness to the prom- ised land.

A flame burned continually on the Temple altar ; an eternal lamp before the holy ark. To rededicate the house of God a menorah was lighted by the Maccabees. These symbolize the faith of our people in the God in whose light we see light.

This is what we symbolize each time we kindle a Sabbath or holy day candle. If we understand this our- selves and teach it diligently to our children, then the act is no trite ritual form. It becomes a glowing and meaningful re-affirmation of our faith.

Let there be light . . . in your home. Let it be warm, Jewish spiritually significant light . . . the gentle light of neighborliness, friend-ship and love . . . the radiant light of knowledge and wisdom . . . the light of justice, truth and peace . . . the light shed by the presence of God in our midst.

ALBERT S. GOLDSTEIN,
Temple Bulletin

The Impact Of Jewish Family Life

In married life it is the attitude toward the institution of the family on the part of husband and wife that determines not only their relationship to each other, but their ambitions and achievements in every one of their other relationships.

What family integrity has contributed to the perpetuation of Judaism, and what Judaism in turn has done to perfect the institution of the family as a socializing and spiritualizing agency in the life of the Jew are matters that should have been given scientific study. But we are on terra firma when we say that as a factor for moral purity Jewish family life has been without equal. Judaism's influence upon the attitude of the greater part of mankind toward chastity has been more far-reaching, perhaps, than upon the attitude toward any other human or cosmic relationship.

MORDECAI M. KAPLAN,
Judaism as a Civilization

Kindling Sabbath Lights In The Soul

A well-known Jewish poet, Philip M. Raskin, has written a nostalgic poem entitled "Kindling the Sabbath Lights." In it, he sketches from memory a touching childhood picture of his mother lighting the *Shabbos* candles. She is screening her face and in a half whisper is praying to God. Her heart is full of gratitude for the Sabbath of joy and rest. Then the poet goes on to say :

Of childhood, fair childhood, the years are long fled :

Youth's candles are quenched, and my mother is dead.
And yet ev'ry Friday, when twilight arrives,
The face of my mother within me revives :
A prayer on her lips, "O Almighty be blessed.
For sending us Sabbath, the angel of rest."
And some hidden feeling I cannot control
A Sabbath light kindles, deep, deep in my soul.

Here the poet has movingly pictured the deep and lasting impression of a beautiful Jewish home observance which even the passage of years cannot erase. In a dramatic way he has emphasized the simple truth that, like charity, Jewish living begins in the home. It is there that the Jewish child makes his first contact with Judaism. Through the home symbols and ceremonies the historical dramas of Judaism are regularly re-enacted. Through the holidays he learns the appealing story of his people and its heroes. The very atmosphere of the Jewish home exercises a profound influence in molding the attitude of the child toward his heritage.

If, therefore, we are genuinely concerned with Jewish survival, we should pay careful attention to the spiritual interior decoration of our homes. A truly Jewish home is not only a place where Jews live but a place where Judaism is lived.

Far too many Jewish parents today feel that their obligation to their child's Jewish education begins and ends when they enroll him in a Hebrew or Sunday school for a few years. How little do they realize the inadequacy of the religious school without the active cooperation of the Jewish home. The child spends a comparatively short period in the school but his home is his constant environment. The school can only teach textbook Judaism that is abstract. How much meaning can that have if the child sees no evidence of Jewish living at home ?

In fact, without a truly Jewish home the school can only confuse the child. It teaches him how Jews should live and yet the Jews he worships most, his parents, do not live in the way he is taught. Can it be that his parents are wrong or is the school wrong ? Obviously they cannot both be right. In this way, the school which should inspire and guide the child, finds itself at cross-purposes with the home and this battle is waged on the battle field of the child's confused soul. In the end both the child and Judaism are the losers.

This loss to the child is usually greater than would appear on the surface. Something very vital is missing from his life for he has failed to come to terms with his heritage. In later life, an unkind world may penalize him for his heritage. If that happens, he will be paying a price for something which he hardly understood and rarely enjoyed. He shall be lacking the necessary defense which can only come from a whole-hearted acceptance of his Jewishness based on a knowledge and appreciation of it. No parent would deliberately expose his child to winter's cold without adequate protection. Yet many parents think nothing of exposing their children to the icy winds of intolerance without the necessary inner protection of Jewish values, Jewish learning and Jewish pride.

Throughout the ages the Jew's home has been his castle. Frequently it contained only the poorest furnishings—a few benches, a wooden table and hard beds or straw for the floor. But the home was sacred because it contained a *mezuzah* on the doorpost, religious books on the shelves, a *Tzedakah* box above the oven, candlesticks and a wine-cup ready for the Sabbath and the Festivals. With these ornaments, the home was beautiful. From these homes came Jews with a great love of God and a quiet dignity born out of a pride in their legacy. Our homes have added beautiful furnishings.

Their comforts have increased. But will they produce Jews with the same love of their faith ? Will they evoke the hidden feelings that kindle Sabbath lights deep in the Jewish soul ? To the extent that they do, will they contribute to the enrichment of the lives of their inhabitants and strengthen the faith upon which they must draw for meaningful creative living.

SIDNEY GREENBERG,
Temple Sinai News

7

Learn and Live

For the Jew, Life has always been dependent upon
knowledge.

ISRAEL H. LEVINTHAL,
Judaism

Learning! Learning! Learning! That is the secret of
Jewish survival.

ACHAD HA'AM,
Essays, Letters and Memoirs

For others, a knowledge of the history of their people
is a civic duty, while for the Jews it is a sacred duty.

MAURICE SAMUEL,
The Professor and The Fossil

A Requisite For Jewish Existence

Literature for us Jews is not an aspect of recreation or ornamentation. It is one of the requisites of Jewish existence. The quite significant library of Jewish subject matter now available in English makes Jewish knowledge more accessible to Jews of the Western world than ever before.

For the Jew to know is to live more fully as a Jew.

For the Jew to know is to strengthen his bonds with Jewish history and to enlarge his understanding of the contemporary Jewish scene.

For the Jew to know is to translate Jewishness into an edifying and stimulating force.

For the Jew to know is to help raise the standards of our collective life.

For the Jew to know is to be armed against the misconceptions and distortions which are to be found in the cultural environment about us. Sooner or later an American Jew is bound to meet the words "Pharisee" and "Pharisaic." Will they strike his ear with all the negative Christian connotations with which they have become associated or will he know them in reference to Hillel, Akiba and the great Talmudic tradition? He will know Judaism either as it has been misunderstood by its detractors or as it has been lived by its adherents. We are too integrated in Western culture to escape its persistent misinterpretations of Judaism and Jews. Jewish knowledge becomes an indispensable corrective in such a situation.

Another consideration gives the call of the Jewish book supreme value. In the world of the spirit it is as true that readers create writers as that writers attract readers. Give us loyal discerning readers and some of the energy of our Jewish men of talent will be devoted to creative Jewish work. Let us heed the call and play our part in enriching Jewish life generally even as we enrich our own.

MORRIS ADLER,
Shaarey Zedek Recorder

If you have acquired knowledge, what do you lack?
If you lack knowledge what have you acquired?
Leviticus Rabbah 1 : 6

Learning—The Sole Claim To Distinction

Learning was for two thousand years the sole claim of distinction recognized by Israel. "The scholar," says the Talmud, "takes precedence over the king." Israel remained faithful to this precept throughout all her humiliations. Whenever, in Christian or Moslem lands, a hostile hand closed her schools, the rabbis crossed the seas to reopen their academies in a distant country. Like the legendary Wandering Jew, the flickering torch of Jewish scholarship thus passed from East to West, from North to South, changing every two or three hundred years, from one country to another. Whenever a royal edict commanded them to leave, within three months, the country in which their fathers had been buried and their sons had been born, the treasure which the Jews were most anxious to carry away with them was their books.

ANATOLE LEROY-BEAULIEU,
Israel Among The Nations

The Book And The Jew

Jews, surveying their own past, often express astonishment at the breadth and depth of the civilization which they have inherited. It seems unreasonable that such exquisite and variegated flowers should have blossomed on a sterile soil and in an uncongenial atmosphere. Amazement disappears when one considers the urgency which impelled Jewish cultural life. For, since the Jew would not die, he had his choice of only two alternatives. He must either cultivate a compensating culture or go stark mad. This accounts for the passionate devotion of the Jew to ideas, for his intense absorption in books, for his reverence for scholarship. With other peoples, culture was an afterthought, a by-product of normal living, an amusement for leisure hours. With the Jew it was a condition for sanity.

Out of rigid necessity the Jew concerned himself with study and instruction. In no other society was education taken so seriously as in the ghetto. Mothers in their lullabies assured their infants that Torah was the best of all wares. Jewish parents held always before themselves the example of the mother of Rabbi Joshua ben Chananyah who " used to take her child to the door of the academy in his crib so that he might early become accustomed to the sound of learning."

MILTON STEINBERG,
The Making of the Modern Jew

A Mind Rooted In Jewish Wisdom

Only a Jewish mind rooted in Jewish wisdom, a Jewish soul purified by Jewish ideals, and a Jewish life disciplined by Jewish law, can make a maximum contribution to the solution of the essentially ethical and moral questions plaguing modern society. Only such Jews can hope to withstand the onslaught of the enemy. And when the day of ultimate human reconciliation will at last arrive, when all men will share the blessings of peace and justice and goodwill, only such Jews will survive to share in those blessings, to vindicate Israel's martyrdom, and humbly to glory in the luster of Israel's heroic devotions to its divinely inspired ideals.

SIMON GREENBERG,
Living as a Jew Today

If We Fail To Respond

If we, the Jewish people, ever come to the stage where we fail to respond to the call of Jewish education, we will have done what our enemies never succeeded in doing .... We will have destroyed ourselves. We will have written our own death-warrant.

LOUIS MARSHALL,
The New York Times

Jewish Study Is Indispensable

Earlier than among any other people, Jewish law and custom ordained the provision of elementary instruction to all the children of the community, rich and poor alike. "Be ye heedful of the children of the poor, for from them does the Torah go forth," was the warning of the Rabbis. And the Jewish knowledge which is to endow every Jewish boy or girl with the Jewish outlook and Jewish loyalty cannot be acquired in the few hundred hours of instruction they receive in the current Religion Classes. It must extend over years, and not end with adolescence.

The continuous teaching of the Jewish youth and the Jewish adult need not necessarily be carried on in formal classes. But a deep yearning, and constant striving for acquaintance with Jewish thought, and the classical sources of Jewish inspiration, are indispensable for real, conscious, and not merely accidental membership in the House of Israel.

JOSEPH H. HERTZ,
The Pentateuch and Haftorahs

If We Want To Go On Living

The heart of the Jewish people has always been in the Bet Hamidrash ; there was the source from which they drew the strength and the inspiration that enabled them to overcome all difficulties and withstand all persecutions. If we want to go on living, we must restore the center to the Bet Hamidrash, and make that once more the living source of Judaism.

ACHAD HA'AM,
Essays, Letters and Memoirs

Jewish Life Depends Upon Knowledge

For the Jew, Life has always been dependent upon Knowledge. There is the almost childlike but beautiful tale that the Bible tells us in its opening pages, of the trees of life and knowledge, which were placed in the center of the Garden of Eden : " The tree of life also in the midst of the garden, and the tree of the knowledge of good and evil." How few grasp the true meaning of this very simple description ! The Rabbis, however, saw deeper into these words. "Where was the tree of knowledge ?" they ask. In fact, when Eve addressed the serpent, she said : " But of the fruit of *the tree which is in the midst of the garden*, God hath said, Ye shall not eat of it." Evidently, that too was in the midst of the garden. How can both be in the same place ? And they give the interesting answer to their own query : " The tree of life was *inside* the tree of knowledge !" These Rabbis went to the very heart of the problem. For the Jew, the tree of life is *within* the tree of knowledge. With the tree of knowledge growing and blossoming, the tree of life, too, will thrive and bloom. Without the tree of knowledge, the tree of life must die and disappear !

The future of Judaism is thus even a more serious matter than the future of the Jew. As Zangwill put it : " There is worse than oppression — there is inward stagnation of the spiritual life." Our enemies may see to it that we remain Jews. A hostile world may decree : " You are compelled to remain a Jew !" But to remain Jews without Judaism would be worse than death itself. It would indeed be what the Rabbis so aptly picture as " A body preserved, but the soul consumed." We would then be nothing more than ghosts, phantoms of a dead past, not dead, and also not alive !

With Judaism vital and alive, the Jew, despite the efforts of a cruel world to destroy him, will be — must be — triumphant ! For the old truth remains : " Not only did the Jews carry the Ark of the Law, but the Ark carried the Jews !" Today, too, Judaism can keep alive those who keep it alive ! . . .

Judaism — What of the future ? To this we would reply : The Jew must learn to say again in the words of our ancestors standing at the foot of Sinai : *Na'ase Venishma !* Not as the ordinary translation would have us read these words — " We shall do and we shall hear " — but in the more original and more fundamental *meaning* of the word *She'mah* — " We shall do and we shall *understand !*" Let the Jew endeavor to do, to practice, to live his Judaism and to understand it, to know it ; let him keep the light of Judaism burning in his life and kindle it in the lives of his children, and the future of Judaism will be assured.

ISRAEL H. LEVINTHAL, *Judaism*

Torah Is Light

A young Rabbi complained to his Master : " During the hours when I am studying I feel filled with light and life, but as soon as I cease to study this mood disappears. What ought I do ? "

Thereupon the Rabbi replied : " It is like a man who journeys through a forest on a dark night, and part of the way is accompanied by a companion who carries a lantern. At length they come to the point where their paths divide, and they must go on alone. If each carries his own lantern, he need fear no darkness."

The Hasidic Anthology

How We Can Help Humanity

Jewish historical - ethical monotheism, expressive of the unity of God, of the universe and mankind, is needed more than ever in our divided world. Perhaps the greatest task now confronting humanity is how to establish the supremacy of the moral order above all other sovereignties, including that of the state. A history-oriented and messianically driven religion alone can counteract the destructive forces of nature, nowadays magnified by the new man-made means of destruction.

In the service of that religion and with this ideal in mind, the Jewish people still has a tremendous mission to perform. Its destiny has made it not only a world people in the course of its history, but has also placed it in a strategic position for service — service to be sure combined with suffering — in this critical epoch of human history. Destiny willed it that the two largest agglomerations of Jews should be found today in the United States and the Soviet Union, the two world powers whose rivalry or cooperation will fatefully determine the whole course of human evolution. The third largest group of Jews, which before long may outstrip the second, is located in Israel, at the edge of the turbulent Asiatic - African populations, and has an irresistible drive toward reshaping existing international relations. Before the Jewish people a great book of human and Jewish destiny stands open : in it is mirrored its millennial experience in its progression through many civilizations. If only our present generation and its successors can become fully cognizant of their heritage, if only they will delve ever deeper into the mysteries of their people's past and present, they will not only make certain of that people's creative survival, but also significantly help in charting mankind's path toward its ultimate, let us hope messianic, goals.

SALO W. BARON,
Great Ages and Ideas of the Jewish People

The Aim Of Jewish Education

We should utilize the Jewish cultural tradition for helping the individual Jew to live happily as a Jew, and to contribute to the welfare of the Jewish and American communities and of mankind in general. The content of such an education will inevitably include the Hebrew language, Jewish history, Jewish literature, Jewish current events, Jewish music, and Jewish art. Above all, it must stress that aspect of Jewish civilization which expressed the Jew's conception of his place in the world, his relation to the Jewish people and its relation to the rest of humanity. In short, education in Jewish religion is to be not merely instruction in beliefs and ritual practices. Its aim is to develop a sincere faith in the holiness of life and a sense of responsibility for enabling the Jewish people to make its contribution to the achievement of the good life.

MORDECAI M. KAPLAN,
The Future of the American Jew

An Understanding Heart

If God had appeared to our pious mothers and said to them, as He did to Solomon of old, " Ask, what shall I give thee " — they would have answered, " I ask for no riches nor honors to myself ; but O may it be Thy will, Lord of the Universe, that Thou give my children an understanding heart in Torah and Wisdom, so as to discern the eternal difference between good and evil."

CHAIM N. BIALIK

Religion—Something To Be Discovered

What is it we want for our children ? What is it we want their Jewishness to mean to them ?

We want them to be at home in their Jewishness, to have that comfortable sense of belonging which is such a rarity among us.

We want their Jewishness to be neither a burden, nor a source of shame or contempt to them. Nor do we want them to wear it too ostentatiously, to flaunt it before the world, to insert it clumsily into every situation. We want their Jewishness to be as natural to them as their breathing.

We want our children to have a religious attitude toward life, to have a reverence for all that enhances life ; to develop a sense of awe and mystery about the known as well as the unknown, to be warmed by the sun of knowledge; to have a feeling for beauty, and all that issues from being a part of this earth and this life. We want life and the religious understanding of it to be a joyous thing.

We want our children to appreciate the beauty and the richness of our customs and ceremonies, and to observe them, not out of a sense of guilt, not out of a belief in their magical quality, not even to hallow the memory of an ancestor; but rather as an expression of their own felt needs, as a part of their own recognition that a symbol or a ceremony is a technique of concretizing certain values, a way of clothing ideals with flesh. We want them to understand that the custom or ceremony is not as important as the feeling tones which surround it.

We want them to appreciate that their religion is concerned with all reality; that it can flourish only when the mind is open and free; that it can be destructive when it enslaves men to outworn beliefs and archaic patterns of thought; and that no religion is worth its salt unless it can liberate rather than shackle. We want them to understand that their religion (as our Prayer Book states it) welcomes all truth, whether shining from the annals of ancient revelation or reaching us through the seers of our own time.

We want our children to learn how to love, to love themselves, to love one another, to love humanity — for the world needs so much love.

We want them to sense their bond of union with the Jewish people and with all the children of men.

We want them to look upon religion not as something to be inherited, but rather as something to be discovered.

LEONARD I. BEERMAN,
Temple Bulletin

The Strategy Of Survival

Our forefathers have taught us the strategy of survival. In every crisis, exile, war or disaster, they turned not to statesmen, generals or philanthropists but to schoolmen and teachers — Ezra the Scribe, in the trying days of the First Restoration; Jochanan ben Zakki and his school at Yamnia after the Second Destruction. Teachers were always their captains, pupils their soldiers, schools their fortresses. Whenever one center of Jewish life was destroyed, men of the spirit and of the Book carried the seeds of national resurrection to the new center. America is today the greatest center of Jewish life in all our history. The Old World centers have been destroyed by fire and sword. Those who build here Jewish schools, academies and seats of learning are the saviours of our people, for they are faithful to the tried and tested technique of Jewish survival.

ABBA HILLEL SILVER

To be self-sustaining, a people has to attend to its economy. To be self-renewing it has to attend to the education of its youth.

The Reconstructionist

What Is Torah ?

Torah is the attempt of a people covenanted with God to fulfill its obligation. It is the quest of the mind for understanding and of the spirit for fulfillment. Torah is the ladder by which the Jew seeks to ascend to God. It is the bridge he builds between himself and humanity. Torah is the worship of God by means of study. It is the prayer of the mind. It is the science which seeks to discover the laws of the moral universe and thus it deals with the realities that lie above and beyond the world of visible nature. It is man's pilgrimage through life in search of himself. Torah is the shrine which the Jew builds of thought and feeling and aspiration. It is the tree of life and in its shade alone can the Jew find completeness, peace and serenity.

MORRIS ADLER,
Shaarey Zedek Recorder

Adult Jewish Education

It must become a major objective of Adult Jewish Education so to revitalize our magnificent traditional Jewish attitude to Jewish learning that the range of Jewish education shall be extended to include the whole of the life of the Jew. If heretofore the education of youth has been the first goal of Jewish education, it is imperative that henceforth its final goal shall be the education of the adult. For the only way that we can achieve any intelligent, vital and vibrant Jewish living is to education the whole Jew ! . . .

If our first objective in Adult Jewish Education is to educate the whole Jew, our second should be *to make the Jew whole*. We must bring integrity to Jewish personality. As we know, the word " integrity " is derived from the Latin " integer." This latter word occurs in the English language in the noun " integer." " Integer " means a complete whole number. It is not a fraction. For a fraction is one number above the dividing line and another number below it. It can be said that, since the period of Emancipation, the major problem of Judaism in the modern world has been and ever must be to bring completeness, wholeness, to the Jewish spirit. Since the breakdown of the Ghetto walls many Jews have been leading fractional, broken spiritual lives. There has been a stabbing dividing line in their souls. They have been one thing on one side of the line, and something else on the other side. Many Jews have been human bodies with split souls. They have been suffering from a sort of spiritual schizophrenia . . . .

The learned Jew is the complete Jew. For him the temptations of physical assimilation, spiritual hyphenation, or any of the other forms of Jewish escapisms have no lure whatsoever. Learn well! The cultured Jew is the sound, healthy Jew. For him the terrors of attempts at concealment of his Jewish identity or the torments of Jewish self-hate are non-existent. Learn well! The understanding Jew is the whole Jew whether he lives in America or in Germany or in Russia. Learn well! The Jew who knows Jewish culture is the Jew who knows himself. To know oneself is to have integrity.

It must therefore become the objective of Adult Jewish Education to bring at least a minimum quantity of the content of Jewish knowledge to every adult Jew. It must be the aim of Adult Jewish Education to familiarize the adult Jew with the thought-life of the Jewish people as expressed in its classic texts. It must Judaize the mind of the Jew so that he shall know who he is and what he is and thereby be made spiritually whole.

Closely allied with our above aim, it must also be the objective of Adult Jewish Education *to make the Jew feel the worthwhileness of Jewish life. . . .*

One of the undermining influences of anti-Semitism to Jewish survival is that many Jews tend to adopt our enemies' estimates of ourselves. It is no wonder that Judaism gets to be a misfortune to such Jews . . . .

Where are we to find the truth about ourselves if not in the Jewish book ? Where are we to find the true estimates and evaluations of Jewish life, and Jewish ideals, if not in our Jewish cultural heritage ? Where are we to get inspiration and strength to live lives of Jewish dignity if not in Jewish education ?

The real worthwhileness of Jewish living cannot be experienced merely by contributing to Jewish relief or by donating to Jewish charity, or by paying dues to philanthropic institutions or even by belonging to a Synagogue. The quality of joy can only be achieved through Jewish knowledge. . . .

Adult Jewish Education must aim to give the Jew a sense of kinship and integration with the Jewish community and also with *Kelal Israel*—the whole Jewish people. Furthermore, through such association the Jew must be able to find the maximum of personal self-realization and self-fulfillment. This was very easy to achieve for the Ghetto-Jew who lived in a world all his own. But it is very difficult to achieve for the modern Jew. He lives and mingles everywhere as a member of a minority group. The pull of the overwhelming majority tends both consciously and unconsciously toward the disintegration and destruction of those distinctive forms and patterns of Jewish life and thought, which alone offer kinship, cohesion, a sense of belonging and opportunities for self-realization to the individual Jew. In other words, the affirmative, positive aspects of Jewish life are in danger of disappearing. . . .

Adult Jewish Education must be, and can be, a great agency for teaching Jews those positive common interests of Jewish life which yield advantages and opportunities for self-fulfillment to the individual Jew. . . .

A further objective of Jewish Education for adults may well be to train and enlist the Jew to become an intelligent, responsible and active factor in the solution of Jewish problems.

Education in general has until very recently been making the serious mistake of putting all its educational eggs into the one basket of child-training. Too many generations have thought that the problems of mankind could be solved by centering education upon youth. It was believed that even though we can't solve our problems, we will give our children a good education, and they will solve the problems for us. Well, they won't! If the adults are not learning at the same time when the children are, the children will grow up to be just the same as the adults are. And the problems of life will not be nearer solution by one iota.

The new note which Adult Education brings is the emphasis on the thought that the hope of the world does not lie in children, for the children live in the patterns and grooves made for them by parents. It is the adults who must continually be stimulated to learn, to think, to keep sensitive to the ever-changing processes of life. . . .

It was the American poet, Walt Whitman, who prayerfully sang, " O to Be Self-Balanced for Contingencies." That might well be the prayer of the modern Jew, " O to be self-balanced for the ever-recurring contingencies in Jewish life." The host of urgent Jewish problems of our times — whether they be local, Palestinian, European, international — requires information, discussion, and the creation of an intelligent Jewish public opinion. By the education of our adults along some such lines we may yet come nearer to the realization of the Rabbinic hope that all our sons shall be builders of the Jewish people, for they shall have been taught of the Lord.

ISRAEL M. GOLDMAN,
Address before the Rabbinical
Assembly, 1938

If you do not want to bear the light burden of education, you will have to bear the heavy burden of ignorance.

MOSES IBN EZRA

The Role Of The Jewish School

The school is the most original institution created by post-biblical Judaism — a magnificent institution, a veritable fortress unshaken by the storms of the ages. To borrow a simile from the Midrash, the school was the heart that kept watch while the other organs slept. Ideals pass into great historical forces by embodying themselves into institutions, and the Jewish ideal of knowledge became a great historical force by embodying itself in the Jewish school.

LOUIS GINZBERG,
Students, Scholars and Saints

The Rediscovery Of Judaism

Give our children their total heritage — the copious bounty of Judaism — the Torah, the synagogue, the prayer book, the noble literature and the beautiful language of their people. Give them the millennial companionship of their kinsmen and their kinsmen's heroic faith and dreams and their matchless saga, and they will be matched with their great hour. They will then come to understand what it is in our heritage that has kept us alive. . . .

For each young heart will say I stood with Abraham in his lonely vigil and read the destiny of my people in the stars. With Isaac I built the altar of a patriarch's stern faith and ultimate sacrifice. At Jabbok's ford I learned to wrestle through the night with the dark angel of despair and to wrest a blessing at the break of dawn. With Joseph I dreamt the dream of sheaves and stars and climbed the steps from the dungeon's pit to a prince's throne. I wandered with Moses, an alien prince among an alien people. Unshod, I knelt with him before the vision in the wilderness, and from within the inextinguishable fires of God I heard the Voice summoning to duty and freedom. I saw the lightnings and the clouds and heard the thunder roll around Mt. Sinai, and witnessed the everlasting covenant between my people and its God. I learned how to suffer and hunger in long and weary marches to reach a promised land. I was with Joshua fighting at Gibeon, and with Deborah by the waters of Megiddo, when the stars in their courses fought against Sisera. I stood with the blind Samson in his agony, and heard the wild cry of his desperate courage as he pulled down the temple over the Philistines. I heard Samuel admonish his people to remain free, and not to reject God by enslaving themselves to a king. I listened to the harp of the shepherd king, David, and saw the great king bow before the righteous wrath of the prophet, and before the majesty of the over-arching Law of God. I prayed with Solomon in the Temple which he dedicated as a House of Prayer for all peoples, and I learned of a God Whom Heaven, and the Heaven of Heavens, cannot contain, and Whose compassion extendeth to all, even to the stranger who cometh out of a far country.

I marched with the resolute band of the prophets who came to destroy old worlds and to build new ones. I shuddered at the wrath of their spirit as they lashed out against oppression and injustice, against false gods and gilded idols, against blind leaders and lying prophets. I warmed at their infinite compassion for the weak, the denied, and the wronged. From them I learned the nature of mission and what a raging fire within one's bosom an unfulfilled mandate of God may become.

I wandered with my people by the slow-moving rivers of Babylon, and I heard their oath of deathless loyalty, " If I forget thee, O Jerusalem, may my right hand forget her cunning." I entered their humble and improvised synagogues, and I discovered that prayer and devout study are beautiful, and as acceptable to God as the sacrifices of the priests in the Temple, and the songs of the Levites.

I returned from captivity, and standing with those who rebuilt the walls of Jerusalem, I learned how a people can build upon ruins. I sat with the sages and scribes who

piously taught and interpreted the word of God, and molded a people's reverence for its spirit enshrined in a timeless Book. I moved among the mountains of Judea, pulling down the heathen altars, with the lion-hearted sons of Maccabees. I saw the miracle of a single cruse of spiritual oil inexhaustibly illumine the rededicated temple of their faith. I was a companion of the gentle Hillel who revealed to me the whole of the Law in the single kernel of neighborly love ; and of Akiba who knew how to inspire a revolution, defy an empire and die a martyr.

And then into the long dark exile I wandered with my people, into many lands over which cross and crescent reigned, and I walked with them the weary highways of the world. I was with them when they drank deep out of the bitter chalice of pain, humiliation, and hate. But never did I fail to sense the stress of their imperious vision, their pride of a great past, their hope of a greater future, their superb courage, their unflinching faith. Philosophers, poets and saints never failed them in the lands of their dispersion, and the light of their Torah was never extinguished.

And then I saw the night lift and the dawn break ; and into a reborn world, drenched with a new light of freedom and justice, I marched with them exaltingly. I heard the shackles fall from off their limbs. I saw the radiance of their emancipated minds and hearts. I beheld them, mounting as on eagles' wings, rising to bless the world with matchless gifts of heart and mind in every field of human creation. . . .

Shall I leave my people now? Can I leave them now? Shall I part company with this immortal band? They have become too dear and precious to me. The urgency of their pilgrimage is now coursing through my own blood. Their beckoning shrine is now also the shrine of my quest. Like unto the first pilgrim, out of Ur of the Chaldees, I, too, seized by the hand of God, am listening to the Divine summons: "Get thee out of thy country and from thy father's house into a land which I will show thee . . . and I will bless thee, and thou shalt be a blessing."

ABBA HILLEL SILVER,
The World Crisis and Jewish Survival

That man is best able to advance on the road to moral perfection, who starts with the accumulated spiritual heritage of righteous ancestors.

FELIX A. LEVY

The American-Jewish Community

Since neither forcible elimination nor voluntary disappearance seems to be a realistic possibility, the only genuine question is what kind of Jews there will be in America and elsewhere a century hence. No one in his senses will have the temerity to predict the type of Judaism and Jewish community which is likely to emerge from the great turmoil of our present world. Yet one thing may confidently be asserted: If American Jewry turns from quantity to quality, if it builds its communal coexistence less upon the quantitative criteria of financial success, statistically measurable membership or school attendance, and costly and outwardly impressive buildings and institutions, and devotes more attention to the cultivation of the genuinely creative personality and of the substantive and enduring values in religion and culture, the new type of American Jewry will be a cause of pride and satisfaction. To put it bluntly, if someone were to guarantee that in the next generation American Jews will harbor one hundred truly first-rate scholars; one hundred first-rate writers and artists; one hundred first-rate rabbis; one hundred first-rate communal executives; and one hundred first-rate lay leaders — the total number would not exceed five hundred persons, a negligible and statistically hardly recognizable segment of the Jewish population — one could look forward confidently to American Judaism's reaching new heights of achievement.

SALO W. BARON,
Great Ages and Ideas of the Jewish People

The Gravest Sin

The Jewish people is represented by every individual Jew. We need to remember where we came from, and the way to do this is by study of our great books. We are God's stake in human history. We must reawaken our consciousness of being involved in a history that transcends the interests and glories of particular dynasties and empires. The gravest sin for a Jew is to forget — or not to know — what he represents.

ABRAHAM J. HESCHEL,
The Earth Is the Lord's

A Community Based On Memory

We Jews are a community based on memory. A common memory has kept us together and enabled us to survive. This does not mean that we based our life on any one particular past, even on the loftiest of pasts; it simply means that one generation passed on to the next a memory which gained in scope — for new destiny and new emotional life were constantly accruing to it — and which realized itself in a way we can call organic. This expanding memory was more than a spiritual motif; it was a power which sustained, fed, and quickened Jewish existence itself. I might even say that these memories realized themselves biologically, for in their strength the Jewish substance was renewed. . . .

Much has disappeared from Jewry in the past one hundred and fifty years, but nothing is so ominous as the disappearance of the collective memory and the passion for handing down. All attempts to replace this vital force with substitute morals or forms have been inadequate and will prove more and more so. But more misleading than these attempts was the notion that it might be possible to dispense with this force altogether, to make a fresh and " unburdened " start — best of all in Palestine. Why cling to a community based on memory when it is possible to live as a nation among other nations! But we cannot become a nation like other nations, For the magnetism of Palestine itself, and even its power to call forth sacrifice, are due to nothing but organic memory. And from the generation which is just now growing up — let alone from future generations — the *Yishuv* (Palestinian community) will discover that it cannot establish a new continuity unless the age-old bond of memory is revived in a new form. As for the Diaspora — it will disintegrate if the connection between the generations is not restored, if the organic bond with " Israel " is not made real again, if the words of the Passover Haggadah : " We, all of us, have gone forth out of Egypt," are not rescued from being a mere phrase, and reinstated in their authenticity.

But how can all this be done? What the fathers no longer hand down the sons must get as best they can — they must study it. In times gone by, all we really had to learn was the Oral Law. Everything else we needed to know was handed down and remembered without any particular effort. Today what was once matter of course — our language, the Scriptures, our history — must become curriculum of the most crucial importance. The passion to hand down can be replaced only by the passion to study, the passion of the fathers only by that of the sons, who must work unremittingly to regain the approach to the ancestral treasure, and thus re-establish the bond of memory that joins the community together. Whether there are many such sons or few, they constitute a beginning.

MARTIN BUBER,
Israel and the World

Study—A Religious Exercise

The most important part of the ritual is *study* : and the difference between Jewish and other study is clarified once for all when we remember that for others a knowledge of the history of their people is a civic duty, while for Jews it is a sacred duty. It is considered God's will not only that we shall be good, but that we shall know what He did to us and what we did about Him. The view is that we cannot, in fact, know what He wants us to do without that knowledge of what happened between Him and us, between Him and the world, and among all three of us. There is a sense in which Jews consider *all* knowledge sacred, and all study — unless it leads toward apostasy — a religious exercise.

MAURICE SAMUEL,
The Professor and The Fossil

Education—The Very Essence Of Life

Education or the study of Torah is not a plus or an addition to human life ; it is part of its very essence. It is not something you can take or leave alone without affecting your humanity. There are some qualities in a person which constitute an asset, a plus. Their absence in a person is not a minus. To be able to sing well, for instance, is an asset. One who is unable to do so, is not defective. It is not a minus. What about education ?

" If thou hast learned much Torah,

ascribe not any merit to thyself, for thereunto wast thou created." (*Abot*, II, 8). Study is part of the essential nature of man. That is what raises him above the animal level. Its presence is not a human plus but its absence is a human minus. Without Torah, man is reduced to animal. We have then this equation: "Animal + Torah = man ; Man — Torah = animal." DAVID ARONSON, *Occasional Talks*

We cannot rid ourselves of our past without destroying our present and ruining our future.

HARRY WOLFSON,
Escaping Judaism

The Torah—Fountain And Fortress

For any community of people to be, and to remain, Jewish, they must be brought up from their tenderest childhood to regard the Sefer Torah as the title-deed of their birthright and pedigree, which they are religiously to hand down unaltered from generation to generation. For is there a Jewish community anywhere, however safely domiciled, which has relinquished the Torah for even one generation and has survived that separation ?

Those who forsake the Torah, bringing it into disrepute and weakening the hold it has on us, are working at the destruction of the brotherhood that cradled and sheltered their fathers and forefathers through all the vicissitudes of the bygone ages, to whom they owe their own life and presence on earth. The Torah is a fountain of life. In it is protection greater than in fortresses.

WALDEMAR HAFFKINE,
Quoted in *The Sabbath and Festival Prayer Book*

The Symbolic Power Of Hebrew

It is because of the Jew's great and enduring love for the Hebrew language that there has come to pass the great marvel of the renaissance of the Hebrew language in our generation. And through this revival has come, in part, the rebirth of the Jewish state, for it was the Hebrew language that was a powerful force in the revival and redemption both of the people and of the land.

It was the Hebrew language, that, through all the vagaries of time, was the fortress of strength in which the Jew, cleaving to the rock whence he was hewn, entrenched himself. Through the language of the prayers and hymns, the lamentations and penitential psalms, his heart would cleave not only to his father in heaven but also to the desolate land for which he yearned and to whose redemption he looked forward. This land would live in his heart through the poetic descriptions of the Bible that were included in the prayer book and that became the daily bread of the Jew. It is possible to say without exaggeration that the essence of the chant of the prayers in their gentle and soulful language would quiet the sighing of the heart and calm the storm of longing. Thus the uttering of the Hebrew words of the prayers was not only a means to an end but in no small measure an end in itself. It became a great individual and national achievement. Because of it, Zionist sentiment lived in the heart of every Jew through all the years of the Exile.

MENACHEM RIBALOW,
Hebrew Revival and Redemption

The Jews of America cannot live without English but will not survive without Hebrew.

SOLOMON SCHECHTER

Hebrew—A Spiritual Home

In our time, almost simultaneously with the Jewish State, one of the oldest and noblest nations in the world, India, also experienced its national rebirth. I am revealing nothing everyone here did not already know when I note that the official language of the Indian Union is still English, the language of the former occupying power, the invader, from whose yoke the great country has just been freed. India still lacks a common national language that could bind together all its provinces and ethnic components, even though the Indians—let us remember—lived continuously in their own land for the whole extent of their long history. Take a second example: Ireland. Nominally, independent Eire has its own official language, Gaelic. But, in fact, how many of the Irish can speak Gaelic? How large and how widely distributed is their Gaelic literature? In what language are their newspapers and journals published? What language is chiefly used in their Parliament? If there exists a "friends of Gaelic" society, it cannot boast of any great accomplishments even in the period of full political independence, and English, the language of the historic "foe," is still actually the language of Ireland. The Irish, like the Jews, have their own Diaspora, and by no means a small one, but the several million Irishmen who live in their homeland have always lived there, have never emigrated, have been continuously rooted in their own soil and milieu. Why then were they unable to do for Gaelic what we did for Hebrew? We succeeded not because we are more skilled than they, but because Hebrew in all generations was our sacred tongue, while Gaelic was never more for the Irish than a folk tongue, part of a local ethnographic culture. For many centuries, since the days of St. Patrick, the Irish sacred tongue was the same as in all Roman Catholic countries, the universal, denationalized Latin language, not their own tongue. Hebrew was able to exist for two thousand years, and not as a museum exhibit but as a functional organ, without state or territory, because the language itself was a kind of "territory" a spiritual home, and because the pathos of Jewish life and creativity, of inner Jewish struggles and victories was chiefly expressed in the Hebrew language. Hebrew in our own time has the power of becoming a secular vernacular — not in spite of but because of the fact that for so many generations it was our sacred tongue. If Hebrew (together with its sister language, Aramaic, in certain periods) had not been the organ of sublimation in Jewish life, it would long have become a dead language. If one takes the modern Hebrew of Israel, of which we are so justly proud, it is not simply a fresh new growth sprouted "from the soil" in a few decades. Modern Hebrew would have been impossible if it had not sprung from the stock of "*galut* Hebrew" — the prose of Mendele Mocher Sforim, the essay style of Ahad Ha'am, the poetry of Bialik, and the recreation of Sholom Aleichem by Berkovits. But this "*galut* Hebrew" itself drew its sustenance from the depths of traditional Hebrew, from the *lingua sancta*, from the spiritual stream which contained much more than nationalism, from the Jewish reservoir of great collective and individual spiritual endeavors.

HAYIM GREENBERG
Jewish Culture and Education in the Diaspora

Language Is The People

We accept the statement of the ethnologist that the first and irrevocable tie that binds a people together is language, and we must act upon it. Not only does its language constitute the "index to a people's soul," it is the only way to become acquainted with that soul. In our treasure house, in our national literature, we preserve only works in the Hebrew language. Alexandrian literature, even though its content was Jewish, failed to influence the course of Jewish life because its form was not Jewish. But for a few able translators, that might have been the fate of the medieval Spanish-Jewish group. Style may be the man, but language is the people.

SOLOMON GOLDMAN,
A Rabbi Takes Stock

Hebrew, key to the casket which holds the precious treasure.

HEINRICH HEINE,
Confessions

The Bond Of Hebrew

That ancient community (Alexandrian Jewry) had all the characteristic types of Jewish activity that are found in America. Its members were "proud" of their Jewishness. They were constantly face to face with anti - Semitism, which some observers erroneously imagine is the guarantee, if not the only prerequisite, for Jewish survival. They, therefore, had to engage in the defense of Jewish rights, through delegations to the government, propaganda and good will movements. They carried on a great deal of cultural activity, producing in Greek a large and valuable literature, the work of men of genuine talent and profound Jewish loyalty. Yet Alexandrian Jewry was completely lost, probably absorbed by the early Christian Church. Undoubtedly, an important factor was that they permitted themselves to become translation - Jews, whose contact with the sources of Jewish living was only through secondary mediums. The Bible they knew only in the Greek version called the Septuagint. . . . . Alexandrian Jews, without the bond of Hebrew, found themselves imperceptibly wandering away from all that was fundamental and unifying in Jewish life. They lost touch with the great evolving "tradition of the rabbis, then developing in Palestine. . . ." The Jews in Mohammedan Spain, on the other hand, had the same problems as Alexandrian Jewry, but they never lost contact with Palestine and the world of Hebraic culture. On the contrary, Spanish Jewry made Hebrew the vehicle of literary, scientific, and scholarly expression, rivaling the biblical period in the profusion of its genius. Hence Spanish Jews were able to produce the kind of community life that was creative and self-sustaining and never succumbed to the Inquisition and the Expulsion. Even in their martydom they were not defeated ; they were only killed. Their contributions to the treasury of the Jewish spirit are imperishable.

ROBERT GORDIS,
The Reconstructionist

Hebrew Has Blessed Us

Jewish survival is bound to Hebrew to an even higher degree than to the Jewish homeland, for Hebrew has always been with us in our territorial homelessness. It has blessed us, under many strange skies, with a sense and feeling of home and belonging, while infusing us with the indomitable will to go on — despite the frustrations and sufferings that are our lot in exile. There can be no Jewish survival without Hebrew ! The strengthening of our ties with Hebrew is therefore imperative. TRUDE WEISS-ROSMARIN,
Jewish Survival

Why Hebrew Is Indispensable

There are religious, cultural and practical reasons why Hebrew is indispensable to the Jew concerned with the fate of Jewry and Judaism. To the religious Jew, Hebrew is the language of worship and Jewish religious thought. To men of letters, Hebrew is the key to a classic literature which records the intimate experiences and memories of an ancient people. To lovers of Israel, Hebrew can serve as a bond of unity with world Jewry and the State of Israel. To Jewry at large, Hebrew can serve as a potent factor in Jewish survival, for it links the Jew to his past, binds him to the present, and enables him to share in the vision for a creative Jewish life in the future.

SAMUEL M. BLUMENFELD,
Congress Weekly

The Hebrew language . . . is the only glue which holds together our scattered bones. It also holds togeher the rings in the chain of time. . . . It binds us to those who built pyramids, to those who shed their blood on the ramparts of Jerusalem, and to those who, at the burning stakes, cried *Shema Yisrael!*

ISAAC L. PERETZ,
Alle Verk

Hebrew—The Bridge

There must grow up in the spirit of c u l t u r a l interaction between American Jewry and the State of Israel a unity far more organic than the partnership which we needed in the political and military and the economic spheres. There is a difference between partnership and integration. In military, political, and economic matters it was enough that you stood by our side. In this question of constructing a broad stream of new Israelic culture with all the essence of these three elements of the Hebrew tradition, the Jewish exilic tradition and the Western tradition, this we can do with nothing less than your most active participation. Perhaps, therefore, the worst menace both to Israel's culture and to the unity of the American Jewish Community is the depressed state of Hebrew studies in the American Jewish Community. The Hebrew language by itself does not of course exhaust the whole story. The fact is that the Hebrew language is the common factor in every single element of our common tradition.

Whether you think of Judaism in religious terms, or in terms of a great and distinctive literature, or in terms of a modern national revival, in each case Hebrew is the only key which unlocks both the religion and the literature and the unfolding pattern of a modern national life. It is the only bridge whereby a man crosses in one moment from a world which is all Gentilic to a world which is entirely Israel.

Therefore, it seems to me, that a close concentration upon the revival of Hebrew studies as an essential element in the mass life of the American Jewish Community is an essential prelude to our partnership in any of these spheres. If this task is neglected any longer, Israel and American Jewry will become foreign to each other, and we shall become overshadowed and separated by a widening gulf of alienation. You might not notice the gulf so much in this generation, in which Israel's citizens still retain the attributes of an immigrant community. You will notice it in the second generation which is built upon a mono-lingual pattern, and the day when an American Jew, however deep and ardent the passion of his Zionist spirit, is a foreigner to Israel and Israel is foreign to him, that terrible day becomes imminent upon the horizon unless somehow the Hebrew movements in this country can gather a far greater momentum.

ABBA EBAN,
Address before the Rabbinical
Assembly, 1952

One cannot understand Israel without understanding Hebrew.

EDMUND FLEG,
Why I Am A Jew

Hebrew Must Be Sacred

The Synagogue service is essentially the expression of the soul of collective Israel. In the Synagogue we meet as Jews, in prayer, in aspiration, in confession of faith, to carry on the stream of spiritual effort which has flowed unbroken through the ages ever since Israel became conscious of himself. Therefore, the prayers will not merely voice private needs and modern ideas, but will chiefly speak of Israel.

And so they will largely be in Hebrew, Israel's historic language. You may get rid of Hebrew, but with it you will get rid of the Synagogue, too, of the Synagogue as a living organism, as the well-spring of Jewish feeling and the inspiration of Jewish life. Nor is this all. The claim of Hebrew, though bound up with the interests of public worship, yet transcends them. It will meet you whenever you open your Jewish history, whenever you open your Bible. As long as we remain Jews and call the Bible our own, the Tongue in which it is written must be inestimably sacred to us.

MORRIS JOSEPH,
Judaism as Creed and Life

Hebrew—The Golden Hinge

The knowledge of Hebrew is the golden hinge upon which our national and religious existence turns. Flowing down from the hills of eternity, the Hebrew language has been set apart by God as the receptacle of truths destined to sway mankind and humanize the world.

SABATO MORAIS

Why I Studied Hebrew

My family was Orthodox. They had settled in Newark, New Jersey, after emigrating from Russia. My *zeida* was a Talmudist and earned a sketchy living in a gas-mantle factory. My *bubah* was a typical *shtetel* grandmother who toiled to keep a kosher house and my mother maintained the tradition.

In these years my family built a kosher catering business called Schary Manor. To this day I meet people who were married in our place or whose parents were. I am constantly reminded by men that they recited their "Today I am a Man" Bar Mitzvah speech in our rococo banquet rooms. My life was full of Jewish *simchas*.

So Jewishness was in my bones, my heart, my soul—but alas—I cannot say as much for Judaism. Perhaps it was the business we were in—perhaps because when I was twelve I began working in the checkroom—or perhaps because everybody took for granted that since I was a Jew, I would be a religious one. Whatever the reasons for my dereliction, the fact is I tried *chedder* and was a sorry failure at it. Though I learned some Siddur Hebrew by sheer dint of repetition. I started cheating very quickly by tying the *tefillin* tightly about my arm, holding it for a few minutes, meanwhile mumbling some of the prayers.

Meanwhile, the years rushed by. I soon forgot my abbreviated Hebrew lessons. With the exception of the *Sh'ma* and my nightly *k'rishmeh*, my religious education was limited to my ability to recognise kosher.

Then I entered the world of my ambitions—the theater—and my lessons and my life were confined to the mediums in which I worked. While I remained intensely Jewish, I still had no inclination to pursue the study of Judaism.

Miriam and I were married. Our family began to arrive—first two daughters and then a son. We began to form our Jewish home. Having a need for a Chanukah service that would translate the holiday for me and my family into something they would feel and enjoy in the only terms I knew, I began to work on one and after some years completed it.

The Jewish Theological Seminary thought it had sufficient formal religious substance to publish it.

Some years ago, I suffered the sad loss of my beloved parents and suddenly Kaddish was something I had to learn and recite each night. This, too, I learned phonetically. Only recently have I learned to read it properly.

About two years ago I began to prepare for my journey to Israel. A year before my departure I began to take Hebrew lessons. I began with a primer. Each day I found an hour's time to work with my rabbi or with the child's book he had given me.

Soon I was able to read haltingly. That year at Seder I read Hebrew to our guests and was able to understand a bit of what I was reading.

I felt I would understand Israel better if I could speak the language. So I began a high-pressure course in Sephardic Hebrew. I learned the hard way. I made my own phonetic notes. My grammar was, and still is, appalling, but my vocabulary increased and my knowledge broadened.

The study of Hebrew started me on the path to a knowledge that I had witlessly barred from myself. I remembered when my son Jeb was called to the Torah for the first time as a Bar Mitzvah. Thinking back, I wish I had known more Hebrew then so that I could have understood completely what he had said.

I suppose to many of us it seems that the unique religious civilization which is Judaism has always existed and will continue to live eternally. We assume that all our agonies must surely guarantee the survival of the Jewish approach to life because the price paid for survival was so costly.

But this is not so. It will not endure unless it is guarded, protected and nourished. When Judaism was still young and when the Torah was on the lips of only a small segment of the eastern world, Rabbi Yose warned; "Devote yourselves to the study of the Torah, for it will not come to you by inheritance."

The Torah will not come to us by inheritance, any more than will Americanism or the practice of the worldly virtues. It must be taught and then studied.

I am well aware of "the Jews who are Jews at heart." I respect these Jews. But the generations who come after them will not be as Jewish "at heart" because there will be fewer memories from which they can draw. The number of these "Jews at heart" will diminish and suddenly there may be a group of Jews who will be identified as Jews but will have no idea of what they are, why they are, or who they are.

Nothing in the way of ideals or convictions is transmitted through the genes. Blue eyes, yes — but brotherhood, no. Long legs, yes — but democracy, no. If we do not devote ourselves to studying the Jewish ideals and values, then they, too, can in one generation, be swept away.

My concern, is that the life, culture and faith of our people be preserved for generations to come — so that all those treasures encompassed by Torah (the Bible, the Talmud, the Law, the lore, the mores, the art, the music, the poetry, the wisdom and the inspiration of Judaism) shall surge with life in the minds and hearts of our children and theirs after them.

I know it is not enough for me merely to learn some Hebrew and to have my ego satisfied that I have mastered some of its mysteries. My aim is to better understand the large concepts that will seem less complex once I am able to contact them on basic levels.

Finally, I feel deeply that what I shall learn is not for me alone. The broad concepts of Judaism are not a private domain. They have been related, and in the future will be even more related, to our kinship with the world at large.

DORE SCHARY

Torah Must Live In Its Native Medium

Torah in America must be strongly Hebraic in tone and content. This does not mean that it is feasible or desirable for Jewish learning to be exclusively Hebraic under the civilization in which we live. The Torah speaks to the heart of Israel; but its message must be carried to the world. We may well hail as historic witnesses the Jewries of medieval Spain and Italy. A great Jewish literature which derives its nurture and inspiration from the Hebrew source may also be created in other friendly languages. We too may find translations useful and even indispensable for the transmission of Jewish thought to the world and to large masses of Jews, who, even as in Spain, may remain Hebraically unlettered. But for original creative power, Torah must live in its native medium. It must strike deep into the original sources of Judaism. Above all, the channels of communication with the overflowing Hebrew spirit of the new Israel must be kept open.

ABRAHAM A. NEUMAN,
Landmarks and Goals

As no man is dead so long as the mirror put to his lips reveals a breath, so no race is extinct so long as there comes from its lips the breath of speech.

ISRAEL ZANGWILL,
Voice of Jerusalem

Hebrew — The Means Of Self-Identification

The function of worship is not only to commune with God. If that were its sole purpose, there would be no need for public worship. In worshipping as a congregation, we seek a sense of fellowship with those who share our religious tradition. The sense of togetherness which is effected by public worship is of incalculable worth in laying the basis for communion with the Divine. The interdependence of the elements of a civilization — peoplehood, culture and religion — is as evident in respect to all other aspects of Jewish life. In worship, the whole of us should be engaged. When we pray as Jews, therefore, our worship must express our self-identification with the Jewish People. That self-identification which expands our spiritual horizon to embrace the whole history and destiny of our People, is as indispensable a part of our religious experience as the contemplation of Deity.

To achieve that self-identification, the use of the Hebrew language is indispensable. It is the language that, from the beginnings of Jewish history, has helped to express and to shape the religious thought and feeling of our People. Whatever other languages they came to use in their widespread Diaspora, they always and everywhere cherished Hebrew as the *leshon Hakodesh*, the sacred language of Judaism. To be sure,

we want our worship to stress the universal ideals of Jewry and not be limited to its collective interests. But the use of the Hebrew language enables us, through our worship, to maintain our ties with Jewry everywhere and in every age, while leaving us free to express the most universal thoughts and sentiments.

On the other hand, we must reckon with the fact that we can hardly expect all Jews to have a knowledge of Hebrew adequate for expressing spontaneously their religious feelings and thoughts. And we are right in insisting that our prayers should sincerely express our own thoughts and emotions. We should be defeating our own purpose, were we to confine the services wholly to Hebrew. They would then fail to arouse the personal emotions that evoke our faith in God. For that reason, the principle governing the actual conduct of our worship would be to maintain a balance between the use of Hebrew and that of the vernacular.

MORDECAI M. KAPLAN,
Questions Jews Ask

We Need Hebrew For Revival

It is a fundamental mistake to assume that we have to revive Hebrew. It does not need our efforts. Hebrew has always remained alive, even if not spoken. Hebrew is at present very much alive, not only in Palestine, but also in many countries

of the Diaspora. Therefore it is not our Hebrew which needs revival, but we, who need this language of the past and present, its classical and modern literature, for our revival.

SIMON RAWIDOWICZ

Hebrew Has Never Been Dead

The Hebrew language, mysteriously preserved like Israel, the people after whom it is called, through the tempests of many centuries, politically annihilated, but spiritually full of vigor, has never ceased to be a vehicle for the expression of sublime thoughts and sentiments. Not only in the brilliant epoch of Hebrew literature in Spain, from the tenth to the fifteenth centuries, but since then, Hebrew has been written in prose and in poetry with power and effect unattainable in any of the languages that have ceased to live.

It is entirely wrong to consider Hebrew a dead language. Hebrew has never been dead. At no time in its long history has it ceased to be employed by the Jewish people as a medium for the expression, whether in speech or writing, of the living thoughts and the living feelings of the Jew. Its use as a national medium of everyday speech came, indeed, to an end with the destruction of the political organization of the Jewish people. But that catastrophe did not destroy the life of the language any more than it destroyed the life of the nation. The marvelous revival of the Hebrew language in our times in Palestine, which is one of the greatest achievements of the Zionist movement, ·shows that the language was only neglected, and that it was essentially a living language.

The Hebrew language, with its naturalness and noble simplicity, has exerted an influence no less powerful than that of biblical ideas on the English mind. Knowing little of artificial forms, it has a natural sublimity of its own, and a great logical clearness in discriminating between nice shades of meaning. It appeals strongly to the English mind, because it is the holy language, bringing the Divine Word and coming from the sanctuary of that ancient covenant, whose faithful guardians are the people of Israel. The Semitic word has within historic times exercised on the civilization of the whole human race an influence to which no parallel can be found, and which, if the future may be measured by the past, is destined triumphantly to extend, for the incalculable benefit of mankind, to the uttermost bounds of the earth. The poetry of the Bible has no rival.

NAHUM SOKOLOW

It is worth studying the Hebrew language for ten years in order to read Psalm 104 in the original.

J. G. HERDER

Why The Jew Prays In Hebrew

The Jew prays in Hebrew, not because God understands no other language, but because it is his language, and therefore is both the form and the content of his thought. His holiest sentiments must be expressed in the tongue that links him with his ancestors and his brothers everywhere. As Schechter said of Bible translations prepared by Gentiles, " We cannot afford to have our love-letters written for us by others."

ROBERT GORDIS,
The Jew Faces a New World

Why Study And Teach Hebrew ?

Why should we study Hebrew and teach it our children ?

1. Hebrew is the language of our past. It was the instrument of expression employed by the creative genius of our people throughout the generations. It is the master key whereby one may unlock the storehouses of original literary sources. Without a knowledge of Hebrew it is impossible to attain ready and direct access to the bedrock of the Jewish soul, or to study its evolution and embodiment in the writings of the Bible, the Talmud, the medieval and modern philosophers and poets.

2. Hebrew is the nerve - center which unites and integrates the Jewish people in time and in space. It serves as an intellectual and emotional bond among all Jews throughout all ages and generations, and throughout all the lands of dispersion. Its granite syllables are personal links to the timeless message of Moses or Isaiah. And by means of the Hebrew Bible and prayerbook, Jews of the remotest corners of the earth are banded together. As the universal language of study and prayer, Hebrew is a major unifying force of the people

of Israel. It is not difficult to imagine what would happen if, for example, the Jews of America would use only English as the language of worship, the Jews of China would employ Chinese, and the Jews of France would worship in French. This would certainly mean the end of the unity of the Jewish people.

3. Hebrew is the symbol of regeneration and self-assertion in Jewish life. The Jewish will to live, and undying faith in its creative destiny in face of all difficulties, are symbolized by the revival of Hebrew as a spoken language. The sacred language of the past is now the vernacular of 700,000 Jews in Eretz Yisrael. The thick horizontal strokes and thin verticals of the Hebrew alphabet are blazoned all over the country on stamps, coins, advertising signs, and posters ; on highways, shops, stores, and hotels. Periodicals are published in Hebrew. Theatrical companies offer regular performances, all, of course, in Hebrew.

The language lives in the mouths of tens of thousands of school children, bootblacks, busmen, cab-drivers, cabaret singers, etc. Hebrew slang, colloquialisms and even curses are freely coined, while the *Vaad Ha-Lashon*, a sort of Hebrew language Academy, composed of outstanding Jewish scholars and writers, is vigilantly on guard against the intrusion of any solecisms or barbarisms that might impair the purity of the language. At the same time this Academy from time to time publishes lists of technical terms covering every branch and aspect of science, industry, technology, etc.

None of the modern attempts to revive old languages, such as Gaelic, Welsh, and Ukrainian, can boast of anything approximating the progress made by Hebrew. Yet the Irish, the Welsh, and the Ukrainians are rooted on their own soil and are free from all the political, physical, and economic difficulties with which the young, struggling *Yishuv* has to cope.

4. Hebrew is a potent medium of revitalizing the Jewish community of America ; of rendering it dynamic and creative, and a source of spiritual satisfaction and security for the individual American Jew. By means of it channels are established leading directly to the fountainhead of Jewish creativity throughout he generations. Through these channels the living stream of the accumulated Hebraic wisdom of the past and the new creative resources of modern Palestine will flow pure and untainted, constantly refreshing and regenerating.

WILLIAM CHOMSKY,
Hebrew : The Story of a Living Language

The Power Of A Language

The power of a language can scarcely be gauged. Language is more than language. Within language lie concealed magic forces of nature and of blood . . . a heritage of emotions, habits of thought, traditions of taste, inheritances of will — the imperative of the past. It is impossible to measure the power and influence of all this upon the soul, upon its consciousness and upon its subterranean strata.

SHALOM SPIEGEL,
Hebrew Reborn

Hebrew—The Touchstone

Hebrew is gradually becoming and will in time develop fully into the most pronounced sign by which one will be able to differentiate between a Jew fully integrated with his people and one who maintains only loose connections with it. Adherents of conflicting theories of Jewishness may go on endlessly discussing their points of view in the abstract, but the Jew familiar with the Hebrew language and the great stores of ancient and modern Jewish knowledge in that language will feel and act like a Jew whatever label the theorists of one or another camp may place on him.

MENAHEM BORAISHA,
Notes on Jewish Survival

Qualifications For The Well-Educated

I hope the time will come when the laws and literature of the ancient Hebrews will be studied in all of our schools as now are studied the laws and literature of the ancient Greeks and Romans, and when it will be universally recognized that no man ignorant of the laws and literature of the ancient Hebrews is a well-educated man.

LYMAN ABBOTT,
The Outlook (1905)

8

Truth to Live By

I call heaven and earth to witness . . . that I have set
before thee life and death, the blessing and the curse;
therefore choose life, that thou mayest live, thou and
thy seed.

DEUTERONOMY 30: 19

Knowledge is imperfect without faith.

THE BRATZLAVER RABBI

What is the worst thing the evil urge can achieve?
To make man forget that he is the son of a king.

RABBI SHLOMO OF KARLIN

How Free Are We?

Jewish ethics is rooted in the doctrine of human responsibility, that is, *freedom of the will*. "All is in the hands of God, except the fear of God," is an undisputed maxim of the Rabbis. And "to subject our will to the will of our Father in Heaven" is the great purpose of man's life on earth. Josephus states that the doctrine of Free-will was maintained by the Pharisees both against the Sadducees who attributed everything to chance, and the Essenes who ascribed all the actions of man to pre-destination and Divine Providence. "Free-will is granted to every man. If he desires to incline toward the good way, and be righteous, he has the power to do so; and if he desires to incline toward the unrighteous way, and be a wicked man, he has also the power to do so. Since this power of doing good or evil is in our own hands, and since all the wicked deeds which we have committed have been committed with our full consciousness, it befits us to turn in penitence and forsake our evil deeds; the power of doing so being still in our hands. Now this matter is a very important principle; nay, it is the pillar of the Law and of the commandments" (Maimonides).

We are free agents in so far as our choice between good and evil is concerned. This is an undeniable fact of human nature; but it is an equally undeniable fact that the sphere in which that choice is exercised is limited for us by heredity and environment. As the earth follows the sun in its vast sweep through heavenly space, and yet at the same time daily revolves on its axis, even so man, in the midst of the larger national and cultural whole of which he is a part, ever revolves in his own orbit. His sphere of individual conduct is largely of man's own making. It depends upon him alone whether his life be a cosmos—order, law, unity ruling in it; or whether it be chaos—desolate and void, and darkness for evermore hovering over it. Thus, in the moral universe man ever remains his own master. Though man cannot always even half control his destiny, God has given the reins of man's conduct altogether into his hands.

JOSEPH H. HERTZ,
The Pentateuch and Haftorahs

The Hebrews affirmed the reality and importance of time. To them it was not an illusion, something from which man must escape, but something which must be redeemed.

JAMES PHILIP HYATT,
Prophetic Religion

The World's Debt To Israel

Catholicism, Protestantism and the Orthodox Church teach that no salvation is possible outside the Church of Christ and without faith in it. Islam teaches that all those who do not believe in the unity of God and in the Divine message of Mohammed will be damned, that is to say that all non-Moslems (little children, who are considered as Moslems, excepted) will go to hell. The Talmud, on the contrary, teaches us that "the just and pious men of all nations will inherit the world to come" (will be saved), and the Jews therefore no longer make proselytes. People who desire to become Jews are usually dissuaded, and the above talmudical passage is quoted to them, while Christians and Moslems are zealously endeavoring to make proselytes. When a Jew is being baptized the baptizer tells him : HORRESCE JUDAICAM PERFIDIAM, REQUE HEBRAICAM SUPERSTITIONEM. I consider every further comment to be superfluous . . . .

SALUS EX JUDAIS ! Salvation comes from the Jews. It is a profound truth which is unfortunately being forgotten. To millions of men today, as it was centuries ago, this salvation lies in the belief that we are all children of the same primeval parents, and thereafter brothers ; that we are all the creatures of an omnipotent, all-bountiful God who created the world and who rules over us and guides our destiny ; that we possess an immortal soul which is destined for eternal bliss. This belief has come from the Jews. It has been expressed by Jewish prophets, and it was in the language of the Jews that those words resounded which constituted, and still constitute, the salvation, the consolation and the bliss of millions and millions of men, be they Jews, Christians, or Moslems. This belief has consoled and fortified poor humanity in its sufferings, for it dries the tears of widows and of orphans, alleviates the pain of the stick, fortifies them in the hour of death and saves them from despair. That is what the world is indebted for to Israel !

COUNT HENRY COUDENHOVE-KALERGI,
Anti-Semitism Throughout The Ages

Man — The Center Of Creation

"When God had created the world," one of the later Midrashim records, " he produced on the second day the angels with their natural inclination to do good, and an absolute inability to commit sin. On the following days he created the beasts with their exclusively animal desires. But he was pleased with neither of these extremes. 'If the angels follow my will,' said God, 'it is only on account of their inability to act in the opposite direction. I shall, therefore, create man, who will be a combination of both angel and beast, so that he will be able to follow either the good or the evil inclination. His evil deeds will place him below the level of the brutes, whilst his noble aspirations will raise him above the angels'."

In short, it is not slaves, heaven-born though they may be, that can make the kingdom glorious. God wants to reign over free agents, and it is their obedience which he desires to obtain. Man becomes thus the center of creation, for he is the only object in which the kingship could come into full expression.

SOLOMON SCHECHTER,
Some Aspects of Rabbinic Theology

A man is like a letter of the alphabet : to produce a word, it must combine with another.

BENJAMIN MANDELSTAMM,
Mishlay Binyamin

The Optimism Of Judaism

Judaism did not dwell, in the exclusive way of Christianity, on bliss in the afterworld, nor did it consider that the Messianic manifestation at the end of days would be a " day of wrath and destruction." Steadfastness would ultimately receive its reward — in this world ; a state of perfection would ultimately be attained — in this world. Thus there was in the Jewish outlook an inherent optimism. It believed in the perfectibility of humanity. It considered that to despair of redemption was one of the sins that would not be forgiven at Judgment Day. It thought of the Golden Age as being in the future, not in the past. The worse external conditions grew, the more profound and deep-rooted was the certainty of deliverance — and if we examine Jewish history in detail, we see that those few Jewish people who succumbed to the pressure of the environment did so not because they suffered more than the others, but because they gave up the optimistic conviction of ultimate deliverance. It was a conviction that in later times made it natural for Jews to take a prominent part in movements for the abolition of war and the establishment of universal peace, indeed, in many movements aimed at improving the lot of mankind. This optimistic outlook is of the greatest significance too for the present age, when scientific developments have given a grim actuality to Christian conceptions of the Last Day and the destruction of the world. As against this, Judaism teaches that to despair of the future is one of the gravest of all sins, because the perfect age, for which every man must work, still lies before us.   CECIL ROTH, *Great Ages and Ideas of the Jewish People*

Life Is Good

Life is good and a gracious gift of God. To love God one need not hate the world. Life should not be feared or contemned or renounced, but sanctified and enjoyed through wholesome living in which the whole of man — body, mind and soul — is fulfilled.

ABBA HILLEL SILVER, Address, Hebrew Union College, 1952

The Meaning Of Revelation

Revelation means communication ; it requires *two* active participants. It depends not merely upon its infinite and divine source, but also upon its finite and imperfect human instrument. God is unchanged eternally, but man is perpetually in flux, varying in his capacity to grasp the Revelation of his Maker. Hence the idea of a progressive and growing revelation is not merely compatible with faith in its divine origin, but is the only view that reckons with the nature of the human participant in the process.

A Hasidic teacher was wont to say that God tempers His message in accordance with the understanding of the people to whom He addresses Himself, just as a loving father will use baby talk in speaking to his infant. We may suggest a more modern analogy, to be found in one of the wonders of our time, the electronic transmission of sound. Let us imagine a group of people assembled in a room, and a man addressing them in a normal voice. The auditors, if they possess average hearing, can grasp his words without difficulty. But the naked ear of the audience is incapable of catching the radio waves which fill the atmosphere in the room at the same time. Then a boy brings an inexpensive portable radio into the room, and now it becomes possible for the group to hear the sounds emanating from the nearest and most powerful transmitting stations in the vicinity. Nevertheless, the sound waves of distant or weaker stations still remain inaudible until a finer instrument is introduced.

Now, whether the group in the room hears only the human voice of the speaker in their midst or the powerful, nearby stations, or the fainter and more distant broadcasts, depends upon the varying instruments of reception available; all the varied sound waves themselves are within those four walls, whether men are equipped to hear them or not. The objective factor of the sources of sound is unchanged; only the subjective factor of the recipients varies.

That is not all. In no case will the human ear grasp exactly what emanates from the source. Some degree of distortion of the purity of the original sound is inevitable— the finer the instrument, the higher the fidelity, but always the receiving instrument affects the timbre and the tone to a greater or lesser extent.

The implications of this modern parable are clear. God is the source of Revelation, but He works through men, whose capacity to grasp the divine truth depends on their personal insight and on the conditions of their age, whose children they inescapably are. Moreover, what men receive they refract through the medium of their own personality. It will always be the Revelation of God, but never the full Revelation; it will be approaching the divine "infinity," but never quite reaching it. Hence, the content of Revelation vouchsafed to men constitutes a growing and evolving body of truth.

ROBERT GORDIS,
Judaism for the Modern Age

How God reveals Himself to His chosen messengers will scarcely ever be understood. It is the greatest of mysteries: although *that* he reveals Himself is the greatest of certainties.

KARL MARTI

The Meaning Of Faith

To have faith is to perceive the wonder that is here, and to be stirred by the desire to integrate the self into the holy order of living.

Faith does not spring out of nothing. It comes with the discovery of the holy dimension of our existence.

We live by the certainty that we are not as dust in the wind, that our life is related to the ultimate, the meaning of all meanings.

God's existence can never be tested by human thought. All proofs are mere demonstrations of our thirst for Him. Does the thirsty man need a proof for his thirst?

There is neither advance nor service without faith. Nobody can rationally explain why he should sacrifice his life and happiness for the sake of the good.

Faith does not detach man from thinking, it does not suspend reason. It is opposed not to knowledge but to indifferent aloofness to the essence of living.

Faith means to hold small things great, to take light matters seriously, to distinguish the common and the passing from the aspect of the lasting.

Faith is an awareness of divine mutuality and companionship, a form of communion between God and man.

To regard all that happens as workings of Providence is to deny human responsibility. We must not idolize history.

This world is more frequently subject to the power of man than to the love of God.

Its power is revealed when man is able to exercise defiance in the face of adversity.

Our task is to act, not only to enjoy; to change, not only to accept; to augment, not only to discover the glory of God.

What is it that makes us worthy of life, if not our compassion and ability to help?

We do not exist for our own sake.

Life would be preposterous if not for the love it confers.

Faith is a dynamic, personal act, flowing between the heart of man and the love of God.

The man of faith will know when to consent and when to defy.

It is faith from which we draw the sweetness of life, the taste of the sacred, the joy of the imperishably dear. It is faith that offers us a share in eternity.

Faith is the insight that life is not a self-maintaining, private affair, not a chaos of whims and instincts, but an aspiration, a way, not a refuge.

Faith is real only when it is not one-sided but reciprocal. Man can rely on God, if God can rely on man.

We may trust in Him because He trusts in us. Our trustworthiness for God is the measure of the integrity of our faith.

ABRAHAM J. HESCHEL,
Man Is Not Alone

The Innate Dignity Of Man

During the height of World War II, the essence of the democratic outlook was succinctly set forth by President Franklin Delano Roosevelt. He was asked why the war was being fought, and he answered: " In defense of one verse in Genesis: ' God created man in His own image '." President Roosevelt thus focussed attention upon the heart of the tradition which Judaism and Christianity share : the sacred character of life, and the innate and inalienable dignity of each human being.

Eighteen centuries before Roosevelt, the teachers of the Mishnah had utilized the biblical story of the creation of Adam as a basis for their conception of man. Characteristically their discussion occurs in a legal passage dealing with the cross-examination of witnesses in a trial. The judges are instructed to warn witnesses of the heinous character of false testimony, by stressing the sanctity of human life. In this connection, a homily, at once naive and profound, is introduced:

Man was created through Adam, a single human being, in order to teach that whoever destroys a single human life is regarded as though he destroyed an entire world, and he who saves a single human life is as though he saved an entire world.

The human race began with a single individual for the sake of peace among all men, so that no man might say, "My ancestor is greater than yours," and to make it impossible for heretics to say, "There are many heavenly Powers!"

Moreover, the creation of human-ity through one ancester proclaims the greatness of the Holy One, blessed be He. For man strikes off many coins with a single mould and they are all identical. But the King of the King of Kings, the Holy One, blessed be He, stamps each man in the mould of Adam, and yet no one is identical with his fellow.

Finally, the creation of Adam teaches that each human being is obligated to declare, " For my sake was the world created." (Mishnah Sanhedrin, Chapter 4.)

Thus, the Rabbis used the biblical account of creation to buttress the innate dignity of every man, which is the source of his right to freedom, and to establish the equality of every human being, which is the foundation of his right to justice.

ROBERT GORDIS,
Judaism for the Modern Age

The Strongest Thing In The World

There are ten strong things in the world : Rock, but iron cleaves it. Iron, but fire softens it. Fire, but water quenches it. Water, but clouds bear it. Clouds, but wind scatters them. Wind, but the body withstands it. The body, but fright crushes it. Fright, but wine banishes it. Wine, but sleep works it off. Death is stronger than all, and charity saves from it.

Talmud, Baba Bathra, 10a

Whose Blood Is Redder ?

No Jew, however learned and pious, may consider himself an iota better than a fellow-Jew, however ignorant or irreligious the latter may be. This is confirmed by the law that if a learned and pious Jew were commanded to slay the ignorant and impious one, or be himself slain, he must accept death rather than kill the other. No one can tell whose blood is redder and whose life is more important in the eyes of God. If a man in this crucial moment has no right to deem himself superior to another, what right can he possibly have to do so on less critical occasions ?   RABBI BUNAM, *The Hasidic Anthology*

Just Means To Just Ends

The verse : " Justice, justice shalt thou pursue " (Deut. 16: 20) teaches us that we may use only justifiable methods even in the pursuit of justice.   RABBI BUNAM, *The Hasidic Anthology*

Every Person Is Unique

Every person born into this world represents something new, something that never existed before, something original and unique. It is the duty of every person in Israel to know and consider that he is unique in the world in his particular character and that there has never been anyone like him in the world, for if there had been someone like him, there would have been no need for him to be in the world. Every single man is a new thing in the world and is called upon to fulfill his particularity in the world.

MARTIN BUBER,
The Way of Man

The Paradox That Is Man

In the Hebraic view, there is no aspect of life so exalted, so spiritual, that it is without its roots in material nature. But, on the other hand, there is nothing, literally nothing, that is simply and exclusively material in man. In Man, every natural impulse is transformed, every organic vitality is transmuted, into a spiritual force that operates in indeterminate forms along a new dimension of freedom. Sex becomes love or lust ; kinship becomes racialism or fraternity ; gregariousness becomes free community or totalitarian regimentation ; the will-to-live becomes the service of love or the drive, however transfigured in spirituality, is grounded in the natural conditions of life. Such is the paradox that is man, a natural organism that is more than nature because it is transformed through spirit and is thus able to achieve a new level of freedom.   WILL HERBERG, *Judaism and Modern Man*

No sin is too great for God to pardon, but none too small for habit to magnify.   BAHYA IBN PAKUDA, *Hobot Halebabot*

What Is Faith ?

What is faith ? As the word is generally understood it means acknowledgment of the existence of a supreme being and the reality of a divine order in the world. It means a religious system or a religious group to which one belongs. But faith means more than this. It means also fidelity to our promises. It conveys the idea of the certainty of goodness. To have faith in some person or thing means to be sure of his or its goodness. It means to accept as true that which cannot be demonstrated by rational proof or tangible evidence.

What is faith ? It is the ability to say in the hour of sorrow that life is good, and that pain and bereavement are a natural part thereof. It is a rendering of thanks for the blessings we have enjoyed rather than a vain yearning after those we might have had.

What is faith ? It is the recognition that the quality of a life is infinitely more important than its number of years. It is the memory of precious moments stored up in the heart, unforgettable experiences which punctuate the ordinary prose of life and give it meaning.

What is faith ? It is the determination to make ideals live long after one who professed them is no longer in existence. It is the ability to find solace in the association of the afflicted.

What is faith ? It is the ability to feel the touch of a hand made cold by death, to hear across the great barrier the gentle, soothing voice of those we loved. It is the ability to face the trials of life with courage and to confront its problems with undimmed eye.

This is the meaning of faith.

HARRY HALPERN,
East Midwood Bulletin

Two Pockets

Everyone must have two pockets, so that he can reach into the one or the other, according to his needs. In his right pocket are to be the words : "For my sake was the world created," and in his left : "I am but dust and ashes."

RABBI BUNAM

Man — Creature And Creator

That which characterizes man as man, namely his moral freedom, lifts him at once out of the universe of mere objects. Because man can freely decide, because he can liberate himself from the web of the conditioned and rise into the world of the unconditioned — therefore is he the chariot of God. This freedom of man would not be possible if in his life there did not exist a Yes and a No, a good and an evil. It is by virtue of his power to say No to the conditioned, to refuse to be tempted, that he is man. " In the image of God created He him " . . .

Thus according to the Jewish conception man is creature and creator at once. He is mere creature so long as, like a thing, he is thrust into action from without. He becomes creative when, liberating himself from the chains of alien force, he rises to the freedom of ethical action.

HUGO BERGMANN,
quoted in *Rebirth*

Where Judaism Differs

Religion are ways of life ; every prophet says implicitly or explicitly : I am the way . . . the way to salvation, to reconciliation with one's soul, one's fellow-men, with pain and death and the inscrutable universe. There are three ways of life in the Western world — the pagan, the Christian, the Jewish.

The pagan accepts man and the universe as given. He accepts nature as implacable and fortune as mad and blind and brutal. Cicero, seeking in Euripides a passage of universal truth and weightiness to turn into Latin verse, selects : " There is no mortal whom pain does not touch or many ills . . . earth must return to earth and life is to be feared by all ; we are as the fruits of the field. Thus necessity decrees."

Paganism omitted almost wholly both the fact and the problem of human suffering. It accepted pain as incurable and bade man make the best of it. Hence the triumph of Paul and of the Christian way of life. For the pagan acceptance of man and nature it substituted a complete repudiation, for truth vision and reason faith. It is needless to rehearse here the great and terrible seventh chapter of the first Epistle to the Corinthians or the seventh chapter of the Epistle to the Romans. Doom was at hand. The fashion of this world passeth away. What mattered nature which was about to be shrivelled up like a scroll or man who was an immediate candidate for either heaven or hell ? What need was there except to crucify the body of this death ? . . . A perfect way of life, perhaps, under the shadow of a last day. Remain as you are, married or unmarried, slave or free. Watch and pray. But the fashion of this world remained. And the Christian repudiation of nature and reason remained too. Hence sprang the incurable antinomy and dualism at the heart of Christianity and the failure of Christianity to humanize life. For force and war and empire and injustice and the pagan cult of glory and all the actions and passions of the natural man continued, and Christianity declaring all these purely evil and wholly damned had no power upon them. It lost the world by repudiating the world.

There is a third way of life, that of the Jew. This Jewish way of life neither accepts nor repudiates without discrimination the natural man and his world. To it both are materials of which a new life is to be wrought. This sanctified human life is to be lived within the law, but not indiscriminately or regarding the dead letter. " The Sabbath is given to you ; but you, you are not given to the Sabbath." This attitude, wrongly held to be a Christian contribution, is further elaborated and universalized : " Of such importance is the duty to respect man, one's fellow-being, that it is permitted to transgress precepts explicitly announced in the holy law, if these are at variance with that duty." The Jewish way of life seeks flexibly and sanely to sanctify the natural world within which it exists and which it accepts. Its emphasis is not on kind, but on quality of action. It knows human life to be what it is. " If one were to kill the passions the world would perish." It goes soberly into detail. Among good things are " beauty, strength, wealth, honour, wisdom, old age, white hair, and sons." Among things " which are good when used in moderation and

harmful when abused are wine, work, sleep, wealth, travel, sexual love." The Jewish teaching has nothing to say of faith, but much of wisdom. But it demands that wisdom issue in action. In a thousand forms and on a thousand occasions it reiterates the principle : " Woe unto the disciples of the law who possess wisdom and do not practise virtue." And what is virtue ? " Filial piety, charity, hospitality, the establishment of peace among men." Peace — the four Hebrew letters that symbolize that word are sprinkled up and down these pages. " The blessing of God is peace." But this peace is not a metaphysical peace of grace wrought by a miracle. It must be achieved within the actual world by love. " The day of Atonement expiates your offences against God ; it does not expiate an offence against a fellow-man unless you have reconciled him to you." . . . " Benevolence and love are worth as much as the observation of all the other precepts of the divine law." . . . " Lovingkindness is worth more than all sacrifices." A thousand precepts, examples, and legends drive home the same point. With infinite spiritual delicacy the duty toward one's fellow-man is defined. One's beneficence shall not hurt his pride nor one's kindness be emphatic. For the aim of one's life is to bring peace and to diminish the suffering that is under the sun. A Mishna of the tractate Sanhedrin, of great antiquity to judge by its legendary naïveté, symbolizes the whole matter : "God feels pain each time that a man suffers. When the blood of a man is spilt, be it even of an impious man, God groans and shows upon his head or arms the very wounds by which one of his children was wounded." And all our actions are to be done, according to the sayings of the fathers, "for the sake of God," for the sake of this wounded God . . . .

The Western World has tried the pagan acceptance of man and nature ; it has tried the Christian repudiation of man and nature ; there is a third way — the sanctification, the humanization of the natural. That way has been tried by only one people. LUDWIG LEWISOHN, *Rebirth*

A life of seclusion, devoted only to meditation and prayer, is not Judaism. S. R. HIRSCH, *Nineteen Letters*

Faith And Deed

Religiousness embraces both faith and action, and action is often primary, and it provides a basis for faith ; the more we do good, the more we grasp the meaning of duty and the meaning of life, the more profoundly we believe in the good and the divine. The more too are we imbued with the feeling of humility — in regard to our deeds as also in regard to the consciousness of having been created—of our significance before God. The moral and morally acting man becomes humble and believing. In this way, but in this way alone, does faith become commanded : "believe thou ever more profoundly in God by ever doing more good !" In the sphere of morality it is the same as in the sphere of knowledge. The more knowledge we acquire, the more we learn how much we do not know. The more good we do, the more urgently obvious it becomes to us how much good there remains to be done, and how far we lag behind the command of God. The service of God is unending ; "the day is short, and the task is great ". . . .

That is why the Hebrew Bible places faith and deed, as a single religious unit, into close juxtaposition with one another. "Keep love and justice, and wait on thy God continually." "Trust in the Lord, and do good." "Wait on the Lord, and keep his way." "Offer the sacrifices of righteousness, and put your trust in the Lord." "Let integrity and uprighteousness, and me ; for I wait on Thee." "Seek ye the Lord, all ye meek of the earth, who have wrought his justice ; seek righteousness, seek meekness," "He has shown thee, O man, what is good ; and what does the Lord require of thee, but to do justly, and to love mercy, and to walk humbly with thy God ?" Humility is put here in this sentence of the Prophet at the end, as the spiritual result of the righteousness and of the love which have been practiced, and yet it becomes also the beginning, for it is the humility which never stands still, but walks with God, which not only learns that God is with it, but knows also and as well that it should be with God. Out of the ethical deed arises humility, and it in turn begets the fresh ethical deed.

LEO BAECK,
The Essence of Judaism

We Claim No Monopoly On Truth

Jews regard Judaism as the *only* religion for *Jews*. But we neither judge nor condemn the honest, devout worshiper of any faith. The Talmud tells us : " The righteous of *all* nations are worthy of immortality."

We believe in certain basic ethical concepts : decency, kindliness, justice and integrity. These we regard as eternal verities. But we claim no monopoly on these verities, for we recognize that every great religious faith has discovered them. That is what Rabbi Meir meant some eighteen centuries ago, when he said that a Gentile who follows the Torah is as good as our High Priest.

There are many mountain tops and all of them reach for the stars.

MORRIS N. KERTZER,
What Is A Jew ?

The Unity Of Mankind

" This is the book of the generations of Adam." (Gen. 5 : 1)

One of the early Rabbis, Ben Azzai, translated these words, " This is the book of the generations of MAN," and declared them to be " a great, fundamental teaching of the Torah." As all human beings are traced back to one parent, he taught, they must necessarily be brothers. These words, therefore, proclaim the vital truth of the Unity of the Human Race, and the consequent doctrine of the Brotherhood of Man. " This is the book of the generations of Man " — not black, not white, not great, not small, but MAN. In these Scriptural words we have a concept quite unknown in the ancient world — Humanity. And only the belief in One God could lead to such a clear affirmation of the unity of mankind.

JOSEPH H. HERTZ,
The Pentateuch and Haftorahs

None of us has solid ground under his feet ; each of us is only held up by the neighborly hands grasping him by the scruff, with the result that we are each held up by the next man, and often, indeed most of the time, hold each other up mutually.

FRANZ ROSENZWEIG

Religion Helps To Keep Man Human

Religion subserves many purposes. It is a principle of explanation of the universe, in the light of which the individual can find meaning for his own career and that of mankind. It is a sanction for morality. It is an esthetic, and much else besides. But not the least of its utilities is this: by positing God it inhibits man from laying claim to being God. It prevents his becoming less than man through the arrogance of claiming to be more. In brief, it helps to keep man human.

MILTON STEINBERG,
A Believing Jew

Moral Law Cannot Be Defied

Passover has a message also for the conscience and the heart of all mankind. For what does it commemorate? It commemorates the deliverance of a people from degrading slavery, from most foul and cruel tyranny. And so it is Israel's, nay, God's protest against unrighteousness, whether individual or national. Wrong, it declares, may triumph for a time, but even though it be perpetrated by the strong on the weak, it will meet with its inevitable retribution at last. "For One higher than the high regardeth." This is a truth which mankind has still to lay to heart even in these days. The world is thousands of years older than it was when the first Passover was celebrated; but the lessons taught by the ancient Deliverance retain their original force. Injustice and cruelty have by no means vanished from the world. But the Passover brands all such crimes as an abomination in the sight of God, who will avenge them now even as He interfered to avenge them on rebellious Egypt. Still, as of old, His children " sigh by reason of their bondage " ; and still " their cry goes up to God; and He remembers." Nor can the moral law be defied with impunity because it is a people that defies it. Nations have their responsibilities no less than individuals. Guilt does not cease to be guilt because it is impersonal. If it be true that " righteousness exalteth a nation," it is equally true that " sin is a people's shame," shame that must inevitably be expiated in national humiliation.

MORRIS JOSEPH,
Judaism as Creed and Life

We are not punished for our sins, but by them.

LEON HARRISON,
The Religion of a Modern Liberal

Reward And Punishment In Judaism

Judaism teaches that obedience to the will of God is rewarded, and disobedience punished. This doctrine is bound up with the fundamental belief of Judaism in a God of Justice. Because God is just, He will not treat the righteous and the wicked in the same manner. In some way, it must be better with the former than with the latter, through the justice of God. But such reward— whether conceived as material blessing or, as in later ages, when it became more and more spiritualized — is not made the motive for virtue. That must be love of God and His commandments, a free enthusiasm for doing His will. . . .

How far there is correspondence in actual life between righteousness and happiness, and between misery and sin, is a recurrent problem both in biblical and post-biblical Judaism. Deuteronomy and Ezekiel declare that men get in this world exactly what they deserve. Job, Jeremiah, Habakkuk, the Psalms, and Ecclesiastes courageously face the bitter facts of life, and point out how often it goes well with the wicked and ill with the righteous. This world-riddle becomes less distracting under the influence of the belief in the immortality of the soul.

Since the time of the Maccabees, the belief in immortality had become wellnigh universal among the masses of the Jewish people. R. Jannai could thus remain quite unperturbed by his recognition, that " it is not in our power to explain either the prosperity of the wicked, or the affliction of the righteous." " Faithful is thy Employer," says R. Tarphon, " to pay thee the reward of thy labor, and know that the grant of the reward of the righteous will be in the future life." New spiritual conceptions become prominent ; such as the great saying of the illustrious Babylonian teacher Rab, " In the world to come there is neither eating nor drinking . . . but the righteous enjoy the radiance of the *Shechinah*."

In connection with this world-riddle, the Rabbis never lost sight of two things. One, that suffering is not an absolute evil ; it educates, it purifies, it can be an instrument of Divine love. Through it, Israel came into possession of the best gifts — the Torah, the Holy Land, and Eternal Life. Rab declared, " He who suffers no affliction and persecution does not belong to Israel," i.e., has not known the highest spiritual experience of God's chosen ones. And the second thing, is that in the deepest sense, righteousness is its own reward. Ben Azzai taught that even as one sin begets another, so the reward of a good deed is that it leads to another good deed ! The Rabbis would have rejected the thought that in this world righteousness should permanently produce misery, and wickedness invariably lead to happiness, as both irrational and blasphemous. Nevertheless, they taught men to disregard the thought of reward altogether; and to do their duty, lishmoh, for its own sake. Rabbi Eleazar explained the opening verse of Psalm 112, " Blessed is the man that delighteth greatly in His commandments," to mean, " he delights greatly in His commandments, but not in the reward connected with them." This is in line with the teaching of one of the earliest Sages, Antigonos of Socoh, " Be not like servants that minister to their master with the condition of receiving a reward; but be like servants who minister to their master without the condition of receiving a reward; and let the fear of Heaven be upon you." (*Ethics of the Fathers*)

" It is true that the ordinary man may be incapable of such pure devotion; and in his case, promises of reward and punishment are necessary. But such promises are merely a means to an end, the end being the attainment of such spiritual exaltation in which the love of good will be the sole stimulus to good. Let men serve God at first for reward; they will end by serving Him without any such motive. He who desires to serve God from love must not serve to win the future world, but he does the right and avoids the wrong, because he is a man, and owes it to his manhood to perfect himself." (Maimonides)

JOSEPH H. HERTZ,
The Pentateuch and Haftorahs

In Judaism social action is religiousness, and religiousness implies social action.

LEO BAECK,
The Essence of Judaism

God And Freedom

Faith in God is the strongest bulwark of a free society. Human freedom began when men became conscious that over and above society and nature there is a God who created them, who breathed His spirit into them, who fashioned them in His likeness, and that they are, therefore, possessed of intrinsic and independent significance and are endowed, as individuals, with original and irrevocable rights and authority. When in the long past men challenged the right of kings or magistrates or restrictive customs and traditions, they did so in the name of some higher mandate derived from the spirit of God within them, in the name of some moral sanction which emanated from their relationship to God. Men became free when they acknowledged a higher authority than that of state, class, system or ruler.

ABBA HILLEL SILVER,
The World Crisis and Jewish Survival

Resisting The Environment

Like Joseph, the Jew has been the dreamer of the ages, dreaming Israel's dream of universal justice and peace and brotherhood. Like Joseph, he has everywhere been the helpless victim of the hatred of his step - brethren, hatred that drove him from home and doomed him to Exile. In that Exile, he has, like Joseph, times without number resisted the Great Temptation of disloyalty to the God of his fathers. In the dreams of Joseph, the sun, moon and eleven stars bowed down to him. It is the stars that bow to *him*, and not he to the stars. This is characteristic of both Joseph and Israel. An Israelite should be ashamed to blame his star, his environment, or any outward circumstance for his moral downfall or his religious apostasy. Man is captain of his own soul ; and wherever there is a will to Judaism, there is a way to lead the Jewish life.

JOSEPH H. HERTZ,
The Pentateuch and Haftorahs

The Last Coin Or The First ?

In medieval Jewish literature there is to be found an exquisite and illuminating parable.

Once, we are told, a traveler making his way through a difficult and perilous countryside came to the bank of a river too deep to be forded. Return he could not, nor remain where he was. How, then, was he to come to the other side ? Then he bethought himself of the purse which dangled from his girdle, containing in the form of gold pieces all his worldly wealth. In the extremity of his need he began to toss the coins one by one into the river, hoping so to raise a pathway for himself over its bed.

In vain ! The bag emptied ; the river still could not be crossed.

Finally one gold piece remained. Holding this in his hand, the traveler cast about for some other device. Looking here and there he espied a ferry boat far down the river which in his frenzy he had failed to notice earlier. Regretting that he had wasted his treasure to no purpose, yet fortunate in that one coin was left to him for passage money, he hastened to the boat, gave the gold piece to the ferryman and crossed to the other side, so saving his life and going on his way.

Bahya ibn Pakuda, the eleventh-century Spanish Jewish moralist who told this tale, has atonement in mind as its point. He was trying to say that penitence ought to be man's first expenditure, but that it proves too often his last — the sole remaining device available to him when all else has been spent.

With no violence to the parable,

it can fittingly be applied to the role of religion in life, of Judaism in Israel.

This is the function of faith among men, of the Jewish faith among Jews.

For the wise and the prudent it is the first coin in the purse — that disbursement of the spirit which makes possible the negotiating of life's most dreadful passages — which enables men to go on their way safe and rejoicing.

But for the foolish, the insensitive, the reckless, the undiscerning, it is the last coin in the purse, the one which — when every resource has been exhausted, when man is left with only his need and desperation — purchases a secure crossing to fresh possibilities and new hopes.

MILTON STEINBERG, *Basic Judaism*

Time Is Life

In the inside cover of Professor Israel Davidson's watch was the inscription, "It is later than you think." Once, addressing the students of the Jewish Theological Seminary at a Commencement, he said, "There is an American proverb which I think is not only false but pernicious in its implication. America prides itself on having coined the saying, 'Time is money.' This is a false statement and leads to serious error. The only case in which time and money are alike is that there are some people who do not know what to do with their time and some who do not know what to do with their money, and still others who are so unfortunate as not to know what to do with either. But, otherwise, time is infinitely more precious than money, and there is nothing common between them. You cannot accumulate time : you cannot regain time lost ; you cannot borrow time ; you can never tell how much time you have left in the Bank of Life. Time is life."

LOUIS FINKELSTEIN

Human Life Is Sacred

Judaism demands recognition of the dignity of man on the strength of the exalted dignity of the Creator. Every man is infused with a spark of the Spirit in whose image man was created. To degrade man thus becomes tantamount to degrading God. Thanks to this identification of the dignity of man with the honor of God, the religious-ethical spirit gained early ascendancy in Israel. It became the mainspring of Jewish social ethics and the legislation informed by it. Over and over again, biblical, talmudic and rabbinic literature emphasize that every human being has infinite value by dint of his endowment with a spark of the Divine in whose image all men are created. Wrong inflicted upon any man thus becomes a transgression against God, and "he who sheds blood diminishes something from the Likeness in which man is made." Lest one assume that God sorrows, as it were, only for the hurt inflicted upon the righteous, the Sages stressed that he mourns also for the blood of the sinners for they, too, are "His children."

Man as such is the highest value of Judaism. The degradation of any man to the level of "an animated machine" is unthinkable in the Jewish setting. To the Jew, every human life is sacred because every man partakes of the holiness of God. This is why all commandments of the Torah must be ignored when a human life is in the balance.

TRUDE WEISS-ROSMARIN,
Jewish Survival

If God Is One

"Hear, O Israel, the Lord is our God, the Lord is One." These words enshrine Judaism's greatest contribution to the religious thought of mankind. They constitute the primal confession of Faith in the religion of the Synagogue, declaring that the Holy God worshipped and proclaimed by Israel is one ; and that He alone is God, who was, is, and ever will be. That opening sentence of the *Shema* rightly occupies the central place in Jewish religious thought ; for every other Jewish belief turns upon it : all goes back to it ; all flows from it. The following are some of its far-reaching implications, negative and positive, that have been of vital importance in the spiritual history of man.

Its Negations

Polytheism. This sublime pronouncement of absolute monotheism was a declaration of war against all polytheism, the worship of many

deities, and paganism, the deification of any finite thing or being or natural force. It scornfully rejected the star-cults and demon worship of Babylonia, the animal worship of Egypt, the nature worship of Greece, the Emperor worship of Rome, as well as the stone, tree and serpent idolatries of other heathen religions with their human sacrifices, lustful rites, their barbarism and inhumanity. Polytheism breaks the moral unity of man, and involves a variety of moral standards ; that is to say, no standard at all. . . .

This is true of even its highest forms, such as the heathenism of the Greeks. . . . Despite the love of beauty that characterized the Greeks, and despite their iridescent minds, they remained barbarians religiously and morally. . . . The fruit of Greek heathen teaching is, in fact, best seen in the horrors of the arena, the wholesale crucifixions, and the unspeakable bestialities of these same pupils, the Romans of Imperial days.

Quite other were the works of Hebrew monotheism. Its preaching of the One, Omnipotent God liberated man from slavery to nature; from fear of demons and goblins and ghosts; from all creatures of man's infantile or diseased imagination. And that One God is One who "is sanctified by righteousness," who is of purer eyes than to endure the sight of evil, or to tolerate wrong. This has been named ethical monotheism . . . the sublime idea that morality is something Divine, spiritual in its inmost essence — that is the distinctive teaching of the Hebrew Scriptures. In Hebrew monotheism, ethical values are not only the highest of human values, but exclusively the only values of eternal worth. . . . The *Shema* excludes dualism, any assumption of two rival powers of light and darkness, of the universe being regarded as the arena of a perpetual conflict between the principles of Good and Evil. This was the religion of Zoroaster, the seer of ancient Persia. . . . In the Jewish view, the universe with all its conflicting forces, is marvelously harmonized in its totality; and in the sum, evil is overruled and made a new source of strength for the victory of the good. . . . In the same way, the *Shema* excludes the trinity of the Christian creed as a violation of the Unity of God. Trinitarianism has at times been indistinguishable from tritheism; i.e.,

the belief in three separate Gods. To this were added later cults of the Virgin and the saints, all of them quite incompatible with pure monotheism. Judaism recognizes no intermediary between God and man; and declares that prayer is to be directed to God alone, and to no other being in the heavens above or on the earth beneath.

Its Positive Implications

Brotherhood of Man. The belief in the unity of the Human Race is the natural corollary of the Unity of God, since the One God must be the God of the whole of humanity. It was impossible for polytheism to reach the conception of One Humanity. It could no more have written the tenth chapter of Genesis, which traces the descent of all the races of man to a common ancestry, than it could have written the first chapter of Genesis, which proclaims the One God as the Creator of the universe and all that is therein. Through Hebrew monotheism alone was it possible to teach the Brotherhood of Man; and it was Hebrew monotheism which first declared, "Thou shalt love thy neighbor as thyself. And the stranger that sojourneth with you shall be unto you as the homeborn among you, and thou shalt love him as thyself" (Lev. xix, 18, 34).

Unity of the Universe. The conception of monotheism has been the basis of modern science, and of the modern world-view. Belief in the

Unity of God opened the eyes of man to the unity of nature; "that there is a unity and harmony in the structure of things, because of the unity of their Source" (L. Roth). . . . Likewise, A. N. Whitehead declares that the conception of absolute cosmic regularity is monotheistic in origin. . . .

Unity of History. And this One God — Judaism teaches — is the righteous and omnipotent Ruler of the universe. . . . As early as the days of the second temple, the idea of the Sovereignty of God was linked with the *Shema.* The Rabbis ordained that the words, " Hear O Israel, the Lord is our God, the Lord is One," should be immediately followed by " Blessed be His name, Whose glorious kingdom is for ever and ever " — the proclamation of the ultimate triumph of justice on earth. Jewish monotheism thus stresses the supremacy of the will of God for righteousness over the course of history : " One will rules all to one end — the world as it ought to be " (Moore).

The Messianic Kingdom. The cardinal Jewish teaching of a living God who rules history, has changed the heart and the whole outlook of humanity. Not only the hallowing of human life, but the hallowing of history flows from this doctrine of a Holy God, who is hallowed by righteousness. It is only the Jew, and those who have adopted Israel's Scriptures as their own, who see all events in nature and history as parts of one all-embracing plan ; who behold God's world as a magnificent unity ; and who look forward to that sure triumph of justice in humanity on earth which men call the Kingdom of God. And it is only the Jew, and those who have gone to school to the Jew, who can pray, " May His kingdom come."

Highest among the implications of the *Shema* is the passionate conviction of the Jew that the day must dawn when all mankind will call upon the One God, when all the peoples will recognize that they are the children of One Father. Nine hundred years ago, Rashi commented as follows on the six words of the *Shema :* " He Who now is our God and is not yet recognized by the nations as their God, will yet be the one God of the whole world."

JOSEPH H. HERTZ,
The Pentateuch and Haftorahs

The Essence Of Israel's Dignity

What I have learned from Jewish life is that if a man is not more than human then he is less than human. Judaism is an attempt to prove that, in order to be a man, you have to be more than a man, that, in order to be a people, we have to be more than a people.

Israel was made to be a "holy people." This is the essence of its dignity and the essence of its merit.

Judaism is a link to eternity, kinship with ultimate reality.

ABRAHAM J. HESCHEL,
God in Search of Man

My Neighbor And I

The essential features of faith in our neighbor have already become manifest in what has been shown to be the true basis of faith in ourselves. We cannot attribute to ourselves that high nobility which we consider to be ours in virtue of its source, without also attributing it implicitly to others. Were it not essentially theirs, it could not be ours. We are created in the image of God; we are the children of God; and that which we are, they are as well. The source of our life, and the way which we are commanded to follow, are also theirs. The recognition of ourselves and the recognition of them are inseparable; they are one and the same. The religious conception of "man" necessarily implies the conception of fellow man or "neighbor," and the latter is likewise one of the great discoveries of Israelite genius. Judaism created the fellow-man or "neighbor," and with it the conception of humanity in its true sense, in the sense of respecting the life of our neighbor, of esteem for human dignity, of reverence for the Divine in all who wear the face of man.

In Judaism "neighbor" is inseparable from "man." I and my neighbor constitute in Judaism a religious and ethical unit. Fundamentally, any opposition between me and my neighbor is impossible. Here, too, as in all the conceptions of Judaism, the unity, with all its tension, with all its simultaneity of far and near, arises out of the contrast. My neighbor is the other man, and yet he is not the other; he is different from me, and yet the same; he is separated from me, and yet united with me. All that is comprised in the meaning of the word existence : place and vocation, craving and longing, have separated him from me, his life from mine. Yet everything which is contained in the word existence : content and form, source and aim of life, lead him to me, bring his life into mine. The meaning and value, the creation and task, of his life and of mine are not to be separated. He is understood by me only if like me, he is apprehended as the image of God, as the man of God. In the belief in the One God, the meaning of his life, as of mine, is revealed. He is the other, but the covenant of God with me is at the same time the covenant of God with him, and therefore the covenant which links me with him.

In Judaism there is no " man " without " fellow-man," no faith in God without faith in neighbor as well as in myself. Thus one of the Rabbis of the generation following the destruction of the Temple, Ben Asai, referred to the sentence concerning man being created in the image of God as the great fundamental principle of the Torah. Ben Asai said, " This is the history of man : when God created man, He made him in His image " — this sentence bears the weight of the whole Torah.

LEO BAECK,
The Essence of Judaism

For My Sake Was The World Created

Therefore but a single man was created in the world, to teach that if any man has caused a single soul to perish Scripture imputes it to him as though he had caused the whole world to perish ; and if man saves alive a single soul Scripture imputes it to him as though he had saved alive the whole world. . . . For man stamps many coins with the one seal and they are all like one another ; but the King of Kings, the Holy One blessed is He, has stamped every man with the seal of the first man, yet not one of them is like his fellow. Therefore every one must say, For my sake was the world created.

Mishna, Sanhedrin 4 : 5

A Passion For Social Justice

The passion of social justice runs through Judaism from the earliest writings to the present day. No modern attack upon economic exploitation can equal in earnestness and power the denunciations of the prophets against those who " grind down the faces of the poor." No modern warning against the evils of authoritarianism is so arresting as the words of Samuel rebuking the people of Israel for desiring to subject themselves to the yoke of kingship. And the numerous rabbinical provisions protecting workers against their employers and helping to mitigate the lot of the poor, the friendless and the underpriviliged are a sign that the original biblical impetus was not lost in later Judaism.

The prophetic passion for social justice and the Scriptural emphasis upon the utter reality of this life of ours have had a powerful influence on our entire culture. Perhaps no aspect of biblical religion is more striking, particularly in contrast to the otherworldly quietism of Oriental spirituality, than its restless discontent with existing conditions and the perpetual striving for something better — indeed, for perfection. The social dynamic of Hebraic religion is certainly a dynamic of social progress. The serious concern with social justice, so characteristic of the West, is one of its fruits. The social activism of Western life and its sense of the reality of history constitute another.

WILL HERBERG,
Judaism and Modern Man

The Four R's Of Repentance

The High Holidays constitute a rich spiritual symphony in which many heroic motifs are blended. The celebration of the birthday of the universe, the coronation of the King of Kings, the remembrance of the merit of the ancestors, the emphasis upon life's brevity, the yearning for more life. These motifs are all interwoven in the liturgy. The dominant and recurrent theme, however, is the insistence upon the need for repentance. Indeed the ten-day period from Rosh Hashanah to Yom Kippur constitutes the *Aseret Yimay T'shubah*, the ten days of Penitence.

The mood of these days is contrite and sober. How could it be otherwise when we focus the spotlight of conscience upon ourselves? Moral inventory, honestly taken, is rarely conducive to heightened self-appreciation. The gulf between what we could be and what we are, between our vast potentialities and our limited achievements, underscores the need for *T'shubah* — a return to God, an upreaching for the Highest. Like the angels in the thrice-repeated *Unsaneh Tokef* prayer, we too are dismayed, fear and trembling seize hold of us too when the great trumpet is sounded and the still small voice is heard.

But fear does not yield to despair. The awareness of our sins and our human frailty is relieved by the comforting faith that we can conquer sin. The accusing voice is silenced long enough to enable us to hear the whispered assurance that atonement is within reach. We need not remain the unwilling captives of our own transgressions. Given a determined will on our part we can count on Divine assistance to liberate us from the shackles of our own fashioning. Thus our Sages taught: "If a man opens his heart even so slightly as a needle's eye, God will open it as wide as the gateway to the Temple Hall."

Thus God is not only our Judge but also our Ally in the struggle for moral regeneration. Yom Kippur was traditionally referred to as the "white fast" because it held out the promise of victory on the fierce battlefield of the soul. The Jerusalem Talmud put the thought this way : " When men are summoned before an earthly ruler to defend themselves against some charge, they appear downcast and dressed in black like mourners. Israel appears before God on the Atonement day attired in white as if going to a feast because he is confident that as soon as he returns penitently to his Maker, He will not condemn but will abundantly pardon."

By which pathway does the penitent return ? How is *T'shubah* effected ? The discipline of repentance consists of three distinct steps. Initially there must be the conscious awareness of having sinned. Rationalization, concealment, projection — these and other mental masks we use to disguise our inadequacies must be removed. We need firstly the courage to accuse ourselves.

The consciousness of sin must be followed by its confession — directly to God without benefit of human mediator. The ennumeration of sins found in the *Al Chet* is sufficiently exhaustive to touch upon the personal transgressions of each of us. It has been suggested that the reason for the alphabetical arrangement of the sins in the *Al Chet* was to assure a conclusion to the list. For the alphabet does have an end whereas the sins of men do not. This may be true of the number of human sins but not of their variety. The Yom Kippur confessional seems to cover the types of human transgressions with terrifying thoroughness.

Having thus confessed his sins, the true penitent must determine in his heart of hearts not to repeat the sin. Remorse without resolution is inadequate. Morris Joseph accurately reflected Jewish teaching when he wrote : " We may be truly sorry for our shortcomings, sincere in our entreaties for pardon, earnest in our desire for reconciliation with the Highest, but unless to crown all this we solemnly resolve to make a better fight for Duty henceforth, the Day will have done little for us." True atonement involves amendment.

This then is the three-fold spiritual strategy to rid ourselves of sin — recognition, recitation, renunciation.

Where the sin is against a fellow man, a fourth step is required — reparation. " If thou hast sinned against thy brother go first and appease him, otherwise the Day of Atonement cannot absolve thee."

The prayers of these holy days are beautiful and moving. The spiritual reveille sounded by the *Shofar* is dramatically stirring. The pathos and sorrow of the *Kol Nidre* chant strike some sympathetic note in every Jewish heart. The self-imposed austerity of the fast drives home most effectively the moral significance of the season. All these, however, are only the prelude to something bigger. Beyond prayer, rite and ritual is the arena of human action. It is there that true repentance is achieved, the human triumph made secure.

The keynote of the Days of Awe, their solemnity and their hopefulness, is eloquently sounded in the message of Isaiah read on Yom Kippur morning :

Is not this the fast that I have chosen?
To loose the bonds of wickedness
To undo the bands of the yoke
And to let the oppressed go free?

Is it not to deal thy bread to the hungry

And that thou bring the poor that are cast out to thy house?

When thou seest the naked that thou cover him
And that thou hide not thyself from thine own flesh?

Then shall thy light break forth like the morning
And thy health shall spring forth speedily ;
And thy righteousness shall go before thee
The glory of the Lord shall be thy reward.

SIDNEY GREENBERG,
Jewish Telegraphic Agency

9

The Good Life

Which is the right course which a man should choose
for himself? That which he feels to be honorable to
himself and which also brings him honor from mankind.

Ethics of the Fathers, 2 : 1

The divine test of a man's worth is not his theology
but his life.

MORRIS JOSEPH,
Judaism as Creed and Life

The Jewish way in the world has consistently and unswervingly pursued the idea and technique of the good
life. Not beauty but goodness is the central problem and
theme of Judaism.

TRUDE WEISS-ROSMARIN,
Jewish Survival

On Contentment And Forgiveness

The ethical person is content with what he has; the unethical one is never satisfied. If a man is satisfied with his lot, he is likely to live a happy life. For one thing, he will not be too dependent on others. None is so rich as one who is content with little. There is no wealth like generosity; no treasure like wisdom; no glory like self-mastery; no sin like pride; no poverty like the love of money; no ornament like health.

In order to have contentment one must have faith. If a man has no faith he is likely to worry constantly. He will be afraid to spend even a little of what he has lest he lose everything and become poor. But the man of faith is confident that God will supply his needs at all times and so he is always cheerful. He will not be tempted to steal from others and will enjoy a peaceful life. Happy indeed is he who has learned to rely upon God rather than upon man.

Contentment frees a man from greed and envy. Greed leads to many evils; envy and contentment can never be found together. If you are envious, you court all kinds of trouble and ailments. Be generous toward your neighbor; be as concerned about his welfare and reputation as you are about your own.

He who controls his anger shows that he is intelligent and follows the example of the great men of Jewish history. One saintly man, for example, used to say every evening before retiring: " I forgive all those who have offended me." Thus he never passed a night in hatred of any man. ISRAEL AL-NAKAWA, *Menorath Hamaor*

Keep discontent far from thee, envy a man nothing save his virtues. ELAZAR OF WORMS, *Sefer Rokeah*

On Loving One's Neighbor

Do not displease God by hating him whom He loves. A father's love for his child is only a drop in the ocean compared with God's love for man. How, then, can you slander your neighbor or raise your voice against him ?

If your neighbor is guilty of a misdeed, do not hate him for it, since it is quite possible that you in his position would act much worse. Instead, your great love and mercy for him should fill you with sorrow and sympathy because of the misfortune that has befallen him.

If you know in your heart that you are not well disposed toward your neighbor, shut your eyes and do not look at his faults with malicious pleasure in order to shame him with stinging reproof. Close your lips, do not rebuke him, lest you destroy your soul. God's anger turned against tyrants who tormented our souls, even though we deserved to suffer the evil done to us. Those tyrants were punished because of their malicious intent, because they rejoiced in seeing us suffer.

If you have a good heart, you will be sorry for the wrongdoer; you will pray for him and seek to rehabilitate him. If this is not possible, leave him in the care of God who will have mercy on him and direct him in the right path so that he may come to a good end. Seek to love him for the sake of the good he will do in time to come. Enrich your heart with love and friendship.

Love your neighbor as yourself and wish him well. Have mercy upon him in his misfortune, and do all you can for him.

JACOB KRANZ,
Sefer Ha-Middoth

Most people are concerned about their own bodies and their neighbors' souls. This is a serious error.

In order to improve our world we must leave our neighbors' souls alone. We must instead worry about our neighbors' bodies and our own souls.

ISRAEL SALANTER,

In our law it is a greater sin to rob or defraud a stranger than a fellow Jew. A Jew must show his charity to all men.

MENASSEH B. ISRAEL,
Vindiciae Judacorum

Our Neighbor Is Any Human Being

Not only theoretically is the character of Jewish ethics universally human, but in an eminently practical sense is it so. The Mosaic legislation, upon the spirit of which the later, more amplified, purified, and deepened Jewish ethics was built up, is the noblest code of antiquity in its treatment of the stranger. Again and again is the Israelite reminded that there is one law for the stranger and the native. In the great institution, the Sabbath, which perhaps more than anything else

made for the dignity and equality of man, the stranger is included, so that he, though he might be bondman, should have his day of rest. Every time the Israelite is enjoined to deal lovingly and helpfully with his poor, the stranger is included: " To the poor and to the stranger shalt thou leave them." When the Israelite is commanded to rejoice on his festival, he is to include in his joy the widow and the orphan, and the poor and the stranger. When he is commanded to " love they neighbor as thyself," he is immediately also commanded to love the stranger, thus implying that neighbor included stranger. That the law not only was addressed to all men but that it embraced all men in its operation is made clear once for all by a striking saying of the Rabbis. In the course of a discussion the question is asked as to which is the most important sentence in the Bible. One Rabbi answers by saying, "And thou shalt love thy neighbor as thyself," quoting from the nineteenth chapter of Leviticus. Another Rabbi replies that there is a sentence that reaches even deeper than this. He quotes from the fifth chapter of Genesis: "This is the book of the generations of man." For this sentence tells us who is our neighbor. Our neighbor is any human being.

SAMUEL SCHULMAN,
Jewish Ethics

No One Must Be Wronged

Deceive no one, be he Jew or non-Jew. Do not argue and quarrel with people, regardless of what religion they confess. Be honest in business. Do not say that a certain price has been offered for your merchandise when it is not so, and do not pretend to be unwilling to sell when you are. Such conduct is unbefitting a Jew. . . .If a contract is concluded between Jews and non-Jews, mutually binding, the former must live up to it even if the latter do not. . . . No one must be wronged, whether he belong to our religion or to another.

JUDAH HE HASID,
Sefer Hasidim

The Hand Of Compassion

God has willed that there be two hands in the matter of charity; one that gives and one that receives. . . .

Thank God that yours is the hand that gives. . . .

Open a hand of compassion to the poor. Say not, "I will miss what I give." Be like the sheep who give their wool and have no less the next year because they have given.

LOUIS I. NEWMAN,
The Talmudic Anthology

Justice For The Orphan

The wife of Rabbi Wolf of Zbaraz accused her maidservant of having stolen a costly vessel. The girl denied the deed. The woman, being wroth, prepared herself to go out and appeal to the rabbinical court. Rabbi Wolf, seeing her preparations, put on his Sabbath garment also. His wife said that it was not fitting for him to go, too, and that she knew well enough how to bear herself in the court's presence.

"Truly," replied the Zaddick, "you do. But the poor orphan, your maid, as whose counsel I am going, does not. And who but I will see that justice is done her?"

The Hasidic Anthology

On Loving The Wicked

A Zaddick once cried from the depth of his heart: "Would I could love the best of men as tenderly as God loves the worst."

The Hasidic Anthology

Royalty And Humility

A king was told that a man of humility is endowed with long life. He attired himself in old garments, took up his residence in a small hut, and forbade anyone to show reverence before him. But when he honestly examined himself, the king found himself to be prouder of his seeming humility than ever before. A Philosopher thereupon remarked to him: "Dress like a king; live like a king; allow the people to show due respect to you; but be humble in your inmost heart."

THE BAAL SHEM,
The Hasidic Anthology

To sin against a fellow-man is worse than to sin against the Creator. The man you harmed may have gone to an unknown place, and you may lose the opportunity to beg his forgiveness. The Lord, however, is everywhere and you can always find Him when you seek Him.

THE AMSHINOVER RABBI
The Hasidic Anthology

The Meaning Of Love

Rabbi Moshe Leib of Sassov declared to his disciples: "I learned how we must truly love our neighbor from a conversation between two villagers which I overheard.

"The first said: 'Tell me, friend Ivan, do you love me?'

"The second: "I love you deeply.'

"The first: 'Do you know, my friend, what gives me pain?'

"The second: 'How can I, pray,

know what gives you pain ? '

" The first : ' If you do not know what gives me pain, how can you say that you truly love me ? '

" Understand, then, my sons," continued the Sassover ; " to love, truly to love, means to know what brings pain to your comrade."

The Hasidic Anthology

What Is Hateful To Thee

Rabbi Schmelke interpreted the famous saying of Hillel (*Sabbath* 31a) : " What is hateful to thee do not cause to be done to thy neighbor." He paraphrased it saying : " What is hateful to thee in thy neighbor, do not do thyself."

The Hasidic Anthology

The good man should himself be the Torah, and people should be able to learn good conduct from observing him.

LEIB SARAS,
The Hasidic Anthology

A Prescription For Goodness

We are told by the Psalmist first to leave evil and then to do good. I will add that if you find it difficult to follow this advice, you may first do good, and the evil will automatically depart from you.

THE GERER RABBI
The Hasidic Anthology

Failure To Repent

Failure to repent is much worse than sin. A man may have sinned for but a moment, but he may fail to repent of it moments without number.

RABBI BUNAM,
The Hasidic Anthology

The Meaning Of Humility

The essential meaning of humility, as it grew up in the Jewish soul, is the knowledge of the position which man has in infinity and eternity ; it is the full religious feeling of life in the man who knows that he has been created by God. Thus there is in it nothing deliberate or intentional, nothing which crushes or oppresses ; it is no self-humiliation, but it is insight into man's own existence, the realization that it has come into being through God. It is the mood which pervades life when it becomes conscious of its profoundness, when it listens within to itself ; it is the sound in which the harmony of the great creation — the music of the spheres one is inclined to say — rises up in the human soul.

LEO BAECK,
The Essence of Judaism

If ever man becomes proud, let him remember that a gnat preceded him in the divine order of creation !

Tosefta, Sanhedrin 8 : 8

The End Of Man

Thus spoke Rabbi Meir, when he had ended the Book of Job :
The end of man is death,
the end of cattle is slaughter.
Everything that is, dies.
Happy is he who has grown in the Torah,
whose labors are concerned with the Torah,
who gives satisfaction to his Maker,
who has grown up with a good name,
and with a good name departs from this world.

About him Solomon says :
" A good name
is better than precious oil ;
and the day of death
than the day of one's birth."

NAHUM GLATZER
adapted from the *Talmud*

Man was created with two eyes, so that with one he may see God's greatness, and with the other his own lowliness.

SAMUEL J. AGNON

How To Remove Rancor

I have often made it my practice . . . to look over those present [at a religious service] one by one, to ask myself whether in truth I loved everyone, whether indeed my acceptance of the command to love my fellow was genuine. With God's help I often found such to be the case. Whenever I noticed one who had done me some wrong I made it my rule to forgive him at that very instant, undertaking to love him nevertheless. But if my heart refused to allow me to love him, then I would force myself to say great goodnesses concerning him until I had removed rancor from my heart.

JOEL BEN ABRAHAM SHEMARIAH,
quoted in *Basic Judaism*

Honesty And Eternity

Above all, my children, be honest in money matters with Jews and non-Jews alike. If you have money or possessions belonging to other people, take better care of them than you would if they were your own. The first question that is put to a man on entering the next world is whether or not he was faithful in his business dealings. A man may work ever so hard to amass money dishonestly; he may, during his lifetime, provide his children with rich dowries and leave them a generous inheritance at his death; and yet, I say, woe shall it be to that wicked man who, because he tried to enrich his children with dishonest money, has forfeited his share in the world to come! In one fleeting moment he has lost eternity!

GLUECKEL OF HAMELIN,
Memoirs

First Things First

Let a man first do good deeds, and then ask God for [knowledge of] Torah: let a man first act as righteous and upright men act, and then let him ask God for wisdom: let a man first grasp the way of humility, and then ask God for understanding.

TANNA DEBE ELIYAHU

What Is Compassion?

Compassion is the pain a father feels when his son hurts his hand playing ball; the pang a mother knows when her daughter is not invited to the party she had her heart set on; the concern a lover has for the least concern of his beloved; the anguish which touches a man when his friend bares his troubles to him; the tears a child sheds for the limp foot of his dog or the broken arm of her doll; the sigh a judge heaves when he must pronounce strong sentence; the care a doctor exerts toward a patient in pain; the dull tug at the heart of a soldier when he sees the destruction he has wrought; the help a businessman extends towards a failing competitor; the forgiveness a man grants toward one who has hurt him; the pleading of Moses when the people were to be destroyed because of their golden idol; the weeping of Rachel for the exiles who trudged by her grave on the bloody way to Babylon. It is the eternal mercy of the Lord toward the folly and misery of man.

SAMUEL H. DRESNER
Prayer, Humility and Compassion

The Golden Flute

In the Temple at Jerusalem there was a flute fashioned out of reeds, an old flute, having come down from the days of Moses. The sound of the flute was sweet and beautiful, ravishing the souls of the worshippers. But one day the priests at the sanctuary decided to decorate the flute, and they covered it with gold. The flute was never the same again. Its sweet, clear, cool tones were now harsh, metallic and jarring. Gold had coarsened its melody.

ABBA HILLEL SILVER,
Religion In A Changing World

The Heart Of The Jew

"Thou shalt not take vengeance" (Leviticus 19 : 18) forbids repaying evil with evil. "If a man finds both a friend and an enemy in distress, he should first assist his enemy, in order to subdue his evil inclination," i.e., man's inborn passion for revenge (Talmud). Scripture inculcates this virtue both by precept and illustrious example. Joseph's conduct to his brethren, and David's to Saul, are among the noblest instances of forgiveness to be found in literature. Such examples are not confined to the Biblical period. Samuel ibn Nagrela was a Spanish-Jewish poet of the eleventh century, who was vizier to the king of Granada. He was one day cursed in the presence of the king, who commanded Samuel to punish the offender by cutting out his tongue. The Jewish vizier, however, treated his enemy kindly, whereupon the curses became blessings. When the king next noticed the offender, he was astonished that Samuel had not carried out his command. Samuel replied, "I have torn out his angry tongue, and given him instead a kind one." The Rabbis rightly declare, "Who is mighty ? He who makes his enemy his friend."

The Jew is not "a good hater." Shylock is "the Jew that Shakespeare drew." He is not the Jew of real life, even in the Middle Ages, stained as their story is with the hot tears — nay, the very heart's blood — of the martyred race. The medieval Jew did not take vengeance on his cruel foes. The Jews hunted out of Spain in 1492 were in turn cruelly expelled from Portugal. Some took refuge on the African coast. Eighty years later the descendants of the men who had thus inhumanly treated their Jewish fellowmen were defeated in Africa, whither they had been led by their king, Dom Sebastian. Those who were not slain were offered as slaves at Fez to the descendants of the Jewish exiles from Portugal. "The humbled

Portuguese nobles," the historian narrates, "were comforted when their purchasers proved to be Jews, for they knew that they had humane hearts."   MORRIS JOSEPH. quoted in *The Pentateuch and Haftorahs*

Whether a man really loves God can be determined by the love he bears toward his fellow men.
LEVI YITZHAK OF BERDITSHEV

The Unfilled Cup

One must extend the quality of mercy even to one's enemies. It may be necessary to punish those who wronged us, but one must not rejoice at their suffering. When the Egyptians were drowning in the sea the angels wanted to sing songs of exaltation, but the Holy One, blessed be He, disapproved, saying : " The work of my hands are drowning in the sea, and you are singing !"

The same thought is expressed in a quaint custom of the Passover Eve Seder ritual. When the Jew recites the story of the plagues suffered by the Egyptians, he pours out from his cup of wine a drop for each plague. For the Jew does not consider his " Cup of Salvation " complete when it comes through the suffering of any of God's children. Hence the more plagues the Egyptians suffered, the less full is the Jewish cup and the less complete his happiness.
DAVID ARONSON,
The Jewish Way of Life

Kindness To Animals

Peace, say the Rabbis, is one of the pillars of the world ; without it the social order could not exist. Therefore, let a man do his utmost to promote it. Thus it is that the greatest Sages made a point of being the first to salute passersby in the street. Peace is the burden of the prayer with which every service in the synagogue concludes : " May He who maketh peace in His high heavens grant peace unto us ! "

And so a twofold duty is indi- cated. We are not only to be peace- ful ourselves, but to help others to be peaceful also. . . . Peace is not only a personal, but a national ideal. There are, doubtless, occasions when war is defensible as a lesser evil than a disastrous and dishonorable peace. There are worse things, it is true, than war ; but the worst of them is the belief that war is indispensable. Such a belief is fatal to the ultimate establishment of universal peace. The Jew who is true to himself will labor with especial energy in the cause of peace. The war-loving Jew is a contradiction in terms. Only the peace-loving Jew is a true follower of his Prophets, who set universal brotherhood in the forefront of their pictures of coming happiness for mankind, predicting the advent of a Golden Age when nations should not lift up sword against nation, nor learn war any more.

MORRIS JOSEPH,
Judaism as Creed and Life

Bringers Of Comfort And Harmony

A Talmudic legend tells how a Rabbi once meets Elijah in the crowded market - place. "Master," he asks, "who among this throng are most sure of eternal life?" The Prophet, in reply, points out two men of homely appearance. The Rabbi accosts them. "What," he asks, "are your special merits?" "We have none," they answer, "unless it be that when people are in trouble we comfort them, and when they quarrel we make them friends again."

MORRIS JOSEPH,
Judaism as Creed and Life

God grant that you neither shame nor be shamed.

Talmud, Moed Katan 9b

The Aim Of Jewish Ethics

Jewish ethics aims to create social-mindedness in its followers. That is why the Jew plays such an important role in the social development of human society. Not salvation for yourself alone but for the world, for human society — that is the goal of Judaism. But though social in its philosophy, it is healthy and practical-minded nevertheless. It has never asked complete self-effacement or the total neglect of oneself in the interest of others. Charity has its limitations. To give away all of one's possessions and thus to pauperize oneself is prohibited. Hillel strikes the true ideal when he says: "If I am not for myself, who will be, but if I am only for myself, what am I?"

Jewish ethics, too, we are proud to claim, is universal in its teaching and in its appeal. It is not limited in its application to members of one group, or one color, or one faith. "Justice, justice shalt thou pursue." "Why," ask the Rabbis, "is the word justice written twice? To teach us that we must practice justice at all times, whether it be for our profit or for our loss, and toward all men — toward Jews and non-Jews alike!" Jewish ethics makes no distinction between Jew and non - Jew. "The Holy One Blessed be He rejects no human being. The portals are open, and who desires may come and enter. For thus it is written : ' Open ye the gates that the righteous nation that keepeth faithfulness may enter in.' Note that the Prophet does not say that the priest, or the Levite or an Israelite may enter, but that the righteous nation may enter in, for the portals of heaven are open to the righteous of any nation, to the worthy of all humankind." A certain heathen once asked Rabbi Judah, the Patriarch : " Will I have a share in the world to come ? " To which the latter answered : " Yes." " But is it not written," the heathen demanded, " And there shall not be any remaining of the house of Esau ?" " Yes," came the quick reply of Rabbi Judah, " but that applies only to those who commit Esau's acts of violence ! "

Jewish ethical ideals are so universal in scope that they even include the dumb animals, the beasts of the field. Judaism coined a phrase, to which there is no adequate translation — Za'ar Ba'ale Hayyim, " Pity toward a living creature " ; it made of a whole people a " Society for the Prevention of Cruelty to Animals." The Jew was commanded to feed his household animals before he sat down to his own meal. Even the trees of the field were objects of life in Jewish teaching, and Jewish ethics did not neglect man's duty toward them. Cutting down fruit-bearing and useful trees is a transgression forbidden by Jewish law.

Even in time of war, when wood is vital for the building of defenses, fruit trees about besieged cities may not be destroyed or injured. All life comes under the beneficent wings of Jewish ethical teaching.

And here I come to the concluding fact that must be noted. Jewish ethics was not just taught as abstract moral sayings either in the Bible or Talmud. These ethical principles underlie the whole of Jewish life ; they penetrate all of Jewish teaching and every branch of Jewish study. Even the strictly juristic sections of our Halakah exemplify these ideals in various and manifold ways. The Halakah, too, to quote the words of Professor Ginzberg, " is a true mirror reflecting the work of the Jew in shaping his character." " There was no need " — to quote him further — " to give moral instructions directly. . . . The pupil was not called upon to compose his face solemnly while moral exhortations were poured down upon his devoted head. In the regular course of study the Talmud offered him ethical observations of fundamental importance, while ostensibly propounding an intricate judicial question which requires fine dialectic reasoning." Ethics permeated his law, his philosophy, his theology, aye, even his folk-lore ; everything in his life was saturated with ethical ideals and ethical principles. . . .

With the Psalmist, the Jew could ever proclaim : " I shall walk before the Lord in the lands of the living."

Not only in the privacy of the home, not only in the sacred precincts of the Synagogue, but "in the lands of the living," which the Rabbis in the Talmud translate : "this refers to the Market-Places." Yea, everywhere and at all times and with all men, he walked before the Lord, in the ways of the Lord, which Jewish ethics interpreted to mean, in the ways of mercy and truth !

ISRAEL H. LEVINTHAL
Judaism

In The Stranger Man Discovered The Idea Of Humanity

A stranger *shalt thou not wrong* (Exodus 22). The Rabbis explain this term to mean that nothing must be done to injure or annoy him, or even by word to wound his feelings. The fact that a man is a stranger should in no way justify treatment other than that enjoyed by brethren in race. "This law of shielding the alien from all wrong is of vital significance in the history of religion. With it, alone, true Religion begins. The alien was to be protected, not because he was a member of one's family, clan, religious community, or people ; but because he was a human being. In the alien, therefore, man discovered the idea of humanity " (Hermann Cohen).

JOSEPH H. HERTZ,
The Pentateuch and Haftorahs

God Is With The Persecuted

Seest thou a wicked man persecuting a wicked, know thou that God is with the persecuted. If a righteous man persecute a righteous, God is with the persecuted. And even when the righteous persecute the wicked, by the very fact of their persecution, God is still with the persecuted.

Midrash, Koheleth Rab 3 : 1

Duties To Animals

In Judaism man owes certain duties not only to God and his fellow-men, but also to his fellow-animals. Kindness to animals is with the Jews no mere sentimentality. Like charity it is part and parcel of justice, of righteousness, of piety. They advocate it as a religious injunction to be obeyed not for the sake of economic or material benefit. They feel that sympathy with the weak and dependent of any species reflects back, and promotes, as is pointed out in a Talmudic parable, peace and happiness among human species. Above all they believe that the best service one could render Him is in being kind to His handiwork, that

> He prayeth best who loveth best
> All things, both great and small ;
> For the dear God who loveth us
> He made and loveth all.

JACOB S. RAISIN

Vision looks inward and becomes duty. Vision looks outward and becomes aspiration. Vision looks upward and becomes faith.

STEPHEN S. WISE,
Sermons and Addresses

The Good Life

The perils to which man is exposed in the nuclear age differ from those of earlier times in their depth and in their extent. It is a truism to say that the world is becoming a neighborhood and that unless we can learn to be good neighbors we shall end in mutual destruction. It is in just such an age that the message of Bible and Talmud is so urgent and significant. This message requires each of us to transform himself into a master of the art of life so that each of us can become the means of helping the world and fulfilling the will of God.

The task which Conservative Judaism sets before itself in this age is the raising of the level of conduct by its members so that they may achieve the standards set by the great teachers of Judaism of old. Ethical life is too vital a matter to be left to specialists. This Movement will not have fulfilled itself until the man of affairs, no less than the specialized student of the sacred texts, sees the fulfillment of his life in the achievement of saintliness.

In Judaism, the life process is one of continuous education for character and, therefore, requires not only practice of good deeds but constant preparation through study for situations which cannot be anticipated. The discovery of what is right under complicated conditions is not easy and does not come from intuition. It comes from a discernment born out of continuous concern with precedents established generation after generation by dedicated spirits.

We are fortunate in having in the literature bequeathed us by our fathers a vast storehouse of religious and ethical experience. The more we study the cases with which our ancestors dealt the better we will be able to handle the complications of our time, as individuals and as a group. The code of conduct now adopted at this convention [United Synagogue's Convention, 1955] is an important step in raising the level of conduct of our members. But an even greater step will be taken when each of us, following in the footsteps of our great teachers, sets aside time each day for the contemplation of man's moral dilemmas and tries to prepare himself to achieve greatness in the art which alone is common to all people — the art of the good life.

Nothing we can do for our fellow-men outranks in importance the transformation of ourselves into " a kingdom of priests." The world today needs, as Solomon Schechter said in his day, a sprinkling of saints, whose very example will help the rest of mankind in its struggle to attain spiritual life.

LOUIS FINKELSTEIN,
United Synagogue Review

Aaron : The Peace-Maker

In later Jewish thought, Aaron is the ideal peace-maker ; and Hillel bids every man to be a " disciple of Aaron, loving peace and pursuing peace, loving his fellow men and bringing them near to the Torah." According to rabbinic legend, he would go from house to house, and whenever he found one who did not know how to recite the *Shema*, he taught him to recite it. He did not, however, restrict his activities to " establishing peace between God and man," but strove to establish peace between man and his fellow. If he discovered that two men had fallen out, he hastened first to the one, then to the other, saying to each : " If thou didst but know how he with whom thou hast quarreled regrets his action ! " Aaron would thus speak to each separately, until both the former enemies would mutually forgive each other, and as soon as they were again face to face greet each other as friends. This kindness of his led many a sinner to reform, who at the moment when he was about to commit a sin thought to himself, " How shall I be able to lift up my eyes to Aaron's face, I, to whom Aaron was so kind ! "

JOSEPH H. HERTZ,
The Pentateuch and Haftorahs

Whoever has a generous eye, a humble mind, and a modest spirit is a disciple of Abraham our father.
Ethics of The Fathers 5 : 19

Torah And Character

Judaism is distinctive for its theory of education. We have a Hebrew word for knowledge which is virtually untranslatable because its deepest and fullest meaning has not yet been grasped by other peoples and tongues. That word is Torah. By Torah, Jewish tradition did not mean essentially the dis-interested acquisition of factual information or the cultivation of skills of the body and mind, or even the scholarly exploration of the multi-roomed mansion of worldly wisdom. All these were deemed desirable and necessary only insofar as they expanded the soul, stimulated the moral sensitivity of man, and were channeled in the direction of the promotion of human welfare. Thus Jeremiah declares, " Let not the wise man glory in his wisdom, neither let the mighty man glory in his might, let not the rich man glory in his riches; but let him that glorieth glory in this, that he understandeth and knoweth Me, that I am the Lord who exercises mercy, justice and righteousness on the earth ; for in these things I delight, saith the Lord."

Universal literacy is not moral intelligence. The three R's do not spell righteousness. Popular education in our day teaches young people how to make a living, but it largely ignores the necessity of teaching them how to live, and what to live for. Judaism can, in our time, make a significant contribution through its unrivaled tradition of the pre-eminence of Torah, the character-building, soul-cultivating emphasis in learning, calling on man to develop ethical alertness, to master himself rather than to rule over others.

Our religion goes beyond the formulation of universal postulates and idealistic ends. It translates the poetry of moral aspiration into the prose of every day life. It is a religion of behavior as well as of beliefs. It brings down the holy tablets from the heights of Sinai to the valley of decision and the plain of realization. It translates the Torah into life.

MAX ARZT,
Sabbath and Festival Prayer Book

Religion And Conduct

Religion is not so much knowledge of God as godly living. What distinguishes a religion from a system of science or philosophy is its concern with man's behavior. Theories of reality are vital to it only to the degree to which they help transform the lives of men and to affect their conduct. . . .

Unless religion affects human life and conduct, it is of small worth.

SAMUEL S. COHON,
Judaism : A Way of Life

The Glory In Forbearance

Fear the Lord the God of thy Fathers and serve Him in love, for fear only restrains a man from sin, while love stimulates him to good. Accustom thyself to habitual goodness, for a man's character is what habit makes it.

If thou find in the Torah or the Prophets or the Sages a hard saying which thou canst not grasp, stand fast by thy faith and attribute the fault to thine own intelligence. Place it in a corner of your heart for future consideration, but despise not thy Religion because thou art unable to understand one difficult matter.

Love truth and uprightness — the ornaments of the soul — and cleave unto them ; prosperity so obtained is built on a sure rock. Keep firmly to thy word ; let not a legal contract or witnesses be more binding than thine verbal promise, whether in public or in private. Disdain reservations and subterfuges, evasions and sharp practices. Woe to him who builds his house upon them. Abhor inactivity and indolence — the causes of bodily destruction, of penury, of self-contempt — the ladders of Satan and his satellites.

Defile not your souls by quarrelsomeness and petulance. I have seen the white become black, the low brought still lower, families driven into exile, princes deposed from their high estate, great cities laid in ruins, assemblies dispersed, the pious humiliated, the honorable held lightly and despised — all on account of quarrelsomeness. Glory in forbearance, for in that is true strength and victory.

MOSES MAIMONIDES

If I am not for myself, who is for me ? And if I am (only) for myself, what am I ?

Ethics of the Fathers 2 : 4

Resistance To Evil

If the means of thy support in life be measured out scantily to thee, remember that thou hast to be thankful and grateful even for the mere privilege to breathe, and that thou must look upon that suffering as a test of thy piety and a preparation for better things. But if worldly wealth be lent to thee, exalt not thyself above thy brother ; for both of you came naked into the world, and both of you will surely have to sleep at last together in the dust.

Bear well thy heart against the assaults of envy, which kills even sooner than death itself ; and know no envy at all, save such envy of the merits of virtuous men as shall lead thee to emulate the beauty of their lives. Surrender not thyself a slave to hate, that ruin of all the heart's good resolves, that destroyer of the very savor of food, of our sleep, of all reverence in our souls.

Keep peace both within the city and without, for it goes well with all those who are counselors of peace. Be wholly sincere ; mislead no one by prevarications or words smoother than intention, as little as by direct falsehood. For God the Eternal is a God of Truth.

If thou hadst lived in the dread days of martyrdom, and the peoples had fallen on thee to force thee to apostasize from thy faith, thou wouldst surely, as did so many, have given thy life in its defense. Well then, fight now the fight laid on thee in the better days, the fight with evil desire; fight and conquer, and seek for allies in this warfare of your soul, seek them in the fear of God and the study of the Torah. Forget not that God recompenses according to the measure wherewith we withstand the evil in our heart. Be a man in thy youth; but if thou wert then defeated in the struggle, return, return at last to God, however old thou mayest be.

ELAZAR OF WORMS,
Sefer Rokeah

He who sustains God's creatures is as though he had created them.

Tanhuma

If you want to praise, praise God; if you want to blame, blame yourself.

BAHYA IBN PAKUDA,
Hobot Halebabot

A Father's Legacy

My son, give God all honor and the gratitude which is His due. Thou hast need of Him, but He needs thee not. Put no trust in thy mere physical well-being here below. Many a one has lain down to sleep at nightfall, but at morn has not risen again. See that thou guard well thy soul's holiness; let the thought of thy heart be saintly, and profane not thy soul with words of impurity.

Visit the sick and suffering man, and let thy countenance be cheerful when he sees it, but not so that thou oppress the helpless one with gaiety. Comfort those that are in grief; let piety where thou seest it affect thee even to tears. . . .

Respect the poor man by gifts whose hand he knows not of; be not deaf to his beseechings, deal not hard words out to him. From a wicked neighbor, see that thou keep aloof, and spend not much of thy time among the people who speak ill of their brother-man; be not as the fly that is always seeking sick and wounded places; and tell not of the faults and failings of those about thee.

Take no one to wife unworthy to be thy life's partner, and keep thy sons close to the study of Divine things. Dare not to rejoice when thine enemy comes to the ground; but give him food when he hungers. Be on thy guard lest thou give pain to the widow and the orphan; and beware lest thou ever set thyself up to be both witness and judge against another.

Never enter thy house with abrupt and startling step, and bear not thyself so that those who dwell under thy roof shall dread thy presence. Purge thy soul of angry passion, that inheritance of fools ; love wise men, and strive to know more and more of the works and the ways of the Creator.

ELIEZER BEN ISAAC,
Orhot Hayyim

How can we tell when a sin we have committed has been pardoned ? By the fact that we no longer commit that sin.

RABBI BUNAM

The Friends Of God

Whosoever does not persecute them that persecute him, whosoever takes an offense in silence, he who does good not because of reward but out of love, he who is cheerful under his sufferings — such are the friends of God.

Talmud, Shabbat 88b

Self-complacency is the companion of ignorance.   SOLOMON SCHECHTER,
Seminary Addresses

Be open-eyed to the great wonders of nature, familiar though they be. But men are more wont to be astonished at the sun's eclipse than at its unfailing rise.   HAYIM LUZZATTO,
Orhot Tzaddikim

Guideposts For Living

No crown carries such royalty with it as doth humility ; no monument gives such glory as an unsullied name ; no worldly gain can equal that which comes from observing God's laws. The highest sacrifice is a broken and contrite heart ; the highest wisdom is that which is found in the Torah ; the noblest of all ornaments is modesty ; and the most beautiful thing that man can do, is to forgive a wrong.

Cherish a good heart when thou findest it in any one ; hate, for thou mayest hate it, the haughtiness of the overbearing man, and keep the boaster at a distance. There is no skill or cleverness to be compared

to that which avoids temptation ; there is no force, no strength, that can equal piety.

Let thy dealings be of such sort that a blush need never cover thy cheek ; be sternly dumb to the voice of passion ; commit no sin, saying to thyself that thou wilt repent and make atonement at a later time. Follow not the desire of the eyes, banish carefully all guile from thy soul, all unseemly self - assertion from thy bearing and thy temper.

Speak never mere empty words ; enter into strife with no man ; place no reliance on men of mocking lips ; wrangle not with evil men ; cherish no too fixed good opinion of thyself, but lend thine ear to remonstrance and reproof. Be not weakly pleased at demonstrations of honor ; strive not anxiously for distinction ; be never enviously jealous of others, or too eager for money.

Honor thy parents ; make peace whenever thou canst among people, lead them gently into the good path ; place thy trust in, give thy company to, those who fear God.

ELAZAR OF WORMS,
Sefer Rokeah

A man should so live that at the close of every day he can repeat : " I have not wasted my day."

ZOHAR

An Ethical Testament

Be not ready to quarrel ; avoid oaths and passionate adjurations, excess of laughter and outbursts of wrath ; they disturb and confound the reason of man. Avoid dealings wherein there is a lie ; and make not gold the foremost longing of thy life ; for that is the first step to idolatry. Rather give money than words ; and as to ill words, see that thou place them in the scale of understanding before they leave thy lips.

What has been uttered in thy presence, even though not told as secret, let it not pass from thee to others. And if one tell thee a tale, say not to him that thou hast heard it all before. Do not fix thine eyes too much on one who is far above thee in wealth, but on those who are behind thee in worldly fortune.

Put no one to open shame ; misuse not thy power against any one ; who can tell whether thou wilt not some day be powerless thyself ?

Do not struggle vaingloriously for the small triumph of showing thyself in the right and a wise man in the wrong ; thou art not one whit the wiser therefor. Be not angry or unkind to anyone for trifles, lest thou make thyself enemies unnecessarily.

Do not refuse things out of mere obstinancy. Avoid, as much as may be, bad men, men of persistent angry feelings, fools ; thou canst get nothing from their company but shame. Be the first to extend courteous greeting to every one, whatever be his faith ; provoke not to wrath one of another belief than thine.

ASHER BEN YEHIEL,
Hanhaga

Rabbi Hanina, son of Dosa, said: He in whom the spirit of his fellow-men takes delight, in him the Spirit of the All-present takes delight ; and he in whom the spirit of his fellowmen does not take delight, in him the Spirit of the All-present does not take delight.

Ethics of the Fathers 3 : 13

Bear Thyself In This World Like A Guest

Sooner be a servant among the noble-minded than a leader among the vulgar; for some of the honor of the former will remain with thee, while thou must share the contempt of thy unworthy followers. If thou too earnestly seek pre-eminence and power, be sure that they will flee from thee; but if thou bearest thyself in this world like a guest receiving its hospitality, men will try to find for thee a place of honor.

If, because of beauty or riches that are thine, thou raisest thy head above neighbor or brother, thou feedest hateful envy, and the beggar whom thou despisest may yet triumph over thee. Better enough in freedom, than plenty at the table of another.

Love thy children with an impartial love; the hope oft errs that you place on the more promising, and all the joy may come from him that thou hast kept in the background.

BERAHYAH HA-NAKDAN,
Mishlay Shualim

What God Wants

Rabbi Akiba, when asked by a Roman general, " Why does your God who loves the needy not provide for their support Himself ? " answered: " God, the Father of both rich and poor, wants the one to help the other so as to make the world a household of love."

Talmud, Baba Batra 10a

The Day Is Short

Rabbi Tarphon said: The day is short, and the work is great, but the laborers are idle, though the reward be great, and the Master of the work is urgent. It is not incumbent upon thee to complete the work; but neither art thou free to desist from it. . . . Faithful is Thine Employer to pay the reward of thy labor.

Ethics of the Fathers 2 : 20, 21

The Hero And The Saint

The hero is one who kindles a great light in the world, who sets up blazing torches in the dark streets of life for men to see by. The saint is the man who walks through the dark paths of the world, himself a " light."

FELIX ADLER,
Creed and Deed

The Good Life

The Jewish way in the world has consistently and unswervingly pursued the idea and technique of the good life. Not beauty but goodness is the central problem and theme of Judaism. Not the amassing of physical power, but the generation of spiritual energy is the ideal of which the builders of our civilization have dreamed. Not man in his animal strength and expression, but man as the highest ethical purpose has been their perennial theme. Not self-indulgence, but self control and abnegation in the service of a higher goal inspired the greatest works of Jewish literature.

TRUDE WEISS-ROSMARIN,
Jewish Survival

Every judge who renders righteous judgment, Scripture deems him a co-partner of the Holy One, blessed be He, in the work of Creation.

Mekilta to Exodus 18 : 13

The Wisdom Of Creation

If we would only think we could easily find God's lofty purpose in all His handiwork. For example, since God is omnipotent He could have enabled man to see through one eye. Why did He give us two ?

The answer is: one eye is for observing our neighbor's virtues, and the other for detecting our own failings.

MEIR PREMISHLANER

Where Is Holiness ?

Many are the ways of holiness ; varied are its paths.

There is holiness in a lab when a vaccine is discovered to destroy diseases.

There is holiness when nations meet to beat swords into plowshares.

There is holiness when we strive for purity and harmony in family life.

There is holiness when men of different backgrounds work together for a common future.

There is holiness when men seek justice and struggle for righteousness.

There is holiness when men lift up the fallen and free the captives.

There is holiness when men bring consolation to the sorrowing and comfort to the silent sufferers.

There is holiness when men create lasting poetry or song or philosophy.

There is holiness when men gather to seek Thee, oh God, through prayer.

Holy, holy, holy is the Lord of hosts.

National Federation of Temple Youth

How To Measure A Deed

If you have done your fellow a little wrong, let it be in your eyes great; if you have done him much good, let it be in your eyes little; if he has done you a little good, let it be in your eyes great; if he has done you a great wrong, let it be in your eyes little.

Aboth of R. Nathan 41a

One who thinks he can live without others is mistaken. One who thinks others cannot live without him is more mistaken.   Hasidic saying

The Serpent's Reply

Resh Lakish said, In the future day of judgment, all animals will be assembled and will ask the serpent why he poisons his prey. They will say, "The lion destroys, so that he may eat. The wolf tears his prey for food. What do you gain, through your poison?" And the serpent will reply, "Ask the slanderer, for he too destroys without benefit to himself."

Talmud, Taanit 8a

Degrees Of Charity

Moses Maimonides outlines eight degrees of charity : the highest form is to strengthen the hands of the poor by giving him a gift or a loan, or to join him in partnership, or to find him work, that he may not become a public charge. In brief, to help him be independent. It is with reference to this degree of charity that Scripture says, "Thou shalt uphold him" (Leviticus 25 : 35).

The next degree in charity is to give in such a way that the giver should not know the individual to whom he gives; nor should the receiver know from whom he receives. The Community Fund is substantially on this level.

A somewhat lower form is a situation where the giver knows to whom he gives but the receiver knows not from whom he receives. Many of our sages acted thus when they secretly threw money into the doors of the poor.

A still lower form is an arrangement whereby the poor knows from whom he takes, but the giver knows not to whom he gives.

A still lower form is where one gives directly, but before being asked by the poor man.

Next, is to give directly after being asked, but giving a sufficient sum.

Next to this is giving not enough, but cheerfully.

The lowest form of charity is to give grudgingly.

DAVID ARONSON,
The Jewish Way of Life

The Strings Of Pearls

The thread on which the different good qualities of human beings are strung as pearls, is the fear of God. When the fastenings of this fear are unloosed, the pearls roll in all directions, and are lost one by one. Even a single grave moral fault may be the ruin of all other advantages ; as when, for example, one is always setting off his own excellence by bringing into prominence his neighbor's failings. Never put in words anything which can call up a blush on thine own cheek or make another's grow pale.

MOSES HAYIM LUZZATTO,
The Way of The Righteous

The road to pleasure is downhill and very easy, so that one does not walk but is dragged along ; the way to self-control is uphill, toilsome no doubt, but exceedingly profitable.

PHILO

A Declaration For Each Day

It is because man is half angel, half brute, that his inner life witnesses such bitter war between such unlike natures. The brute in him clamors for sensual joy and things in which there is only vanity ; but the angel resists and strives to make him know that meat, drink, sleep are but means whereby the body may be made efficient for the study of the truths, and the doing of the will, of God. Not until the very hour of death can it be certain or known to what measure the victory has been won. He who is but a novice in the fear of God will do well to say audibly each day, as he rises : " This day I will be a faithful servant of the Almighty. I will be on my guard against wrath, falsehood, hatred, and quarrelsomeness, and will forgive those who wound me." For whoso forgives is forgiven in his turn ; hardheartedness and a temper that will not make up quarrels are a heavy burden of sin, and unworthy of an Israelite.

MOSES OF COUCY,
Sefer Mitzvot Hagadol

He who gives a penny to a poor man receives six blessings: he who shows his sympathy with the poor man receives eleven blessings.

The Bratzlaver Rabbi

The Pious Man

What is piety ? Is it abandonment of the world ?
Is it scrupulous performance of rites, or fanatical zeal ?

Let us observe the pious man and probe into his soul.
We shall discover in it that which transcends man,

That which surmounts the visible and available,

Steadily preventing him from immersing himself in sensation or ambition,

From yielding to passion or slaving for a career.

For him life takes place amid horizons beyond the span of years.

He senses the significant in small things; he is alive to the sublime in common acts and simple thoughts.

He feels the hidden warmth of good beneath the thick crust of evil.

In the rush of the passing, he notes the stillness of the eternal.

He complies with destiny; he is at peace with life.

Every experience opens to him the door into a temple of light, though the vestibule be dark and dismal.

His responsibility to God is the scaffold on which he stands, as daily he builds his life.

He serves family, friend, community and nation.

These never become for him blind alleys; they ever remain thoroughfares to God.

With sacrifice and single-mindedness, he continues on the way.

His conscience is attuned to listen to the voice of God;

His concern is for the will of God;

He turns his back on human vanity.

He disdains the shabbiness of human selfishness, and deplores the meagerness of human service.

He abhors shining garments, a smiling countenance or miracles of art, when they cover vice or blasphemy.

He loathes great temples and monuments of worldly glory, when built by sweat and tears of suffering slaves.

The pious man lays no claim to reward.

Engrossed in the beauty of what he worships, he shuns self-display.

The wise man, master of himself, oft deems himself author of his mastery;

Not so the pious, who, no less master of himself, administers his life in God's name.

The wise man seeks to penetrate into the soul of the sacred:

The pious man ever strives to be penetrated by it.

Faith engages a man's mind;
Piety, his entire life.

Faith precedes piety; piety is faith's achievement.

Faith desires to meet God; piety to abide by Him.

Faith strives to know His will; piety to do it.

Faith yearns to hear His voice; piety, to respond to it.

The pious man is never alone, for God is within reach of his heart.

In affliction, though desolate for a moment, he need but turn his eyes,

To discover his grief outflanked by God's compassion.

Having achieved understanding, he believes;

Having acquired, he gives away;

Having lived, he knows how to die. He craves not vainly for the endless rotation of his own life's wheel ; He is content to merge his being into that of the God he loves.

ABRAHAM J. HESCHEL,
Reconstructionist Prayer Book

A life without guiding principles and thoughts, is a life not worth living.

SOLOMON SCHECTER

Shaming another in public is like shedding blood.

Talmud, BaBa Metzia 58b

Jewish Ethics Embraces All Men

The ethical ideas of Judaism are *universal*. They are intended to appeal to all human beings. And in their practical application they are to embrace all human beings. The Jewish consciousness produced them. But in their scope and in their practical realization they are not limited to Jews. Huxley said the best definition ever given of religion was that provided by the Prophet Micah, in the famous passage, " It hath been told thee, O man, what is good, and what the Lord doth require of thee : only to do justly, and to love mercy, and to walk humbly with thy God." This passage is a climax to a controversy which the Prophet describes as dramatically taking place between God and Israel. In the course of it Israel asks, " Wherewith shall I come before the Lord ? " And we should expect as an answer, " It hath been told thee, O Israel, what is good." It is very significant that the Prophet does not say this. He uses the " Adam," " man." He thus indicates clearly that what Israel stood for in history is not limited to the Jew, but is intended for all men.

Isaiah tells us that the justice and righteousness which were to be observed are intended for all men. " Happy is the *man* that doeth this, and the son of man that holdeth fast by it." It is interesting to observe that some of the noblest characters in Scripture are not presented as Jewish in race. The type of perfect womanhood, realizing the ideal of love and self-sacrificing loyalty, is given in Ruth, a Moabite and not an Israelite woman. The hero of the great drama of Job, the perfectly righteous man who is wrestling with destiny, and out of the depths of his matchless suffering argues with God, and with it all maintains his immovable faith in a Redeemer that liveth, is not presented as a Hebrew. Job thinks and talks like a Hebrew. The book is Jewish from beginning to end. But the hero is purposely made to represent man without any tribal or national limitation. The Rabbinical literature, including the Talmud, Midrashim, and later literature, fairly teems with statements emphasizing the universal character of the Jewish law and its aim to appeal to and to reach man. We are told that the Torah, or the Law, was given in the desert, in no-man's-land, so that he who would could come and accept it. It was not intended to be limited to any country or to any nation. If a non-Jew obeys the law he is equal to the High Priest. If a stranger accepts the law of his own free will, he stands higher in the eyes of God than the hosts of the children of Israel who surrounded Mount Sinai. This law is, in its essence, ethical. For the Rabbis developed the idea of the "commandments of Noah." This meant that there were certain commandments which were applicable for all sons of men, technically called "the sons of Noah." Noah was conceived as the ancestor of the human race after the flood. Humanity, in order to lead the right life and to earn salvation, need not become Jewish. All it has to do is to obey the fundamental laws of righteousness. This is in accordance with the conception of Judaism that man is not saved by creed, but by deed. Therefore, the ethics of Judaism is an ethics for all men, though all men need not observe the Jewish ceremonial law or accept the historic obligation imposed upon Israel to witness as a distinct religious community to God. The righteousness amongst the Gentiles is their sin-offering. That is to say, it is as valuable in the eyes of God as any particular ceremonial service of the Jew. It is not only as valuable, but it is quite sufficient. The law, we are told, is given not to Priest, not to Levite, not to Israelite, but to man.

SAMUEL SCHULMAN,
Jewish Ethics

Fear God by day, and you'll sleep soundly at night.

JOSEPH ZABARA,
Sefer Shaashuim

The Dignity Of Labor And The Laborer

The Talmud (*Rosh Hashana* 1 . 8) puts the usurer on the same level with the gambler, and declares both to be vicious men, unfit to bear testimony in a court of justice.

Ancient Judaism honored labor and handicraft. When the Holy One, says a passage in the Talmud (*Pes.* 118a), pronounced his sentence on fallen Adam, he burst into tears at the words, "Thorns also and thistles shall it bring forth to thee. . . ." But when God added, "In the sweat of thy face shalt thou eat bread," he was comforted. "Love labor," was a maxim of Hillel's teacher, Shemaya (Ab. 1.10). "Great is labor," says another (Ned. 49b; cf. Kamma 79b), "for she honors her master."

Domestic servants were treated as members of the family. Kindness and consideration for them is recommended both by precept and example. "Beware," it is said, "to eat fine bread and to feed thy servant upon black bread; to sleep on cushions while he lies on straw" (Kid. 20a). . . . Righteousness was already then understood . . . to consist, not in strict adherence to the law, but in following the law of kindness.   FRANZ DELITZSCH, *Jewish Artisan Life in the Time of Jesus*

To be a Jew is to be a friend of mankind, to be a proclaimer of liberty and peace.
                    LUDWIG LEWISOHN,
                                Israel

The Honor Of Your Fellow Man

When Rabbi Nehumya's disciples asked their master to what he ascribed his longevity, he replied: "I never sought honor by disgracing my fellow men and I never retired with a curse against any one." The effect of this conduct on physical vigor is not very insistently stressed. But that it is the road to the good life is emphasized by all Jewish teachers. Judaism categorically demands that we guard our fellow man's honor. In the same tenor, it is commanded that his property "be as dear to you as your own." This outlaws any improbity through which another person might suffer loss. Integrity and honesty in business are part of the commandment to love one's neighbor as oneself. According to the Rabbis, honesty in business is so important that in the world to come, the first question directed to the soul will be: "Have you dealt honestly and faithfully with your fellow men?"
                    TRUDE WEISS-ROSMARIN,
                                Jewish Survival

Whenever night falls, whenever day breaks, search well into your dealings, so will your whole life be one Day of Atonement.
                    MOSES OF EVREUX

Consideration For The Poor

Consideration for the poor distinguishes the Mosaic Law from all other ancient legislations, such as the Roman Law. The object of the latter seems to be primarily to safeguard the rights of the possessing classes. In the Torah, the poor man is a brother, and when in need he is to be relieved ungrudgingly not only with an open hand but with an open heart. In his noble self-defense, Job (XXXI, 17 : 20) protests :

Never have I eaten my morsel alone,
Without sharing it with the fatherless ;
Never saw I any perish for want of clothing

But I warmed him with fleece from my lambs,
And his loins gave me their blessing. The Rabbis continued this doctrine, and declared pity to be a distinguishing trait of the Jewish character. If a Jew — they held — shows himself lacking in consideration for a fellow man in distress or suffering, we may well doubt the purity of his Jewish descent. " There is no ethical qual-ity more characteristic of Rabbinic Judaism than Rachmonuth — pity. The beggar whose point of view is that you are to thank him for allowing him to give you the opportunity for showing Rachmonuth, is a characteristically Jewish figure " (Montefiore).

JOSEPH H. HERTZ,
The Pentateuch and Haftorahs

10

Duties for Our Day

We must ever be mindful that our behavior . . .
determines the name and fame, the fate and faith of
Israel.

DAVID ARONSON,
The Jewish Way of Life

The Nazi beasts considered as Jews those who had a
Jewish grandfather and grandmother. We consider as
Jews those who do something about assuring for our
people that our children and grandchildren remain
Jewish.

MEIR BAR ILAN

To be a Jew . . . is to be strong with the strength that
has outlived persecutions.

PHYLLIS BOTTOME,
The Mortal Storm

Which Minyan Will You Join?

We Jews have a more pressing responsibility for our lives and beliefs than perhaps any other religious community.

Don't shelter yourself in any course of action by the idea that " it is not my affair." It is your affair, but it is also mine and the community's. Nor can we neglect the world beyond. A fierce light beats upon the Jew. It is a grave responsi- bility this — to be a Jew ; and you cannot escape from it, even if you choose to ignore it. Ethically or religiously, we Jews can be and do nothing lightheartedly. Ten bad Jews may help to damn us ; ten good Jews may help to save us. Which minyan will you join ?

CLAUDE G. MONTEFIORE,
address, Cambridge, 1900

What Can I Do?

As a Jew let me be conscious of the honor of my religion, and so live that I will do nothing to besmirch it.

As a member of a congregation, let me be quick to discharge my responsibilities to it, even if sometimes this may involve sacrifices.

As one who regards the House of Worship as my spiritual center, let me devote to it that time necessary for congregational worship and communion with my Maker.

As a human parent, let me be sure that I show my child how best to attain the highest human ends, and to desist from unjust and inhuman practices.

As an American parent, let me be quick to impress upon my child, the greatness of our American heritage and its way of life, and the importance of being loyal to them.

As a Jewish parent let me not be negligent in helping my child to secure a religious training in the history, the essentials and the aspirations of my religion.

As a member of a group persecuted in other lands, let me impress upon my child through my good example, the necessity of aiding and assisting all men whether of my faith or not, who are suffering because of their ideals, their religion or their racial origins.

Exchange

When the individual values the community as his own life and strives after its happiness as though it were his individual well-being, he finds satisfaction and no longer feels so keenly the bitterness of his individual existence, because he sees the end for which he lives and suffers.

ACHAD HA'AM

Every Jew A Trustee

What is being achieved in Palestine can perhaps be achieved only there in the fullest degree; but the lesson applies to the Jews all over the world. We have our obligations, the same *noblesse oblige*. Our traditions are the same. They have been transmitted also to us. We have not applied them in the same degree as those of our people who have returned to our ancestral home. But the ages of sacrifice have left us with the sense of brotherhood. That brotherhood has given us the feeling of solidarity which makes each one of us ready and anxious to fulfill his obligations. And we know, from the lesson of history, that the traditions we cherish depend for their life upon the conduct of every single one of us.

It is not wealth, it is not station, it is not social standing and ambition, which makes us worthy of the Jewish name, of the Jewish heritage. To be worthy of them, we must live up to and with them. We must regard ourselves as custodians. Every young man here must feel that he is the trustee of what is best in Jewish history. We cannot go as far as the pioneers in Palestine, but we must make their example to radiate in our lives. We must sense our solidarity to such an extent that even an unconscious departure from our noble traditions will make us feel guilty of a breach of a most sacred trust.

Here then is the task before you. . . . It is to promote the ideals which the Jews have carried forward through thousands of years of persecution and by much sacrifice. We must learn to realize that our sacrifices have enhanced the quality of our achievements, and that the overcoming of obstacles is part of our attainments.

Men differ in ability, however great the average ability of the Jews is, but every single Jew can make his own contribution to the Jewish way of life. Every single one of us can do that for himself. Every one of us can declare : " What is mean is not for us." We bespeak what is best, what is noblest and finest in all civilization. This is our heritage. We have survived persecution because of the virtues and sacrifices of our ancestors. It is for us to follow in that path. It is the Jewish tradition, and the Jewish law, and the Jewish spirit which prepare us for the lessons of life.

Louis D. Brandeis
Brandeis on Zionism

A Prescription For Health ?

We Jews become once more conscious of our nationality, and regain the self-respect which is necessary to our national existence. We must learn once more to avow our ancestry and our history; we must once more take upon ourselves, as a nation, cultural tasks of a kind calculated to strengthen our feeling of solidarity. It is not sufficient for us to take part as individuals in the cultural work of mankind : we must also set our hands to some work which conserves the ends of our corporate national existence. In this way, and in this way only, can the Jewish people regain its health.

ALBERT EINSTEIN

Israel's Miniature Bible

"And ye shall not profane My holy name ; but I will be hallowed among the children of Israel " (Leviticus 22 : 2). This verse has been called "Israel's Bible in little" (*Jellinek*). It contains the solemn warning against the Profanation of the Divine Name (*Chillul Hashem*), and the positive injunction to every Israelite to hallow the Name of God (*Kiddush Hashem*) by his life and, if need be, by his death. Although spoken in reference to the priests as the appointed guardians of the Sanctuary, this Commandment, both in its positive and negative forms, was early applied to the whole of Israel.

"Ye shall not profane My holy name." Be ye exceedingly guarded in your actions, say the Rabbis, so that ye do nothing that tarnishes the honor of Judaism or of the Jew. Especially do they warn against any misdeed toward a non-Jew as an unpardonable sin, because it gives a false impression of the moral standard of Judaism. The Jew should remember that the glory of God is, as it were, entrusted to his care ; and that *every Israelite holds the honor* of his Faith and of his entire People in his hands. A single Jew's offense can bring shame on the whole House of Israel. This has been the fate of Israel in all the ages ; and nothing, it seems, will ever break the world of its habit of putting down the crimes, vices, or failings of a Jew, no matter how estranged from his people or his people's Faith he may be, to his Jewishness, and of fathering them upon the entire Jewish race. The Rabbis say : "Wild beasts visit and afflict the world because of the profanation of the Divine Name" (*Ethics of the Fathers*, v, 11). And, indeed, wherever Jews are guilty of conduct unworthy of their Faith, there the wild beast in man — blind prejudice and causeless hatred — is unchained against Israel. No student of Jewish history will question the truth of the judgment. The Rabbis, in a striking apologue, picture a boat at sea, full of men. One of them begins to bore a hole in the bottom of the boat and, on being remonstrated with, urges that he is only boring under his own seat. "Yes," say his comrades, "but when the sea rushes in we shall be drowned with you." So it is with Israel. Its weal or its woe is in the hands of every one of its children. "I will be hallowed." Not to commit *Chillul Hashem* is only a negative virtue. Far more is required of the Israelite. He is bidden so to live as to shed luster on the Divine Name and the Torah by his deeds and influence. Rabbi Simon ben Shetach one day commissioned his disciples to buy him a camel from an Arab. When they brought him the animal, they gleefully announced that they had found a precious stone on its collar. "Did the seller know of this gem?" asked the Master. On being answered in the negative, he called out angrily, "Do you think me a barbarian that I should take advantage of the letter of the law by which the gem is mine together with the camel? Return the gem to the Arab immediately." When the heathen received it back he exclaimed: "Blessed be the God of Simon ben Shatach! Blessed be the God of Israel!"

The highest form of hallowing God is martyrdom; and Jewish Law demands of every Israelite to surrender his life, rather than by public apostasy desecrate the Name of God (*Shelchan Aruch, Yore Deah*, CLVII). When during the war of annihilation which the Emperor Hadrian waged against Judaism, the readiness for martyrdom on the part of young and old began to imperil the existence of the Jewish nation, the Rabbis decreed that only with regard to three fundamental laws—idolatry, incest and murder—should death be preferred to transgression. . . . "The Jewish martyrs of olden days, who bore witness to their God at the stake, are described as having yielded up their lives for the "sanctification of the Divine Name." Such testimony is within the power, and constitutes the duty of the Jew, in these times also. If he is not called upon to die for the sanctification of the Name, he has at least to live for it. His life must give glory to God, vindicate his God-given religion" (M. Joseph).

JOSEPH H. HERTZ,
The Pentateuch and Haftorahs

Our quarrel is not with Jews who are different but with Jews who are indifferent.   STEPHEN S. WISE,
Rededication

Definite, Concrete Acts

The American Jew who has re-allied himself to his people and its history, who has identified himself with the uniqueness of that people's character and destiny . . . will begin, if he has not yet begun, to rebuild in pride and joy for himself and his children, the form of his life. He will set his feet once more upon the eternal road of Israel's tragic but luminous persistence in the world. For this purpose he will perform definite, concrete acts.

He will fasten a *mezuzah* on his door.

He will usher in the Sabbath, if only simply and haltingly, if only with lit candles and a *kiddush* in English.

He will cease eating the forbidden foods — swine's flesh and shellfish.

He will say the blessings over food and drink.

He will keep in his house within easiest reach Jewish books. . . . . These he will read and ponder as the permanent record and expression of his people and therefore of himself.

He will read a passage of the dawn-prayer in the morning and teach his children or repeat with them the exquisite last evening prayer when slumber falls upon the eyelids.

He will not separate himself from the congregation of Israel but be active in his synagogue.

He will find that these affirmative *acts* will give meaning to what has hitherto been meaningless. They will identify him with that eternal community which is his road to mankind ; they will reassure him of his having been created in the image of God ; they will lead him to those universal affirmations concerning God, freedom and immortality, which alone explain man and the universe, which alone keep man and his history from dust and defeat.

LUDWIG LEWISOHN,
The American Jew

What Kind Of A Witness Are You ?

Israel's "Heroic History," as Manasseh ben Israel called it, is in truth never-ending. Each Jew and each Jewess is making his or her mark, or his or her stain, upon the wonderful unfinished history of the Jews, the history which Herder called the greatest poem of all time." "Ye are My witnesses, saith the Lord." Loyal and steadfast witnesses is it, or self-seeking and suborned ones ? A witness of some sort every Jew born is bound to be. He must fulfil his mission, and through good report and through evil report, he must add his item of evidence to the record.

KATIE MAGNUS

The Object Of Education

The object of education is not merely to enable our children to gain their daily bread and to acquire pleasant means of recreation, but that they should know God and serve Him with earnestness and devotion. Are you thus training your children ? Is it your care that they be educated as Jews and Jewesses ?

HERMANN ADLER

The Obligation To Understand First

We, as Jews, feel free to reject the totality of the Jewish tradition or any single part of it. We may if we are so minded withdraw from participation in Jewish life, individual and collective. These are privileges which have come to us as persons born in our age.

But what most modern Jews fail to perceive is that the right to reject Judaism in whole or in part carries with it a prior obligation — the obligation first to understand. A Jew has the right to reject Jewish religious attitudes but not until first he has come to comprehend their logical validity and psychological values. He has the right, if he sees fit, to abandon traditional observances, but not until he has first made an effort to understand their place in the Jewish scheme of things. He is free to embark upon a deliberate policy of assimilation. But he owes it to himself, to the Jewish group and to mankind, first to evaluate the possible implications of his program and the grounds on which it is rejected by protagonists of Jewish survival. . . .

The obligation resting upon the Jew to understand before he rejects is real enough. No Jew who has any respect for his own intellect, no Jew who wishes to live as rich a life as he can, no Jew with any sense of realism or with any feeling of responsibility to the past of mankind and to its future, can avoid that responsibility.

It is possible, of course, that a Jew may come to understand and still reject. With such an individual, Judaism can have no quarrel. It must say to him, Go thy way in peace ; we shall reason with each other again tomorrow. Judaism has no complaint against honest, intelligent, and informed rejection of itself. But Judaism does have a quarrel with the man who accepts no responsibility, who rejects Judaism without a proper understanding of it. It is in the last analysis not freedom of thought which endangers Jewish values, but the freedom which some people arrogate to themselves not to think at all.

From many points of view it is much easier to be a Jew today than it was four or five hundred years ago. For all the persecution of our time the Jew, even in the lands of darkest repression, enjoys now a measure of liberty and security such as the medieval Jew scarcely dared envisage. But from another point of view, ours is the heavier burden. In one respect at least our ancestors were more fortunate than we are. They accepted what was taught to them and their problem was at an end. Their minds were so conditioned that it never occurred to them to claim the right to accept or to reject faith in God, standards of morality, patterns of observance, and their identification with the

Jewish group. The times have thrown us intellectually upon our own resources. We are driven, often against our will, to subject our Jewish heritage to bold inquiry. We are the children of the modern world, free to believe or disbelieve, to accept or reject as our reason determines — a glorious freedom. But we are also the heirs of an obligation which, difficult though it may be, is equally glorious — the obligation of understanding before judging. Of that responsibility let the Jews or our day be reminded, for their own sake, for the sake of the Jewish group and its future, and for the sake of mankind to whose spiritual resources Israel may have further contributions to make.

MILTON STEINBERG,
A Believing Jew

Unless it is a present which forms a link between two eternities, representing an answer of Amen to the past and an Opening Prayer to the future, it will be a very petty present indeed.

SOLOMON SCHECHTER
Seminary Addresses

The Search To Which We Are Committed

The Bible nowhere calls upon men to go out in search of peace of mind. It does call upon men to go out in search of God and the things of God. It challenges men to hunger and thirst after righteousness, to relieve the oppressed, to proclaim liberty to the captives, and to establish peace in the world. These objectives must be elaborately sought. As often as not, such enterprises are attended by persecution and suffering. Judaism as a prophetic religion could not offer its faithful the compensation of peace of mind, except insofar as the confidence of faith lessens the tensions of doubt and despair ; but it did offer them other and more precious compensations — the nearness of God, an uplifting interest in life, a nourishing pride and dignity and, on occasion, the ineffable ecstasy that derives from moments of spiritual daring and adventure. There is a lyrical vibrancy to such moments when man drinks of the wine of life and partakes of the very manna of heaven.

Personal sacrifices are often involved in the pursuit of the good life. Sometimes even martyrdom is called for. The moral commitments of the faithful are never of a limited liability. The Jewish people gave the first religious martyrs known to mankind, and through many dark and weary centuries of exile and persecution its noblest sons and daughters never denied God the supreme tribute of martyrdom. True love of God is to serve Him " with all your heart, with all your soul and with all your might " (Deuteronomy 6 : 5). Akiba defined the term "with all your soul" to mean "even if He takes away your life."

He attested it with his own martyrdom.

ABBA HILLEL SILVER,
Where Judaism Differed

To Be A Jew

To be a Jew. . .

It is to look back over one's shoulder at patriarch, prophet and psalmist.

It is to feel about the earth the presence of one's brothers bound to one in deep ways. Even if I wish to repudiate them, the world will not let me. Tragedy binds me to them even when dreams do not.

It is to be the result of a severe process of selection to be the scion of those who have breasted the billows of ages.

It is to feel many things blended in one's heart : people, faith, mission, martyrdoms. Fear is in it for the weak, glory for the strong, confusion for the bewildered and clear vision and simple faith for the stout of heart.

It is to love one's own people and to know that this love conflicts in no wise with utter loyalty to lands like America which have given us liberty and equality.

It is to realize that one has been chosen to be a touchstone of the progress of the human soul to live through some days that witness the recrudescence of the evil in men, to see it wreak itself upon my people.

Israel is partly a legacy, partly a social entity, most deeply and fully a religion coextensive with life. It is all these fused into unity, into one way, one vision.

Israel is as diverse as life and as unitary as life ; as plural as history and as consistent as God's purpose in history ; as mysterious as the union and interaction of body and spirit.

This is my people and my faith which I love, and in which I take deep pride. JAMES HELLER

Maintaining Jewish Distinctiveness

The Jewish Heritage Must Be Transmitted

On most of the basic concerns of the day, the modern Jew can reaffirm his tradition, and thus maintain Jewish distinctiveness, which is not merely a difference of entity, but a distinction in quality. Not being biological in character, the Jewish heritage is not transmitted automatically like the animal instincts, but is dependent for its preservation upon the process of education. A well-conceived and integrated program for Jewish living is essential, if these ideals are to function effectively in the Jewish community and the world as a whole.

Judaism is worthy of the loyalty of the modern Jew, because it is not just another version of the same body of ideals that he can find elsewhere. The evidence is at hand that Judaism offers him the means to a richer and more satisfying life, because it contains certain elements, lacking in other civilizations either in whole or in part, in content or in emphasis. This is not merely the proper psychological approach calculated to arouse and maintain Jewish loyalty ; it is validated by the facts.

Moreover, this affirmation of Jewish distinctiveness serves the larger purposes of humanity as well. It is an ancient Jewish hope that the day will come " when the Lord will be one and His Name one," when the great human ideals will be shared alike by all men. When that day dawns, all civilizations will differ from one another in entity and not in quality. We shall minister to that great goal the more effectively, if we recognize that it has not yet been achieved.

ROBERT GORDIS,
The Jew Faces a New World

Ten Commandments For Friday Evenings

1. I am the Sabbath Eve that takes thee out of bondage from lowly pursuit into the realm of life's highest values.

2. Thou shalt have no other appointments on Friday evening but home and Synagogue.

3. Thou shalt not take the name of the Sabbath in vain. Thou shalt avoid all card playing, movie attendance and other weekday pursuits on Sabbath Eve.

4. Remember the Sabbath to keep it holy through worship and cultural pursuit.

5. Honor the faith of your father and mother by attending Friday night services with unfailing regularity.

6. Thou shalt not kill the Sabbath spirit by following secular activities on Friday evenings.

7. Thou shalt not be unfaithful to Jewish home life by banishing the Sabbath candles and *Kiddush* from your home.

8. Thou shalt not steal from the precious hours that belong to the synagogue and Judaism for unworthy, unspiritual pursuits.

9. Thou shalt not bear false witness against the Jewish people by showing irreverence and unconcern for the Sabbath.

10. Thou shalt not covet the pastimes of pleasure-seekers who live as if Judaism has no meaning and message for the modern world.   *Exchange*

Man Is Here For The Sake Of Others

Strange is our situation here upon earth.
Each of us comes for a short visit, not knowing why, yet sometimes seeming
to divine a purpose.
From the standpoint of daily life, however,
there is one thing we do know :
That Man Is Here for the Sake of Other Men. . .
Above all, for those upon whose smile and
well - being our own happiness depends, and also
for the countless unknown souls with whose
fate we are connected by a bond of sympathy.
Many times a day I realize how much my own
outer and inner life is built upon the labors
of my fellow men, both living and dead, and
how earnestly I must exert myself in order to
give in return as much as I have received
and am still receiving.

ALBERT EINSTEIN

Handouts From Heaven

No wonder so many of our Jewish young people are confused. We, the parents have told them that they should study and know their Jewish history and Jewish literature — but how much do we know, and how much time do we take to study ?

We have told them that they must take pride in being Jews — but how much pride and joy do we manifest ? When we talk about Judaism it is about the trouble, the heartache, the misery of being a Jew. It's about anti - semitism and prejudice and discrimination. It's about the evil of the Zionists or the depravity of the anti-Zionists ; the old-fashioned stupidity of Orthodoxy, the muddled mediocrity of Conservatism, or the modern heresy of a cold and empty

Reform. It's about what we eat and don't eat ; whether we wear hats or we don't ; who gives enough to the United Jewish Appeal and who doesn't. In all this, where is the sense of mission ? Where is the poetry and the beauty of a dynamic faith ? Where is the zeal for exalted purpose that will feed the hungry souls of our youth, and nurture their spirit with religious sustenance ?

We say that we are Jews by religion. We aren't a race. We aren't a nationality. It is religion that glorifies and fulfills Jewish destiny, and then after all the glowing affirmation of Judaism as a religious faith, when we are too self-conscious to pray, or read the Bible, or attend the Temple Services except during the High Holydays or children's programs, shall we expect our youth to burst into a flame of religious fervor ?

We say that we predicate our religion on the ethical teachings of the prophets and yet we hide in the corners of timidity and scuttle into cellars of fear, we temporize, equivocate and rationalize when we are called upon as Jews to take a stand on controversial social issues : racial segregation, bible and religion in the public schools, civil liberties, the freedom to write and think and believe and speak as Americans. No wonder our young people look at each other in perplexity and doubt.

And if a young person should say to his parents : " GOD ISN'T SO IMPORTANT IN MY LIFE," I'm sure that the parents would be shocked at such apparent blasphemy and rush the offending offspring to the Rabbi, with a how-could-this-happen-to-us gleam in their eyes. And yet, if the Rabbi should reply : " You say, dear friends, that your child contends that God isn't important to him. Tell me, how important is God to you ? How much do you think about God, or pray to God, or make God a factor in your lives leading you and directing you in what you do and say ? " What do you think the answer of the parents would be ?

You see, there aren't any handouts from heaven even for parents—and I can't offer sweet and packaged platitudes to youth to be good, to be obedient, to be reverent ; I can't separate youth from their parents because Judaism is a family religion — and without the help of the parents our youth will continue to look one upon the other in perplexity and doubt. It is a Jewish family that we go forth in search of God and share the mystery and adventure of the quest for a living faith.

Let no one deceive himself that faith is to be acquired as spiritual manna from above, a gift of God, a handout from heaven. The great spiritual teachers of mankind had to struggle, wrestle, and suffer to achieve their faith. Let no one think that a love of Judaism as a living faith can be acquired without practice, study, thought, and even the agony of doubt. Let no one delude himself into thinking that all we have to do is shout, "God ! God !" and because we have rubbed the cover of a prayerbook or repeated the magic words, God will appear to inspire us, help us, and solve our problems for us offering faith as a handout from heaven.

WILLIAM B. SILVERMAN,
Temple Bulletin

Kiddush Hashem

Throughout the centuries the Jew regarded himself not only as an individual but also as a member of a particular and distinctive group.

No other people in the world has organized its life around this group feeling as did the Jewish people. As a result those around him have also considered the Jew not as an individual but as a representative of all Jewry. This strong group consciousness saved the Jew from disappearing in the melting pot of history. But it has also placed a great responsibility on every Jew. It has made each of our actions not only a matter of personal merit or fault but a *Kiddush Hashem* or *Hillul Hashem*, something which sanctifies or desecrates the name of Israel and the God of Israel.

This strong group feeling created a condition where, *Yisrael Arevim zeh bazeh*, Jews are responsible for each other. The act of each Jew reflects on the character of all Israel. No man is perfect, but when a Jew misbehaves, the seriousness of the act is greatly increased by the fact that it is charged against the character and reputation of all Jews. This is a great responsibility indeed. But it has its compensation when we remember that every noble act we perform is not only a fine thing in itself but that it also helps to overcome, at least in part, the prejudice and ill-will to which Israel is exposed.

This responsibility which history imposes upon every individual Jew is even more serious when we no longer live isolated in ghettos. We are in daily contact with those of other groups and the spotlight of their judgment is constantly turned upon us. We must ever be mindful therefore that our behaviour is not a personal matter only. It is a daily opportunity for *Kiddush Hashem*. It determines the name and the fame, the fate and the faith of Israel.

DAVID ARONSON,
Sabbath and Festival Prayer Book

Lest We Burn The Bridge

In order to attain an adequate appreciation of the preciousness that the Jewish way of living is capable of bestowing upon us, we should initiate a thorough cleaning of the minds. Every one of us should be asked to make one major sacrifice : to sacrifice his prejudice against our heritage. We should strive to cultivate an atmosphere in which the values of Jewish faith and piety could be cherished, an atmosphere in which the Jewish form of living is the heartily approved or at least respected pattern, in which sensitivity to *kashruth* (dietary laws) is not regarded as treason against the American Constitution and reverence for the Sabbath is not considered conspiracy against progress.

Without solidarity with our forebears, the solidarity with our brothers will remain feeble. The vertical unity of Israel is essential to the horizontal unity of *Kelal Israel* (the community of Israel). Identification with what is undying in Israel, the appreciation of what was supremely significant throughout the ages, the endeavor to integrate the abiding teachings and aspirations of the past into our own thinking will enable us to be creative, to expand, not to imitate or to repeat. Survival of Israel means that we carry on our independent dialogue with the past. Our way of life must remain such as would be, to some degree, intelligible to Isaiah and Rabbi Yochanan ben Zakkai, to Maimonides and the Baal Shem.

Let us be under no illusion. The task is hard. However, if it is true that the good cannot exist without the holy, what are we doing for the purpose of securing holiness in the world? Can we afford to be indifferent, to forget the responsibility which our position as teachers bestows upon us?

A wide stream of human callousness separates us from the realm of holiness. Neither an individual man nor a single generation can by its own power erect a bridge that would reach that realm. For ages our fathers have labored in building a sacred bridge. *We who have not crossed the stream must beware lest we burn the bridge.*

ABRAHAM J. HESCHEL,
Man's Quest for God

Enriching The Heritage

The difference between the non-Jew and the Jew rests on the fact that the Jew constantly subjects himself to a spiritual and ethical regimen which helps him conquer the evil in himself. The minute the regimen is abolished the Jew is no better and may become worse than others. Being a Jew therefore means perpetual, constant effort in maintaining a trend of thought, an attitude toward the world, a control of a spiritual discipline that help cultivate the good in man. There is no denying that in the course of many generations of such efforts Jews developed certain abilities, inclinations, talents, which provide them with the power to conquer evils in themselves. The former generations did leave us a heritage. But living on that heritage alone without constantly enlarging upon it means, in the first place, to live as parasites and, secondly, to squander the heritage. Were it not for all former generations that worked upon enlarging that heritage, our youth of today would have no chance to boast of Jewish progressivism and to rely upon Jewish perseverance. And if our youth of today have real intention to survive as Jews, chauvinistic boasting will not achieve it. Like all former generations this generation too, must become active and make itself not only the guardian but also the builder of new values to enrich and enlarge its heritage.

MENAHEM BORAISHA,
Notes on Jewish Survival

The Return To Judaism

I was once — thirty-five years ago — a young returning intellectual. And I didn't stay "returning." I returned. I returned so with my whole soul and heart and mind that today, when somebody reminds me of once having been in a state of alienation and is kind enough to assign to me the merit — unmerited — which our sages grant to a *Baal Teshuvah*, it seems to me like a legend, like a dream, like something that has no relevance to the man I am. And perhaps these present younger returning intellectuals, who are nearly all scholars and writers, sensitive and gifted, have a faint notion of that peace within Israel which can be found today as in every age and yet being, for strange and varied reasons, impotent to approach even the source whence that peace springs, feel a natural and pardonable and understandable irritation in the presence of a result which is the object of their desire but not within their power to attain.

It is a great pity. The American Jewish community is not too rich in lay leadership. Younger scholars and writers would be a very precious accession to its ranks. But the first quality that is needed for one who desires indeed to return is humility. He must "learn"; he must sit at the feet of the sages and saints of Israel, the living and the dead. And the second prerequisite is a true abjuration of pagan idols — of nihilist Utopias, not because they have failed but because God forbid, they might have succeeded. But even humility and the abjuration of pagan idols will not suffice — I warn my young contemporaries — without the spontaneous love of Israel. They will know that they are Jews again and no more lonely and no more alienated when the humblest Jew and the most recalcitrant Jew is dear and precious to them for the sake of that eternal bond of pain and glory, of aspiration and even of defeat, of service to man and of suffering for that service which constitutes the fellowship of Israel through the ages.

LUDWIG LEWISOHN,
To the Young Jewish Intellectuals

The Danger Of Indifference

What may endanger our Jewish future here is not conscious escapism or deliberate assimilationist tendencies. . . . Rather, a too facile adaptability, an unconscious drift and a care-free relaxation of all disciplines—not out of conviction but out of sheer indifference—such as belonging to Synagogues and not attending them, or sending children to schools which are so limited as to time that they cannot really give them an adequate Jewish education, or in very many instances, not giving them any instruction at all, or emptying our homes of all Jewish content. What we should fear most is the rise of a generation of prosperous Jews who have no spiritual anchorage, or a generation of clever restless Jews of quick ferment and, high voltage, rooted in no religious tradition, reverent of no moral code, ignorant of all Jewish learning and held to social responsibility by no spiritual inner restraint. . . . Such floating mines are a danger to any people, but especially to a minority group.

If American Jewry of tomorrow will restore what has become peripheral in our life, to the center again — the Synagogue, the school, the academy and the religious disciplines of Judaism — then American Jewry is destined to enjoy a resplendent century of spiritual growth in this gracious land.

ABBA HILLEL SILVER,
Address, 1954

A Sign Of Maturity

We have succeeded in teaching large numbers of Jews to carry their communal obligations, in terms of their contribution to Israel, overseas national and local causes, as a normal and constant item in their annual budget. We shall have reached maturity as a Jewish community when equally large numbers of Jews include in their personal budget of time and duty such responsibilities as Jewish study, the Jewish education of their young, Jewish symbols and disciplines in the home and a commitment to the advancement of Jewish learning, art and literature.

MORRIS ADLER,
Shaarey Zedek Recorder

11

How Beautiful
Is Our Heritage

Happy are we. How goodly is our portion, how pleasant
our lot, how beautiful our heritage.

Daily Morning Service

When sometimes our own unchristian prejudices flame
out against the Jewish people, let us remember that all
that we have and all that we are we owe, under God,
to what Judaism has given us.

Lyman Abbott

Far from having become 1900 years ago a stagnant
religion, Judaism has ever remained "a river of God
full of living waters," which, while running within the
river-bed of a single nation, has continued to feed anew
the great streams of human civilization.

Kaufmann Kohler

The Bible And The Jew

There are no words in the world more knowing, more disclosing and more indispensable, words both stern and graceful, heart-rending and healing. A truth so universal : God is One. A thought so consoling : He is with us in distress. A responsibility so overwhelming : His name can be desecrated. A map of time : from creation to redemption. Guideposts along the way : The Sabbath. An offering ; contrition of the heart. A utopia : would that all people were prophets. The insight : man lives by his faithfulness : his home is in time and his substance in deeds. A standard so bold : ye shall be holy. A commandment so daring : love thy neighbor as thyself. A fact so sublime : human and divine pathos can be in accord. And a gift so undeserved : the ability to repent.

ABRAHAM J. HESCHEL
God in Search of Man

The Universal Significance Of Judaism

The two religions which control the larger portion of the inhabited globe, Christianity and Islam, are both based on the religion of the Jews.

Yes, in a certain sense it is indisputable that we are indebted to the religion of Moses for a large share of the culture which we now enjoy. Through it, a precious truth became popularly known, the doctrine of one God, which, if left to the intellect alone, would have been discovered only after a slow process of evolution.

The Hebrew system enjoyed this extraordinary advantage, that the religion of its sages and the religion of its folk were not in direct mutual contradiction, as was the case among the enlightened pagans. From this standpoint, the Jewish nation must appear to us historically as of universal significance. All the evil which has been imputed to them, all the efforts of literary men to disparage them, will not prevent us from doing them justice.

FRIEDRICH VON SCHILLER,
Die Sendung Moses

The Life-Giving Soil

I am persuaded that the national character of Judaism not only does not exclude humanity and true civilization, but leads to these as its necessary consequence. If, nevertheless, I emphasize the nationalistic roots of Judaism at the expense of its humanitarian blossoms, that is because in our day people are too apt to adorn their buttonholes with the handsome flowers of civilization, and never dream of cultivating the soil from which they draw their life.

MOSES HESS,
Rome and Jerusalem

The Inspiration Of Jewish History

The first part of Jewish history, the Biblical part, is a source from which for many centuries, millions of human beings have derived instruction, solace, and inspiration. Its heroes have long ago become types, incarnations of great ideals. The events it relates serve as living ethical formulae. But a time will come — perhaps it is not very far off — when the second half of Jewish history, that people's life after the Biblical period, will be accorded the same treatment. The thousand years' martyrdom of the Jewish people, its unbroken pilgrimage, its tragic fate, its teachers of religion, its martyrs, philosophers, champions — this whole epic will, in days to come, sink deep into the memory of men. It will speak to the heart and conscience of men, and secure respect for the silvery hair of the Jewish People.

SIMON DUBNOW,
Jewish History

I Am A Jew

I am a Jew because the faith of Israel demands no abdication of my mind.

I am a Jew because the faith of Israel asks every possible sacrifice of my soul.

I am a Jew because in all places where there are tears and suffering the Jew weeps.

I am a Jew because in every age when the cry of despair is heard the Jew hopes.

I am a Jew because the message of Israel is the most ancient and the most modern.

I am a Jew because Israel's promise is a universal promise.

I am a Jew because for Israel the world is not finished ; men will complete it.

I am a Jew because for Israel man is not yet fully created ; men are creating him.

I am a Jew because Israel places man and his unity above nations and above Israel itself.

I am a Jew because above man, image of the divine unity, Israel places the unity which is divine.

EDMOND FIEG,
Why I Am a Jew

A Contribution In Two Parts

What is fascinating in the contribution which comes from the Jewish civilization is that it comes in two sections, separated by more than two thousand years. There is the contribution which comes from the Old Testament, as it was interpreted by Christians; and there is that which comes from actual living Jewish communities. These show how Jewish thoughts, hammered in the mills of generations of rabbinic understanding and interpretation, have developed what we find in the Hebrew Bible itself. These two contributions are not identical; for, in spite of Toynbee, Judaism has not been a fossil for the last two thousand years. There is, however, a more curious reason why they are not identical: *we often had to wait until Jewish emancipation to understand what the real Jewish inheritance was; what the Christian was presenting was a misunderstanding.*

The most obvious example of this perversion is to be found in the field of law. Christians still contrast the " love " of the Gospels with " an eye for an eye and a tooth for a tooth," which is supposed to be characteristic of Judaism. They do not realize that " an eye for an eye " was out of date in Judaism before Jesus of Nazareth was born, whereas in Christian Europe it took centuries of work to emancipate legal conception from the tyranny of verbal adherence to some Old Testament text.

We should exaggerate if we took such a situation as typical over the whole field. Europe got its sense of history from the Jews; for the Greeks history was simply a meaningless and endless repetition. One could say that every social reformer in European history drew his inspiration and his support from the Jewish prophets. In neither case was there misunderstanding of the Jewish contribution. And though it constantly misunderstood individual laws, yet it was from the Jewish sense of law as the basis of God's relation with men in community that Europe built up the so-called Christian sense of justice. A Roman could say " caveat emptor " — " let the buyer look out " — and so justify sharp practice on the part of the seller. To the Christian (whatever his practice) the eye of God saw the cheat, even if the eye of man did not. And this the Christian had learned from Jewish law.

JAMES W. PARKES,
Jewish Contributions to Civilization

Israel's Conception Of Justice

A distinguished American judge, referring to the Jewish contributions to civilization, says :

" Israel's idea of justice has taken permanent possession of the human mind. Torn asunder by faction, driven from his country, scattered to the four winds of heaven, scourged up and down the highways of the world, stretched upon the rack, burned at the stake, massacred by the hundred thousand, a wanderer, friendless and homeless through the centuries, despised by the world he was liberating from its idols, Israel has stamped his ideal of justice on the human consciousness itself, and lives in every upward movement of the race. I do not forget what other races have contributed to the common store—Athens and Italy their sense of beauty, Sparta and Rome their love of discipline and order, Gaul and Germany their zeal for liberty, England and America their ever-blessed union of liberty under law. I do not forget what your gifted race has wrought in other ways—in war and statecraft, in music, art, poetry, science, history, philosophy — but, compared with the meaning and majesty of this achievement every other work you have accomplished, every other triumph of every other people, sinks into insignificance. Give up every other claim to the world's gratitude before you surrender this : the world owes its conception of justice to the Jew."

MAURICE H. FARBRIDGE,
Judaism and the Modern Mind

Melodies Of Israel

Where is there a holy book in which
   you do not hear
The swish of Jordan's waters and the
   rustle of the Lebanon ?
Where is there a chapel or a shrine
Wherein you do not catch the echo
Of the son of Amram's voice or
   Psalms of David's praise ?
Where is the canvas, marble or the
   bronze
Which does not speak the language
   of the ancients —
The low-voiced stirring of awaken-
   ing matter

That heartfelt something of my
   treasured prophets
And the dreams and visions of their
   light,
The gentle dropping of Creation's
   dew
From out the pages of our Genesis,
The sad-sweet vintage of Kohelet
The exultation of the Song of Songs ?

ZALMAN SHENEOR,
quoted in *A History of Jewish
Literature*

Justice Akin To Holiness

" Justice, justice shalt thou follow " (Deuteronomy 16 : 20). These passionate words, may be taken as the keynote of the humane legislation of the Torah, and of the demand for social righteousness by Israel's

Prophets, Psalmists and Sages. "Let justice roll down as waters, and righteousness as a mighty stream," is the cry of Amos. Justice is not the only ethical quality in God or man, nor is it the highest quality ; but it is the basis for all the others. "Righteousness and justice are the foundations of Thy throne," says the Psalmist : the whole idea of the Divine rests on them.

It must be noted that the idea of justice in Hebrew thought stands for something quite other than in Greek. In Plato's *Republic*, for example, it implies a harmonious arrangement of society, by which every human peg is put into its appropriate hole, so that those who perform humble functions shall be content to perform them in due subservience to their superiors. It stresses the inequalities of human nature ; whereas in the Hebrew conception of justice, the equality is stressed. To understand the idea of justice in Israel we must bear in mind the biblical teaching that man is created in the image of God ; that in every human being there is a Divine spark ; and that each human life is sacred, and of infinite worth. In consequence, a human being cannot be treated as a chattel, or a thing, but must be treated as a personality ; and, as a personality, every human being is the possessor of the right to life, honor, and the fruits of his labor. *Justice is the awe-inspired respect for the personality of others, and their inalienable rights ;* even as injustice is the most flagrant manifestation of disrespect for the personality of others (F. Adler). Judaism requires that human personality be respected in every human being — in the female heathen prisoner of war, in the delinquent, even in the criminal condemned to death. The lashes to be inflicted on the evil-doer must be strictly limited, lest "thy brother seem vile unto thee" (25 : 3) ; and, if he be found worthy of death by hanging, his human dignity must still be respected : his body is not to remain hanging over night, but must be buried the same day (21 : 23).

It is thus seen that whereas in Greek the idea of justice was akin to harmony, in Hebrew it is akin to holiness. Isaiah (5 : 16) has for all time declared "The Holy God is sanctified by *justice.*" In brief, where there is no justice, no proper and practical appreciation of the human rights of every human being as sons of the one and only God of righteousness — there we have a negation of religion. The oppressor, the man who tramples on others, and especially on those like the orphan and the stranger who are too weak to defend themselves, is throughout Scripture held forth as the enemy of God and man. The final disappearance of injustice and oppression is represented in the New Year Amidah as the goal of human history, and as synonymous with the realization of God's Kingdom on earth.

However, justice is more than mere abstention from injuring our fellow-men. " The work of justice is peace ; and the effect thereof quietness and confidence forever " (Isaiah 32 : 17). It is a positive conception, and includes charity, philanthropy, and every endeavor to bring out what is highest and best in others. Just as " truth " is usually preceded in Scripture by " loving-kindness," to remind us that the truth must be spoken *in love ;* even so is " justice " often accompanied by some synonym of " loving-kindness " — to teach that strict justice must, in its execution, be mitigated by pity and humanity. " To do justly *and* to love mercy," is the Prophet's summing up of human duty toward our fellow-men. The world could not exist if it were governed by strict justice alone — say the Rabbis ; therefore, God judges His human children by justice tempered with mercy. Such being the Jewish understanding of justice it is but natural that in later Hebrew that same word came to denote " charity " exclusively.

Nor is justice limited to the relation between individuals. It extends to the relation between group and group, and it asserts the claims of the poor upon the rich, of the helpless upon them who possess the means to help. And even as there is *social* justice, prescribing the duties of class to class, so there is *international* justice, which demands respect for the personality of each and every national group, and proclaims that no people can of right be robbed of its national life or territory, its language or spiritual heritage. It is this wider recognition of justice that has called into existence the League of Nations. " I do not know whether you are aware that the League of Nations was first of all the vision of a great Jew, almost three thousand years ago — the prophet Isaiah " (J. C. Smuts).

JOSEPH H. HERTZ,
The Pentateuch and Haftorahs

Every inheritance of the Jewish people, every teaching of their secular history and religious experience, draws them powerfully to the side of charity, liberty and progress.

CALVIN COOLIDGE,
The Spiritual Foundation of America

The Joy Of Being A Jew

A Jew who is not always full of joy because he is a Jew, is ungrateful to the Lord.

THE ALEXANDER RABBI,
The Hasidic Anthology

The Key To Human Salvation

I submit that Judaism, the Mother Religion, can take its place alongside of the most enlightened and most virile of the world's creeds as a source, in fact the chief source, of inspiration for mankind. Judaism furnishes the key to human salvation. It points the way to the establishment of the Kingdom of Heaven on earth. And when Scripture states that the seed of the Patriarchs was destined to become a blessing to the world, it means just this, that by means of our sublime Faith we are to lead the human race heavenward, Godward, to the state designated as the Millennium, the Messianic period when the world's yearnings for peace and universal brotherhood will be realized.

As a matter of fact, this message is preached from every Jewish pulpit, on every occasion, on every Sabbath and Festival of the year. Almost every page of our Bible, the Torah, the Prophets and the Holy Writings, stresses the ideals essential for bringing on the Messianic era. Every one of our Festivals has its distinct message for humanity. Passover stresses freedom, freedom from bondage, physical and political. *Shabuoth* with its emphasis on the Revelation at Sinai, underscores spiritual freedom. *Sukkoth*, the Feast of Ingathering, focuses attention on the importance of material and economic freedom and security.

Chanukah glorifies the Maccabean struggle for religious freedom. Thus all the freedoms indispensable to human progress and happiness are the themes taught by our Festivals.

Israel's code repeatedly and vigorously proclaims the exalted doctrines of the Oneness of the Deity and the unity of mankind. It demands that we pursue justice, promote peace, love the stranger, pity the poor and the needy, the helpless and the dependent, and compassionate even the dumb beast. The Prophets urge equity and righteousness, faith and humility. Says Isaiah: " Learn to do well ; seek justice, relieve the oppressed, judge the fatherless, plead for the widow." Israel's Seers foretell the era of peace when " they shall beat their swords into plowshares, and their spears into pruning-hooks ; nation shall not lift up sword against nation, neither shall they learn war any more." They also portray the glorious future when, " the wolf shall dwell with the lamb — They shall not hurt nor destroy in all My holy mountain ; for the earth shall be full of the knowledge of the Lord, as the waters cover the sea."

Malachi pleads: " Have we not all One Father ? " The Psalmist rhapsodizes : " How good and how pleasant it is when brethren dwell together in unity." On the afternoon of our holiest day, *Yom Kippur*, we read the Book of Jonah, the sublimest plea for tolerance and compassion and forgiveness respecting even the sinful people of Nineveh. On *Shabuoth*, the Book of Ruth is read in the traditional synagogue, a charming idyl setting forth Judaism's universal appeal; "Thy people shall be my people, and thy God my God."

Has any people ever proclaimed a nobler message than has Israel, the "prophet unto the Nations," the "light unto the Nations?" Ours is truly the Gospel of love, of faith, hope and charity, incomparably the sublimest mission to turn men's hearts heavenward, to effect the world's salvation. Oh, if only the world heeded the message of Judaism!...

Let us ever remember that ours is the noblest Gospel, the most comprehensive, most world-embracing, most comforting and most inspiring. Ours is the task to preach this doctrine, everywhere and always, to apprise our friends of the blessed message of which we are the bearers, with the hope in our hearts, and on our lips the prayer, that Isaiah's prophecy may be fulfilled in our day;

> And many people shall go and say;
> Come ye, and let us go up to the mountain of the Lord. . . .
> And He will teach us of His ways,
> And we will walk in His paths.

ELIAS L. SOLOMON,
The Message of Judaism

The Jews are probably the greatest of all peoples. Has any other so persistently produced an almost ceaseless string of great men for three or four thousand years? Has any other produced so many great men in proportion to its numbers? Certainly no other, unless it be the Chinese, have so consistently maintained a prominent position for millennium after millennium.

ELLSWORTH HUNTINGTON,
Pulse of Progress

The Wonderful Book Of Psalms

There is one history, and that the most touching and most profound of all, for which we should search in vain through all the pages of the classics — I mean the history of the human soul in its relations with its Maker; the history of its sin, and grief, and death, and of the way of its recovery to hope and life and to enduring joy. For the exercises of strength and skill, for the achievements and for the enchantments of wit, of eloquence, of art, of genius, for the imperial games of politics and war — let us seek them on the shores of Greece. But if the first among the problems of life be how to establish the peace, and restore the balance, of our inward being; if the highest of all conditions in the existence of the creature be his aspect toward the God to whom he owes his being and in whose great hand he stands; then let us make our search elsewhere. All the wonders of the Greek civilization heaped together are less wonderful, than is the single Book of Psalms.

WILLIAM EWART GLADSTONE,
Gleanings of Past Years

The Greek grasped the present moment, and was the artist; the Jew worshipped the timeless spirit, and was the prophet.

ISAAC M. WISE,
Selected Writings

The Music Of The Heart Of Man

Above the couch of David, according to Rabbinical tradition, there hung a harp. The midnight breeze, as it rippled over the strings, made such music that the poet King was constrained to rise from his bed, and until dawn flushed the eastern skies he wedded words to the strains. The poetry of that tradition is condensed in the saying that the Book of Psalms contains the whole music of the heart of man, swept by the hand of his Maker. In it are gathered the lyrical burst of his tenderness, the moan of his penitence, the pathos of his sorrow, the triumph of his victory, the despair of his defeat, the firmness of his confidence, the rapture of his assured hope. . . .

They alone have known no limitations to a particular age, country or form of faith. In the Psalms the vast hosts of suffering humanity have found the deepest expression of their hopes and fears.

ROWLAND EDMUND PROTHERO,
The Psalms in Human Life

The Origin Of Religious Thought

If Jewish thought had never existed the world would have been without Christianity and Islam. By this is not meant that Christianity and Islam are solely Jewish in nature and origin. Far from it. They are surely themselves. To be oneself is to be distinct from others; and so far as they are products at all, they are products of other factors besides the Jewish. And yet Jewish thought is all important both for them in particular and in the general history of religion.

We may take the latter point first, illustrating it by a conventional analogy. . . .

According to the tradition, explicitly phrased in Proclus, the Greek Pythagoras was the first to treat number by and in itself, i.e., he was the creator of mathematics as a science. Mathematics as a craft or as a business device, or as a pre-requisite to religious rites, was known to the Egyptians and Babylonians. But mathematics in the " pure " sense is Greek ; and it is the vision of Pythagoras which was taken up long after by Kepler and Descartes and the mathematical physicists of our own day. Mathematics may therefore be fairly called Greek, although the thought may have changed in its content and detail and although no one can say whether, if Pythagoras and the Greeks had never existed, there might not have arisen other individuals, or another people, to think the same or similar thoughts.

It is somewhat in the same way that we may call religion Jewish. It is in Jewish thought that what is recognised as religion received basic expression. If we are asked what religion is, we can point to certain ideas, or figures, in Jewish thought, much as, when asked what mathematics is we point to the Greek tradition and the Greeks.

But we may go further than this. It is not only a matter of " type " or " inspiration " or " vision." The positive content of Greek mathematics is an integral part of modern mathematics, and whole sections of it are given in modern textbooks as its essential ground-work. It is not a mere survival taught for historical reasons like the theory of Phlogiston in chemistry. Its value for humanity lies in itself, in its own demonstrated propositions.

Similarly, Jewish thought as such is embedded in Christianity and Islam. It fills their sacred books ;

and if it were removed, their essential content would be different. Christianity, indeed, on the lips of its founder, proclaimed itself the fulfillment of Judaism ; and the Prophet of Islam declared that he was the true successor of Moses and, like Moses, a "Prophet with a book." Thus we may fairly reaffirm the accepted judgment that Judaism is the " mother " religion, Christianity and Islam its " daughters." Without Abraham, Moses and the Prophets, both Christianity and Islam, if they could have come into being at all, would have been strangely other than they are.

But, again, this is not all. Children often break with their parents and, whether in sorrow or in anger, go their own independent ways ; and yet retain for all that, in the very fibers of their being, their parents' characteristics. Whatever be finally accepted as the detailed connection between the three great monotheistic religions it is clear that they have, and still preserve, a strong family resemblance. They are all vitally interested in conduct ; they all conceive the material universe as dependent on spiritual reality ; they all see this one and unique spiritual reality as the source of good and of right conduct. There is between them much more in common than this ; but it will be agreed that there is at least this, and that this is all-important.   LEON ROTH,
Jewish Thought as a Factor in Civilization

The Hebrews have determined our literature more than all other influences combined; the English heart and mind are now partly made of Hebrew thought and ideals.

THOMAS G. TUCKER,
The Foreign Debt of English Literature

In The Withered Head Bloomed Dreams Like Roses

Israel has always been a nation of aristocrats, working out its own conception of the common life, and in tacit protestation against whatever seemed false and wrong in the ideals and morals of the world outside. This modern surrender to contemporary civilization, this spiritual intermarriage with the ideals and customs of the environments, while keeping up the meaningless tradition of physical intermarriage with one another, is more inglorious than a graceful lowering of the flag of Judah before a civilization and a culture proved and acknowledged superior. Now, if I say that the old Judaism had much still adequate for this age, much that is not yet, and can never be superceded, you will not suspect me of being a professional pulpiteer. You know me, I trust as a friendly observer, who, disliking the dogmatism of all religions, has preferred to express himself through art, which bends with the tolerance of the sky over everything human. Yet, if we must formulate creeds, I should say that that would be nearest to the final creed which has in it — first, the pervasive recognition of the mystery of the universe; secondly, the truest expression of the laws of the universe, both spiritual and physical; thirdly, the code of conduct that is best adapted to harmonize with those laws, physical and spiritual; and fourthly — since some of the laws of nature work not outside us, but through us — the evolutionary ideal best fitted to carry on the race toward higher developments.

A natural metaphor, which occurs to me on account of my recent voyage, is that of sailing on the ocean. We need first a recognition of the poetry and mystery of the sea; secondly, charts and maps of the rocks, currents, winds and streams; thirdly, a reduction of this knowledge to practical seamanship; and fourthly, a goal toward which we are sailing. It is the first requisite, the sense of wonder and poetry, that is most easily deadened, and more, perhaps, in the saloon than in the steerage. For in the gilded dining rooms and smoking rooms, which shut out the loneliness and terror of the deep, one easily subsides into the commonplace, and it takes storms and collisions to rouse us to a sense of the awe and mystery. If most religions have degenerated into cut-and-dried schemes, by which people imagine they can get first - class passages to heaven, this was rarely the idea of their founders, who left vistas opening on the infinite. Judaism has been represented both by Jews and Christians as the most cut-and-dried scheme of all ; but the truth rather is that half the Jews have been engaged in drying Judaism and the other half in cutting it. "Judaism is not a religion, but a misfortune," said Heine ; and the vulgar comedy of little souls who have changed "Moses Moses" to "Montmorency," is paralleled by the high tragedy of those great souls that have found themselves distracted between a parochial something which they did not understand and the great free world of ideas and institutions and aspirations calling them without. And yet—here is the irony—all those ideals and aspirations were already within. Judaism was never the mummy that Heine figured it. Beneath that yellow parchment skin the blood beat and tingled, and in that withered head bloomed dreams like roses.

ISRAEL ZANGWILL,
Speeches, Articles and Letters

Compassion And The Mosaic Law

The strongest impulse in the character of Moses appears to have been that of protective justice, more particularly with regard to the helpless and down-trodden classes. The laws of Moses, if carefully examined, are a perfect phenomenon ; an exception to the laws of either ancient or modern nations in the care they exercised over women, widows, orphans, paupers, foreigners, servants, and dumb animals. No so-called Christian nation but could advantageously take a lesson in legislation from the laws of Moses. There is a plaintive, pathetic spirit of compassion in the very language in which the laws in favor of the helpless and suffering are expressed, that it seems must have been learned only of superhuman tenderness. Not the gentlest words of Jesus are more compassionate in their spirit than many of these laws of Moses.

HARRIET BEECHER STOWE,
Moses and His Laws

Moses — The Master Artist

I did not particularly like Moses at first, I suppose, because I was under the complete sway of the Hellenic spirit and could not forgive the Jewish Lawgiver his hatred of all imagery and plastic art. I did not realize that Moses in spite of his enmity for art was, nevertheless, himself a great artist endowed with the artist's true spirit. His art, however, like that of his Egyptian countrymen was directed to the colossal and indestructible. But he did not, like the Egyptians, mold his masterpieces out of brick and granite, rather did he build human pyramids. He carved human obelisks. He took a poor shepherd tribe and out of it created a people, that even like the pyramids defies the centuries, an eternal, holy people, God's people, that might serve as model to all other peoples, indeed, as the prototype of humanity ; he created Israel ! . . . The writer of these pages might well be proud that his ancestors belong to the noble house of Israel, that he is a descendant of those martyrs who gave the world a God and an ethic, who struggled and suffered on all the battlefields of ideas.

HEINRICH HEINE,
Confessions

The Jew And Brotherhood

The Jews did not worship idols ; they alone did not prostrate themselves before nature ; they condemned, despised that pantheism, that idol-worship, which sanctified the vices and the passions, and which the Greeks and Romans embraced with such ardor. The dignity and regularity of their habits formed a striking contrast to pagan dissipation. They opposed in their individuality the beauty of their rigorous law to the impure teachings of paganism. They never presented a disgraceful spectacle in the time of their prosperity ; they never participated in the bloody games of the ring ; they held human sacrifices in horror.

The Jews did not profess the principle of equity, of which the Greeks and Romans boasted so much — themselves absolute partisans of slavery. They simply upheld the institution of family hierarchy, the paternal authority. Their habits and institutions, inspired by the parental sentiment — were they not full of kindliness and foresight ? Could they overlook the feeble and the poor ? Among them brothers could not know contention and strife, because they were equals in reality. Without the parent, fraternity would disappear.

In order to subsist it is necessary that children should always have before them the image, the memory, the principle of the paternity from which they emanated, which formed the bonds of their friendship. Their unity proceeds from thence, a unity sweet, lively, inculcated in infancy, formed by the heart before the mind could grasp it. . . . The Jews never forgot, and had they done so, the law would have reminded them, that the earth belongs to the Lord and that in God they are all brothers. The constitutional wars between the poor and the rich in Rome and Athens were caused by extortion. This question of extortion fills Roman history with its pale shadow; it is at the bottom of all the troubles, dissensions, periodical massacres and revolts. . . . The Jewish fraternity condemned extortion as a principle of tyranny.

This fraternity, so powerful a principle, led the Jews to love their fellow-beings, to see in them colleagues and brothers ; they received the stranger willingly, extended to him their hospitality, even a share in the benefits of their law — something that was foreign to all other nations. . . . The dogma of Divine creation exhibited to the Jews all men as brethren. They did not treat the stranger therefore as a barbarian. They, the Israelites, alone of all the nations of antiquity, did not carry on aggressive wars ; once established upon their soil, they had no other desire than to live in peace by living out their laws. This is the object of all their institutions. They do not make war upon the stranger, because they have no hate against him. . . .

By their habits in the government of the State, the Jews were separated completely from Greece and Rome. They never brooked the insults of the ancient and modern mobocracy, because they respected the principle of the family, the foundation of their political, judicial, administrative and military organization. They alone in antiquity repudiated slavery. They practiced a national brotherhood which the Christian people are hardly capable of comprehending ; it is so sublime, and almost beyond human nature. . . .

The Jewish nation has survived all its victors ; it alone, says Jean Jacques Rousseau, withstood the power of time, fortune and defeat. Greece and Rome were enveloped in a system of superstition which weighed heavily upon the actions of public and private life. The Jews lived beyond the pale of that ignominy. The causes of this intellectual and moral superiority became the subject of jealous depreciation generally.

Le Monde (Catholic Journal)

We are perhaps the sons of dealers in old clothes, but we are the grandsons of Prophets. CHAIM WEIZMANN, address, 1923

The Noble Demands Of Judaism

The religion preached by Moses taught the concept of a true God, not of the sky as the pagans thought, not of a world structure as the philosophers envisaged, but of a God who was above the heavens and the world. . . .

The descendants of Abraham

represent humanity in its purest form, without brutish giants, just as their religion is pure of superstitious rites. All the religious institutions of the Hebrew people were designed to maintain and promote the knowledge of God and to shield man against sinking into pagan vulgarity. While the pagan priests concealed carefully their religious mysteries, the prescriptions of the Jewish religion were put down in writing, and made accessible to all who could read. . . .

The pagan religions prescribed certain purification ceremonies and ritual ablutions, but these pertained only to the body. The purity of the soul, the contrition of the heart crushed by the consciousness of its moral impurity, was demanded only by the religion of the Hebrews.

GIOVANNI BATTISTA VICO

As long as the world lasts, all who want to make progress in righteousness will come to Israel for inspiration, as the people who have the sense for righteousness most glowing and strongest.

MATTHEW ARNOLD,
Literature and Dogma

I have never seen a country or a culture which was not the better for having the contribution of the Jewish people.

PEARL BUCK

The Light Shed From Palestine

All the greatness of the white races comes from that sublime Judeo-Christian idea whose light was shed over the world from Palestine through the agency of the Bible and the great teachers of the Pharisees. Through its influence the State lost its divine character and put itself at the service of mankind ; the spirit of criticism and the desire of better things were given the freedom of the world ; the thirst for truth and justice increased with every effort made to quench it.

GUGLIELMO FERRERO,
Peace and War

Thou Shalt Love Thy Neighbor As Thyself
(Leviticus 19 : 18)

The world at large is unaware of the fact that this comprehensive maxim of morality — the golden rule of human conduct — was first taught by Judaism. No less a thinker than John Stuart Mill expressed his surprise that it came from the Pentateuch. Not only is it Jewish in origin, but, long before the rise of Christianity, Israel's religious teachers quoted Leviticus 19 : 18 either verbally or in paraphrase, as expressing the essence of the moral life. Thus, Ben Sira says, " Honor thy neighbor as thyself." In the Testaments of the Twelve Patriarchs we read : " A man should not do to his neighbor what a man does not desire for himself." Tobit admonishes his son in the words, " What is displeasing to thyself, that do not unto any other." Philo and Josephus have sayings similar to the above. As to the Rabbis, there is the well-known story of Hillel and the heathen scoffer who asked Hillel to condense for him the whole Law in briefest possible form. Hillel's answer is, " Whatever is hateful unto thee, do it not unto thy fellow : this is the whole Torah ; the rest is explanation." In the generation after the Destruction of the Temple, Rabbi Akiba declares " Thou shalt love thy neighbor as thyself is a fundamental rule in the Torah." His contemporary Ben Azzai agrees that this law of love is such a fundamental rule, provided it is read in conjunction with Genesis 5 : 1 (" This is the book of the generations of man. In the day that God created man, in the likeness of God made He him ") ; for this latter verse teaches reverence for the Divine image in man, and proclaims the vital truth of the unity of mankind, and the consequent doctrine of the brotherhood of man. All men are created in the Divine image, says Ben Azzai, and, therefore all are our fellow-men and entitled to human love.

JOSEPH H. HERTZ,
The Pentateuch and Haftorahs

Conscience is, like charity, a Semitic importation. Israel introduced it into the world.

ANATOLE LEROY-BEAULIEU,
Israel Among The Nations

Experience And Tradition

Jewish ideals, like those of any other people, are the result of a specific group experience, of a history, crystallized and transmitted by a tradition. These two factors adequately explain Jewish traits. For two thousand years, the Jew was deprived of the opportunity, and so he has lost the taste, for violence and bloodshed. His fate associated him with the oppressed and downtrodden, and therefore fired him with a passionate hatred of injustice. He was scattered throughout the world, and thus the seeds of an inter-national outlook were sown in him. Einstein is said to have remarked, " Thank God I belong to a small people that has not been strong enough to do much harm in the world." Physical weakness and insignificance have characterized the Jewish people from its beginnings and undoubtedly have helped to confer upon it some of its most distinctive traits.

Once acquired, these impulses were perpetuated from generation to generation, not by the bloodstream but by tradition, by the educative process. This process had many aspects. It was begun in the home, continued through formal schooling in youth and maintained by lifelong study. Through the reading of the Torah and the homilies in the synagogue, the performance of religious rites and, above all, the celebration of the festivals, each Jew experienced vicariously the history of his people. Each generation felt the truth of the Torah's statement, "Not with our fathers alone has the Lord made this covenant but with us, even us, who are all alive this day," and accepted the ideals of its people as its own.

ROBERT GORDIS,
The Jew Faces a New World

The Lifting Power Of The Jewish Prophets

The moral feelings of men have been deepened and strengthened, and also softened, and almost created, by the Jewish Prophets. In modern times we hardly like to acknowledge the full force of their words, lest they should prove subversive to society. And so we explain them away or spiritualize them, and convert what is figurative into what is literal, and what is literal into what is figurative. And still, after all our interpretation or misinterpretation, whether due to a false theology or an imperfect knowledge of the original language, the force of the words remains, and a light of heavenly truth and love streams from them even now more than 2,500 years after they were first uttered.

BENJAMIN JOWETT,
quoted in *A Book of Jewish Thoughts*

I am convinced that the Bible becomes ever more beautiful the more it is understood.

JOHANN WOLFGANG GOETHE,
Wilhelm Meister's Travels

The Native Endowment Of Israel

The Greeks were not all artists, but the Greek nation was alone capable of producing a Phidias or a Praxiteles. The same was the case with Judaism. It is certain that not all Jews were Prophets ; the exclamation, "Would that all the people of the Lord were Prophets !" was a pious wish. Nevertheless, Israel is the people of Revelation. It must have had a native endowment that could produce, that could rear, such men. Nor does Judaism claim to be the work of single individuals ; it does not speak of the God of Moses, nor of the God of the Prophets, but of the God of Israel. The fact that the greatest Prophet left his work unfinished contains a profound truth. *No man knoweth of his sepulcher* unto this day. Thereon our ancient teachers remark : " His grave should not serve as a place of pilgrimage whither men go to do honor to one man, and thus raise him above the level of man."

ABRAHAM GEIGER,
Judaism and Its History

The Incomparable Grandeur Of Jerusalem

None of the resplendent names in history — Egypt, Athens, Rome — can compare in eternal grandeur with Jerusalem. For Israel has given to mankind the category of holiness. Israel alone has known the thirst for social justice, and that inner saintliness which is the source of justice.

CHARLES WAGNER

The Whisper Of God

The uniqueness of the spiritual heritage which is Israel's lies in the truth that no people or brotherhood was disinherited in order that Israel might become a people of inheritors. Truly Israel might say in the words of the poet, " Anybody might have heard it, but God's whisper came to me." Israel might more truly have said, " I followed after the whisper ; I pursued the gleam ; I claimed the heritage, when it promised, even as it became little more than a burden."

And the second peculiarity of the heritage is that, while material things which are inherited are often safeguarded from others, a spiritual heritage must be shared or else its ownership is made null and void. Israel is more truly the bestower of spiritual bounty than an inheritor. In many ways, the world has sought to belittle the priceless heritage of Israel. Sometimes this has been done through denying the validity and the value of the heritage. Again the inheritors have been assailed, even while the assailants coveted and, in truth, lived upon the bounty of the heritage whose possessors they condemned. And there was another way of doing hurt to the heritage and its trustees, namely, to claim and withal deny it at one and the same time, in some wise to alter it and then to reclaim it as something unknown and unique.

And what has been the effect of the heritage upon its possessors, upon the world ? In other words, what is the testimony to the value of the heritage on the part of its inheritors, on the part of them that would not share it and what has been its effect upon the moral and spiritual destinies of the human family ? That this legacy of Israel enriched them to whom it came cannot be gainsaid. If the prophets and the seers and the psalmists made Israel, it is not less true that Israel made it possible for its sons to become among the prophetic and visioning teachers of the world. The Old Testament is only the first of the chapters of an endless story of moral and spiritual courage to which they were ever equal who claimed and prized the heritage. And the world at its justest has not failed by a thousand voices, among the noblest voices of history to bear witness to what this heritage wrought for a God intoxicated people who held it high.

But an awful problem faces Israel in our own time. In the world of material possessions, a legal title is the equivalent of an imprescriptible charter, but in the world of spiritual things a legal title, if such a thing can be, does no more than prove the spiritual poverty of them that hold no other title than the title of possession or tradition.

The business of Israel is not to vaunt itself as the historical possessor of a priceless heritage but to live and serve and teach in the sight of all the world as becomes the bearers of a great name and of a glorious tradition. One of the great English teachers of the eighteenth century declared : " Happy, that while they lay down the rule, we can also produce the example." What shall it profit Israel, if its fathers have laid down the rule and we can no longer produce the example ? And this is not a matter of verbal testimony or of spirited self-defense or of generous bounty to the needy or of boastful affirmation touching the past. This is to live again as did our fathers, as seekers after God, doers of justice, ever fanatical for social righteousness, possessed of childlike purity of heart. Whether the heritage is to be carried on depends upon the life of the Jew today, here and everywhere ; upon the capacity of the individual Jew to give himself to those noble and consecrated ends of life which were the goal and the guerdon of the bequeathing Jew. And near be the day when it shall be said of us and of our children :

And nobleness walks in our ways again
And we have come into our heritage.

STEPHEN S. WISE,
As I See It

The Bible Dominates

From century to century, even unto this day, through the fairest regions of civilization, the Bible dominates existence. Its vision of life molds states and societies. Its Psalms are more popular in every country than the poems of the nation's own poets. Beside this one book with its infinite editions . . . all other literatures seem " trifles light as air."

ISRAEL ZANGWILL,
North American Review

The Book

The Bible, what a book ! Large and wide as the world, based on the abysses of creation, and peering aloft into the blue secrets of heaven ; sunrise and sunset, promise and fulfilment, birth and death, the whole drama of humanity are contained in this one book. It is the book of God. The Jews may readily be consoled at the loss of Jerusalem, and the Temple, and the Ark of the Covenant, and all the crown jewels of King Solomon. Such forfeiture is as naught when weighed against the Bible, the indestructible treasure that they had saved. That one book is to the Jews their country, their possessions — at once their ruler and their weal and woe. Within the well-fenced boundaries of that book they live and have their being ; they enjoy their alienable citizenship, are strong to admiration ; thence none can dislodge them. Absorbed in the perusal of their sacred book, they little heeded the changes that were wrought in the real world around them. Nations rose and vanished, states flourished and decayed, revolutions raged throughout the earth — but they, the Jews, sat poring over this book, unconscious of the wild chase of time that rushed on above their heads.

HEINRICH HEINE,
Ludwig Boerne

The Art Of Living Together

Throughout the ages, Judaism has been vitally concerned with the ethics of human relations. Possibly as a result of this preoccupation with the fundamentals of civilized living, the Jewish contribution to abstract philosophy, science, technique — not to mention art — has been modest. To be sure, standard works on the "Jewish Contribution to Civilization" adduce commendable evidence that Jews have contributed their due share to all departments and spheres of culture and civilization. But the fact remains that collectively the Jews have made only one truly great contribution : they have evolved the ethics of human relations and have taught mankind all that ever will, or can, be known, of the theory and the practice of the good life. Judaism has not excelled in the sensate realm of art and technique, but it has created single-handedly almost, the art of living together. Judaism has not inspired beautiful statues and imposing structures of architecture. In fact, it has been all but indifferent to the fine arts, for it has invariably concentrated its efforts and given its strength to the cultivation of the arts of peace and social justice.

TRUDE WEISS-ROSMARIN,
Jewish Survival

The Protection Of Humanity

The Hebrew commonwealth was based upon the individual — a commonwealth whose ideal it was that every man should sit under his own vine and fig-tree, with none to vex him or make him afraid ; a commonwealth in which none should be condemned to ceaseless toil ; in which for even the bond-slave there should be hope ; in which for even the beast of burden there should be rest. It is not the protection of property, but the protection of humanity, that is the aim of the Mosaic Code. Its Sabbath day and Sabbath year secure, even to the lowliest, rest and leisure. With the blasts of the jubilee trumpets the slave goes free, and a re-division of the land secures again to the poorest his fair share in the bounty of the common Creator. The reaper must leave something for the gleaner ; even the ox cannot be muzzled as he treadeth out the corn. Everywhere, in everything, the dominant idea is that of our homely phrase, "Live and let live."

HENRY GEORGE,
Moses

A quiet, dignified pride in the creative achievements of Jewish history is no ugly chauvinism. It is the only effective answer to the filth of the agitator.

ABRAM L. SACHAR

The Spirit Of The Prophets

In turning toward the Jewish Prophets, Humanity is not retrograding twenty-six centuries ; it is they who are twenty-six centuries in advance. The spirit of the Prophets is in the modern soul. Righteousness was to them an active force ; the idea was converted into a fact before which all other facts paled. The utterances of these old Prophets, though most ancient, remain young, and the new age has not found either among its philosophers, its moralists, or its poets, words with a magic equal to theirs ; in their speech is concentrated all the greatness of conscience and the ideal. They spread over the future, above the storms of the present the rainbow of a vast hope — a radiant vision of a better humanity.

JAMES DARMESTER,
Selected Essays

Yes, I am a Jew, and when the ancestors of the right honorable gentleman were brutal savages in an unknown island, mine were priests in the temple of Solomon.

BENJAMIN DISRAELI,
in reply to Daniel O'Connell

The Bulwark Against Cruelty And Idolatry

The Mosaic legislation aimed to constitute a free people, that shall be subject to no one but the Law ; and in order to insure that none would rob them of liberty, God Himself became law - giver, law-keeper, and king. He dwelt in the midst of His people ; and the much abused term " Temple " stood really for the House of the Code which the Lord guarded. The entire people was a priestly kingdom : every one was the servant of this King and His Law. " And ye shall be unto Me a kingdom of priests ! " (Exodus 19:6) was the cardinal principle according to which Moses conceived his legislation.

To the great spirit of Moses, to his legislation and covenant, we owe a series of excellent works in poetry, history, science and wisdom which no other people possessed. Prophets, sages, teachers, priests, even good kings followed in his footsteps. His theocratic code was the first bulwark against cruelty and idolatry, inhumanity and oppression, and likewise a nursery of the purest conceptions of God, of sublime hymns, psalms, precepts and doctrines. . . . How happy we would have been, if it were fulfilled completely !

J. G. HERDER,
Spirit of Hebrew Poetry

The Legacy Of Israel

The ethical monotheism of Israel is not the product of a natural development, but is a religion that has been *founded*. The " One God " of Israel is not the last word in an *old* way of thinking which has reached this particular stage, but rather the first word of a new way of thinking, a new logic, the moral logic. In so far as this form of religion is a creation, an entirely new and fruitful principle, we are entitled to call it historically — disregarding first of all every supernatural interpretation — a *revelation*, marking a new sunrise in the history of the world.

We may say this the more emphatically because it has remained an absolutely unique phenomenon. There is in the history of mankind nothing like it, nothing like the origin of monotheism as it was born in Israel, out of the moral consciousness and out of the moral imperative. Whether ,therefore, and in what form, it might have come into existence on different soil and in different circumstances is an idle question. Historically it is a fact that it was given to mankind through Israel and through Israel alone. It is not necessary to create and to construct it, for it stands as a real phenomenon, as a revelation before our eyes. . . .

Only in Israel did an ethical monotheism exist, and wherever else it is found later on, it has been derived directly or indirectly from Israel.

LEO BAECK,
The Essence of Judaism

The pursuit of knowledge for its own sake, an almost fanatical love of justice, and the desire for personal independence — these are the features of Jewish tradition which make me thank my stars that I belong to it.

ALBERT EINSTEIN,
The World As I See It

The Informed Jew

A dear friend of those years of the melting away of an illusion was a noble Jew, the late Rabbi Milton Steinberg. He made the point clearly when he said that Judaism must reject communism because communism is ready to sacrifice mercy to attain its ends. "For this is an integral part of the Communist program, that compassion must be suspended for a time. . . ." And to those who claimed that compassion would be reinstated when the classless society was achieved, he replied: "Judaism says of all such counsels that they overlook the crucial fact about man; that man is always pitiable, even man the capitalist, the Trotskyite, the *kulak*. Therefore there is not a time or occasion on which we are free not to pity him."

This element and the re-examination and rejection of the Marxist values led me to withdraw my sympathies from communism, political and philosophic. Of course, one does not sit down coldly and make an analysis and come to conclusions.

The dynamic events of the world intensify and clarify such decisions. For me, too, the break was broadened by an approach to Judaism and the Jewish people to which nowadays even Sunday-school seniors are exposed. I began to read the secular histories of my people. From the histories, I moved to the philosophers, the poets, the statesmen, the prophets, the commentators on the Bible, the Talmudists — all in a language I could understand. Slowly, terribly late, I began to shed the old illiteracy. And in becoming an informed Jew, I found that so interwoven are the semi-secular writings with our religious writings that any conscientious study of the meaning of the former must lead to some kind of attraction, if not affection, for the latter.

The way back to the synagogue can be taken by many roads, and there are many kinds of synagogues and many things to find in each. It is no great wisdom to perceive that God is not the property of the Jews.

(And I love the Jewish thinkers and scholars for saying this so clearly.) Once I was certain as to who God was and what He did. Now, I am not certain that I even understand what I mean when I say that I believe in Him. But one thing I know : He is no longer a God of Fear.

It was with quite understandable joy that after having found this out for myself, I discovered in Maimonides that the purpose of the biblical laws is to lead to the fear of God, and of the biblical truths to arouse love of Him. This love, as Maimonides suggests, depends on a knowledge of God and later becomes the decisive factor in man's relation to Him. (And, I would add, to man himself.)

We who followed other gods, even with all our good intentions, lost the simple knowledge of Micah : " To do justly, and to love mercy, and to walk humbly with thy God." It is particularly apt for our times to note that the commentary on this specific passage in the Chumesh as edited by Rabbi Hertz points out that the Hebrew for the phrase, " to do justly," literally translated means " to execute justice," implying reverence for the personality of every human being as the possessor, by virtue of his humanity, of inalienable rights to life, honor, and the fruit of his toil.

In the communion of Judaism, the identification with my people, my active affection for the Land of Israel, my faltering efforts to live by the precepts of the Prophets, I have found a peace of the spirit. They have combined in a set of values which do not have all the answers and perhaps are yet only barely perceptible to me. It is a way of life and understanding by which, as a human being, an American, a Jew and a writer, I can view with more meaning the world around me and the world within.

MICHAEL BLANKFORT,
The Education of a Jew

The Sun Of The Bible

We must not forget that the Sun of Homer, to use Schiller's well known phrase, smiles only upon the fortunate few who enjoy life's eternal graces, whereas the Sun of the Bible penetrates into the proudest palaces and the humblest shanties ; that the Sun of Homer smiles, spreading a bewitchingly beautiful glimmer over the surface of life, whereas the Sun of the Bible radiates warmth and strength, and has called into being a system of morality, which has become the corner-stone of human civilization.

ISRAEL FRIEDLANDER,
Past and Present

Antiquity And Continuity

Next to the selection that has been in operation for centuries, it is, in my opinion, the antiquity and the continuity of their civilization that throws some light upon the Jews as well as upon the place they occupy in our midst. They were here before us ; they are our elders. Their children were taught to read from the scrolls of the Torah before our Latin alphabet had reached its final form, long before Cyrillus and Methodius had given writing to the Slavs, and before the Runic characters were known to the Germans of the North. As compared with the Jews, we are young, we are newcomers ; in the matter of civilization they are far ahead of us. It was in vain that we locked them up for several hundred years behind the walls of the Ghetto. No sooner were their prison gates unbarred than they easily caught up with us, even on those paths which we had opened up without their aid.

ANATOLE LEROY-BEAULIEU,
Israel Among the Nations

Recently at a public banquet I happened to sit next to a lady who tried to impress me by letting me know that one of her ancestors witnessed the signing of the Declaration of Independence. I could not resist replying ; " Mine were present at the Giving of the Ten Commandments."

STEPHEN S. WISE

Custodians Of The Divine Secrets

The truth is that the Jews were the only people who, from the very beginning, knew God, the Creator of the heavens and the earth ; the only people, consequently, that could be the custodian of the divine secrets, and it preserved them in a religion that is without equal. The books which the Egyptians and the other nations called divine, have long since been lost, and there scarcely remains a hazy memory of them in ancient histories. The sacred books of the Romans, in which Numa, the author of their religion, wrote down the mysteries, perished at the hands of the Romans themselves. The Senate had them burned, believing that they might overturn religion. These same Romans destroyed finally the Sibylline books, long revered among them as prophetic. They had wished the people to believe that these books contained the decrees of the immortal gods concerning their Empire, but they never perhaps showed in public, I do not say a single volume, but a single oracle. The Jews were the only ones whose sacred Scriptures were held in ever greater veneration as they became better known.

JACQUES BENIGNE BOSSUET,
Discours Sur L'Histoire Universelle

Sublimity is Hebrew by birth.

SAMUEL T. COLERIDGE,
Table Talk

The Healing Jew

This bit from *The Nation* caught my eye. Just think of it, in medicine alone how much we owe to the men of a single race! And so far as I know not one of these men is an American:

" A Nazi with heart disease must not use digitalis, discovered by a Jew, Ludwig Traube. If he has a toothache, a Nazi will not use cocaine, or he will be using the work of a Jew, Solomon Stricker. Nor will he be treated for typhus by the discoveries of the Jews, Widall and Weill. If he has diabetes, he must not use insulin, the discovery of a Jew, Mikowsky. If he has a headache, he must shun pyramidon and antipyrin, discovered by Jews, Spiro and Eilege. Nazis with convulsions must avoid chloral hydrate, the discovery of a Jew, Oslar Liabreich."

JUSTUS TIMBERLINE,
Knight's Master Book of New Illustrations

The pure religion which we dream of as the bond that shall in days to come hold together the whole of mankind in one communion, will be the realization of the religion of Isaiah, the ideal Jewish religion, freed from all admixture of impurity.

ERNEST T. RENAN.

The Bible

Is it a book, a world, a heaven ?
Are those words, or flames, or
    shining stars,
Or burning torches, or clouds of fire
What is it, I ask ye — the Bible ?

Who inspired those infinite truths ?
Who spoke through the mouth of
    the prophet ?
Who mapped out the highways of
    ages,

The glorious lines of the Scriptures ?

Who planted the flowers of wisdom
In this sacred soil of the angels ?
O dream of eternity — Bible —
O Light that is all and forever.

MORRIS ROSENFELD

The greatest poem of all time — the history of the Jews.

J. G. HERDER

To What May Judaism Be Compared?

Countless are the figures under which Judaism appears in the Bible and the writings of the sages. Now it is compared to water, because it cleanses men from what is animal and low, and dulls and cools the passions; and now to wine, because time cannot injure it, nay, it increases in power with advancing age; to oil, because it mixes not with foreign elements, preserving ever its distinctiveness; to honey, because it is sweet and lovely, free from religious hatred; to a wall, because it protects its professors from the violence of the wicked; to manna, because it proclaims human equality before God, and asserts His justice; and lastly it is compared to a crown, because it invests every son of earth with sovereignty, and raises him higher than all nature.

ADOLF A. JELLINEK

The Bible is our patent of nobility.

SOLOMON SCHECHTER,
Seminary Addresses

World's Debt To Israel

We Gentiles owe our life to Israel. It is Israel who has brought us the message that God is one, and that God is a just and righteous God, and demands righteousness of his children, and demands nothing else. It is Israel that has brought us the message that God is our Father. It is Israel who, in bringing us the divine law, has laid the foundation of liberty. It is Israel who had the first free institutions the world ever saw. It is Israel who has brought us our Bible, our Prophets, our apostles. When sometimes our own unchristian prejudices flame out against the Jewish people, let us remember that all that we have and all that we are we owe, under God, to what Judaism has given us.

LYMAN ABBOTT

The Bible, that great medicine chest of humanity.

HEINRICH HEINE,
Ludwig Marcus

No Reply

Not long ago I was reading the Sermon on the Mount with a rabbi. At nearly each verse he showed me very similar passages in the Hebrew Bible and Talmud. When we reached the words, " Resist not evil," he did not say, "This too is in the Talmud," but asked, with a smile, "Do the Christians obey this command?" I had nothing to say in reply, especially as at that particular time, Christians, far from turning the other cheek, were smiting the Jews on both cheeks.

LEO TOLSTOY,
My Religion

The Prophet Of Mankind

The whole history of humanity has produced nothing which can be compared in the remotest degree to the prophecy of Israel. Through prophecy Israel became the prophet of mankind. Let this never be overlooked nor forgotten : the costliest and noblest treasure that man possesses he owes to Israel and to Israelitic prophecy.

CARL HEINRICH CORNILL,
Prophets of Israel

The Universal Wisdom

In my early youth I read — I have forgotten where — the words of the ancient Jewish sage — Hillel, if I remember rightly : " If thou are not for thyself, who will be for thee ? But if thou art for thyself alone, wherefore art thou ? "

The inner meaning of these words impressed me with its profound wisdom, and I interpreted them for myself in this manner: I must actively take care of myself, that my life should be better, and I must not impose the care of myself on other people's shoulders ; but if I am going to take care of myself alone, of nothing but my own personal life, it will be useless, ugly, meaningless. This thought ate its way deep into my soul, and I say now with conviction : Hillel's wisdom served as a strong staff on my road, which was neither even nor easy.

I believe that Jewish wisdom is more all-human and universal than any other ; and this not only because of its immemorial age, not only because it is the first born, but also because of the powerful humaneness that saturates it, because of its high estimate of man.

MAXIM GORKY

Among Jews a great civilization of the heart has persisted through two thousand years as an uninterrupted tradition. They have been able to play so great a part in European culture because they have had so little to learn by way of feeling, and needed only to acquire knowledge.

HEINRICH HEINE

Our Great Claim To Mankind's Gratitude

Our great claim to the gratitude of mankind is that we gave to the world the word of God, the Bible. We stormed heaven to snatch down this heavenly gift, as the Puritanic expression is ; we threw ourselves into the breach and covered it with our bodies against every attack ; we allowed ourselves to be slain by hundreds and thousands rather than become unfaithful to it ; and bore witness to its truth and watched over its purity in the face of a hostile world.

SOLOMON SCHECHTER,
Seminary Address

Christianity's Debt To Judaism

In speaking to you this morning, I have two very definite propositions in mind. One is the proposition that Christianity owes a heavy debt to Judaism. The other is the proposition that Christianity ought to be willing to recognize and pay this debt, as any honorable debtor recognizes and pays his obligation.

Christianity — it should be known, is in reality Jewish in origin and content. It is only an accident that it did not remain in the end what it was in the beginning — a part and parcel of the Jewish world. Now that it is one of the separate religions of mankind, its parentage should be confessed, and its heritage duly honored.

Let me begin what I have to say this morning with Jesus. . . . In the first place, I would remind you that Jesus' parents were Jews. The second fact is, of course, that Jesus, as the oldest child of these parents, was thus himself a Jew. . . .

If we know anything about Jesus at all, it is that he was a child of Jewish parents, born in a Jewish home as the first-born of a large family, and thus himself a Jew.

The third thing to be said about the Jewishness of Jesus is that he was reared and trained in the Jewish faith. His parents were pious Jews ; they went up each year to Jerusalem to keep the feast of the Passover ! They taught Jesus, by precept and example, to attend the synagogue where he became acquainted with the Bible of his race. In his early manhood, it was his custom to go to the synagogue on the Sabbath day, which is more than a good many Jews do today ; and he began his public ministry, so the record tells us, by standing up in the synagogue in Nazareth and reading from the Prophet Isaiah. In spirit as well as in blood, this Nazarene was a son of Israel.

It is from these three points of view — his parents, his birth, and his religious training — that we must agree that Jesus was a Jew. It is to the Jews that the Christians owe this peerless leader and founder of their faith. . . .

So much for Jesus! Next only to this august figure of the Nazarene stand three elements which are central in Christianity. For all these three elements the Christians are indebted to the Jews.

In the first place, there is the Bible, the sacred scriptures of the Christian Church. This Bible consists of two parts — the Old Testament, so called, and the New. The Old Testament, which comprises some three-fourths of the Bible, belongs not to Christianity at all, but to Judaism. The Old Testament, let it be said is the Jewish Bible! I know of no more high-handed piece of impudence in all history than the action of the early Christians in taking over the Old Testament into their churches, and saying: "This is ours!" It is as though we Americans should possess ourselves of Shakespeare and Milton, and Dryden, and Poe, and Keats, and Shelley, and Tennyson, and Browning, and solemnly declare that the writings of these men belong to us and were the basic part of our native literature. Saying so, of course, does not make it so! These poets are not Americans — and, by the same token, the Old Testament is not Christian. It is Jewish through and through; and whenever we use it we should remember that we are turning to Jewish sources for instruction and

inspiration. That is the reason why I am careful in our services here to refer to the Old Testament, whenever I read lessons from its text, as "the Scriptures of the Jews." As for the New Testament, this is our own. This portion of the Bible is "the Scriptures of the Christians." But even so, it is only fair to recognize, it seems to me, that the New Testament is throughout a Jewish book. Every word of it, from the first chapter of Matthew to the last chapter of Revelation, was written by Jews, and thus is saturated with the Jewish spirit and ideals.

Next to the Bible comes the church — by which I mean not the hierarchy, which belongs to a later period of history, but the simple fact of the congregation of men and women meeting together on a Sunday morning for the worship of Almighty God. Where did this reality come from? Why, from the Jews — more specifically from that generation of Jews which suffered the tragic experience of the Exile. . . .

Jesus knew the synagogue of Nazareth from his youth up, and in this synagogue began his ministry. When, following his death, his followers carried on his work, it was first in synagogues, and only later in churches of their own, that they proclaimed the Gospel.

But these churches, when they came, were modeled precisely on Jewish example, and thus were the daughters of the synagogue. When Christians meet today on Sunday mornings to worship God and to consecrate their lives to his service, and to preserve the sacred traditions of the faith, they are doing not only what the early Christians did, but what the Jews have done since the sad days of the Exile. We have a church because the Jews first had a synagogue. The former is the direct descendant of the latter.

This brings us directly to the third of these essential elements of Christianity. In addition to the Bible and the church is Sunday as the sacred day of rest and worship — the one day in seven set scrupulously aside for purposes of physical recreation and spiritual regeneration. Where did this Christian Sunday come from? Why, obviously, from the Jewish Sabbath.

It is true that the Jewish Sabbath is the last day of the week — traditionally the day when God rested from his labors after the six days of the creation. " And on the seventh day God ended his work which he had made " (Genesis 2 : 2). The Christian Sunday, in contrast, is the first day of the week, so celebrated because it was on this first day that Jesus is supposed to have risen from the dead. . . .

So the first day among Christians came to take the place of the seventh day among Jews. But this detail is unimportant. The central fact is that the Christian Sunday is the rebirth of the Jewish Sabbath — the Christian once again taking his religious practices from the Jew !

We are beginning now, perhaps, to understand how stupendous is the debt which Christians owe to Jews. Not only Jesus himself, but the Bible, the church, and Sunday all come from Jewish sources. But not yet have we gotten to the heart of the matter. What about the teachings of Christianity — those great truths of the moral and spiritual life which constitute the essence of the Gospel? The things which Jesus taught — were those original with him, or did they spring from the Judaism in which Jesus was born and reared ?

This question reminds me of an experience in the early days of my ministry in this city. I was attending a meeting of the Liberal Ministers Club of which certain Jewish rabbis were members along with the Christian clergymen. I chanced to be sitting beside a very eminent rabbi of that day — the head of the great Temple Emanuel. In the course of our conversation together, I made some reference to what I called " the originality of Jesus." What was my surprise to hear this rabbi retort that there was no originality in Jesus — that the Nazarene was one of the most unoriginal men who ever lived. As a young and ardent preacher, I was greatly shocked by this remark. In late years, however, I came to feel that my friend, the rabbi, was on the whole correct. It is true that Jesus was original in what he said — or rather in the way he said it. . . !

But in the actual content of his teaching, Jesus was not original. The substance of his faith and vision was all derived from Israel! Let me see if I can make this plain:

On New Year's Day, a civic ceremony was conducted at the City Hall by Mayor LaGuardia, in which a Catholic priest, a Protestant clergyman and a Jewish rabbi were the participants. In the course of his remarks, the Mayor referred to the Golden Rule and the Lord's Prayer, and said that if men would only live up to the precepts of these two teachings, there would be no trouble in the world. It would seem as though, in this reference, the Mayor was flattering the Christians and leaving out the Jews. As a matter of fact, he could not have made a better selection, for the Golden Rule and the Lord's Prayer belong quite as much to the Jews as to the Christians themselves. . . .

The Golden Rule, as it appears in the New Testament, is familiar: "All things whatsoever ye would that men should do to you, do ye even so to them, for this is the law and the prophets." The Jewish Golden Rule is negative rather than positive in its formulation, but is identical in meaning. It reads: "Whatever ye do not wish your neighbor to do to you, do not do unto him. This is the whole law, the rest is exposition."

But the Lord's Prayer—this surely is original with Jesus! So it is in its formulation into one of the simplest and most beautiful compositions that can be found in the world's religious literature. But in its content it is derived from beginning to end from Jewish sources. There is not a line in the prayer which cannot be duplicated in these sources. In substantiation of this sweeping assertion, let me cite the testimony of two scholars who have a right to speak, as I do not. The first is a famous German authority, Theodor Keim, whose biography of Jesus, written many years ago, still ranks as one of the greatest studies ever made of the life and teaching of the Nazarene. Referring to the Lord's Prayer, Keim writes: "Not only the address of God, together with the first two petitions, but pretty well all of it in detail, appears here and there in Jewish Talmudic prayers." The second witness is a great Jewish scholar, Joseph Klausner, of the Hebrew University in Jerusalem, whose "Jesus of Nazareth" is regarded as the ablest biography of Jesus ever written by a Jew. In this authoritative work the author says of the Lord's Prayer that it is "a remarkable prayer, universal in its appeal, earnest, brief and full of devotion. Every single clause in it, however, is to be found in Jewish prayers and sayings in the Talmud." So the Golden Rule and the Lord's Prayer alike belong to Jews as well as Christians.

Next only to these two documents, I would name the Beatitudes as the most precious sayings to be found in the Christian Scriptures. Here again we have a formulation of truth which is a supreme illustration of Jesus' poetic and spiritual genius, But the content of what is said is again almost wholly derivative. " Blessed are they that mourn for they shall be comforted " — if you would know where this comes from, turn to Isaiah 61 : 2. " Blessed are the meek, for they shall inherit the earth " — turn to Psalm 37 :11. " Blessed are they that hunger and thirst after righteousness, for they shall be filled " — turn to Isaiah 55 :1. " Blessed are the pure in heart, for they shall see God " — turn to Psalm 24 : 4. Thus are the phrases and thoughts of this great passage all anticipated by the Jews.

If any statement of Jesus is commonly cited as the complete and perfect summary of his religion, it is the dual commandment : " Thou shalt love the Lord thy God, with all thy heart, and with all thy soul, and with all thy strength, and with all thy mind ; and thy neighbor as thyself." Where does this come from ? First of all, from the New Testament story of the lawyer who tempted Jesus, saying : " What shall I do to inherit eternal life ? " But originally from the Old Testament, in two famous passages. The first is from Deuteronomy 6 : 4 : " Hear, O Israel, the Lord thy God is one Lord ; and thou shalt love the Lord thy God with all thy soul, and with all thy might." The second is from Leviticus 19 : 18 : " Thou shall not

take vengeance, nor bear any grudge . . . but thou shalt love thy neighbor as thyself. . . . "

If I were asked to name the most beautiful expression of Jesus' teaching on this point, I would turn to St. Paul's great Epistle to the Romans, and read the closing verses of the twelfth chapter : " If thine enemy hunger, feed him ; if he thirst, give him drink ; for in so doing thou shalt heap coals of fire upon his head. Be not overcome of evil, but overcome evil with good." If there is anything original in Christianity, this would certainly seem to be it. Yet turn to the twenty-fifth chapter of the Book of Proverbs, the twenty-first verse, and what do you find ? " If thine enemy be hungry, give him bread to eat ; and if he be thirsty, give him water to drink, for thou wilt heap coals of fire upon his head." Even in his teaching of love, for enemies as well as friends, Jesus was only faithful to the noblest precepts of the Jews !

All of this shows what Jesus was really doing in his ministry. Not practicing a new religion, but reviving the pure and undefiled religion of Israel ! Not starting a movement of revolt against Judaism, but only a movement of reform inside of Judaism ! Not forsaking the Jewish synagogue, even as he cleansed the Temple of the money - changers ! Nothing would have surprised Jesus more than to have learned after his death that his work had led to a new religion largely hostile to his own. To this day he would not have understood the meaning Christianity and Christian doctrine. Jesus was a Jew, in the great traditions of the Prophets. . . .

He was teaching what was truest and noblest in the tradition of his own people. He sought for nothing but the restoration of Israel to its true faith. What wonder therefore that he was not original, since he did not seek to be original ? " Think not that I am come," he said, " to destroy the law or the Prophets ! I am come not to destroy but to fulfill. For verily I say unto you : Till heaven and earth pass, one jot or one title shall in no wise pass from the law, till all be fulfilled." Here was not a Christian speaking, but a Jew. All that was distinctively Christian came later and was unknown to the Nazarene.

Such is the debt which Christianity owes to Judaism ! Not Jesus merely, nor the Bible, the church and the Sunday, but the whole substance of Christian teaching ! To take account of this debt is to come face to face with two facts, which I would emphasize in closing :

First, we find here one explanation at least, and a very important one, of why the Christians dislike and persecute the Jews. They hate them and would get rid of them because they are so heavily indebted to them. This is a simple law of psychology, illustrated by the experience of every day. Thus, did you ever hear of a tenant who loved

his landlord ? Have you ever encountered a borrower who is devoted to the money-lender who has given him money ? How often do you see a taxpayer who folds in his affectionate embrace the tax-collector ? The publicans in ancient Israel were hated for nothing except that it was their business to receive the taxes for the government. And now the burden has fallen upon the Jews — that they have given so much to the Christians that the latter feel embarrassed and at least outraged that they owe all this to Israel ! There are many reasons for anti-Semitism — for tortures and massacres, the pogroms and exiles, which the Jews have suffered all these centuries from Christendom. The problem is complicated and difficult — the pattern hopelessly entangled. But one strand in the snarl may be unraveled, and that is the one which has to do with the Christian's debt to Judaism. Until that debt is paid, or at least acknowledged, there will be little peace.

The second thing which I would emphasize is this payment of the debt. Is it not time that payment began ? And how shall it be done ?

First, the debt must be acknowledged, somewhat as I have tried to acknowledge it this morning. Why should not Christians everywhere recognize Jesus as a Jew ? Why should they not have the grace to refer to the Old Testament, when they use it, as the Jewish scriptures ? Why should they not acclaim the kinship of the church with the syna-gogue, and of the Christian Sunday with the Jewish Sabbath ? As for the Gospel, what would be lost and what not gained, if the Jewish sources of this teaching were at last made plain ? All this is not very much, perhaps, in the serious busi-ness of paying a heavy debt, but it is at least something. A first step is taken in discharging an obligation when it is acknowledged that it exists.

Secondly, why may we not pay this debt to the Jews by fighting anti-Semitism ? All around us rages this noisome and fatal plague. It works its havoc not merely in Germany and Europe, but right here in America. Half-hidden, half-confessed, whispered rather than shouted, taking shape not in hideous persecutions but in countless little irritations and injustices, but none the less fatal as a prejudice which poisons the soul, this curse is our curse, and it should be ended for very shame. Here the church, in the very name of Jesus, should take the lead in stamping out this pestilence that devours ourselves as well as our victims. To fight and destroy anti-Semitism — this would be a large payment on the debt.

Lastly, as a means of paying Christianity's debt to Judaism, there is the opportunity now abundantly given us to succor the Jewish refugees who wander the world in misery. Christianity has already done much for these refugees. The Catholics and Protestants of Ger-many and the occupied countries have lifted up their voices in protest against the Nazi horrors, and on more than one occasion have identi-fied themselves with those who suffered. In England and in this country have Christians given generously in relief, and offered shelter and sustenance to the home-less hordes of Israel. But all that we have done is little enough. More — more, is needed, until every Jew the world around has found home and country once again, his place in the great body of humanity. To succor the Jews in this their hour of greater distress than they have endured since Jerusalem fell to Titus, this is our plain duty. And it should be our welcome opportunity to discharge the debt which all too long has gone unpaid.

To bring Jews and Christians together, not by converting or merg-ing one with the other, but by recognition of that spiritual kinship which makes them one — this is our holy task. To end the injustice and horror of the ages in finding and binding that "unity of the spirit which is the bond of peace!" Already Jews and Christians are one in all that is central to the inner essence of our faith. Why should we not similarly be one in all that is central to the outer relations of our lives ? In both branches of the severed family there rests the obli-gation to shake off separatism and end isolation — but most heavily and immediately does this obligation rest upon Christians, who have the numbers, the power — and this debt which must be paid!

I keep thinking, as I talk to you, of that great scene in Lessing's drama, *Nathan der Weise (Nathan the Wise)*, which touches upon this truth. Some of you may have seen this drama when it was produced in New York this past winter. If so, you will remember the scene to which I refer — that scene where the Christian Friar has just discovered some great deed of generosity and sacrifice which has been performed by the Jew, Nathan. In his enthusi-asm and gratitude, and desiring to honor Nathan with the greatest praise that he knows how to speak, the Friar exclaims :

"Nathan, you are a Christian. Yes, I swear
You are a Christian — better never lived."

To which the big-hearted and wise Nathan replies :

"Indeed! The very thing that makes me seem Christian to you, makes a Jew to me."

JOHN HAYNES HOLMES,
Sermon preached at the Community Church

12

Comfort in Sorrow

Yea though I walk through the valley of the shadow of death, I fear no evil for thou art with me.

Psalms 23 : 4

Refrain thy voice from weeping and thine eyes from tears. . . . For there is hope for thy future.

Jeremiah 31 : 15, 16

Magnified and sanctified be His great Name in the world which He hath created according to His will.

The Kaddish

The Goal Of Life

The religion of Judaism can teach us . . . how to understand the goal of life in the presence of mortality. That goal is that we should create a pattern that will be a blessing and inspiration to those who come after us. When we die, those who have been touched and illumined by the flame of our being should rejoice to think of us with joyous reminiscence.

We can face death nobly when we resolve so to live and to work in the years allotted to us that no one shall cry in frustration or anger when we have gone, that no one shall silently curse the day of our birth but rather that they shall recall our day upon earth in the concert hall of memory and shall laugh, with the overbrimming joy that a dear one walked the earth bravely and lovingly once upon a time.

The thought of death need not fill us with dark and despairing anxiety but rather with a creative determination to be for the little world of which we are a part the center of the target toward which all the archers shall send the arrows of their aspiration, to be the oak tree, tall and stately, in the shelter of whose branches the young can sit and play and the old can find shade from the heat of the day. Let us live in such a way that our spirit shall be the rain causing the soil of other souls to grow moist and verdant, to be the sunlight making chlorophyll in the filigree leaves of other hearts and other minds, to be the star, the guiding North Star, by which the mariners and the navigators in our family and in our circle of friends can set their compass across the uncharted sea of being. This is the goal of life, so to live that men shall rehearse the story of our being with inspiration and with deep gratitude that we have walked the earth rejoicing to tell of our strong youth, the manliness of our maturity, the wisdom of our old age. Then indeed our memory shall be a blessing.

JOSHUA LOTH LIEBMAN,
Sermon, " Message of Israel "

Light In Darkness

The first time that Adam saw the sun go down and an ever-deepening gloom enfold creation, his mind was filled with terror. God then took pity on him, and endowed him with the divine intuition to take two stones —the name of one was Darkness and the name of the other Shadow of Death — and rub them against each other, and to discover fire. Thereupon Adam exclaimed with grateful joy : "Blessed be the Creator of Light."

Talmud, Avodah Zorah, 8b

We May Trust In His Love

The hope of immortality is the strength of our life on earth. Whenever we yield to the fear that our earthly labor will some day cease forever, we lose the courage to overcome circumstance, and lack the will to resist failure. If our toil is but for a day, we cannot build. But if, as our sages assure us, we may labor on beyond the accident of death into eternity, then no failure is irreparable, no task is too great. When we may include infinity in our plans then no aim is unattainable, no vision is too exalted.

We tend to doubt our immortality whenever life defeats us. When our plans go awry and our efforts fail, when friends disappoint and solitude grows bitter, then our strength seems to vanish, a sense of our frailty overpowers us and there comes the dread that all our hopes will soon be quenched in an eternal darkness. Our disappointments and our discouragements engender the fear that our life will end in a final defeat and the grave will win its ultimate victory. The terror of death grows from our failures in life.

Yet when each morning dawns and our strength is renewed, when our efforts succeed and the spirit of God, calling to our souls, reveals our innate divinity, then our life again seems triumphant and indestructible. Hope revives and we see our spirit entering, beyond the grave, into the gateway of greater life. Death loses its sting and the grave its victory. When life is strong we foresee our immortality.

We are poised between despair and hope. Each day our failures bring the terror of the grave and our victories bring intimations of immortality. We have ever before us both life and death. It is for us to choose the hope of life eternal ; to depart from fear and to be strong in faith ; to assert to our failing hearts that we shall not die, but live, and declare forever the wonders of God.

Our hopes are not delusions, for God is just and merciful. He would not bid us toil in His name, and then deny us the joy of completing our work. He would not bid us prepare in this ante-chamber of eternity, and then close against us the doors of His eternal halls. Since His mercies endure forever, He would not bid us sow in tears, without permitting us to reap in joy. We may trust in His love. We have known bereavement and the pain of death. He will comfort us. He will destroy death forever and wipe the tears from every face. Though the cords of death encompass us, we will yet walk before Him in " the land of the living."

Blessings and Praise

Death Cannot Be The End Of Life

Death cannot be and is not the end of life. Man transcends death in many altogether naturalistic fashions. He may be immortal biologically, through his children, in thought through the survival of his memory; in influence, by virtue of the continuance of his personality as a force among those who come after him, and, ideally, through his identification with the timeless things of the spirit.

When Judaism speaks of immortality it has in mind all these. But its primary meaning is that man contains something independent of the flesh and surviving it; his consciousness and moral capacity; his essential personality; a soul.

MILTON STEINBERG, *Basic Judaism*

Evil Can Be Converted Into Good

Sorrow is as much a part of life as is joy. To live is to suffer as well as to rejoice. Sorrow cannot be avoided; it can only be conquered . . . .

One of the great teachers of Israel, recognizing the inevitability of sorrow and reconciling himself to it, adopted as the maxim of his life the famous phrase, "This also for Good." His maxim has become a vital, necessary part of the religious philosophy and program of Israel throughout the ages — yea, of every Jew; sometimes it is his only source of salvation. It teaches that every experience of man may be of value, that even as the darkness eventually changes into light, so evil may be converted ultimately into good.

LOUIS BINSTOCK

Who Has Lived?

"And Jacob lived" (Genesis 47: 28). Of how few men, asks a famous modern Jewish preacher, can we repeat a phrase like, "And Jacob lived?" When many a man dies, a death-notice appears in the Press. In reality, it is a life-notice; because but for it, the world would never have known that that man had ever been alive. Only he who has been a force for human goodness, and abides in hearts and souls made better by his presence during his pilgrimage on earth, can be said to have *lived*, only such a one is heir to immortality.

JOSEPH H. HERTZ,
The Pentateuch and Haftorahs

God Is Trustworthy

The doctrine of the immortality of the Soul is an integral part of the Jewish creed. It is more; it is a necessary ingredient of every consistent religious creed. It follows as the logical sequel to the very belief in God. One of the most elementary qualities that we associate with the Supreme is His trustworthiness; He will not willfully deceive His creatures. To believe in God is to believe not only in His existence, but also in His faithfulness. He must needs be true to His word, to His promise. " God is not a man that He should lie." This persuasion of the Divine trustworthiness is an instinct of the human mind. We cherish, for example, the profound conviction that the alternation of day and night and the sequence of the seasons will never be broken. It is a conviction which is shared and acted upon by every scientific thinker. And, taking the shape of religious faith, it marks the attitude of the believer toward spiritual things. The moral universe, he holds, is as trustworthy as the physical. Just as God will always fulfil our expectations of an unbroken alternation of day and night, of heat and cold, so He will fulfil those higher expectations which are sown, as part of its very nature, in every human soul. The Prophet of old seems to have taught this truth : "Thus saith the Lord, If ye can break My covenant of the day, and My covenant of the night, so that there should not be day and night in their season ; then may also My covenant be broken with David My servant." If God fulfils His word written in natural law, He may clearly be trusted to fulfil the promise He has written deep in the human heart.

The presentiment of immortality is one of those promises. An invincible instinct bids us :

Trust that good shall fall
At last, far off, at last, to all,
And every winter change to spring.

And this presentiment is universal. It is part of man's very nature to think of his real self as soul, and to think of that soul as imperishable. Experience joins forces with this intuition. Few of us can contemplate this earthly life without a painful recognition of its incompleteness. " This cannot be the end," we cry ; " the disproportion between means and results is too palpable. God cannot possibly have placed us here to suffer, to battle with evil, only to fling us away like an outworn garment, to cast us 'as rubbish to the void,' when our short race is run." And the inadequateness of this life constitutes the clearest promise of another. The mind oppressed by the sorrows, the vanity of this earthly existence, finds relief in the vision of a heavenly state. The problems that vex us here will be fully solved hereafter ; eternity will explain this brief life. This is the wondrous music which we wring from the jarring notes of the world's pain and sin. In it God speaks to us. It is His promise to us, His promise of immortality. And that promise He will fulfil, nay, must fulfil; for He is God.

Moreover the aspiration after goodness foreshadows a larger life in which to realize it. This, too, is a Divine promise which will assuredly be redeemed. . . . These germs of goodness in the human soul, we say, must come to ripening at last. Retarded and stunted in this inhospitable atmosphere, they will expand and thrive in a more congenial clime. Goodness has a nobler destiny than defeat. God has not taught us to dream of success, only to deceive us. Somewhere and somehow our noblest visions will be fulfilled. God will be true to His promise; He will be true to Himself.

That matter and spirit are distinct is proved by actual facts. As old age creeps over us the bodily powers gradually decay, but the higher faculties of the soul are untouched. Physical vigor is impaired; the senses are dulled; the mental flame burns low. But there is a spiritual residuum which seems beyond the reach of the destroyer. Reverence for duty lives on with undiminished strength to the last; the ideal retains its loveliness and its sanctity; and a dying mother's love is as tender and beautiful as it was years ago when she first pressed her child to her bosom.

It is such considerations as these that lend support to the doctrine of Immortality laid down by religion. The flesh is but the garment of the soul; the garment decays and perishes, but the soul lives on. Death is not the cessation of life, but an incident in it. It is but the "narrows," to use the Psalmist's striking expression, through which the soul passes on its fateful voyage. But though straiter than the river of this earthly life, they open at length into a boundless sea. Coming from God, the soul must eventually go back to Him. This is the Israelite's belief, and he gives expression to it in the beautiful prayer which he repeats every morning soon after awaking from his sleep; for sleep, the type of death, foreshadows, as it vanishes, the momentous passage of the soul into the life hereafter. "O God," so the prayer runs, "the soul which Thou hast set within me is pure. Thou hast fashioned it; Thou hast breathed it into me, and Thou dost keep it within me. And Thou wilt take it from me, and restore it to me in time to come. As long as it is within me I will give humble homage to Thee, O Divine Master, Lord of all spirits, who givest back the soul to the dead."

MORRIS JOSEPH,
Judaism as Creed and Life

We Are Not Alone

There are sorrows whose roots the sympathy of the best friends cannot reach. There are burdens that be so low that no other human being can help to lift or bear them. There are some among men, who in their grief shun the company of their fellows, their wounds too raw even for a friendly touch. What must it mean in such cases and to such people to know and to feel that One not man is there with a sympathy silent but how tender! With a balm unseen but how healing. One to whom a heart can pour out its torrents of bitterness without words. A Friend with the tenderness of a mother, with a healing knowledge, and power how healing.

I. I. MATTUCK

The Fox And The Grapes

A hungry fox was eyeing some luscious fruit in a garden, but to his dismay, he could find no way to enter. At last he discovered an opening through which, he thought, he might possibly get in, but he soon found that the hole was too small to admit his body. "Well," he thought, "if I fast three days I will be able to squeeze through." He did so; and he now feasted to his heart's delight on the grapes and all the other good things in the orchard. But lo! when he wanted to escape before the owner of the garden would find him, he discovered to his great distress, that the opening had again become too small for him. Poor animal! Again he had to fast three days, and as he escaped, he cast a farewell glance upon the scene of his late revels saying: "O garden, charming art thou, delicious are thy fruits! But what have I now for all my labor and cunning?"

So it is with man. Naked he comes into the world, naked must he leave it. After all his toil therein he carries nothing away with him except the good deeds he leaves behind.

Midrash, Koheleth Rabbab 5: 1

A Meditation On Affliction

The Psalmist recalls the somber days of his affliction, the sudden disaster, the dazed heart heavy with grief, then the gradual healing of the wounded spirit, the chastened soul, the deepened understanding, and the blessed sense of God's comfort and mercy. All this he recalls and praises the Lord: "It is good that Thou hast afflicted me, for thus have I learned Thy statutes."

When we live at ease we sail carelessly over the surface of life unaware of its deeper undercurrents.

Then calamity overtakes us, and, in the struggle with the waves, we learn how precious is life, how deep is pain, how boundless our gratitude to our Deliverer and Preserver. God brings us to the very gates of death, in order that we may learn, manfully, how to choose life.

It is not only our own affliction which brings us blessing. Our fellow men suffer for our benefit. From their tragedies we learn how to avoid misfortune. Even the material comforts of our life are largely due to the suffering of those who lived before us. The houses in which we live, the fuel we burn, the streets we traverse, all have a history of toil, suffering, danger, and even death. The musician who delights us with his art, the teacher who brings light to our minds, the physician who rescues us from pain, all have endured years of self-denial, toil and trouble. We live by the sufferings of the mother who bore us and the parents who reared us. The beautiful lives which inspire us have been wrought in the furnace of affliction. The call comes to all of us to bless as we have been blessed ; to accept our share of this interblend of pain and benefit. We who profit by the vast linkage of human woe and weal cannot refuse the burden of pain.

We must patiently accept the daily restraints of conscience, and walk the arduous way of virtue. Perhaps others may profit by our strivings and find in our humble lives a blessing.

Blessings and Praise

The Chastisements Of Love

If the good suffer, we may say that this suffering tends to make goodness more independent. It helps us to care for goodness for its own sake, to love it, and to love its Source, for themselves and only for themselves. But there is something more. Suffering brings out and develops character. It supplies a field for all sorts of virtues, for resignation, faith, courage, resource, endurance. It stimulates ; it purifies. This is an old and familiar and never-to-be-forgotten truth. " The chastisements of love," of which the old rabbis spoke, are very real. The discipline of sorrow, the purification of adversity ; preachers often preach about these, and they are right.

CLAUDE G. MONTEFIORE

Tempests And Trials Make The Man

A smooth sea never made a skillful mariner ; neither do uninterrupted prosperity and success qualify us for usefulness and happiness. Shallow and loose-rooted is the tree that has known only sunshine, that has never felt the wrench and shock of the gale. The storms of adversity, like those of the ocean, rouse the faculties — excite the invention, prudence, skill, and fortitude of the voyager. The martyrs of all times, in bracing their minds to outward calamities, acquired a loftiness of purpose and a moral heroism worth a lifetime of ease and security.

It is not the so-called blessings of life — its sunshine and calm, its comfort and ease — that make man, but its rugged experiences, its storms and tempest and trials. Early adversity is often a blessing in disguise. Wherever souls are being tried, there God is hewing out the pillars for His temple.

JOSEPH KRAUSKOPF

Sorrow Can Enlarge The Domain Of Our Life

Our sorrow can bring understanding as well as pain, breadth as well as the contraction that comes with pain. Out of love and sorrow can come a compassion that endures. The needs of others hitherto unnoticed, the anxieties of neighbors never before realized, now come into the ken of our experience, for our sorrow has opened our life to the needs of others. A bereavement that brings us into the lives of our fellowmen writes a fitting epilogue to a love that had taught us kindliness, and forbearance and had given us so much joy.

Sorrow can enlarge the domain of our life, so that we may now understand the triviality of the things many pursue. We have in our hands a noble and refined measure for judging the events and objects we daily see. What is important is not luxury but love ; not wealth but wisdom ; not gold but goodness.

And our sorrow may so clear our

vision that we may, more brightly, see the God, of Whom it was said, " The Lord is nigh unto them, that are of a broken heart." Beyond the hurry and turmoil of life rises the Eternal. There is God in a world in which love like ours could bloom. There is God in a world in which human beings could experience tenderness. There is a God in a world in which two lives can be bound together by a tie stronger than death.

Out of that vision will come a sense of obligation. A duty, solemn, sacred and significant, rests upon us. To spread the love we have known to others. To share the joy which has been ours. To ease the pains which man's thoughtlessness or malice inflicts. We have a task to perform. There is work to be done and in work there is consolation.

Out of love may come sorrow. But out of sorrow can come light for others who dwell in darkness. And out of the light we bring to others will come light for ourselves — the light of solace, of strength, of transfiguring and consecrating purpose.

MORRIS ADLER

To Live Fully

And while we live, we should try to make each day a year as far as beauty, nobility, and a warm sense of brotherhood are concerned. In a time when there is so much cruelty abroad, we must generate the oxygen of love to keep the soul of the world still breathing. Religion should summon all of us to deepen the quality of life as a compensation for the diminution of its quantity, to treasure each other in the recognition that we do not know how long we shall have each other, to make life strong and brave and beautiful as our answer to the forces of death abroad in the world. We must make up for the threatened brevity of life by heightening the intensity of life. The crimes and sin for which there should be little forgiveness during this epoch are hard-heartedness, selfishness, mutual cruelty, lovelessness — all of the little weapons which we use to shorten the lives of others. Our very understanding of each other can serve to deepen life even when we cannot lengthen it.

All men today need the healthy-mindedness of Judaism, the natural piety with which the Jew declares, "One world at a time is enough." For just as we can rely without fear upon the Power greater than ourselves during this earthly journey ; just as we can rest and do rest securely upon the bosom of mystery every time we fall asleep at night — so we can trust the universe beyond time also, recognizing that it is the part of wisdom not to seek to remove the veil from before birth or after death, but to live fully, richly, nobly, here and now, and make possible a society where other men can so live.

JOSHUA LOTH LIEBMAN,
Peace of Mind

Portrait Painters Of The Soul

Judaism is the religion of life which makes no cult out of death, which seeks no private salvation from the grave, which accepts with confidence and trust both the miracle of birth and the mystery of death. Our faith does not close its eyes to tragedy and does not deny that we human beings shall never possess the everlastingness of stone, the silent perduring quality of the mountain peak, but we have other gifts, conscious minds, aspiring hearts, far-visioned souls. Our faith tells us that God has given to each human being the ability to paint a portrait large or small, beautiful or ugly, radiant or blooming, and our faith summons us to become a portrait painter of a soul-landscape that shall be worthy to be hung in any art gallery of the spirit. Judaism proclaims that God has arranged our journey so that in years brief or many we can find love, joy and the fruits of fulfilment, partial and relative though they be, and that when our day is finished, we should accept its final note with the same calm trust that we greet the skylark's song at sunrise. True, " each one of us has his toad to swallow every morning." Yet we can become what Goethe once said is the true task of man — " Life-worthy."

JOSHUA LOTH LIEBMAN,
Sermon, " Message of Israel "

A Pledge From The Living

The father's heart beat no more. The kindly eye was closed forever. . . . The son had stepped into the parent's shoes. He had undertaken the responsibilities for the honor of his house. And there at the open grave . . . he stood in the presence of the whole congregation of friends and strangers, before those of the age passing and those who were to lead in the age after him, and there at the saddest moment of his life he recalled neither sorrow nor his loss, but his duty. As a real Jew he knew the holiness of the moment, and he framed his resolution in the words holiest to Jewish hearts ; there he opened his lips and made a pledge, a holy promise : " Yissgadal Veyisskadash Sh'meh Rabbah, Lord God, I do not murmur against Thy decree, I am a child of Jewry. Lord God, hear my voice at this moment. As my father lived for Thee, as his life was dedicated to Thy glory and Thy name, so do I declare Yissgadal Veyisskadash, ' that Thy great Name may be magnified and sanctified ' as the promise for my future. So do I undertake to remember his fidelity, and never to forget my own duty."

That was the meaning of Kaddish in the times when Jews were Jewish. That is the meaning of the words today when said for mother and father. Not a prayer for the dead, but a pledge from the living ; not a superstitious phrase, but a man's motto of life.

LEO JUNG

Water Spilt On The Ground

"For we must needs die, and our lives are as water spilt on the ground, which cannot be gathered up again ; neither doth God respect any person " (II Samuel 14 : 14).

It is an ancient truth ever new. It has been voiced by saint and cynic alike, by the wisest of men and by the simple-minded. Life is like water spilled upon the thirsty ground. It sinks into the sands and is no more. Never may it be recalled ; never may it be enjoyed again. . . .

Granted that this is true. Are our lives futile therefore ? Is water spilled upon the ground lost ? Is it not true that it is precisely this submerged water that makes life possible ? It is the rain and the dew that fall on the ground and cease to be that make for life. Without it we perish.

Even so, is it with the life of the spirit. Our fathers and the many generations that went before them have poured out the red, sweet wine of their dreams and ideals and high hopes, and have been absorbed by the hungry earth of life ; you and I are the harvest. They have given us not only our bodies ; they have given us our minds, our appreciation of the good and the true, our will to live and achieve. We have absorbed into our personalities the spilled waters of their lives, just as we in turn, will be absorbed in the lives of our children and children's children. Teachers will be absorbed in the lives of their students and disciples ; poets will be absorbed in the lives of the sensitive who appreciate their writings ; the heroes and the martyrs of our social life will be absorbed in the lives of those who fight for the right. Thus the cycle runs its course.

Withhold this water from being spilled on the ground — if we can — and the world perishes ; withhold the influences of parents, teachers, preachers, artists, and the life of the spirit is parched. A menacing dust bowl will develop in one generation. It is precisely in this absorption that we realize ourselves and achieve immortality. Alas for those who are not absorbed in someone else's life !

Is there nobility in our lives ? Do we cherish high hopes ? Is there strength, dignity, loyalty, capacity for whatever the cup of life may hold for us ? That, largely, is the harvest with which our fathers have endowed us ; it is the submerged water of their lives transformed within our souls.

Are we continuing the cycle ? Are we bringing nobility, high hope, courage, loyalty into the lives of those dear to us ? Are we pouring out fresh, sweet water that yields a harvest of goodness ?

BERYL D. COHON

"I Know No Sorrow"

Rabbi Schmelke and his brother once petitioned their teacher, the Maggid of Mezeritz, to explain to them the words of the Mishnah : " A man must bless God for the evil in the same way that he blesses Him for the good which befalls."

The Maggid replied : " Go to the House of Study, and you will find there a man smoking. He is Rabbi Sussya, and he will explain this to you."

When Rabbi Schmelke and his brother placed their question to Rabbi Sussya, he laughed and said : " I am surprised that the Rabbi sent you to me. You must go elsewhere, and make your inquiry from one who has suffered tribulations in his lifetime. As for me, I have never experienced anything but good all my days."

But Rabbi Schmelke and his brother knew full well that from his earliest hour to the present, he had endured the most grievous sorrows. Thereupon they understood the meaning of the words of the Mishnah, and the reason their Rabbi had sent them to Rabbi Sussya.

The Hasidic Anthology

Faith And Grief

I heard from some of the elders who came out of Spain that one of the boats was infested with the plague, and the captain of the boat put the passengers ashore at some uninhabited place. And there most of them died of starvation, while some of them gathered up all their strength to set out on foot in search of some settlement.

There was one Jew among them who struggled on afoot together with his wife and two children. The wife grew faint and died, because she was not accustomed to so much difficult walking. The husband carried his children along until both he and they fainted from hunger. When he regained consciousness, he found that his two children had died.

In great grief he rose to his feet and said, " O Lord of all the universe, you are doing a great deal that I might even desert my faith. But know you of a certainty that — even against the will of heaven — a Jew I am and a Jew I shall remain. And neither that which you have brought upon me nor that which you will yet bring upon me will be of any avail."

Thereupon he gathered some earth and some grass, and covered the boys, and went forth in search of a settlement.

SOLOMON IBN VIRGA,
In Time and Eternity

The Death Of The Young

The grief of a parent for a child is the most difficult of all to bear. Bereaved parents feel keenly the burning anguish of King David's lament: "O my son Absalom, my son, my son Absalom! Would I had died for thee, O Absalom, my son, my son." Almost these very words were found recently by explorers in an Egyptian tomb. Upon the exquisitely carved sarcophagus of a little child there was inscribed the parent's words: "O my life, my love, my little one, would God I had died for thee!"

Jeremiah pictured mother Rachel weeping so bitterly for her children who "are not" that "she refused to be comforted." Indeed is there any comfort equal to the hurt, any solace adequate to the loss?

Nevertheless, the voice of the Divine Comforter speaks softly to the bereft mother: "Refrain thy voice from weeping and thine eyes from tears . . . there is hope for thy future."

There are some genuine sources of hope and courage to tap at such a time. The awareness that other parents have found the strength to endure a similar affliction can be reassuring. Somehow, from somewhere, there comes the endurance and the fortitude equal to our desperate need. The Psalmist undoubtedly experienced this in his own life for he praised .God "who healeth the broken in heart and bindeth up their wounds." A measure of comfort may also be derived from the realization that there is a precious store of memories which death cannot take away and which no mother would surrender even if she could thereby be relieved immediately of all her sorrow. In those memories, the ravages of time and decay no longer hold sway. There the child "grows not older," it remains eternally "fair and kind and young." And perhaps the greatest comfort lies in the thought that all of life is but a loan to us and when the Lender asks for the return of the jewel, He promises to care for it better than we can.

SIDNEY GREENBERG,
A Treasury of Comfort

Meeting Sorrow Upright

According to ancient Jewish custom the ceremony of cutting our garments. when our nearest and dearest on earth is lying dead before us, is to be performed standing up. This teaches: meet all sorrow standing upright. The future may be dark, veiled from the eye of mortals — but not the manner in which we are to meet the future. To rail at life, to rebel against a destiny that has cast our lines in unpleasant places, is of little avail. We cannot lay down terms to life. Life must be accepted on its own terms. But hard as life's terms are, life (it has been finely said) never dictates unrighteousness, unholiness, dishonor.

JOSEPH H. HERTZ,
A Book of Jewish Thoughts

Daily Blessings

In the *Blessings on Various Occasions* we find a very warm jubilation of life—a spontaneous lyric appreciation of earth; joy in the fruits of the tree, the vine and the field; enchantment in the fragrant odors of barks, plants, fruits and spices; exaltation at the sight of stars, mountain, desert, sea and rainbow, beautiful trees and animals, spring-blossoms equally with scholars and sages — all evoke their grace of appreciation. For storm and evil tidings, too, have their graces—in fortitude! The Hebrew genius could find growth through sorrow; and for the Hebrew, good tidings have their grace, no less than fair sights and experience. Everywhere the infiltration of Earth by Heaven.

LOUIS ZANGWILL

We Must Not Expect Miraculous Healing

We must face grief without any expectation of miraculous healing, but with the knowledge that if we are courageous and resolute we can live as our loved ones would wish us to live, not empty, morose, self-centered, and self-pitying, but as brave and undismayed servants of the greater life. Rabbinic wisdom teaches this approach to grief in the following passages: "When the second Temple in Jerusalem was destroyed, many Jews began to withdraw from life and sank into a state of depressed mourning for the sons and daughters of Israel that had perished and also for the Temple that had gone up in smoke. They refused to eat and to drink." Rabbi Joshua said to them: "My sons, I know that it is impossible not to mourn, but to mourn excessively is forbidden." Why? Because that great Jewish sage felt that we human beings must think not only of the past but of the future. We are commanded by our religion to be the servants of life as long as we live.

JOSHUA LOTH LIEBMAN,
Peace of Mind

The Kaddish Raises Downcast Eyes

Judaism possesses a treasured source of consolation in that moment of deepest suffering when death deprives us of the living presence of a loved one. Consolation lies pregnant in the proper pronouncement of the Kaddish prayer.

It is unfortunate that so many contemporary Jews are unable to understand the noble intent of the Kaddish prayer but rather recite its Aramaic polysyllables by rote as if intoning some mystic incantation which will raise their beloved dead to some conjured celestial paradise. The Kaddish has not such intent. It does not, in fact, even mention the dead.

Instead the Kaddish is recited solely that the *living* may gain strength and consolation in the anguish of their bereavement. The Kaddish is a prayer in which we glorify our God. Praise and adulation of our Heavenly Father is adjured at precisely that moment where in the frenzy of our grief we are wont to rail against His decree, aye, even denounce His seeming injustice. "Extolled and hallowed be the name of God throughout the world which He has created . . ." are the words which are placed on the mourner's lips. "Praised and glorified be the name of the Holy One though He be above praises which we can utter. Our guide is He in life and our redeemer through all eternity."

Slowly, with the recitation of the Kaddish and its words of Divine praise, there pierces the shroud of grief the realization that it was God in his endless mercy who had vouchsafed unto us the lifetime of the departed one and thus bequeathed us countless precious hours of exquisite love and sublime companionship. Such treasured memories gleaned in the rich harvest of daily living are not destroyed by death but live on imperishably. Tenderly they minister to aching hearts, these reflections on a life well lived, healing with all the magic of Gilead's balm. Inspiringly, they animate the noblest impulses, these memories of a life which cherished lofty ideals.

In moments when one is cast down, the Kaddish may raise downcast eyes heavenwards offering the surest consolation, reassuring the mourner that He who taketh away, giveth in even greater measure.

JAY KAUFMAN

Out Of The Dark Passages

When suffering comes upon us, as it comes to all, we often fret despairingly and repine. We cannot understand why we should be made the apparent sport of misfortune and calamity. We wonder why tender affection should be created, only to be rudely broken ; why agonizing pain should wreck our nerves and consume our flesh ; In moments of great sorrow, the stricken heart is apt to exclaim : "Surely God does not care, or else why does He inflict upon me such cruel pain!" The presence of evil — how baffling it is to our finite understanding!

Yet it is through struggle and sorrow that we learn to know more of the love and faithfulness of God than in any other way! We know only too well that sorrow often breaks the crust of a superficial life, uncovers its deepest realities. Through the dark cloud that envelops us, there breaks forth a new vision of the aim and purpose of our earthly existence. Not always on the heights, sometimes from the depths do we best see God. And seeing Him, we come to realize that our life is not a haphazard occurrence of chance events and circumstances, that a Divine hand and purpose are discernible in all that befalls us. Out of the dark passages of life, we emerge into the light of faith, purified in spirit, more keenly alert and responsive to the soft whisperings of the still small voice ever striving to speak to our hearts.

Blessings and Praise

Let Us Count The Past As Gain

It is not God's part to spare us suffering — for that is essential to his plan — but to help us to bear it. If the visitation we dread finds us — for it may be for our good that it should find us — then we do right to ask for the strength that will uphold us under the load, for the insight that reveals the wisdom of it, for the magic power that will transform it into blessing. And to that prayer there is always an answer. . . .

Something precious is taken from us, and we think of it as something we have lost, instead of something we have had. We remember only how empty our lives are now, we forget how full and rich they were before; we forget all the many days and years of happiness we lived while the beloved object was still with us. We praise God for our treasures while we have them; we cease to praise him for them when they are fled. But God never gives; He only lends. What is life itself but a loan? "Everything," cry the old sages, "is given in pledge" to be restored when the Master wills. . . . No. When God claims His own shall we rebel or repine? Instead of murmuring because He takes our precious things from us, let us be grateful to Him for having spared them to us so long. Let us count the past happy days not as loss, but as gain. We have had them; and, now that they are ended, let us turn the loss to glorious gain — the gain that comes with new courage, with nobler tasks, with a wider out-look on life and duty.

MORRIS JOSEPH,
Judaism as Creed and Life

The Spark Of Gratefulness

However short, however long the time given to those who are near to us, strength will be fashioned through the gratitude of our hearts for the blessing of life itself. When the days of life are short, shall we curse the moments of beauty for their brevity, or prize them that they came to us all? When toll is taken in the middle years, shall we be bitter for lack of more, or wall our tears with thanksgiving for what has been? When the bridge of three-score and ten has been crossed, shall we be torn with argument for a longer term, or be grateful for the fullness of the granted time?

Our sages said that all things might be lost save one: the spirit of gratitude that is ever present in the heart of man. They further said that as long as thanksgiving lasts, the world will endure. The waters of sadness are deep, but they will never extinguish the spark of gratefulness that is fed by man's inherent recognition of God's goodness toward him. Let us fan that spark into a flame that will guide us happily into the future.

JOSEPH I. WEISS

If Generations Did Not Come And Go

Judaism . . . teaches us to understand death as part of the Divine pattern of the universe. Actually we could not have our sensitivity without fragility. Mortality is the tax that we pay for the privilege of love, thought, creative work — the toll on the bridge of being from which clods of earth and snow-peaked mountain summits are exempt. Just because we are human, we are prisoners of the years, yet that very prison is the room of discipline in which we, driven by the urgency of time, create.

We can face death without dread when we learn that the Angel of Death plays a very vital role in life's economy. Actually there could be no growth, no progress, if generations did not come and go. There also would be very little meaning to existence if the years were not marked off in the calendar of time by childhood, adolescence, youth, and age. There is a time to run gaily with all the intense excitement of a boy with flushed cheeks racing on a summer's day toward the winding river of sport and adventure; there is also the time when that boy, transformed by the alchemy of the years into an old man, no longer seeks to run but is quite content to sit and browse even unto the twilight.

JOSHUA LOTH LIEBMAN,
Sermon, "Message of Israel"

The Power Of The Kaddish

Its origin is mysterious; angels are said to have brought it down from heaven and taught it to men. About this prayer the tenderest threads of filial feeling and human recollection are entwined; for it is the prayer of the orphans! When the father or mother dies, the surviving sons are to recite it thrice daily, morning and evening, throughout the year of mourning, and then also on each recurring anniversary of the death — on the *Yahrziet*.

It possesses wonderful power. Truly, if there is any bond so strong and indissoluble enough to chain heaven to earth, it is this prayer. It keeps the living together, and forms the bridge to the mysterious realm of the dead. One might almost say that this prayer is the watchman and the guardian of the people by whom alone it is uttered; therein lies the warrant of its continuance. Can a people disappear and be annihilated so long as a child remembers its parents? It may sound strange: in the midst of the wildest dissipation has this prayer recalled to his better self a dissolute character, so that he has bethought himself and for a time at least purified himself by honoring the memory of his parents.

Because this prayer is a resurrection in the spirit of the perishable in man, because it does not acknowledge death, because it permits the blossom, which, withered, has fallen from the tree of mankind, to flower and develop again in the human heart, therefore it possesses sanctifying power. To know that when thou diest, the earth falling on thy head will not cover thee entirely; to know that there remain behind, those who, wherever they may be on this wide earth, whether they may be poor or rich, will send this prayer after thee; to know that thou leavest them no house, no estate, no field by which they must remember thee, and that yet they will cherish thy memory as their dearest inheritance — what more satisfying knowledge canst thou ever hope for? And such is the knowledge bequeathed to us all by the Kaddish.

L. KOMPERT

Light For The Dark House

The Dubner Maggid has left us a parable whose wisdom can serve as a beacon of light for the dark hours.

A king once owned a large, beautiful, pure diamond of which he was justly proud, for it had no equal anywhere. One day, the diamond accidentally sustained a deep scratch. The king called in the most skilled diamond cutters and offered them a great reward if they could remove the imperfection from his treasured jewel. But none could repair the blemish. The king was sorely distressed.

After some time a gifted lapidary came to the king and promised to make the rare diamond even more beautiful than it had been before the mishap. The king was impressed by his confidence and entrusted his precious stone to his care. And the man kept his word.

With superb artistry he engraved a lovely rosebud around the imperfection and he used the scratch to make the stem.

We can emulate that craftsman. When life bruises us and wounds us, we can use even the scratches to etch a portrait of beauty and charm.

SIDNEY GREENBERG,
A Treasury of Comfort

The Gate To Eternity

The life of man means more than the narrowness of existence in this world. With all its deficiences and limitations, its pain and suffering, it is, as the old Rabbinic metaphor says, but a place of "preparation," an "ante-chamber"; it is only the "life of the hour." The true life is the "eternal life." Man is created and destined to be different from the world, to be holy. As the image of God he belongs to that other, the higher life; he is "a child of the world to come." The spiritual, the good, is implanted in him as the strength, as the reality, of his existence, and this, the truly real of his life is exalted above death and destruction. His life remains life, even beyond death.

The loneliness of man, that loneliness of him who is different, exalted above the world, and who yet sees himself surrounded by the infinitude of its doings and its destiny, is overcome by this assurance of eternal life. With his faith in God man was able to gain the mastery over his solitude; with the idea of immortality into which this faith develops, trust gains a new note, and the paradox of the eternity of mortal man, the paradox of human divineness, gains a new precision. In death the most lonely loneliness, the silence without response, opens its gate to man, the gate leading to the path which he has to tread for himself, and of which none who have gone before can tell him. But through this gate he now believes that he passes into that eternity to which he belongs, to the great answer in which all the questions of his life, and all its paradoxes, are included. With the first man loneliness first came into the world. For loneliness is always there, where somebody is tied and yet not tied. The flower in the forest, and the animal in the wilderness, are not lonely, and God is not lonely in his heavens. It is only man who is lonely, he who has been created like the rest of the world, and is yet different. Loneliness first began when began the first yearning, the yearning of him who is tied, and yet able to rise above his bondage. This loneliness and yearning are also found in the ethical nature of man ; for there arises their yearning of spiritual striving and struggling, and there arises there too, the loneliness of him who seeks after the ideal, and carries within him the desire for the eternal significance of life, for its sublime and divine quality, for that permanent value of life which has been enjoined upon him. In the conviction of eternal life and of life with God, all this yearning finds its goal, and all this loneliness its fulfilment. The tension in the human soul which gazes upward from earth to the heights, and hears itself summoned thither, can now be appeased. Redemption from loneliness, calm out of yearning, mean peace, and peace is given in the thought of eternal life.

Man's secret and his path now attain their final significance. Concealment and shelter in one, that protecting profundity of existence, were the secret or mystery, as conceived by the Jewish soul. Eternal life now makes that which is most hidden, the darkness of darkness, which is death, the entrance to eternal protection — concealment and shelter in one ; God receives the man whom He created. Beginning and endlessness in one, that constant task of existence, constitute in Judaism the path of man, the abiding firmness and positiveness which make demands even upon his fulfilment, and point out new tasks to his attainment. Eternal life transforms beginning into duration — beginning and endlessness in one ; born to create, man finds his goal in God. Secret and path united in atonement. Man attains once more to the depth of his life, to that which is holy in his existence, and so returns to God ; such is the meaning of atonement. It is likewise the meaning of immortality. Eternity is the great atonement of finitude. The earthly is reconciled with the endless. All atonement is fundamentally this : reconciliation of the finite and the infinite. The secret which becomes the path, and the path which becomes the secret, were recognized in Judaism as " return," as Teshubah. Death means this Teshuba. Death is the great " return," the great liberation from the merely earthly and limiting ; earth vanishes, and eternity receives. " The dust returns to the earth whence it came, and the spirit returns to God who gave it." The true meaning of the idea of atonement in Judaism is that the life of man can begin again. With death there comes the decisive and concluding beginning, the last rebirth, the new creation which contains everything—the whole path and the whole secret. Purity and freedom in their ultimate fulfilment, the great atonement, that is eternal life. It is called, therefore, the great Sabbath, just like the day of atonement, " the day which is wholly Sabbath, and the repose of life in eternity." It is the great peace. In life man seeks and moves "toward peace"; he who has passed away, as it says in the Talmud, is "in peace"; he has attained. The yearning after per- fection is given fulfilment : complete perfection and greatest bliss is one. Life has reached completeness; death becomes the great revelation. Thus the element of atonement and revel- ation enters also into martyrdom. Where God commands death, the sacrifice of mortal existence, He also promises and grants fulfilment, eternal life. The unending task cor- responds to an unending future; commandment and confidence become one.

LEO BAECK,
The Essence of Judaism

Serenely To Accept What Happens

Judaism encourages us . . . to recognize that it (death) is as natural an aspect of human life as birth. When man has established a con- fidence in life and the God of life, he is prepared serenely to accept what happens after death even as he does not worry about what took place before birth. When we become morbidly and obsessively preoccu- pied with the thought of the end of life, we show that we have fallen in love with ourselves to such an extent that we cannot tolerate the idea of a possible final sleep. Yet the fear of death is a deceiver. We think that we are frightened of death, when actually beneath the surface we are frightened of many things that life has inflicted upon us— some forgotten rejection in child- hood, some imprisonment in a dark and foreboding closet as a punish- ment for a childish prank or tantrum, some identification with an annihilationist mother or a pun- ishing father. It should come as a liberation to recognize that it is not death that is to be feared, but many of the scares of life which are to be removed, understood, discarded.

As mature people we must learn not to love ourselves excessively nor to mistrust the universe mor- bidly. The truth is that we change and die every day a little. Yes, we die every day a little bit without fear. Our skins change. The cells in our hands and in our brains perish and are reborn. Our whole life is strewn with the bones of hopes discarded, dreams outgrown, loves broken, friendships embraced. We change and die every dawn and every sunset, yes, without fear. Let us recognize that we are part of nature, both in life and in death. The atoms composing us are arranged differently in the moment of our conception, at the time of birth as we grow and clothe our skeleton with the flesh and muscles, the tendons and the veins of maturity, and then when the curtain is drawn over our earthly frame, the atoms of our being are rearranged and enter once again the treasury of nature and we are at rest. The shock of corn has fallen upon the soil from which it sprang and we are once more in the bosom of the Divine.

JOSHUA LOTH LIEBMAN,
Sermon " Message of Israel "

13

Judaism and Democracy

The Bible is the most democratic book in the world.
THOMAS H. HUXLEY

Dictators are anti-Semitic because they know or sense that liberty is semitic in origin and character.
ABBA HILLEL SILVER,
The World Crisis and Jewish Survival

Their affliction, as well as their religion, has prepared the Jews for democracy.
LOUIS D. BRANDEIS,
The Jewish Problem

Devotion In Peace And War

The American people need no reminder of the service which those of Jewish faith have rendered our nation. It has been a service with honor and distinction. History reveals that your people have played a great and commendable part in the defense of Americanism during the World War and prior wars, and have contributed much in time of peace toward the development and preservation of the glory and romance of our country and our democratic form of government.

For devotion in peace, for devotion in war, Jewish citizenship — as I know it — is a shining example to all the world.

FRANKLIN D. ROOSEVELT

Judaism And Democracy

The law of acting fairly toward one's neighbor is the starting point for all Jewish teachings. Judaism has no elaborate philosophy of justice. Unlike that of Plato and Aristotle, Jewish teaching made little attempt to develop a systematic democratic philosophy. In point of fact, there is no Hebrew word for democracy, except that which is borrowed from the Greeks. But the social creed by which the Jews have lived for centuries is in democracy's highest traditions.

Basic to Judaism are these fundamental principles which are also basic to democracy : (1) God recognizes no distinction among men on the basis of creed, color or station in life ; all men are equal in His sight. (2) Every man is his brother's keeper — we bear responsibility for our neighbor's failings as well as for his needs. (3) All men, being made in God's image, have infinite potentialities for goodness ; therefore the job of society is to evoke the best that is in each man. (4) Freedom is to be prized above all things ; the very first words of the Ten Commandments depict God as the Great Liberator.

The theme of freedom and equality runs constantly throughout the three-thousand-year history of the Jewish people. The frequent taste of injustice, as they wandered from country to country, reinforced a tradition already rooted in their faith. Thus, Jews responded readily to the thrilling challenge of the American Declaration of Independence and the Bill of Rights. And the French Revolution also found Jews sympathetic to the cries of Liberty, Fraternity and Equality. It is no accident that the words, "Proclaim ye liberty throughout the land to all the inhabitants thereof," found on the American Liberty Bell, stem from the Old Testament. For love of liberty is woven into the fabric of Judaism.

The democratic ideal inherent in

Judaism is naturally incompatible with totalitarianism of any kind — not only political totalitarianism, but coerced conformity of any kind. Dictators always found their Jewish citizens indigestible. Fascists and Communisits alike have never tolerated the maintenance of the Jewish tradition because it represents a denial of the repression for which they stand.

The Prophet Jeremiah exhorted his followers to seek the welfare of the country in which they live. And Jews have always felt the obligation to participate fully in the life of the community.

The voice of the synagogue will therefore be heard in all issues that would have aroused the ancient Prophets of Israel: integrity in public office; just labor - management relations; civil rights and civil liberties; equality of economic opportunity; decent education, housing and health standards for all citizens; peace among the nations of the world.

One of the rabbis of the Talmud said: " If a man of learning participates in public affairs, he gives stability to the land. But if he sits at home and says to himself : ' What have the affairs of society to do with me . . . ? Let my soul dwell in peace,' he brings about the destruction of the world."

MORRIS N. KERTZER,
What Is A Jew ?

America's Debt To The Jews

My pen may have some skill, but I could not begin to measure the debt that this country owes to its Jews and to millions of its foreign-born citizens, first for a jealous guarding of American rights and liberties to which the native-born have too often been indifferent; second, for preserving at all times a great reservoir of idealism and liberalism, and, thirdly, for keeping alive a passionate desire for knowledge in every field, which has steadily quickened American life and notably its colleges.

OSWALD GARRISON VILLARD,
*Fighting Years, Memoirs of a
Liberal Editor*

We Shared In The Making Of America

We have had a share in the making of this nation. In the mine and in the mill, at the lathe and at the loom, in counting room and council chamber, the Jew has been at work for two centuries and a half for his America. He has sentried his nation's camp; he has been in the mast's look-out on his nation's ship; he has gone out to battle, and he was among them that fell at the firing line. . . . The future will place new solemn obligations upon us for the country's sake and as Judaism's consecration ; we shall not shirk our duties.

EMIL G. HIRSCH,
On the 250th Anniversary of the Settlement of the Jews in the United States

The Jewish faith is predominantly the faith of liberty.

CALVIN COOLIDGE
Spiritual Foundations of America

The twentieth - century ideals of America have been the ideals of the Jew for more than twenty centuries.

LOUIS D. BRANDEIS,
Menorah Journal

Hebraic mortar cemented the foundations of our American democracy, and through the windows of the Puritan churches, the New West looked back to the Old East.

OSCAR S. STRAUS,
Address, 1905

The Enemy Of Freedom

The burden of our history is unmistakable : the enemy of the Jew is the enemy of freedom. Those who organize the pogrom of today will attack tomorrow the general foundation of freedom. That is why the moral stature of the nation is set by its recognition that the claim of the Jew to freedom is the claim of its own people to strike off its chains. When it is silent before the agony of the Jew, it collaborates in the organization of its future servitude.

HAROLD LASKI,
New Statesman and Nation

The Blessing Of Cultural Cross-Fertilization

America, I am certain, is best served by its Jews when they strive to exploit the special resources of their group.

If the only effects of such a course were to bolster the shaken morale of the Jews and to enrich their personalities with the treasures of a second heritage, the whole effort would have justified itself from the point of view of American interest. Quite obviously America will be benefited if its Jews who constitute one segment of its citizenry respect themselves, if they are psychically adjusted rather than disaffected and if, in addition, they are richer rather than poorer in spirit.

But beyond all such considerations there is a larger promise in this cultural dualism and its analogues. It is out of differences meeting in reciprocal understanding on a shared soul that cultures bloom most luxuriantly. History is replete with precedent for this statement. The age of Pericles, the Renaissance, the eras of Chaucer and Shakespeare, were all, in no slight measure, the consequence of the cross-fertilization of civilizations. The botanist has long known that plants grow best when they pollinate one another. He has for many centuries been doing deliberately what Nature had been wont to do hit or miss. Those of us who are devoted to the ideal of an American flower could, it would seem, properly follow his precedent. We ought to preserve both the common ground of government, language, and culture in which all groups share, and also the second diversities, and then as a matter of planned policy arrange for their mutual meeting. Out of such husbandry of the spirit may well emerge a cultural life richer than any the human past has known heretofore.

I believe in the attainability of this objective. I believe further that Judaism has its contribution to make to the great fruition which is to be. This is the final and climatic reason for a program dedicated to the preservation of the Jewish tradition on the American scene.

MILTON STEINBERG,
A Believing Jew

Mutual Benefactors

Important as our common course may be, I happen to think that America (as other lands and civilizations in the past) has given its Jewry many valuable ideals and ways hitherto unknown to them ; and Jewry, in turn, possesses valuable ideals and ways of which America is ignorant or heedless. Whenever we demonstrate the latter (and not merely write about it, as I am doing), thereby showing how Judaism differs from Americanism in the things that count toward a richer life, we add perhaps to our discomfort — but also to our stature.

MARVIN LOWENTHAL,
Zionist Quarterly

God Called It America

God built Him a continent of glory
    and filled it with treasures untold;
He carpeted it with soft - rolling
    prairies and columned it with
    thundering mountains ;
He studded it with sweet-flowing
    fountains and traced it with long
    winding streams ;
He planted it with deep-shadowed
    forests, and filled them with song.

Then He called unto a thousand peoples and summoned the bravest among them.
They came from the ends of the earth, each bearing a gift and a hope.
The glow of adventure was in their eyes, and in their hearts the glory of hope.
And out of the bounty of earth and the labor of men,
Out of the longing of hearts and the prayer of souls,
Out of the memory of ages and the hopes of the world,
God fashioned a nation in love, blessed it with a purpose sublime —
And called it America !

ABBA HILLEL SILVER,
America

The Scriptures Have Sparked Revolutions

Throughout the history of the Western world the Scriptures have been the great instigators of revolt against the worst forms of clerical and political despotism. The Bible has been the Magna Charta of the poor and of the oppressed ; down to modern times no State has had a constitution in which the interests of the people are so largely taken into account, in which the duties so much more than the privileges of rulers are insisted upon, as that drawn up for Israel in Deuteronomy and in Leviticus ; nowhere is the fundamental truth that the welfare of the State, in the long run, depends on the uprightness of the citizen so strongly laid down. . . .

THOMAS H. HUXLEY,
Controverted Questions

Monotheism And Democracy

There is no historical record of any other nation which, as early as a millennium before the present era, had overcome the forces both of despotism and of unbridled democracy. The Jewish people at large had as keen an outlook and as wide a vision in political as in religious affairs ; and while the modern monotheistic conception of the universe is largely the product of their genius, so the modern conception of a rational, democratic, representative government owes its origin to the same ancestry. The remarkable phenomenon that the English people and their American descendants, the only nations that have really comprehended and utilized the principles of parliamentary government, took the Jewish Bible as their text-book in times of stress and storm, will thus be explained.

MAYER SULZBERGER

Democracy's Debt To Ancient Israel

The debt that democracy in general, and American democracy in particular, owes ancient Israel is indeed vast. For generations of pious Bible readers, the Scriptures created the moral and spiritual climate, in which a free government could function. The basic content of democracy, if not its forms, existed in ancient Hebrew society, with its insistence upon individual dignity, its hatred of caste, its uncompromising love of liberty. Above all, democracy in action would be inconceivable without the Hebrew Prophets, who proclaimed the truth without fear or favor and established the right to dissent, which is the living breath of democracy.

ROBERT GORDIS,
The Jew Faces a New World

The Golden Thread Of Jewish History

"Democracy," declared Hitler, "is fundamentally Jewish, not Germanic." The so-called Aryan must trace his political traditions back to the oriental despotisms and King-worship of ancient Persia and to the caste system of India. Even the Greeks had no strong consistent democratic tradition. Thucydides, Plato and Aristotle opposed the democratic form of government. Aristotle actually defended slavery. . . . But the Semite of the desert, from whom Israel is descended, neither knew nor tolerated any despotism. The democratic motif runs like a golden thread through the whole political, social, economic and religious history of Israel from the earliest nomadic period unto the present.

ABBA HILLEL SILVER,
The World Crisis and Jewish Survival

The Jewish belief in democracy is based simply on the faith that God created man in His image, that all men are His equal children, and that each possesses within him a spark of the divine which may not be violated.

SIMON H. RIFKIND,
Address, American Jewish Tercentenary, 1954

An Affirmation

We reaffirm those ancient truths contained in the Ten Commandments, and rededicate ourselves to them as timeless imperatives. Keenly aware of their cogency at the present juncture in human affairs, we register our firm conviction that the principles of Sinai can achieve salvation for human society.

We affirm that man is the embodiment of the Divine, and that every human being, containing within himself something of God, is of infinite moral worth, too sacred to be exploited or oppressed.

We affirm that all men, being children of God, are bound together in a union in God which is deeper and more essential than any of the interests which may divide them from one another.

We affirm that the career of mankind, since it reflects the creative design of God, is no mere groping from one futility to another, but represents the march of the human spirit toward the achievement of God's kingdom on earth. We have faith that the time will come when all men everywhere shall be free, when every human spirit shall be encouraged to rise to its full stature of humanity and divinity and when human society shall at last be ordered so as to conform with the principles of justice and righteousness, first proclaimed at Sinai.

We affirm our unwavering loyalty to the Biblical teachings of human liberty and human equality, the sanctity of human life, and the universality of moral standards, for which the present war is being waged.

We dedicate ourselves to the service of our country. We are resolved to serve it with our hearts, with our substance and with our lives. We pray that its just cause may be crowned with victory, bringing the day nearer when men everywhere may be redeemed from all evil, and God's Kingdom be realized on earth.

ISRAEL GOLDSTEIN,

The Foundation Of Democracy

I believe in the value of the endeavors to extend and improve religious education among children and youth of the Jewish faith. In teaching this democratic faith to American children, we need the sustaining, buttressing aid of those great ethical religious teachings which are the heritage of our modern civilization. For not upon strength nor upon power alone, but upon the spirit of God shall our democracy be founded.

FRANKLIN D. ROOSEVELT

Education For Democracy

There is the danger of yielding to dictatorial authority. Jewish education has at its disposal a potent means of combatting that danger. It has been a long-standing practice with the Jews to initiate the Jewish layman into as much knowledge as feasible of the law under which he lives, the civil and family law, as well as the ritual law. That knowledge was to consist not only of the formal rules which he was expected to obey, but of the basic premises underlying them, and of the reasoning by which they were arrived at. In Jewish tradition this study of the law is known as Gemara, in contrast with Mishnah, which is the code. The study of the law, especially when pursued in such a spirit, constituted for the Jew religion, or a means of experiencing the divine. He felt as though he himself stood at Sinai and as though God revealed to him anew what he was to do in order that he might live the life abundant. He was thus saved from falling into the habit of obeying, as Isaiah puts it, " a commandment of men learned by rote." Thus, in commenting on God's saying to Moses : " And these are the ordinances which thou shalt set before them," the Sages add, " Set out these ordinances before them like a well arranged table." That is, let them have an intelligent understanding of the laws.

It was the study of the law, in this spirit that ruled out all dictatorship and self-imposed authority in Israel. No matter how great the prestige of the rabbi who was always both administrator of justice and head of the academy, he could not silence the arguments of the poorest shoemaker or porter who knew the law. That was genuine democracy.

There is nothing the Jews dread more than the evil slogan of mobocracy : " One people, one State, one leader." There is nothing for which Jews yearn more than for the good tidings of democracy announcing : " One humanity, one divine Kingdom, one God."

MORDECAI M. KAPLAN,
Education for Democracy

The Greater Freedom

There is a freedom greater even than the freedom conferred by citizenship and the possession of full human rights. It is the freedom of the soul — of the soul that "walks at liberty because it has sought God's precepts," that visualizes the best and strenuously aspires after it.

MORRIS JOSEPH,
Song of Songs

The Trumpets Of The Exodus

Four thousand years of history have extended their span between Israel's first nationhood and her restoration to freedom at the turning point of this century. The redemption from Egyptian bondage must be regarded in any serious view of history as one of the authentic points of climax in the progress of mankind. In the words of Henry George : " From between the paws of the rock-hewn Sphinx rises the genius of human liberty ; and the trumpets of the Exodus throb with the defiant proclamation of the rights of man."

These forceful phrases do not overstate the case. The flight across the Red Sea and Sinai preserved a revolutionary idea, which could never have evolved in the idolatrous despotism of the Pharaohs. The idea was the sovereignty of God, the Ruler of the universe. Omnipotent, one and indivisible, the embodiment of righteousness and the loving Father of all creation. From this idea there flowed acceptances and rejections which came to dominate life among the children of man. Recognizing this event as the beginning of our true destiny we, the descendants of those fleeing slaves have, in all succeeding generations, commemorated the ancient saga. Our tradition, to this day, exhorts every Jew to recite the story of the Exodus from Egypt at the appointed season as though he personally had experienced this redemption from servitude to freedom.

This narrative of this rebellion against idolatry by men charged with the custody of an irreplaceable idea also occurs in the history of thought in a more secular aspect. The Exodus is the original and classic episode of national liberation. The memory of Israel's first struggle for freedom has inspired and consoled many subsequent movements for national independence. When Benjamin Franklin and Thomas Jefferson were consulted on the emblem of the future American Union they suggested that the Seal of the United States should represent the Children of Israel fleeing across the parted waters of the Red Sea on their way to freedom. This portrayal was to be surmounted by the uncannily Hebraic slogan : " Resistance to Tyrants is Obedience to God."

It is not, I think, presumptuous to believe that future generations will keep the memories of Israel's modern revival with a similar reverence and tenacity. This will certainly come to pass in the particular domain of Jewish history. Nothing since the miraculous redemption four thousand years ago can compete in our history with this recent transition from martyrdom to sovereignty, this most sudden ascent from the depths of agony to new peaks of opportunity and pride. The attainment of Israel's independence seven years ago is already much more than a political or secular event in the Jewish consciousness. The date is bound to be numbered amid the festivals of a people whose other temporal milestones have endured with rare constancy.

ABBA EBAN,
Address, at the University of Notre Dame, 1955

Since the Exodus, Freedom has always spoken with a Hebrew accent.

HEINRICH HEINE,
Germany to Luther

Our Debt To America And To Ourselves

As we look back on the three hundred-year-road we have traveled, we have a right to feel humbly proud and deeply grateful — grateful to the God of our fathers who provided this safe and bountiful haven in our hard journey, and grateful to this mighty land of freedom and opportunity.

We have marched forward on this road together with America as a whole. We have marched with her bold pioneers across the continent toward her vanishing frontiers. We have toiled and struggled and suffered together with them. We have marched with America onward toward the expanding boundaries of her industry and commerce, her science and invention, her literature, her music, her drama, her art. We have sat in the councils of her statesmen, we have fought and bled and died on her battlefields. Do we owe a debt to America? Indeed we do! It is the same debt that is owed by all others who live under her sheltering wings. It is a continuous debt that is never liquidated. We have paid it and shall continue to pay it gladly and proudly.

But we owe another debt, a debt to ourselves as a community and a debt to our people — " be-chal atar va-atar " — wherever they dwell. Is there a conflict between our obligations to America and our obligations to ourselves and our people? Does America demand of us that we erase our momentous past, renounce a millennial kinship, deny our inner selves?

To ask that question is to answer it with a thunderous no! Such a demand would itself be in conflict with America, in conflict with her noblest traditions, her great ideals and standards of freedom. Free America detests and rejects the pressures on groups and individuals to be other than themselves — pressures that prevail in totalitarian societies on artists, writers, composers and even scientists, and on religious and national groups. Freedom has made America great and freedom will keep her great!

Our obligation to ourselves as a community — a Jewish community — requires us, first and foremost, to insure the continuity of our heritage of faith and traditions by transmitting it to our children. No token transmission, with which so many of us satisfy ourselves, will accomplish that result. This majestic heritage of ours cannot be a mere sauce or side-dish at our cultural table. It is too fundamental to our health, the health of our children, the health of our community life. It provides a vitamin without which we would languish and wither. And with it — with Jewish knowledge and pride, with loyalty to our immemorial faith — we need not be anxious about our other needs and institutions — our philanthropies at home and overseas, for example, or the instruments we must maintain to safeguard our rights and good repute. There is, finally, our obligation to our people the world over. That obligation, in the three hundred years of our life in America, we have never failed to honor. We have raised our voices, and often with good effect, against the oppressor abroad. We have brought relief, and usually in generous measure, to our victims of persecution, relief that has been not only palliative but constructive. And in discharging these obligations we have had the blessings and assistance of our Christian fellow citizens.

In the last several decades these obligations have become more and more manifest and urgent. Who can now doubt the truth of what was so often proclaimed in the past : that America became a City of Refuge for our people that out of it might flow salvation for its harried remnants across the earth ? And what Jew in America will not find new pride in that time-honored role today, when it summons us to further the strength and security of the State of Israel, the consummation of our millennial hope, the harbinger of a new status of dignity and security for Jews the world over ?

May I conclude, my friends, by offering you a paraphrase of the last lines of a great poem, with which I know you are familiar — William Cullen Bryant's *Thanatopsis* :

So live that when the summons comes from men
Or from the Inner Voice you cannot still
To say what loyalties command your heart,
What proud device your noble blazon flaunts,
You will stand forth and hold aloft your shield
With words writ large : " American and Jew ! "

RUFUS LEARSI,
Tercentenial Oration

We Have Earned Our Citizenship

Our fellow - citizens . . . fully appreciate that we are of them and they of us, together constituting a single unit — that of the American citizen ; that our title is as ancient as theirs ; that it is not conferred upon us as a matter of favor or grace ; that we have earned it by fighting for it ; that our blood has been shed upon the battlefields of the Republic for its preservation, and that we cherish it as a priceless possession, and love the country from which we have derived it, because it is our own, and because it is the first in modern times in which the Jew secured the precious boon of full citizenship.

LOUIS MARSHALL,
on the 250th anniversary of Jewish Settlement in America

The Demands Of The New Era

Some sociologists have sentenced American Jewry to disappearance by assimilation, defining it as merely one of the many immigrant groups that have lost their language in the process of Americanization. Others have decreed that Jewish culture should wither away because the Jewish community should only be defined as a religious entity. However, it is time that we repeat the Founding Father's words of understanding that we are not merely an ethnic immigrant group or solely a denomination. George Washington understood the uniqueness of the Jews when he called us the " people whose God is Jehovah " and the " children of the stock of Abraham."

The Tercentenary should therefore afford us the opportunity not only of taking stock of our contributions to America and of our adjustment to American life, but also of the need for thinking and action to further Jewish psychological equality and integration. This process should involve at the minimum level, research, publication and interpreta-

tion in American Jewish history and contemporary life. It should result in the establishment of chairs in Jewish civilization to give Judaism and Jewish culture a chance to be encountered in the university curriculum. It should lead to changes in our communal life and education to fit the conditions of a group that is no longer predominantly composed of newcomers, fearful of their rights, and of their children who are uneasy about identifying themselves with their parents' immigrant past. These changes should reflect the healthy attitudes of American Jews, who are conscious of the right to certain differences in a democratic society.

Ours is the largest Jewish community in the free world. Our very survival is a challenge to political, religious, and cultural totalitarianisms. Let us live up to the demands of the new era in Jewish life and to the demands of a democratically and culturally expanding America.

ABRAHAM G. DUCKER,
Reflections on the Tercentenary

If Democracy Is To Triumph

Anyone who cherishes the richness of cultural life cannot but hope that the identity of the Jewish people will not be lost. They represent one of the most highly civilized and gifted groups. Their sensitivity

toward moral issues, amounting almost to moral genius, constitutes an invaluable asset to the modern world. Quite apart from the great heritage of the Jewish culture, there are men like Brandeis, Cardozo, and

Frankfurter, Albert Einstein, Sigmund Freud, Henri Bergson, and Morris Cohen, not to mention the numerous writers, labor leaders, and medical men without whose work modern democracy would not be what it is. Neither assimilation nor isolation would produce the same striking enrichment as would the individual and collective participation of the Jews in the building of the future. Democracy is, as a matter of fact, a system to which they, along with others, bring peculiar and important capacities. If the democratic world government is to come into existence, the Jewish people certainly have contributed and are contributing their share toward its realization.

CARL J. FRIEDRICH,
Jews in a Gentile World

Our Gift To America

America has done much for its immigrants, but there is another half to the story, namely, what the immigrants have done for America. Jews represent an influence in America, an ethical influence which is the product of their bitter European experience. America, for all its moral decency, is full of prejudice against certain disadvantaged groups and races, of one religion against another. In this regard, the Jews have something to say, for their feelings are strong. Having been the prime victim of prejudice in all the world, they are more sensitive to its presence than any other group. Whenever anybody expresses a brutal hatred for any other group, the Jew feels pained at it, for he feels apprehensive. And whenever some act of generous justice is done, whenever some group hitherto disadvantaged has had the disadvantage lifted from its shoulders by some great legal decision, every Jew in America rejoices. He believes in justice. He rejoices in every act of justice, for the simple human reason that he has sought for justice through long, unjust centuries.

American democracy is real. In a deep sense this is a self-government of a nation of comrades. But even here, tyranny arises from time to time. It is a sort of a democratic tyranny, one based upon the poisoned consent of misled masses. It is a tyranny rooted in demagoguery. It is the type of self-chosen tyranny that Spengler calls " Caesarism." We have had such " Caesars " in America, but fortunately, their time is brief. They rise and quickly fall. Huey Longs do not last in America, but while they flourish and while they preach their hatreds and practice their injustices, the most miserable group of citizens in America are the Jews. They hate all such prejudice - mongering, even though the particular prejudice is not directed against them. Perhaps they are over-timorous. If so, their history has made them sensitive. They are sure that hatreds and prejudices against one group will result in hatreds against other groups. Jews will never be found in the shouting, yelling crowds and mobs which scream for the blood of a whole class. We are the products of our history. Time has made us touchy. We bring this sensitiveness to the altar of America. We are by habit and second nature on the side of justice and kindliness.

I knew, in Illinois, a number of descendants of Jewish immigrants who collected books and mementoes on Abraham Lincoln. He was the figure in American history who appealed to them most. He was a man who, in a time of national crisis, lived and led without hate and prejudice. His memory is written on the heart of America, but he repre-

sents especially the mood of the Jewish citizens of America :

"With malice toward none, and charity toward all."

SOLOMON B. FREEHOF,
Address, "Message of Israel"

No Jew should ever look upon our institutions as an alien. His people have had their tremendous share in making them. If they are imperfect, his is a part of the blame. If they surpass all others, his is a part of the glory. In either event, they belong to him equally with others.

CALVIN COOLIDGE

In a free State, it is not the Christian that rules the Jew, neither is it the Jew that rules the Christian ; it is Justice that rules.

LEOPOLD ZUNZ

I Am An American

I Am An American. I was not ever thus. My Fathers were not Americans. They dwelt on the Continent of Europe for many centuries. But my parents chose, within a year after my birth, to become Americans. My father, on the day after Lincoln's death, announced to his friends at a German University : " Some day I mean to live in the land of Lincoln." When I told that story to President Theodore Roosevelt and added that he did not come to America until ten years later, President Roosevelt said : " Then your

Father was a good American ten years before he arrived in America."

I am an American. I am doubly an American, because I am foreign-born. It may be that native-born Americans take America for granted. Foreign-born Americans like myself do not take America for granted. We look upon American citizenship as the most precious and sacred of boons. We understand what it is that we have left behind us — of denial of the freedoms of man, and we know what it is that has come to be our high destiny, to be a sharer in American freedom, to be a bearer of American responsibility, to be a devotee of the American Democracy, to use American freedom not for one's own advantage but for the service of the American Democracy, and in these days of war, for the preservation of its loftiest ideals and purposes.

I am an American. I thank God that my parents brought me to this country. I thank God that my children and children's children have been born in this country. They have entered into and become sharers in the most precious heritage which can fall to the lot of man, and I have faith that they will prove equal to and worthy of the high opportunities of life which American citizenship affords. They, like me, will give their deepest, truest loyalty to the America which is today, to the greater, freer, nobler America that is to be on the morrow.

I am an American, I say, not boastfully, but with deepest faith in my country's destiny. For more than one hundred and fifty years my country has held aloft the torch of human freedom that other peoples might watch and learn how men live under the law of freedom. Today that freedom is under attack by those powers of darkness whom the light of American freedom offends and moves to derision and to attempted destruction. My country is in the midst of war, a war which it has not willed to wage, which it has not chosen to engage in. But now that America is under attack by the enslaving despotisms, America and its people which hate war, are resolved to spare no effort and substance that world tyranny may be broken, that human enslavement may be halted, and that human freedom may be saved.

I am an American, an American Jew who, because he is a Jew, proudly recalls that on the Independence Bell, which, on the fourth day of July, 1776, proclaimed the gladdest tidings that human ears ever heard, there were inscribed the words of the Hebrew Bible, " And ye shall proclaim liberty throughout the land unto all the inhabitants thereof." On this, " I Am An American " day, I know, and I thank God because I am permitted to know, that the Bible verse " And ye shall proclaim liberty throughout the land unto all the inhabitants thereof" has, since the seventh day of December, 1941, yea since the third of September, 1939, yea since the fourth day of March, 1933, translated itself into the larger term, " And ye Americans shall proclaim liberty throughout the lands unto all the inhabitants thereof."

I am an American. Because I am an American, I am free. Because I am an American, I shall live and labor to the end that all men be set free and that the spirit of American freedom rule over all the sons and daughters of men.

STEPHEN S. WISE, *As I See It*

The Father Of Freedom

Western culture in its Anglo-Saxon form is in itself nothing but an indirect descendant of the original Hebrew tradition. Western democracy is conceived and this world is built upon three concepts, individual morality, social justice and international peace. But where were those concepts produced, when were they proclaimed? They were proclaimed by the people of Israel in the land of Israel, through the language of Israel, in the previous eras of Israel's independence.

We reflect not with boastfulness, but with deep humility that there is nothing original or essential in what we call Western civilization, which you cannot trace back to the hills and valleys of our country, to the rare spirits and immortal voices which issued forth from it.

You do not, therefore, do justice to the facts when you describe Israel as a part of the cause of freedom and democracy. Israel is the father of freedom and the ancestor of the elements out of which democracy is born.

ABBA EBAN,
Address before the Rabbinical
Assembly of America, 1952

The Genius Of Judaism

Democracy is the very genius of Judaism. The very soul of the striving of Judaism is a social order inspired and hallowed by a just and righteous God and based on justice and righteousness in fulfilment of the will of that God. Almost on every page of the Bible the God of Israel is represented as the source and the proprietor of land and life, dispensing these as gifts, and demanding that they be administered in the spirit of the Giver. God is portrayed as sympathizing with the victim of oppression, with the underprivileged, with those who struggle for their rights and their liberties. Of the hundreds of references one might select from the Old Testament, the one pertaining to the Jubilee Year is perhaps the most characteristic and descriptive : " And ye shall hallow the fiftieth year, and proclaim liberty throughout the land unto all the inhabitants thereof . . . and ye shall return every man unto his possession, and ye shall return every man unto his family. . . . And ye shall not wrong one another ; but thou shalt fear thy God ; for I am the Lord your God. . . . And the land shall not be sold into perpetuity ; for the land is Mine ; for ye are strangers and settlers with Me." Since men can never be free politically unless they are free economically, the Scriptures here offer what was deemed to be an ideal economic basis for democracy. It is by no accident that the Prophets who were the inspired spokesmen of God were also the flaming champions of social righteousness. Elijah defies and denounces Ahab, the king, for robbing Naboth of his vineyard. " Thus saith the Lord : hast thou killed and also taken possession . . . ? In the place where dogs licked the blood of Naboth, shall dogs lick thy blood, even thine." Amos predicts a visitation of the wrath of God upon non-Jewish nations for crimes that are social in character ; upon Damascus for threshing Gilead with sledges of iron ; upon Gaza for delivering a whole captivity to Edom ; upon Ammon for ripping up women with child. It was the Prophets who proclaimed : " Let justice well up as waters, and righteousness as a mighty stream " ; " and they shall beat their swords into plowshares, and their spears into pruning-hooks ; nation shall not lift up sword against nation, neither shall they learn war any more." " Have we not all one father ? Hath not one God created us ? Why do we deal treacherously every man against his brother ? " " It hath been told thee, O man, what is good, and what the Lord doth require of thee : only to do justly, and to love mercy, and to walk humbly with thy God." Thus were the Prophets the great Commoners, the tribunes of the people, the consecrated social agitators, proclaiming in the name of God

(*Neum Adonoi*) a social order of justice and peace and freedom, an essential democracy on earth.

The American Revolution was both proof and product of the spirit of liberty and democracy in Judaism. The Revolution was dominated by the Puritan element in American life and that element was nurtured on the teachings of the Old Testament. The Bible, writes W. B. Selbie in the chapter on The Influence of the Old Testament on Puritanism : " moulded their speech, their thoughts, and their lives, and on it they built all their hopes of a better future both in this world and the next. In the bitter experiences of persecution and of civil war they found in the Old Testament in particular language and sentiments which exactly fitted their mood and suited their occasions." Dr. Ezra Stiles, President of Yale College, in his election sermon delivered in 1783 before the Governor and General Assembly of the State of Connecticut, refers to the American people as " God's American Israel. . . . ."

It was under the dominating influence of the spirit of Hebraism that the Committee, consisting of Benjamin Franklin, John Adams, and Thomas Jefferson, appointed, on the same day the Declaration of Independence was signed, to prepare a device for a seal for the United States, proposed as such a device, Pharaoh sitting in an open chariot, a crown on his head and a sword in his hand, passing through the dividing waters of the Red Sea in pursuit of the Israelites, with rays from a fire gleaming on Moses who is represented as standing on the shore, extending his hand over the sea, causing it to overwhelm Pharaoh; underneath being the motto, Rebellion to tyrants is obedience to God. Characteristic, too, is the inscription taken from the Old Testament (Leviticus 25 : 10) and engraved on the Liberty Bell : " Proclaim liberty throughout all the land unto all the inhabitants thereof." Lecky might well say : " The Hebraic mortar cemented the foundations of American Democracy."

LOUIS WITT,
Judaism and Democracy

The Jew In America

The Jew played a part in the discovery of this country, in its settlement and development, and its economic and political progress. The Jew in America played a not ignoble part in its art, literature, and science, in its social and educational movements, in peace and in war. He wishes to be permitted to carry on unmolested. He asks for no favors. He deserves no disfavors. He is eager to co-operate with all his neighbors. He is not clannish, except when intolerance forces clannishness upon him. The Jew in America should not be put on the defensive. He should not be forced to spend his energies in counterpropaganda or in apologetics. It is not good for him. It is not good for America. He should not be forced to fight for those rights which are his, as well as those of every other American citizen, by virtue of the basic law of the land, rights which are his inalienably.

ABBA HILLEL SILVER,
The World Crisis and Jewish Survival

The Message Of The Maccabees

Hanukkah, the Feast of the Maccabees, celebrates a victory — not a military victory only, but a victory also over more dangerous internal enemies. A victory of the many over the ease-loving, safety-playing, privileged, powerful few, who in their pliancy would have betrayed the best interests of the people, a victory of democracy over aristocracy.

As part of the eternal world-wide struggle for democracy, the struggle of the Maccabees is of eternal world-wide interest. It is a struggle of the Jews of today as well as of those of two thousand years ago. It is a struggle in which all Americans, non-Jews as well as Jews, should be vitally interested because they are vitally affected.

The Maccabees' victory proved that the Jews — then already an old people — possessed the secret of eternal youth : the ability to rejuvenate itself through courage, hope, enthusiasm, devotion and self-sacrifice of the plain people. This will bring a Jewish Renaissance.

LOUIS D. BRANDEIS

The Influence Of Hebrew Culture

The influence of Hebrew culture went far beyond the bounds of technical scholarship and professional training for theologians. It would be an impertinence for me to attempt to trace this influence in detail, but it is readily apparent that it has pervaded and colored the thought and feeling of this nation ever since its beginnings. Ezra Stiles, who became President of Yale College in 1778, was a thorough master of the Hebrew language which he wrote and spoke with a fluency and grace unusual even for those days. At the Public Commencement in 1781 he delivered a Hebrew oration. The study of Hebrew was not, to his mind, merely a formal intellectual discipline nor was it only a useful tool for the technical theologian. He regarded it as an important element in a liberal education, as the key to a vast storehouse of knowledge which could make possible an understanding of a highly significant aspect of human culture.

CHARLES SEYMOUR

The Nature Of Prophetic Religion

What was contained in the religion of the Prophets has remained the property of Judaism ; therein lie the determining elements of its being. Characteristic boundary lines can be drawn. Judaism is a religion which seeks verification in life and finds its answers in the union of life with God. In religion all men are to be on an equal footing ; religion is to be a common possession for all. Everybody is to be pious ; not the saint, but " a kingdom of priests and a holy nation " is the ideal. In the depths of the soul of the Prophet there dwells indeed his special secret, and he may and indeed must apprehend what to everybody else remains a closed door, or wholly non-existent. But this his possession, and his right to it, is to him but a duty, a gift, and a commandment to proclaim what, prior to all others, he has heard, to announce what, prior to all others, he has seen. But it was never considered to be a special piety which could be claimed by him alone, which was reserved for him exclusively. He has a mission, for which God created and chose him, but not a special rung of religion, upon which he may stand. He is the Prophet, but not the saint. And even he has not looked upon the face of God. In relation, or as opposed, to God, all men, in the last resort, are equal. However different the degree of knowledge, however different the institutions which go beyond knowledge, the divine unfathomableness and infinitude confront all, revealing themselves to none. But religion, the gift and capacity of piety, may be the possession of all. Everybody can draw near to his God, and a way to God proceeds from every soul.

Hence there cannot arise in Judaism a distinction between consecrated and unconsecrated persons, initiated and uninitiated, possessors and partakers of religion ; moreover,

the absence of any kind of sacrament has served to prevent that. Elsewhere e.g., in Christianity, this has taken place frequently, and in a variety of ways. There an exclusive religion has made its appearance, a special and peculiar type of holiness — not merely and purely a revealed proclamation of the Eternal — on the basis of rapturous and exuberant experiences, special manifestations of divine grace and extraordinary unions with God. Thus the religious community became at last always divided into two classes and grades. . . .

The religion of the Prophets by its very nature seeks to be the religion for all ; it imposes upon everybody the same demand ; it offers to everybody the same promise. The religious personality which it seeks to inform is to be the personality of every man.

LEO BAECK,
The Essence of Judaism

The Spirit Which Toppled Thrones

From the free spirit of the Mosaic law sprang the intensity of family life that amid all dispersions and persecution has preserved the individuality of the Hebrew race ; that love of independence that under the most adverse circumstances has characterized the Jew ; that burning patriotism that flamed up in the Maccabees and bared the breasts of Jewish peasants to the serried steel

of Grecian phalanx and the resistless onset of Roman legion ; that stubborn courage that in exile and in torture held the Jew to his faith. It kindled that fire that has made the strains of Hebrew seers and poets phrase for us the highest exaltations of thought ; that intellectual vigor that has over and over again made the dry staff bud and blossom. And passing outward from one narrow race it has exerted its power wherever the influence of the Hebrew Scriptures has been felt. It has toppled thrones and cast down hierarchies. It strengthened the Scottish Covenanter in the hour of trial, and the Puritan amid the snows of a strange land. It charged with the "Ironsides" at Naseby; it stood behind the low redoubt on Bunker Hill.

HENRY GEORGE,
Moses

The Impact Of The Bible On England

At a time when there was as yet no English literature for the common people, this untold wealth of Hebrew literature was implanted in the English mind as in a virgin soil. Great consequences have flowed from the fact that the first truly popular literature in England — the first which stirred the hearts of all classes of people and filled their minds with ideal pictures and their everyday speech with apt and telling phrases — was the literature comprised within the Bible. . . . To the Englishman who listened to Latimer, to the Scotchman who listened to Knox, the Bible more than filled the place which in modern times is filled by poem and essay, by novel and newspaper and scientific treatise. To its pages they went for daily instruction and comfort, with its strange Semitic names they baptized their children, upon its precepts, too often misunderstood and misapplied, they sought to build up a rule of life that might raise them above the crude and unsatisfying world into which they were born.

JOHN FISKE,
The Beginnings of New England

Our Obligations To Enrich Democracy

Our deep attachment to democracy is prompted by many considerations. In the first place there is the elemental consideration of patriotism. Then again, we are only too cognizant today that democracy alone offers a wholesome climate for Jewish physical, cultural and spiritual survival. And as heirs of the Jewish heritage we correctly see in democracy the truest political translation of our spiritual legacy.

We shall not completely discharge our obligation to American democracy, however, by mere expressions of loyalty and gratitude. It deserves to be enriched by us. And if American democracy is, as has been freely acknowledged, already deeply indebted to ancient Israel for its concept of the dignity of man, its passionate love of freedom, and its emphasis upon human equality, we can yet further enrich that democracy by our unflagging insistence that it be extended to include wider economic opportunites, more equitable social rights and more diversified cultural expressions. As members of a minority group, our concern with unlimited democracy has a special urgency. As the possessors of an eminently humane tradition, we are admirably equipped for the task. Thus our personal needs and our unique endowments coalesce to fit us for the vital service of deepening and broadening American democracy.

SIDNEY GREENBERG,
Address before the Rabbinical Assembly Convention, 1949

The Bravery Of Jewish Soldiers

It is impossible for me to do justice to those who served with me under my command who are known to be of Hebrew extraction. I would hardly be justified without their permission to give their names. I had a Jewish aide-de-camp, one of the bravest and best, in the first battle of Bull Run; he is now a distinguished officer of the army, a man of high scientific attainment. I had another aide who was killed at the battle of Chancellorsville, a true friend and a brave officer. Two of my brigade commanders, who answer to the above description, one of whom you have mentioned, served ably and faithfully at Gettysburg and in other great battles of the war. So many of the German officers and men, the Poles and the Hungarians, were of Jewish lineage that I am unable to designate them. I can assure you, my dear sir, that, intrinsically, there are no more patriotic men to be found in the country than those who claim to be of Hebrew descent, and who served with me in parallel commands or more directly under my instructions.... History affords no example superior to those of the Maccabees and other leaders of the Jews, back to the time of Jacob, the prince, who prevailed with God.

OLIVER OTIS HOWARD,
Letter to Simon Wolf

Abraham Krotoshinsky

Courage in emergencies is heroism, and for extraordinary heroism the Distinguished Service Cross is awarded by the United States Government.

A humble recipient of it is Abraham Krotoshinsky, an infantry private of the Bronx. He volunteered for a service which seemed certain death, for other men had fallen wounded, or had been killed, or were accounted "missing" in attempting the duty which the youngster from New York sprang to perform with no illusions about its perils.

The place was the Argonne Forest, full of "Bloody Angels." Krotoshinsky belonged to the "Lost Battalion." Surrounded by the enemy and cut off from the rest of the American Army, it had decided to die rather than surrender. Runner after runner was sent out. They were all volunteers, to quote from the first despatch, "to get through the enemy's lines and bring relief." Every man was a target as soon as he went "over the top." It was the valor of cold blood that made him run the risk. No man had gone through, for there was no cheer of relieving troops, no signal of aid

coming. When the call for a volunteer was made again, Krotoshinsky spoke first, stepped up to the ordeal, went over in full view of the enemy, and was off to save the "Lost Battalion."

One cannot imagine the Germans cheering the private from the Bronx as he faced their fire, now stumbling, now up again, always going forward undaunted to save the battalion, but if ever a fighting man deserved to be cheered by a generous enemy it was this courier who was "captain of his soul" and dared all for love of his comrades. . . .

If the great war has proved anything, it is that men of all races and from all climes are brave to a fault, and that heroes may wear unfamiliar names — the name of Abraham Krotoshinsky, for instance.

The New York Times, Editorial, 1918

Justice To The Jew !

The foundation stones of our great commonwealth were laid by men who differed widely in race and religion, but who came together for a common cause ; those stones were cemented by the blood of martyrs, who though widely divergent in many respects, shed their blood on a common altar for a glorious cause, and among these men and martyrs were many of Jewish faith. North, south, east and west the sunlight streams o'er the graves of Christian and Jewish dead who perished that

America might live, might take her place among the nations of the world, not the last nor the least, but the foremost and best, great, glorious, and free, invincible and immortal, at one and the same time the envy and the admiration of the world. . . .

As America has given the Jew a haven, let her do more, let her take him to her breast and treat him as she does her other children. . . . Lord Macaulay said, "The Jew is what we made him." He is the handiwork of our own civilization. The American Jew is at the present what America is making him. Not his destiny, but his influence for good or evil, lies in her hands. His race is imperishable; republics may rise and fall, nationalities wither and decay, but ever down the stream of time shall sail the barque of Israel until it loses itself in the illimitable vastness of eternity. Whether that barque shall be freighted with a precious cargo or not, depends to a very great extent on the people of America. It they will they can make it valuable and a blessing to their nation, or they can render it harmful and an evil in the land.

Yes, America can shape the future of the Jew; she can show him kindness, respect his manhood, and give him opportunity; in a word, she can give him justice, and this is all he asks. The oldest civilization stands at the door of the youngest, and with suppliant voice, Zion calls to Columbia for — *justice to the Jew.*

MADISON C. PETERS,
Justice to the Jew

Thoughts At The ' Brith ' Of A New-Born Infant

Just born and he already enjoys the longest geneological record in the Western World. Was he not admitted to the " Covenant of Abraham " ? So-called blue-bloods and their social register are upstarts and parvenues alongside of this little fellow. And the list of his ancestors is studded with the prominent names of creative spirits who enriched the life of all mankind. He seems a little frail to bear so great a patrimony. Yet what possibilities he represents.

He has a capacity for such attachment to Jewish traditions as to enhance his life and to acquire a sense of deep companionship with Jews everywhere.

He can be a good American imbued with profound democratic sensitivities and with a fine awareness of the interdependence of all men.

He is qualified to join in a beautiful synthesis of the two currents of influence in his life, the Judaic and the American.

The symbols of Judaism can add beauty to his daily life and its culture can enrich his ethical and intellectual background.

He can enter American life proudly and with dignity unbent by the centuries of Jewish deprivation, and unhurt by underground streams of misconception and bigotry.

He can feel kinship with the great Jewish communities of the past, without ignoring the fact that the American Jewish settlement must respect the logic of its particular climate and background.

He can hold strongly to convictions without defaming those who differ.

He can live by a system of high values without surrendering in the name of modernity, to the vulgarities and errors from which no society is totally free.

He can be versed in the Bible and help reinstate the Jew as a "people of the Book."

He can build a home, that is not simply a stereotyped copy of the homes of his class, but possesses the distinctive qualities of his Jewishness and the best features of American life.

He can be a faithful Jew without being parochial and a loyal American without being the less Jewish.

What an opportunity he represents !

MORRIS ADLER,
Shaarey Zedek Recorder

The Defender Of Liberty

Democracy was not only in Judaism but also in the Jew. Not only because of the teachings of his religion but also because of the unhappy social and political status in which the profession of his religion placed him, the Jew became the defender and the martyr of liberty and liberalism everywhere. He was everywhere the victim of religious intolerance, of commercial envy, of nationalistic Chauvinism, of racial animosity. In the State he was looked upon as alien ; in the Church as an infidel ; in society as a pariah. He had to fight for the most elementary rights, for the very rights for which oppressed causes and liberal principles were fighting everywhere.

He became thus by necessity as much as by choice identified with the liberal movement everywhere. He contributed of his blood and his passion to liberalism in every land and age. Wherever oppressed minorities or peoples were fighting for the separation of Church and State, for equality under the law, for a juster distribution of economic opportunity, for the universalization of the ballot, the Jew fought at their side. As Jacobs says : " their position as forming the sole exception to the Christian concensus had its influence in promoting the slow development of free thought and religious toleration. Throughout the long struggle the foes of the Jew have invariably been the foes of liberalism and the modern spirit. Every step forward in the emancipation of the Jew has ever been a step forward in the emancipation of the human spirit. The Jew has indeed been the barometer of civilization.

The genius of Judaism and the destiny of the Jew have combined to inspire and to enforce the establishment of that social order which from government by the classes for the classes, and government by the classes for the people, rose to the heights of government by the people for the people, safe-guarded by the prevalence of tolerance, good-will, and justice among the people.

LOUIS WITT,
Judaism and Democracy

14

Anti-Semitism

Pretexts change, but the hatred remains. The Jews are
not hated because they have evil qualities ; evil qualities
are sought for in them because they are hated.

MAX NORDAU,
Max Nordau To His People

It is not at all certain that anti-Semitism would be
weakened to any extent if the Jews were to consist
exclusively of angels in human form.

HUGO VALENTIN,
Anti-Semitism

For the Jews the moral is to answer anti-Semitism with
more Semitism, if by Semitism we mean greater devotion
to the great ideals which Judaism proclaimed to the
world.

ISRAEL ABRAHAMS,
Christian and Jew

The Cause Of Massacres

The vicissitudes endured by the Jewish race, from the period when Christianity became dominant, may well be a subject of pride to the Hebrew and of shame to the Christian. The annals of mankind afford no more brilliant instance of steadfastness under adversity, of unconquerable strength through centuries of hopeless oppression, of inexhaustible elasticity in recuperating from apparent destruction and of conscientious adherence to a faith whose only portion in this life was contempt and suffering. Nor does the long record of human perversity present a more damning illustration of the facility with which the evil passions of man can justify themselves with the pretext of duty, than the manner in which the Church, assuming to represent Him who died to redeem mankind, deliberately planted the seeds of intolerance and persecution and assiduously cultivated the harvest for nearly fifteen hundred years. . . .

Man is ready enough to oppress and despoil his fellows, and, when taught by his religious guides that justice and humanity are a sin against God, spoliation and oppression become the easiest of duties. It is not too much to say that for the infinite wrongs committed on the Jews during the Middle Ages, and for the prejudices that are even yet rife in many quarters, the Church is mainly if not wholly responsible. It it true that occasionally she lifted her voice in mild remonstrance when some massacre occurred more atrocious than usual, but these massacres were the direct outcome of the hatred and contempt which she so jealously inculcated, and she never took steps by punishment to prevent their repetition. . . .

HENRY CHARLES LEA,
A History of the Inquisition of Spain

The Real Problem

When the Semitic question raised such a commotion in Europe, there appeared a pamphlet on that subject which concluded with the suggestion that, in order to remove the difficulties involved, the Jews ought to be civilized.

My personal observations have led me to a different conclusion : the Jew, as a people, has reached the highest point of human development as comprehended by the Mosaic law.

It seems to me that the problem now is how to civilize and Christianize thoroughly the peoples among whom the Jews live, so that the latter may, if not love them, at least respect them. . . .

I wish that, instead of devoting themselves to trace the faults of

Jews, Christian nations would seek to imitate them in their social qualities and religious loyalty. Now, that the Jews' first task, to spread monotheism on earth, has been accomplished, should not their presence in our midst serve the purpose of revivifying moral sentiment and familial affection, attributes that are fast disappearing among us. . . ?

Oh, if the Jews had only a fraction of our vices, even their name would long since have been effaced from the earth !

NATHALIE GORTSHAKOV-UVAROV,
Juifs et Chrétiens

The Strange Inconsistency

Strange inconsistency ! to persecute in the name of religion those who had given the religion. . . . Catholic Spain, Protestant Germany, Greek Russia massacred and murdered Jews while singing the psalmody Jewish patriarchs and prophets had written. Oh ! Christianity, what crimes have been committed in thy name !

MADISON C. PETERS,
Justice to the Jew

The Unprecedented Injustice

Such an injustice as that inflicted by the Gentile Church on Judaism is almost unprecedented in the annals of history. The Gentile church stripped it of everything ; she took away its sacred book ; herself but a transformation of Judaism, she cut off all connection with the parent religion. The daughter first robbed her mother, and then repudiated her.

ADOLF HARNACK,
The Expansion of Christianity

It is for his virtues, not his vices, that the Jew is hated.

THEODOR HERZL

Nothing gratifies the mob more than to get a simple name to account for a complex phenomenon, and the word " Jew " is always at hand to explain the never-absent maladies of the body politic.

ISRAEL ZANGWILL

If You Have To Drown A Dog . . .

It is the practice of human intellect to invent for the prejudices, which sentiment has called forth, a cause seemingly reasonable. Probably wisdom has long been acquainted with this psychological law, and puts it in fairly expressive words : " If you have to drown a dog," says the proverb, "you must first declare him to be mad." All kinds of vices are falsely attributed to the Jews, because one wishes to convince himself that he has a right to detest them. But the pre-existing sentiment is the detestation of the Jews.

MAX NORDAU,
Max Nordau to His People

A Message To The Christian World

At this season when the Christmas message of peace to men of good will is being sounded throughout the world, we Christians of the United States and Canada, mindful that this message was first proclaimed in the land of Israel to the Jewish people and that it has come to us through them, earnestly seek to emphasize its significance for us today ; believing that the message from ancient Palestine, if truly accepted, can mellow and exalt all human relationships and hasten the time when men shall dwell together in peace.

We deplore the long record of wrongs from which the Jewish people have suffered in the past, often from the hands of those who have professed the Christian faith and who have yet been guilty of acts utterly alien to the Christian teaching and spirit.

We declare our disavowal of anti-Semitism in every form and our purpose to remove by every available means its causes and manifestations in order that we may share with our fellow citizens of Jewish heritage, every political, educational, commercial, social, and religious opportunity.

We urge upon Christians everywhere the cultivation of understanding, appreciation, and good will toward the Jewish people to whom we owe so much. We call upon all Christians as they commemorate the birth of Jesus at Christmas this year, to join us, through personal influence, the teaching of the young at home and school and in other ways, in earnestly seeking the removal of anti-Jewish prejudices and their consequences and the advent of a new era of friendly fellowship and cooperation worthy of the faith we profess.

Signed by the heads of the leading Protestant Church bodies of U.S. and Canada, 1931,

Quoted in *Judaism at Bay*

Perhaps the saddest thing to admit is that those who rejected the Cross have to carry it, while those who welcomed it are so often engaged in crucifying others.

NICHOLAS BERDYAEV,
Christianity and Anti-Semitism

A Curious Caricature

Last year it happened to the writer that he began a conversation about the Jews with a good Nordic salesman in a Pullman car. The salesman began by telling about the Jews on his route, hard, unscrupulous fellows who pressed every advantage in order to increase their profits. Yes, the Jews were a hard lot to deal with. Curious to see the reaction, I told my fellow traveler that I knew a number of Jews who were conspicuous failures in business, because they were too kind-hearted and gave everything away. The salesman immediately cited two examples among his own customers who were " just like that." And how many Jews did he serve on his route ? Exactly three — and two of these were too kind-hearted to be good businessmen. Yet his first and subconscious reaction was to tell about the hard-driving Jews in business. Why ? Tradition, of course. Like all non-Jews he had imbibed a curious caricature of a tradition about the Jews and he repeated this parrot-like, although it actually did not square with his experience.

H. C. ENGELBRECHT,
Opinion

How strange ! The very people who had given the world a God, and whose whole life was inspired by devotion to God, were stigmatized as deicides !

HEINRICH HEINE,
Confessions

Anti-Semites In Embryo

In large part, anti-Semitism is the direct result of religious indoctrination. For centuries the church has taught the Christian to regard the Jew as the deicide. To this day the Christian child, during his earliest and most pliable years, is subjected to the same instruction. Nor does the typical Sunday School instructor take the trouble to indicate to his pupils that biblical criticism has raised serious doubts concerning the historic truth of the story of the crucifixion, and that in any event, the Jews who supposedly crucified Jesus are dead almost two thousand years. The child naturally confuses ancient Jews with those he knows. At the age of seven or eight, he is an anti-Semite in embryo. As a result, the Christian Sunday School is packed with social dynamite. Teaching the saving efficacy of love, it has tended generally to inculcate hatred of the Jew. It goes without saying that many ministers and teachers of all denominations are keenly aware of the danger, that they attempt cautiously and carefully to " obviate " the transmission of a prejudice. And yet, many a sincere follower of the Christ who taught love has inadvertently helped to poison the minds of a rising generation. Once the damage has been done, it is largely irreparable. A deep prejudice has been created which numberless sermons on human brotherhood cannot eradicate. The child may grow into an adult, he may be exposed to all sorts of educational experiences. He may even turn skeptic or agnostic and break with the religion of his youth. But there exists a large presumption that the bias of infancy will survive all changes, that he will continue to suspect and dislike Jews without being conscious of the long obscured cause of this dislike.

MILTON STEINBERG,
The Making of the Modern Jew

Hatred for Judaism is at bottom hatred for Christianity.

SIGMUND FREUD,
Moses and Monotheism

The Echoes Of History

A cursory reading of early Christian history will easily teach Christians that their own first forerunners in the faith were exposed to the very prejudice and hatreds of which the Jews have suffered throughout Christian centuries. There is hardly a charge or libel against the Jew which is not an echo of the accusations made against Christians in the first three centuries of their history. These accusations persisted as long as Christians remained a minority in the Roman Empire. Christians were accused of using children's blood in their initiation ceremonies; they were charged with thievery, with the corruption of the morals of men and the disintegration of religion. They were regarded as the bringers on of decay, and as a menace to the State. Under similar circumstances they suffered almost to the letters the same persecutions of which the Jews have been the victims. . . . Christians were made the scapegoat because they differed from the majority.

SOLOMON GOLDMAN,
Crisis and Decision

Anti-Semitism is a form of Christian hypocrisy. The Christian whitewashes himself by attributing his vices to the Jew.

BERNARD LAZARE,
Antisemitism

The Perennial Source Of Anti-Semitism

If we consider all the reasons for anti-Semitism advanced by the Christian nations, we find that they are all superficial and transitory. But if we go deeper, we find that there is one deep and unconscious reason that is true for all periods of the exile. It is, that there has entered and become dispersed among them a people carrying a charge from heaven which is written in a book which became sacred for them too when they became Christians. It is unique in human history, strange and awesome, that heaven should make a specific demand in reference to human behavior, and that the demand should be recorded in a book, and that the book should be the heritage of a people which is dispersed among all the nations with this, its holy book, which is holy for all the nations as well. The demand stands above and remote from the nations, a comprehensive demand, differing entirely from the quality characteristic of their own lives ; it hovers high over them as the demand which their God makes of them. And the nations refuse to submit to it. To be sure, they wish to retain the God they have received, but at the same time they would reject his demand. In so doing they rely upon the teachings of Saul, a Jew from Tarsus, who asserted that it was impossible to fulfil the Torah and that it was necessary to cast off its yoke by submission to another Jew, Jesus of Nazareth, who had died during Saul's lifetime and was the Messiah, who had indeed fulfilled the Torah

and abolished it at the same time ; and who demanded nothing of its true believers save faith. Such was the argument of the nations who went in the footsteps of Saul, and a large part of their theology has been nothing but a detailed interpretation of the utterance of Saul, the apostle of the Gentiles.

Yet against all their opposition to the Torah stood that unfortunate Jewish people bearing the book which was its own book and at the same time part of the holy book of the nations. That is the real reason for their hatred. Their theologians argue that God rejected this people, who no longer have any heritage because that heritage has now passed over to Christianity. But the Jewish people continued to exist, book in hand ; and even though they were burned at the stake, the words of the book were still on their lips. That is the perennial source of anti-Semitism. In this sense there is an essential truth in the verse of the medieval Hebrew poet, Yannai, " Hated we are, for thee we love, O Holy ! "   MARTIN BUBER,
Israel and the World

When the ledgers of a people show red, the outlook for minority peoples is black.   MARVIN LOWENTHAL

They Were Both Wrong

George M. Cohan, the famous Irish entertainer and songwriter, was once mistaken by the manager of a swanky hotel for a Jew. When his request for reservations was refused, he wired the management as follows : " We are both wrong. You thought I was a Jew, and I thought you were a gentleman."

The Injustice Of Anti-Semitism

The character of the Jews is utterly irrelevant ; what they do or fail to do is equally so. Hence it is futile for them to seek to oppose anti-Semitism by any kind of human behavior. If they seek to avoid the strictures of their foes by avoiding any imputed fault, their new attitude will be equally attacked because it is a Jewish attitude and they will be mocked in the bargain for assuming virtues that are not theirs. Under exceptionally favorable circumstances the Jew may temporarily hide from the results of hatred ; he can never please his foes and the attempt to do so will only cause him to incur the last reproach of servile weakness.

And since it is not real lacks or vices that evoke anti-Semitism, it is an error to believe that a Jew can get the better of this hatred by personal qualities or achievements. Conspicuous success may occasionally be accepted as the price of entrance into Gentile society ; anti-Semitism as such is diminished by no success, no virtue, and no achievement ; it is like a tropic sun that sears the unjust and just Jew alike.

FRITZ BERNSTEIN,
quoted in Rebirth

How Logical Are The Pretexts ?

In former centuries the pretext for plundering Jewish homes and massacring Jews was that they had crucified Jesus. This pretext was about as logical as that of the black Haitians, who, during the massacre of the white inhabitants of the island of Santo Domingo, ran about with an image of the crucified Savior and shouted : " The whites killed him ; let us kill the whites." The real incentive for the Negroes' acts of violence was the desire for the wealth of the whites.

SOL LIPTZEN,
Germany's Step-Children

The Invalid

The anti-Semite is an invalid who will not go to the doctor. He goes only to the Jew. The Jew is his patent medicine guaranteed to cure him. If he is weak, the Jew will make him strong. If he is stupid, he has only to swallow a few Jews and become brilliant. If he is suffering from being unknown, he can find fame out of Jews. They are a magic indispensable to fools.

BEN HECHT,
A Guide for the Bedevilled

Neo-Paganism And The Spirit Of The Jew

The neo-pagans of the twentieth century wish to destroy the Jew because they hate and fear the spirit of the Jew, which has been the implacable and indefeasible foe of paganism throughout the ages and which will not rest until it has destroyed the new paganism also. They are not afraid of the Jews' physical power. The Jews were never numbered among the conquering peoples of the earth. They never built empires. Their legions never swept over continents with fire and sword. No Cyrus sprang from their loins, no Alexander, no Hannibal, no Ghengis Khan and no Napoleon to shake the world. Against such conquerors one can protect oneself ; one can build Siegfried lines of defense and fashion weapons in Krupp and Skoda works. But the Jews are foes of another stamp, and the fear which they inspire is a greater fear, and at bottom a justifiable fear. The neo-pagans sense a real menace, a threat to them and to their world.

ABBA HILLEL SILVER,
The World Crisis and Jewish Survival

Can We Learn From Our Enemies ?

Not rarely a Jew is heard to murmur that we must learn from our enemies and try to remedy our failings. He forgets, however, that the anti - Semitic accusations are valueless, because they are not based on a criticism of real facts, but are merely due to the psychological law according to which children, savages, and malevolent fools make persons and things against which they have an aversion responsible for their sufferings.

MAX NORDAU,
Max Nordau to His People

The Honest Anti-Semite

Anti-Semitism is a mad passion, akin to the lowest perversities of diseased human nature. It is the will to hate.

The Emperor Hadrian was an honest anti-Semite. One day, the Talmud records, on his journey in the East, a Jew passed the Imperial train and saluted the Emperor. He was beside himself with rage. " You,

a Jew, dare to greet the Emperor! You shall pay for this with your life." In the course of the same day another Jew passed him, and, warned by example, he did not greet Hadrian. "You, a Jew, dare to pass the Emperor without a greeting!" he angrily exclaimed. "You have forfeited your life." To his astonished courtiers he replied : "I hate the Jews. Whatever they do, I find intolerable. I therefore make use of any pretext to destroy them."
So are all anti-Semites.

LEO TOLSTOY,
quoted in *A Book of Jewish Thoughts*

If there were no Jews they would have to be invented, for the use of politicians — they are indispensable, the antithesis of a panacea ; guaranteed to *cause* all evils.

ISRAEL ZANGWILL,
The Voice of Jerusalem

The Source Of Jewish Vitality

Anti - Semitism, as it has often been pointed out, plays a role in the preservation of the Jewish group. It cannot, however, be overemphasized that while anti-Semitism may be able to keep the Jewish community from dying, it cannot stimulate it to life. The sources of Jewish vitality are to be found exclusively in our tradition, our history and our own will to live as Jews.

MORRIS ADLER,
Shaarey Zedek Bulletin

If All Jews Were Angels

The view widely prevalent in Jewish and non-Jewish circles that by acting in this way or that the Jews might have been able to avert anti-Semitism is based on an illusion. For it is not the Jews who are hated, but an imaginary image of them, which is confounded with the reality, and the Jews' actual "faults" play a very unimportant part in the matter. It may indeed be true that the Jewish people, like all others, is in duty bound to work at its moral improvement ; even more than others, in fact, since distress and oppression, of which it has had more than its share, easily lead to demoralization. . . .

But a nation of sixteen millions can never avoid including in its midst unsympathetic and inferior elements. When the non - Jewish world feels the need of hating, of finding a scapegoat, it judges unfairly by these. In fact it is not at all certain that anti-Semitism would be weakened to any extent if the Jews were to consist exclusively of angels in human form.

HUGO VALENTIN
Anti-Semitism

An anti-Semite may prove "logically" that Jesus never existed and may yet continue to prove "historically" that the Jews had crucified him.   HERMANN COHEN,
quoted in *The Inner Eye*

The Stupidity Of The Bigot

Of all the bigotries that savage the human temper there is none so stupid as the anti-Semitic.

In the sight of these fanatics, Jews of today can do nothing right. If they are rich they are birds of prey. If they are poor they are vermin. If they are in favor of a war, that is because they want to exploit the bloody feuds of Gentiles to their own profit. If they are anxious for peace they are either instinctive cowards or traitors. If they give generously — and there are no more liberal givers than the Jews — they are doing it for some selfish purpose of their own. If they don't give — then what would one expect of a Jew ? If labor is oppressed by great capital, the greed of the Jew is held responsible. If labor revolts against capital — as it did in Russia — the Jew is blamed for that also. If he lives in a strange land he must be persecuted and pogrommed out of it. If he wants to go back to his own he must be prevented. . . .

It will be long ere Canaan becomes once more a land flowing with milk and honey. The Jews alone can redeem it from the wilderness and restore its ancient glory.

They belong to a race which for at least nineteen hundred years has been subjected to persecution, pillage, massacre and the torments of endless derision ; a race that has endured persecution which for variety of torture — physical, material and mental — inflicted on its victims, for the virulence and malignity with which it has been sustained, for the length of time it has lasted, and, more than all, for the fortitude and patience with which it has been suffered, is without parallel in the history of any other people.

Is it too much to ask that those among them whose sufferings are the worst shall be able to find refuge in the land their fathers made holy by the splendor of their genius, by the loftiness of their thoughts, by the consecration of their lives and by the inspiration of their message to mankind ?

DAVID LLOYD GEORGE

Playful Brutality

My father once told me that in the 1840's in a village along the Rhine, a boy had thrown a stone at a Jew. The missile did not hit the Jew but it broke a window pane ; and the Jew was made to pay for the damage, because if he hadn't dodged, the pane would not have been broken—the playful brutality of healthy children maltreating a cat.

HANS ZINSSER,
As I Remember Him

"Please Send Us Some Jews"

There is more psychological truth than fiction in the story concerning an official high authority in Fascist Japan who is reported to have cabled to his ally, Germany's (sinister) Minister of Propaganda, "We are starting an anti-Semitic movement in Japan. Please send us some Jews."

ISRAEL GOLDSTEIN,
Toward a Solution

The Ungrateful Daughter

Anti-Semitism, of course, has its religious roots. The Christians have not been able to forgive the Jews for the fact that Judaism is the mother of Christianity, and that the mother disowned the daughter for fraud and ingratitude. No amount of Christian theological casuistry has been able to hide this, and the more honest among the Christian theologians openly admit the ingratitude —for they know that all that is true, good and beautiful in Christianity is basically Jewish ; but most of them still haven't it in their heart to question the concept of the divinity and divine mission of Christ.

CHARLES ANGOFF,
Troubled Intellectuals

The Christian Attitude Toward Anti-Semitism

Every thoughtful Christian must gratefully acknowledge his spiritual indebtedness to the Hebrews. We Christians have inherited the ethical and religious insights of Israel. We hold them with a difference—at one point with a momentous difference —but we can never forget that the historic roots of our faith are in the Hebrew people.

From Israel we inherit the Ten Commandments, which are still our basic moral standards. From Israel we inherit the priceless treasure of the Psalms, which are an essential part of Christian worship around the world. From Israel we inherit the vision of social justice which has come to us through Amos and Isaiah and Micah. From Israel we inherit even our own unique Christian classic, The New Testament, nearly all of which (if not all) was written by Jews.

A Christian who faces the modern world must also be conscious of a present spiritual kinship with his Jewish neighbors to whom their religious heritage is still a vital force. That kinship is grounded in our common faith in the ultimate spiritual foundations of the universe. Over against those who adhere to a materialistic philosophy of life and a mechanistic conception of human destiny, we recognize ourselves as at one with the Jews in the first sublime affirmation of Pentateuch, "In the beginning God." Over against current disillusionment and despair Christian and Hebrew stand together in their belief in the one Holy God who is the Creator of all and whose righteous will gives meaning and direction to life.

A Christian who knows anything of history must also speak a word of confession. For he cannot help recalling how grievously the Jewish people have suffered at the hands of men who have called themselves Christians. The record of the treatment of Jews in Europe through long centuries is one which Christians of today view with penitence and sorrow. One has also regretfully to admit that the day of cruel treatment of the Jews by some who call themselves Christians is not yet a thing of the past. Even in our own country there are misguided groups which circulate statements that spread a poison of mistrust and hate which is antithetical to the true genius both of America and of the Christian religion. Anti-Semitism is inherently unchristian, contrary to the plain teaching and spirit of our Lord, and it can be asserted with confidence that an intolerant attitude toward the Jews is opposed by the great body of Americans who are Christians.

A Christian today must also recognize the practical interests which he shares in common with the Jewish people. If there was formerly any doubt on this point, the tragic events in Germany during the last five years must make the fact as plain as noonday. In that unhappy land the National Socialist regime began by proclaiming itself the friend of what it called "positive Christianity" and the enemy of the Jews. But everything which has happened since shows that what started as a movement against the Jews turns out to be a movement against Christianity also. Today in Germany the whole future of Christianity as well as of the Jews is at stake. The new religious trend known as the "Germanic faith movement," under the leadership of anti-Semites like Alfred Rosenberg and Baldur von Shirach, scorns Christianity as of Jewish origin and would substitute for both Judaism and Christianity a new religion based on German blood. The attempt to de-Judaize a nation threatens to de-Christianize it also.

THE FEDERAL COUNCIL OF THE
CHURCHES OF CHRIST IN AMERICA
Federal Council Bulletin

Anti-Semitism is not to be overcome by getting people to forget us, but to know us.

MEYER LEVIN,
In Search

The Jew Spoiled Everything

However it may express itself on the social, economic, cultural and political levels, whatever may be its involvement with other factors in the ongoing life of society, anti-Semitism is, at the bottom, the revolt of the pagan against the God of Israel and his absolute demand. This was obvious in pre-Christian anti-Semitism, but it is equally true of anti-Semitism in the Christian world, where "hatred of Judaism is at bottom hatred for Christianity" (Sigmund Freud). That is how Rosenzweig understood anti - Semitism. "Whenever the pagan within the Christian soul rises in revolt against the yoke of the Cross, he vents his fury on the Jew." And that is how the most penetrating modern thinkers, Jewish and Christian, have understood it. "It is of Christ that the (anti-Semites) are afraid. . . . Therefore they make their assault on those who are responsible for the birth and spread of Christianity. They spit on the Jews as Christ-killers because they long to spit on them as Christ-givers" (Maurice Samuels). "We reject the Jews in order to reject Jesus as the Christ. Hatred of the Jews is a result of our hatred of Christ" (A. Roy Eckardt). "Hatred of Jews and hatred of Christians spring from a common source, from the same recalcitrance of the world. . . . That is why the bitter zeal of anti-Semitism always turns in the end into bitter zeal against Christianity itself" (Jacques Maritain). "Western civilization, which represents the wedding of Greco-Roman culture with Hebraic culture, has ever since been trying to effect a divorce. Hebraism, as a prophetic and transcendent view of history, has made it difficult for our Western civilization to rest lightly in its pretensions. Anti-Semitism is our answer. . . . Destroy the symbol of Hebraic culture, and the uncertainty of our conscience as well as the reality of our guilt are obliterated. Resisting our destiny we must destroy those who call that destiny to mind. Until we surrender to that destiny, the Jew will not be safe. . . . The Jew is always the enemy of an idolatrous culture" (Fred Denbeaux). But it is Houston Stewart Chamberlain, the forerunner of modern neo - pagan anti - Semitism, who, in a burst of self-disclosure, puts the whole thing in one illuminating phrase : "The Jew came into our gay world and spoiled everything with his ominous concept of sin, with his Law and his Cross."

WILL HERBERG,
Judaism and Modern Man

I Awoke To Find Myself A Jew

One day I awakened from a dream. I had lived among a certain people and thought myself to be of the same blood. I had been raised to rejoice in its joys and to sorrow in its sorrows. Its earth was mine and I had seen no sky more beautiful than the soft sky above it. I thought myself the brother of those about me and only on the day of my awakening did I hear it said that I was of another blood, another earth, another sky, another brotherhood. I awoke to find myself a Jew and I did not know what it was to be a Jew. . . .

It was evening at a friend's house. The crowd in the streets was roaring, " Death to the Jews ! "

Said my friend : " You are not a Jew ; you do not even know what that is, and yet you are persecuted as such. Make over your soul ; then you will find in your soul the strength to bear what your ancestors, too, have borne."

BERNARD LAZARE,
quoted in *Rebirth*

What We Can Do About Anti-Semitism

Though the Jew cannot control the forces of anti - Semitism, he should be able to control its effect upon him. He can, if he wants to, prevent it from injuring his mental health and self-respect. To be able to do that, however, he needs the strength of character which only the cultivation of his Jewish spiritual heritage can give him. The Jew, who is illiterate in matters pertaining to his People and its way of life, is bound to be cursed with a sense of inferiority, and to be forever at war with himself. The illiterate Jew is a living illustration of what it means for a man to be his own worst enemy. The only way the Jew can ever make peace with himself is for him to be literate as a Jew, to know his People and its religion.

The illiterate Jew is his worst enemy, because he himself is to blame for the breakdown of his morale under the impact of anti-Semitism. Morale, as courage in the face of difficulty and danger, presupposes an undivided mind and a self-confident spirit. When the enemy succeeds in getting us to doubt ourselves, it is entirely our own weakness, and not his strength, that undermines our self-confidence. The ignorant Jew is likely so to hate himself as to be something of an anti-Semite. He resents being continually dunned by Jews for Jewish causes. What do they want of him ? They have burdened him with a liability for no good reason. Before one knows it, he finds himself joining the hue and cry of the anti-Semites.

Learn To Know Your Jewish People

Let the Jew, however, learn the inner meaning of the Patriarchal stories and the recorded experiences of Israel in Egypt and the Wilderness. Let him learn to appreciate the towering spiritual genius of a Moses. Let him scan the forces that molded ancient Israel into a nation. Let him discern the unique traits of the Jewish People, that reveal themselves in its return from Babylonian captivity, and its renascence during the Maccabean revolt, in its rejection of Christianity, in the rise of Rabbinism, in its endless wanderings and in its repeated recoveries. He will then realize how, throughout the centuries, the Jewish spirit kept on growing in clearness of vision and in strength of resolve to carry on against all odds. It will then dawn upon him why a People with such an exceptional career, scattered among so many nations, is chosen as a convenient scapegoat for the world's sins. The Jew who knows the facts which give the lie to all the Pharaohs, the Hamans, the Apions, and the Hitlers, can never lose confidence in himself and in his cause.

The illiterate Jew is a traditionless person. The fact that he is known as a Jew prevents him from identifying himself with the Christian tradition. Even, if through conversion, he is formally made an heir to that tradition, it can never become part of his subconscious, or of his inner being. A Jew is not likely to find himself at home in a tradition which still continues to declare all his ancestors deicides and doomed to eternal torment in hell. Thus by keeping aloof from the tradition of his own People, the Jew condemns himself to spiritual homelessness.

On the other hand, the Jew who cultivates the tradition of his People does not merely inform his mind. He gains for himself an ancestry ; he acquires status ; he satisfies the need of belonging to a permanent kinship and to be a part of a spiritual fellowship. The Jew who can rise to his feet and before all the world proclaim, " Our God and the God of our fathers," is heir to *noblesse* which excels any that the proudest titles could confer. The parchment scroll of the Torah out of which he reads in the Synagogue, then becomes his *lettres patentes*. When he consecrates the Sabbath over the Kiddush cup, he rightly claims his share in the tradition which has bestowed on the human race the greatest gift of bodily and spiritual recreation, provided he has learned what the Sabbath means. And when he recounts, on Passover night, the story of the Exodus from Egypt, he identifies himself with ancient Israel, provided he has learned to grasp the full significance of the Jewish teaching that God, the creator, is also God the redeemer. Such a Jew can be trusted to acquit himself worthily before God and man. *Noblesse oblige.*

The realization of the immense possibilities for good that are latent in our people, and of their actual achievements, even in these days of unrelieved universal anxiety, cannot but win the Jew's admiration and love for his fellow Jews. The late Justice Brandeis, during his earlier years, had taken little interest in Jewish life. He got to know his People, however, when he came in contact with them in the course of his efforts to arbitrate their labor disputes. He then noted what wellsprings of justice and kindness flowed from their tradition and the way of life to which it had given rise. As a result he became an ardent Jew, and one of the warmest pleaders of his People's cause.

What Jews have accomplished within the last fifty years in the State of Israel, in reclaiming the least promising of lands, in reviving a language that had been moribund, in laying the foundation of a modern Hebraic civilization which embraces all aspects of human culture, all this is tantamount to the creation of a new world. It is a world in which cooperation, pioneering, and the creative spirit figure as the traits that had long been dormant within the soul of the Jew. To become part of this world one must have a knowledge of contemporary Jewish life and movements.

Know Your Religion

The illiterate Jew is his own worst enemy, because he completely misunderstands the religion of his People. If he is a worker, and is drawn into one of the radical groups, he readily adopts their jargon about religion as "an opiate to the masses." He is led to misinterpret the fact that the Jews have played a leading role in the history of religion and in supplying at least half of mankind with the basic principles of their faiths. In his ignorance, that fact makes them all the more responsible for having contributed to the enslavement of the masses. The Jewish ignoramus, who belongs to the professional or business world, generally judges the Jewish religion by a few observances which have no meaning for him. He dismisses them as survivals of ancient superstition. He cannot forgive the Jews for having stubbornly held on to them at the cost of great hardship.

One does not have to know much about comparative religion to realize that the resort to religion as an opiate represents its abuse rather than its intrinsic use, or that the superstitions in which all religions abound are not the product of religion as such, but rather of the mental inertia which man has inherited from his pre-human ancestors. The truth is that the Jewish religion has been foremost among the religions of the world in combatting superstition, stupidity and aggression.

The most significant trait of the Jewish religion of which we can become aware only through first-hand experience is its creative spirit. By virtue of this trait, it has been able to achieve, in ever progressive fashion the synthesis of social righteousness with faith in God as creator and redeemer of mankind. What more could one ask of a religion ?

Have In Mind Your Children

The illiterate Jew is not only his worst enemy, but also that of his children. To them he transmits merely the name " Jew," emptied of all challenging and inspiring significance. Being a Jew is to them more of a burden and handicap than it is to him, because they are a generation further removed from the last trace of endearing reminiscence. As soon as they leave their home they come in contact with people in high places who make them feel that Jews belong to an inferior species of mankind, unwanted and superfluous. As a result, they are doomed to a life of perpetual inner conflict.

If their parents, however, had known the symbolic significance of the Jewish home observances and had sought to foster an atmosphere of holiness in their homes, their children would never come to such a pass. No religious civilization can compare with Judaism in the opportunities it offers to render the home spiritually beautiful and sustaining. The preoccupations of work business and entertainment generally leave little room for spiritual values. Where, then, if not in the home are those values to receive sanctuary ? Modern industry, the growing division of labor, and the spirit of individualism that is bred in the young threaten to undermine the home. Some way will have to be found to save the home from disintegration. It is the indispensable builder of ethical character and nursery of the human soul. If the Jewish home is to survive as a humanizing agency, the parents will have to learn how to Judaize it by transmitting and interpreting the Jewish heritage to their children.

The tendency of many American Jews, to assume that one can live as a Jew without a life-long process of self-education in Judaism, is fraught with tremendous harm to their own character and happiness, and lays up a burden of misery for their children. They have in their Jewish heritage a rich spiritual estate which they can ill afford to abandon. For their own good, as well as for that of their children and of all whose lives touch theirs, they should cultivate it, im-prove it, and make it their own. This is the work of a lifetime.

MORDECAI KAPLAN,
Questions Jews Ask

The Defense

A communicable disease . . . can be combatted not only by fighting the germs but also by strengthening the resistance of the body under attack. Jews can do very little about fighting anti-Semitism. . . . But they certainly can go on strengthening the morale of their own people.

SALO W. BARON,
The American Zionist

Tablets Without Letters

Everything I am trying to say about the indispensability of knowledge to the Jewish tradition has been anticipated by the tradition itself. In myriad epigrams and metaphors, the teachers of Israel from Moses on insisted that only as Jewry was informed could it be assured of life. But nowhere has this been stated more colorfully than in a legend spun by ancient rabbis.

When Moses descended from Mount Sinai, they relate, he held in his arms, as Scripture informs us, the tablets of stone engraved by the finger of the Holy One, blessed be He. And such was the virtue of the inscription, that it was not Moses who carried the tablets, but the tablets which carried Moses. So it came to pass that his descent over jagged rocks, on the verge of crags and yawning chasms, was effortless and safe. But when the Prophet neared the mountain's base and caught his first glimpse of the Golden Calf, when God's words and the idol were brought into confrontation with each other, a wonder ensued. The sacred letters detached themselves from the stone in which they had been inscribed and vanished into thin air. Moses was left holding a blank, inert thing, too heavy for him. It is not true, the sages assert, that Moses threw the tablets to the earth, so shattering them. The fact is that he had to let them go or be crushed. The lettered stone which had carried Moses was, once letter-less, too much for him to bear.

It is not difficult to discern what the ancient rabbis are trying to say in their parable : given knowledge and insight, Judaism sustains the Jew ; without them it is a crushing burden, too heavy for even the strongest to withstand.

MILTON STEINBERG,
A Partisan Guide to the Jewish Problem

Jewish institutions of learning are the laboratories where weapons are forged to repel anti-Semitism to the degree that such a course is possible.

ABRAHAM A. NEUMAN,
Landmarks and Goals

Strengthening Resistance

The advancement of social and economic progress, the dissemination of the truth regarding Jews and Judaism, the furthering of community movements in which all groups can participate and the utilization of legal means against the embattled forces of prejudice, these constitute the most effective means of fighting anti-Semitism. But their efficacy depends upon utilizing not one or two, but all these means in unison, in a broad, unified attack on the menace.

It must be confessed, however, that even the most effective campaign cannot possibly banish anti-Jewish prejudice within our lifetime or that of our children. The virulence of the disease may be reduced, but it is too much to hope for its early extirpation.

Under these circumstances it is obvious that the resistance of the victims must be strengthened, so that they may be better able to endure the ravages of the affliction. Increased Jewish loyalty and courage can come to American Jewish youth and its elders only through a growing understanding and love of the Jewish heritage. In no other way can a harried generation avoid the crumbling of morale. The Jew who is ignorant of his religion, history and culture is an easy prey for the shafts of prejudice. It is not that he remains entirely uninformed on things Jewish. On the contrary, the world about him is only too eager to fill the void with misinformation. From spheres which he has been taught to regard as beyond reproach, the university, the lecture forum, the public press and the printed page, comes propaganda which persuades him that the Jewish heritage is worthless and even dangerous. For this reason, the most cultured and sensitive spirits within the Jewish group, when they lack any Jewish background that would enable them to evaluate their heritage fairly, are often the first victims of self-hate.

Moreover, without meaningful Jewish values in their lives, all Jews are in imminent danger of identifying Jewish life with "anti-anti-Semitism" and Jewish activity with an unending process of fund-raising. That would be a tragedy not only for Judaism, but for the Jew, whose heart would be filled with bitterness and suspicion. On the other hand, in striving to build Jewish loyalty and self-respect, American Jewry is taking the most constructive step toward protecting the psychic health of four and a half million men, women and children. Efforts in this direction still fall woefully short of the necessary maximum in extent and in resourcefulness.

An active program for fighting anti-Semitism and a positive attitude toward Jewish values are the only sure means of preserving the Jewish people in a dark age. But the modern Jew who observes anti-Semitism at large in the world knows that he is fighting for more than his own preservation. Destiny has made him the custodian of those dynamic ideals which alone offer promise of a better world and the fate of which quivers in the balance today. Self-defense needs no apology, but the proud consciousness of serving a cause beyond oneself gives this desperate task a touch of glory.

ROBERT GORDIS,
The Jew Faces a New World

Civilization Or Complex

Where Jewish education is neglected, the whole content of Judaism is reduced to merely an awareness of anti-Semitism. Judaism ceases then to be a civilization, and becomes a complex.

MORDECAI M. KAPLAN,
The Reconstructionist

The Rewards Of Jewishness?

What do I get out of my Jewishness to justify the expenditure of time and energy upon it? How am I the better off for my adherence to it?

From the Jewish heritage, I derive my world outlook, a God-centered interpretation of reality in the light of which man the individual is clothed with dignity, and the career of humanity with cosmic meaning and hope; a humane morality, elevated in its aspirations yet sensibly realistic; a system of rituals that interpenetrates my daily routines and invests them with poetry and intimations of the divine.

Beyond this, my life is enriched by the accumulated treasures of over three millennia of Jewish history — a large literature in which I read extensively, not as an outsider but with a sense of belonging; music for me to sing, art for me to enjoy. I have the privilege of companionship with the great personalities of Jewish history. At my disposal is a second fund of folklore when I spin tales to my children. Mine literally is a double past — the American and the Jewish. My horizons are distant, not in one direction but in two. I am twice anchored in traditions, and hence twice secured against the peril of being rootless and "unpossessed."

And because my Jewishness is something positive, anti-Semitism looms less large in my life than in that of many of my fellows. I am not hagridden by it as they are. To them it is the whole of what is otherwise a senseless identification ; to me it is an unfortunate, a tragic incident in an inherently worthwhile enterprise. Like them, I am prepared to do anything I can to resist it. I, too, man the walls. But I have shrines, libraries and family altars to defend as well as jobs, legal rights and memberships in clubs. And I know that while much will be taken from me in the event of defeat, my Jewish heritage will still remain to sustain and give me direction. The de-Judaized Jews, on the other hand, recognize quite clearly that they will be left with nothing. Little wonder that their preoccupation with anti-Semitism approaches a hysteria.

I am furthermore quite confident that by virtue of my attitudes, I am less susceptible than escapist Jews to infection by self-contempt. I am undeniably exposed to the same psychic influences that play over them. But in my case, as I have already indicated, participation in and appreciation of the Jewish tradition operate as immunizing elements. I am not tempted to flight from myself, nor bitter because I know in advance that it will prove futile. I cannot despise my identity : it is associated with a process I enjoy and respect. Not the least of the significances for me of a meaningful Judaism is its contribution to my mental health.   MILTON STEINBERG, *A Partisan Guide to the Jewish Problem*

Pleading Guilty To Imaginary Sins

Nothing is more dangerous for a nation or for an individual than to plead guilty to imaginary sins. Where the sin is real — by honest endeavor the sinner can purify himself. But when a man has been persuaded to suspect himself unjustly — what can he do ? Our greatest need is emancipation from self-contempt, from this idea that we are really worse than all the world. Otherwise we may in course of time become in reality what we now imagine ourselves to be.

ACHAD HA'AM

The Lesson Of History

Suffering is intolerable only when it is not suffused with a purpose. To large sections of contemporary Jews, Jewishness has neither rhyme nor reason — and so, quite naturally, they chafe under the disabilities this " accident of birth " entails. The integrated Jew, imbued with the sense of the worthwhileness of the rationale of Judaism, is also discriminated against, at best, and persecuted and hunted, at worst. However, and this is decisive, he knows why he suffers. He knows that all that is inflicted upon him is the dark and lesser side of his great fortune of being a Jew. The tragedy of modern Jewish life is not anti-Semitism, but the loss of the sense of the worthwhileness of being a Jew. Not suffering *per se*, but its seeming meaninglessness breaks the morale of the modern Jew and gives rise to his many psychological difficulties.

The history of Anti-Semitism and the record of the Jewish fight against it prove soberingly that Jew-hatred is the inevitably recurring reaction of the majority to the Jewish minority. All serious students of the psychology of anti-Semitism know that, with the given factors of human nature, the chances for the eradication of anti-Semitism are infinitesimal. Obviously, in the democracies the physical security of the Jewish minority is well assured. We need fear no pogroms in this country, but there are large, painful and, probably, incurable areas that cannot, and dare not, be ignored. As the Jewish survivalist sees it, anti-Semitism can neither be wholly cured nor dare it be left to the devices of its progenitors. We do need organizations defending our civil rights guaranteed by the Constitution. As for the rest, i.e. social discrimination, overt and disguised anti-Semitic expression in private areas, there is not much that can be done. Even yesterday's panacea of " education " has failed, for recent statistical surveys prove that anti-Jewish prejudice is more widespread among the upper classes, with high school and college backgrounds, than among those on the lower rungs of the social ladder and of education.

Jewish historical experience for over two millennia and in virtually all lands, drives home the point that there is only one real defense against anti-Semitism : the strengthening of Jewish survival determination by means of the rationale of Judaism.

At this juncture of history, the first line of Jewish defense must be erected in the areas where doubt in the rationale of Judaism has wrought fatal havoc. It thus becomes imperative for Jewish survivalists to bolster the Jewish national will to live by giving the individual Jew a satisfying sense of worthwhileness.

TRUDE WEISS-ROSMARIN,
Jewish Survival

The Preservation Of Emotional Health

A Jewish child or adult is in one way or another made conscious daily, and often hourly, of the fact that he is a Jew. Indeed that consciousness in the present state of affairs is constantly with him, if not at the very center of attention, then immediately next to it. To a Jew ignorant of his own history and culture such an imposed self-consciousness is an agonizing mental burden under the best of circumstances. How infinitely more burdensome this Jewish self-consciousness becomes when vicious propaganda, unrelenting persecution and ever-present discrimination associate the concept "Jew" with numerous repugnant characteristics and unpleasant experiences. In the mind of many a Jew, the word "Jew" is a synonym for "handicaps in life." It represents an obstacle to be overcome when seeking a position in industry, the professions, the political or the social life. To those more susceptible to the influence of anti-Semitic propaganda "Jew" becomes synonymous with moral turpitude, with greed, despicable cunning and restless social destructiveness.

If nothing is done to counteract these unpleasant associations clustering around the consciousness of one's Jewishness, the result is inevitable. There must follow a sense of inferiority, ending either in self-pity or self-hate or in the compensatory reactions of blustering braggadocio.

An intensive and comprehensive Jewish education is the only means at our disposal whereby to resist the spiritual evils to which the economically impoverished, legally disinherited and publicly humiliated are prone to fall prey.

Hence the supreme stress placed by our fathers upon education for the young and upon the unceasing pursuit of knowledge as the noblest quest of any individual regardless of his age. Study was a sacred occupation. It was not pursued for the practical purposes of earning a livelihood. Our fathers studied Torah with reverence and love because they recognized that that alone preserved their essential humanity. "If thou hast studied much Torah," Rabbi Jochanan ben Zaccai warned his disciples, "do not boast of it, for thereunto wast thou created." The wisdom and the injunctions of the Torah, the manner of life it enjoined upon us, frustrated all the efforts of our enemies to turn us into criminals. In the meanest ghetto alleys the Torah introduced laws of health and cleanliness. It strengthened hearts broken by poverty to eschew murder, or theft, drunkenness or adultery as an escape from the undeserved misery. The light of the Torah turned hovels into homes, dark dank basements into learned academies, and abject hucksters into scholars and saints.

Above all, the study of the Torah and obedience to its precepts preserved the Jew from the most unbearable of all suffering, that which tortures a soul burdened by a feeling of inferiority and turned against itself in hate. It was able to do that because the Torah emancipated the Jew from spiritual subjection to the standards of excellency set up by his tormentors.

Like Jacob's children, the ghetto Jew put away the strange gods. He did not judge himself in the light of their teachings. He had no respect for the morals, the beliefs, nor the social code of his persecutors. Their blows pained him physically, even as does the kick of a donkey or the bite of a wild dog, but they did not humiliate him spiritually. A donkey's kick may hurt. It does not insult.

Jewish education must do the same for our children and for us. It must eradicate from the hearts and minds of our people the last bit of respect that may be there for our tormentors. We need not hate them, even as we do not hate a beast. We might perhaps learn to pity them, even as we pity the moron for being deprived of the world's greatest blessing, a normal mind. But we ought not to be misled by any of their other achievements whether it be in the field of science or military conquest, industry or commerce, to admire them or their way of life. The only standard we should use to judge a fellow man is the standard set by our tradition — the standard of his dealings with his fellow men.

SIMON GREENBERG,
Living As a Jew Today

15

Israel : The Dream and the Fulfilment

The Lord shall set his hand a second time to recover the remnants of His people. . . . And He shall set up an ensign for the nations and shall assemble the outcast of Israel and gather together the depressed of Judah from the four corners of the earth.

Isaiah 11 : 11, 12

The Jews wish to have a state, and they shall have one. . . . The world will be freed by our liberty, enriched by our wealth, magnified by our greatness.

THEODOR HERZL,
The Jewish State

No one can doubt that an incandescent moment has been kindled in the life of the Jewish people in our day and age. Beyond our expectations and perhaps beyond our merits we belong for all time to the generation of Israel's founding fathers.

ABBA EBAN,
address, 1952

The Scandal Of History

What grieved me most was not the Arabic opposition to the Zionist enterprise — I understood the Mufti's motives thoroughly — but the fact that the insinuations of the oily-tongued spokesman of the Arabic feudal order were being accepted at their face value by certain of my journalistic colleagues — men who subsequently cried out their indignation in books, not over the slaughter of Jewish scholars and little Jewish children, the wanton destruction of agricultural colonies, the uprooting of eucalyptus forests and the general terrorism of bands of savage hoodlums directed against an essentially peaceful community, but over the " injustice " of Zionism's indirect interference with the absolute hegemony of a small group of Arabic landlords who kept their mass of destitute peasants on a level comparable only with that of chattel slaves and just a little above that of the beast of the field.

That the Zionists had made clinics available for the healing of the Arabs' diseases, that the Jewish laboratories had prepared serums for the improvement of the miserable breed of native cattle, that their agricultural experimental stations had heightened the quality of Arabic wheat and barley and citrus fruit, that the Jews had supplanted the straggling goat-paths of the past with a system of modern roads, that hydroelectric stations had been installed by Jewish capital and initiative for the comfort and betterment of all, that the swamps which annually claimed thousands of Arab lives had been cleaned up at an immense cost of money and of young Jewish lives, that innumerable wells had been dug by Jews in that land which had become parched and barren through centuries of Arab neglect and suicidal deforestation, that on top of that not a single Arab had been asked to contribute as much as one cent or make the least sacrifice for the work that had led in the first place to his own betterment — all that was considered a mere bagatelle which did not compare to the mental sufferings of the handful of feudal Arab nobles who had suddenly discovered that they wanted self - determination and democratic freedom for the Arabic people.

Humbly and patiently the Jewish pioneers have set about to make the Land of Israel, the hope and prayer of their people for two thousand years, a habitable place not only for the weary wanderers still in Europe, but first of all for the destitute and disease-ridden masses of Arabs. They had not come with weapons of war, building forts and strongholds as a conqueror who protects his gains in a captured province. Spontaneously the Jewish people had rejected the counsel of those who urged, for the sake of national prestige, the bloody panoplies of imperialism. Instead of arsenals and military bastions, the first foundation on Zion's hill had been a school of learning, a tribute to the universality of the spirit, the Hebrew University. Israel had returned to the land of his fathers by virtue of a decree of the civilized world, which in a moment of high idealism had conceived the will to set right an ancient wrong.

Not to trample underfoot, therefore, to crush or to break the bruised reed had those pioneers come, but to fight the battle of the Lord which is to open the eyes of the blind, to bring out those that sit in the darkness of the prison house and to intone a new psalm of peace and human brotherhood. Not domination, not outward success, not even possession was the *Halutzims'* goal. Zionism's object was to bring to a close Israel's two thousand years of exile, to terminate the scandal of history, to end our own Christian shame of a people of human brothers being hounded and hunted from pillar to post.

Not all the Jewish people were expected to come to Palestine. The geographical limits of the country would not have permitted the settlement of so great a number. Only a kernel of the Jewish people, withdrawn from the *Galuth*, was to build there a civilization marked by the ethos of the Hebraic spirit and make a contribution to the sum total of human civilization in accordance with the national character and the national genius of the Jewish people. This, it was expected, would also fill with new meaning and a new dignity the life of the Jews who remained behind in the Diaspora. The deeper significance of Zionism was therefore that the thing called Judaism should not disappear from the earth, but that Israel in a personal - national sense would become again one of the collaborators in the building of humanity's fatherland — the Kingdom of God, "the world to come," a world wherein not one man shall plow and another reap, not one man build and another inhabit, and not one man cause hurt or damage to another man.

And what had been the world's answer?

Blood and terror! Lies and sneers and calumny! The liberals were turning over their specious shibboleths about the rule of the majority. The British talked of striking a balance between two groups of "natives" and of protecting Arab rights. In a land where some of the finest movements of Socialism had been started, the Communists supported the henchmen of the reaction and stabbed the Jewish working community in the back. Others pretended to be concerned over the safety of the dust - covered holy places which nobody menaced. The Christian Church as a body stood aside. In the presence of Albert Schweitzer, the great savant who had given up his scholarly work in Europe's universities to devote himself, in a spirit of expiation for the white man's sins, to his black brethren, and who had gone to work as a medical missionary among them, the Protestant community was full of praise and admiration, but on the work of the Zionists who had freed the Arabs of trachoma — that terrible scourge of the Near Eastern peoples, it turned its back.

Must this — " the scandal of history " — continue forever ? Is there then no balm in Gilead and is there no physician ?

PIERRE VAN PAASSEN,
Days of Our Years

Israel's Agricultural Settlements

I have seen these Jewish agricultural settlements. They are one of the most wonderful moral demonstrations of the human race. . . . I came back with a humble feeling that I should like to give up this game of House of Commons and politics and join them in the clean, healthy life they are living.

HERBERT STANLEY MORRISON,
Address, 1936

With Justice Shall Zion Be Redeemed

At this great moment of our history, let us give thanks and praise to the God of Israel who, in His mercy, granted us the privilege of witnessing the redemption of our people after centuries of affliction and suffering.

Today we stand on the threshold of a new era. From the outset we are building on the fair and solid foundations of freedom, equality, collective responsibility, and national self-discipline.

The nation was conceived for the gathering in of the exiles. Every day, to our heart's joy, thousands and tens of thousands of our brethren from countries near and far are entering the gates of this country which stand wide open to receive them. It is our hope and prayer that this gathering of exiles will increase and will embrace ever larger multitudes of our people who will strike roots here and work side by side with us in building the State and making our desolate places fruitful.

It has fallen upon our generation to weld anew the links of that life of freedom snapped by the tyrants' force nearly nineteen hundred years ago. I know not why it is precisely our generation that has been privileged to bring about what all generations before longed for and cleaved to in the darkness of exile, unless it be that we earned it by the hardship and weariness, sorrow and tribulation that have been our portion in the last seventy years, years when our body was stricken limb by limb until one-third of the entire nation was annihilated. We have suffered torture and affliction such as befell no other nation in the world until, at long last, the prophecy was fulfilled : " The remnant shall return." But because we are a remnant, no more than a remnant, double and treble responsibility is laid upon us to fill the terrible void in our national life that has been created by the slaughter of the best sons of our people, the guardians of her spirit and the bearers of her culture.

It is our people who once gave the world a spiritual message fundamental to civilization. The world is watching us now to see the way we choose in ordering our lives, how we fashion our State. The world is listening to hear whether a new message will go forth from Zion, and what that message will be.

A new message is not born without some sore travail of the creative spirit. It does not see the light without much toil and weariness and difficulty and pain. The creative force of our nation will soon meet a new and serious challenge.

Having taken part in the great battles of the human spirit, having shed our blood and given our lives for the liberation of many peoples, we have finally won the right to toil and labor in order to give expression to our distinct national identity and to make a contribution as a free people among other free peoples to the spiritual treasure of the world.

Today is a great day in our lives. Let us not be thought too arrogant if we say that it is also a great day in the history of the world. This, our message of hope and good cheer issues from this place, from this sacred city to all throughout the world who are persecuted and oppressed and who are struggling for freedom and equality. A just struggle is indeed of avail. If we, the people of sorrows and affliction, have been vouchsafed today's event, then truly there is hope at the end for all who long for justice.

Let us be mindful that the eyes of the entire Jewish People are lifted up toward us and the longings and prayers of past generations attend our steps. May it be given to all of us to be equal to the hour and to our heavy charge.

Let us recall the great leaders and teachers of our people, the fathers of our movement and the architects of our constructive endeavor whose vision and labors brought us here. Let us honor the memory of all the other men and women of the *Yishuv* and the Zionist Movement who have gone to their rest and have not been privileged to come this far with us. With sacred reverence, let us recall the memory of our sons and daughters, precious and beloved, who bravely died in order that Israel might live. CHAIM WEIZMANN, Address, 1949.

The Jews Shall Have A State

I believe that a wondrous generation of Jews will spring into existence. The Maccabees will rise again.

Let me repeat once more my opening words : The Jews wish to have a state, and they shall have one.

We shall live at last as free men on our own soil, and die peacefully in our own home.

The world will be freed by our liberty, enriched by our wealth, magnified by our greatness.

And whatever we attempt there to accomplish for our own welfare will react with beneficent force for the good of humanity.

THEODOR HERZL,
The Jewish State

A Zionist is a Jew who, though not persecuted by Gentiles, wishes to revive Israel, because of his inner need and voluntary choice.

ELIEZER LIVNEH (formerly Liebenstein),
Jewish Frontier

The Jew's Love For Palestine

The Jew, even though he was driven from the land, never surrendered his love for it. The Jew literally transplanted Palestine into his very consciousness. He imagined that he continued to live in the land of his dreams. He might be living in the cold north or in the sunny south, yet he prayed for rain or for dew when it was the season for these in Palestine. He celebrated his Arbor Day when the trees were beginning to blossom in Palestine. In whatever clime he lived, he was always under the illusion that he was still in his ancient home. His very name Jew was a living protest that he still held his lien upon the land of Judea, from which, though he was torn physically, he was never separated in heart or mind. He sang

of Palestine, dreamed of Palestine ; it was uppermost in his thoughts in time of supremest joy and darkest sorrow.

The Jew mourned for his ancient land as he would for the dead, and yet he never regarded Palestine as altogether dead. If dead, then it would rise again and experience the resurrection of the dead. . . .

And strange as it may seem, Palestine itself seemed to feel the same — that she belonged to Israel and to Israel alone. Pagan, Christian, Mohammedan, Romans, Egyptians, Turks, all conquered the land and tried to make it their own. But none succeeded. With a stubborn resistance the land refused to prosper in their hands and preferred to remain in its desolation. She waited patiently for her own beloved. "The land without a people," to use the phrase of Zangwill, "waited for the people without a land."

ISRAEL H. LEVINTHAL,
Sabbath and Festival Prayer Book

The Jews are a tiny people. Palestine is a tiny land. But when the tiny people will be reunited with the tiny land great things will come to pass.

MANAHEM USSISHKIN

We Did Not Forget

The oath which the first exiles pronounced at the streams of Babylon . . . Jews did not forget! Eras came and went, civilizations grew and decayed, empires rose and fell, historic trends flowed and ebbed, but Jerusalem was yet prized above all joys and remembered in all sorrows. Under the hupah (the wedding canopy) when two hearts are beating in unison, when joy reigns supreme, there comes from the depth of the soul the prayer, "May there soon be heard in the cities of Judah and in the streets of Jerusalem the voice of gladness, the voice of bridegroom and the voice of bride." And when in the house of mourning sorrow oppresses the heart and longing tests faith, the lips murmur, "He who fills the world, comfort ye together with all those that mourn for Zion and Jerusalem. . . ." And when death claimed the Jew and the cold earth opened its mouth . . . the head (of the Jew) rested on a bag of Palestinian soil.

SOLOMON GOLDMAN,
A Rabbi Takes Stock

The Price Of Homelessness

Among the economic losses due to the lack of soil, the loss of men is not the least ; for men are after all true riches of a country. I am not speaking merely of the myriads washed away by the waters of baptism, but of the men of distinction who are the salt of the race. In Palestine, although Judaism was the national religion, there were at least four varieties of it, some sufficiently apart to amount to quite different religious conceptions. Thus in Palestine there was room for men of every school of religion, and even if they had dropped religion altogether they could still have remained patriots. When Palestine was lost and became metaphorically incorporated in the religion, not only were large parts of the religion fossilized by being thus removed from the vital influences of reality, but the resulting platform of a mere religion proved too small to afford a standing-place to all the sons of Israel, especially as the thoughts of men went widening with the process of the suns. Hence, the loss of men like Spinoza, who, stepping off the narrow religious platform, found themselves outside Jewry, whereas in a land of our own such men in future, instead of being excommunicated, would still find themselves among their own brethren.

Since neither birth nor marriage now definitely determines who is a Jew and who not, the chronicler of Judaism is reduced to the test of whether a man is buried with the Jews. We take our census in our cemeteries. But the test of Judaism must be not death but life: how a man lives, not how he is buried.

ISRAEL ZANGWILL,
Speeches, Articles and Letters

Israel — The Focal Center Of All That Is Vital

The Jewry of Israel enjoys a unique advantage over other Jewries, which makes it of more vital significance for Judaism as the civilization of the Jewish People than any other Jewish community. Because it represents a majority of Israel's population, it alone is in a position to control all the factors — political, economic, social and cultural — that enter into the totality of Jewish life. This makes it possible for Israeli Jewry to exemplify Judaism as a civilization in all its aspects, and to impress the character of Judaism on the entire life of the people in Israel. That makes the relation of Israeli Jewry to other aggregates of Jews like that of the heart to other less vital organs.

Zionism became necessary, among other reasons, because Judaism everywhere was living on the momentum of the past, and that momentum was being rapidly exhausted. It thus became necessary,

before the momentum was entirely spent, to create a central organ for world Jewry, by establishing a community where Jews could, as a majority, control all the vital forces that operate in modern life. Israel is today the focal center of all that is vital in Judaism. It is the heart from which currents of that vitality can be circulated through all the Jewries of the Diaspora, provided that arteries of communication are kept open so that the vital blood-stream of a living and creative Jewish culture can circulate freely throughout the entire body of world Jewry.

MORDECAI M. KAPLAN,
Questions Jews Ask

Palestine needs a people; Israel needs a country. If, in regenerating the Holy Land, Israel could regenerate itself, how should the world be other than the gainer?

ISRAEL ZANGWILL,
Zion, Whence Cometh My Help

The Power Of The Spirit

There is no doubt that the emergence of the first Jewish state in two thousand years has changed the course of our history. But to my mind it also represents one of the great achievements of the conscience of the world. It is the more noteworthy in that it occurred in a century characterized by such human and spiritual devastation that many men had lost hope for the future. That a people, however bitterly used, could rise again, must give heart and courage to us all. It is proof of what will and spirit and dedication to a cause can bring about in spite of towering odds.

BARTLEY CRUM

The Spiritual Climate Of Israel

There is one thing that Israel possesses in greater abundance than any other country and that is the freedom to be Jewish. In Israel the environment is your ally. There are no economic considerations to reconcile with observing the Shabbat or the festivals. There is no counterpull of a dominant and often aggressive Christian civilization. There are no problems arising from the delicate problem of balancing loyalties and contributions to two civilizations. The calendar is Jewish, the radio is Jewish, the language is Jewish, the headlines are Jewish, the names of streets and boulevards are Jewish. The largest crane in Haifa harbor with a lift capacity of one hundred and twenty tons has a Jewish name. It is called " Samson." Israel is a place where you can attend, as I did, a Talmud lesson on Shabbat morning in Jerusalem and share a volume of Baba Metziah with the President of the State; a place where you can attend a magnificent all-youth service, replete with choir, cantors and Torah readers in the Bilu Synagogue in Tel Aviv on Shabbat morning and a lecture in the " Ohel Shem " in the afternoon on " Aristotle and Maimonides "; a place where a Lag B'omer pilgrimage to Miron can become an unforgettable and thrilling experience; a place where Bikkurim on Shevuot is not a faded memory but an exciting reality; a place where your radio brings you Bible lessons and Talmud lessons, the music of the synagogue, the classics of our heritage; a place where bank entrances have Mezuzot and post-office clerks feel free to wear Yarmulkes; a place where the ideals of the Prophets have been translated into political and social realities; a place, in brief, where Am Yisroel Chai — the people of Israel lives. When you get caught up in its rhythm and its people insinuate themselves into your heart, you can begin to understand the embarrassingly chauvinistic statement of our sages that " he who dwells in Eretz Yisroel is like one who has a God while he who dwells outside of Israel is like one who has no God."

We must have faith in the inherent religious genius of our people which has already begun to assert itself in a hundred ways and will do so with ever-increasing vigor as Israel strikes firmer roots in the soil in which its spiritual productivity once found its most impressive flowering. The sainted Rabbi Kuk, a passionate believer in the spiritual future of the *Yishuv*, once made the crisp prophecy : " The ancient will be revitalized ; the contemporary will be sanctified." That prophecy is already on the road to fulfilment. We can shorten that road.

SIDNEY GREENBERG,
Address before the Rabbinical
Assembly of America, 1956

The Reward Of Love

Our love for Zion is one of our proudest titles. For no nation has ever loved its country with such a surpassing love as the people of Israel has loved the land of Israel. Though driven from Palestine nearly two thousand years ago, the Jewish people, which the world, knowing it only on the surface, considers a nation of hard-headed, sober-minded traders, has loved its ancient land with an undying love, with a romantic love, with a love one reads of in books of fiction, a love that expects no reward, a love that is happy in the privilege of loving. And yet, though expecting no reward, Israel received the amplest reward for its love. For it is this love which has enabled the Jewish people to survive until this day. The love of Eretz Yisroel was the torch that illumined the thorny path of our people. It was the anchor that kept our ship from drifting out into the boundless ocean. And when the eternal wanderer seemed to sink under the burden of his suffering, he looked up into the sky and saw the light that shone from Zion, and with renewed courage he continued on his journey.

ISRAEL FRIEDLANDER,
Past and Present

The Miracle Of Israel

A few weeks ago I went to Israel. . . . I am a Catholic. . . .

While in Israel we met Carl Alpert, Assistant to the President of the Technion in Haifa. After talking with him, and others in other parts of Israel, and keeping an open mind, I was suddenly and deeply impressed at the miracle of Israel. She is the only country now in the world which practices the ancient admonition of " faith with work." I was overwhelmed at the heroism and dedication of the Jews there, and they now not only have my deepest respect but a gratitude that they have reawakened in me the knowledge that the human spirit, in conjunction with God, cannot be overcome or destroyed.

I have been asked by a national syndicate to do an immediate series of columns on Israel from the reverent Christian point of view and I will get at this work at once. When I saw what the Jews are doing in Israel and their pride and their humility and endless work I could only pray for the preservation of this heroic country and to go out and give talks about it.

Shalom
TAYLOR CALDWELL,
Hadassah Newsletter

Who Believed ? Who Imagined ?

Who believed decades ago that Jews who for centuries had lived in towns and for generations had been strangers to labor and the soil, would become the builders of a country ? Who imagined that a people which had been scattered and dispersed for over two thousand years would reassemble in its ancient homeland under foreign occupation and in it renew its sovereign independence ? Who believed that a dead tongue, embalmed in songs and books of prayer, would once again become the living tongue of a people which spoke a Babel of Languages ? Who dreamed that a people oppressed, degraded and helpless for generations would suddenly reveal a heroic spirit and crush a hostile army forty times its superior in numbers ?

The faith — bold and naive at the same time — which the early pioneers showed eighty years ago, and the force of the creative initiative which they showed in establishing new Jewish villages in the ancient, captive homeland ; the pioneering impetus which grew steadily stronger in the course of the last three generations until it achieved the revival of the Jewish State and the brilliant victories of the War of Independence ; the daring involved in settling tens of thousands of immigrants from backward countries, who for thousands of years had been foreign to the fragrance of the fields, in the desolate wastes of the South ; the cultural, social and economic transformations which took place in the lives of hundreds of thousands of immigrants in two or three generations, transformations unparalleled either in the life of our own people since its beginnings or in the life of any other people in our own day — all these are the fruit of that great human miracle which has taken place in our modern history, and which we call *halutziut*, which is nothing else than the profound faith of man in his power and capacity, and a burning spiritual need to transform the natural order, as well as the order of his own life, for the sake of the redeeming vision.

Israel cannot survive without strength and power, so long as the human race is divided into warring blocs and nation lifts up sword against nation. But the profound truth of the supremacy of the spirit, the most incontrovertible proof of which is the long history and the manifold experiences of the Jewish people, remains unchallenged. It is on this truth that the faith of the Jewish people in its future is based, and the supreme test of Israel in our generation lies.

State of Israel Government Year Book

A Link In The Chain Of Mankind

It is said by some that Palestine does not have room for all the Jews. I do not know. I am no political scientist, and I cannot say how many of our people Palestine can or cannot contain. But one thing I can say : even if Palestine has not room for all the people, and not even for the majority, even if only a considerable part of the people take root there, develop there, live as a living people, working and creating, like a tree that draws its life from its own native soil, I shall not consider it a misfortune if the shade of its leafy crown falls upon other lands.

Every country has sons and daughters in other countries. So there is nothing to dread if a part of the people, or even a majority, must live dispersed in other lands, if we only have our roots in Palestine. And then those scattered abroad will not be parasites in a foreign body, but they will be the branches that draw their shape from our own roots and spread out beyond the soil that sustains them. Then we shall again be a link in the chain of mankind, an organ in the body of humanity.

ARON DAVID GORDON,
Quoted in Harthern's *Going Home*

Zionism And Americanism

Let no American imagine that Zionism is inconsistent with patriotism. Multiple loyalties are objectionable only if they are inconsistent. A man is a better citizen of the United States for being also a loyal citizen of his state, and of his city; for being loyal to his family, and to his profession or trade; for being loyal to his college or his lodge. Every Irish American who contributed toward advancing home rule was a better man and a better American for the sacrifice he made. Every American Jew who aids in advancing the Jewish settlement in Palestine, though he feels that neither he nor his descendants will ever live there, will likewise be a better man and a better American for doing so. . . .

There is no inconsistency between loyalty to America and loyalty to Jewry. The Jewish spirit, the product of our religion and experiences, is essentially modern and essentially American. Not since the destruction of the Temple have the Jews in spirit and in ideals been so fully in harmony with the noblest aspirations of the country in which they lived.

America's fundamental law seeks to make real the brotherhood of man. That brotherhood became the Jewish fundamental law more than twenty-five hundred years ago.

America's insistent demand in the twentieth century is for social justice. That also has been the Jews' striving for ages. Their affliction as well as their religion has prepared the Jews for effective democracy. Persecution broadened their sympathies. It trained them in patient endurance, in self-control, and in sacrifice. It made them think as well as suffer. It deepened the passion for righteousness.

Indeed, loyalty to America demands rather that each American Jew become a Zionist. For only through the ennobling effect of its strivings can we develop the best that is in us and give to this country the full benefit of our great inheritance. The Jewish spirit, so long preserved, the character developed by so many centuries of sacrifice, should be preserved and developed further, so that in America as elsewhere the sons of the race may in future live lives and do deeds worthy of their ancestors.

LOUIS D. BRANDEIS,
Brandeis on Zionism

There Is Singing On Mount Scopus

Upon this mountain (Mount Scopus) eighteen hundred and fifty-five years ago, the Roman general Titus Vespasian, pitched his tent the better to direct the attack of his cohorts upon Jerusalem. It was from Mount Scopus the order came to

pierce the walls with battering-rams, to place ladders against them, and for hordes of Roman soldiers to grapple with the brave defenders upon the parapets. Resistance was gradually broken down. The invaders set fire to the Holy Temple.

Jerusalem was taken amid the slaughter of thousands of zealots, who resisted to the last. Masses of the vanquished were taken captive and dragged to Rome, where they were set in mortal combat with wild animals, and their blood crimsoned the sand of the arenas. As a memorial of victory, Titus Vespasian caused an arch to be erected in Rome, and a coin was struck off in his honor on which were inscribed the words, Judaea Devicta.

The wandering Jew, bearing the stigma of national defeat, has traversed the world these eighteen hundred and fifty-five years, nursing the hope that in God's time he would return to the scene of his former glory. He bore with fortitude and patience the burdens of life rendered all but intolerable by continued oppression. The evergreen sprig of memory made suffering endurable. Faith gave incentive to struggle. Before the storms of adversity, conscious of his inner strength, he bent his shoulders and lowered his head, but his spirit was never conquered. He made terms with conditions, but never lost hope. He embodied his hope in precept, in prayer, in ceremony, in physical habit, in the everyday duties of life. He determined to outlast enmity. He pressed through adversity in order that when the Day of Days arrived, he would be identifiably the man of Judea, able to recover the straight back, the clear upright head, the ability to begin again the making of new life, with a consciousness of living traditions and ideals still virile and forceful.

The great Empire of Rome today is ashes. It is the dust of a dim past. The conqueror, Titus Vespasian, owes his place in history to the act that sent the Jews once more out of their land. Titus is tyrant forever in Jewish legend, a figure of incarnate cruelty. He is the god of the machine that intervened, unknowingly, in the drama of Jewish life, and through his intervention sent the ball of Jewish existence rolling into the tragic depths of a long and terrible exile. The Arch of Titus crumbles. And on the mountain which saw Jerusalem in flames, the descendants of Judea Devicta gather in the year 1925 to dedicate an edifice which proclaims to the world the Return of the Exile, again head up, again shoulders erect, the light of renewed life glistening in his eyes. They dedicate the Return on Mount Scopus.

The generations that kept the faith and retained the inner fire of Jewish devotion and passion— hiding their light so that none could see and, unseeing, could not destroy — that never saw the Promised Land, but died and were buried in alien soil, will forget humiliation and suffering ; and their spirits, rising, passing through all the lands of persecution, will make their way back again to the land of their origin. And as the shofar is heard on Mount Scopus, they will join in the psalms of praise and jubilation that will resound throughout the Holy Land. They, too, will rise — the generations who died in the Galuth.

The invisible witnesses of the Rededication !

There is singing again on Mount Scopus. And there is rejoicing in the Holy City of Jerusalem.

LOUIS LIPSKY,
Address, 1925

Thorns And Thistles Garbed In Glory

Hearken, O my people !
From the very depths of my soul
I speak unto you ;
From the core of life where lies the tie
That binds us one to the other,
With devotion, deep and profound,
I declare unto you
That you, each one of you,
All of you, the whole of you,
Your very souls, your generations,
Only you are the essence of my life.
I live in you, in each of you, in all of you ;
In your life, my life has deeper, truer meaning ;
Without you I am as naught.
Hope, aspiration and life's intrinsic worth,
All this I find only when I am with you.
I am bound up inextricably
With the soul of all of you,
And I love you with infiinte love ;
I cannot feel otherwise.
All life's loves, small and great,
Are treasured in my love of you,
In my love of all of you,
Each one of you, each individual soul

Is a glowing spark of that torch eternal,
Kindling the light of life for me.
You give meaning to life, to labor,
To learning, to prayer, song and hope ;
Through the channel of your being, life pulsates in me ;
On the wings of your love I rise to the Love of God.
Everything becomes crystal-clear to me, unequivocal,
Like a flame in my heart purifying my thoughts.
With you, O my people, my kin-folk, my mother,
Source of my life,
With you I soar the wide spaces of the world ;
In your eternity I have life eternal.
In your glory I am honored, in your sorrow I am grieved,
In your affliction, I suffer anguish,
In your knowledge and understand-ing,
Behold, I am filled with knowledge and understanding.
Every footstep, wherever you have trod is a treasure of life.

Your land, the land of your hope, is sacred to me ;
Its heavens a source of beauty, of eternal splendor ;
Its Carmel and Sharon are the spring of hope,
The fountain of blessing, the source of life's joy.
Even its thorns and thistles are garbed in glory.
In deathless beauty !

ABRAHAM ISAAC KUK,
Sabbath and Festival Prayer Book

Zionism Was The Sabbath Of My Life

Zionism was the Sabbath of my life.

I believe that my influence as a leader is based on the fact that while as man and writer I had so many faults, and committed so many blunders and mistakes, as a leader in Zionism I have remained pure of heart and quite selfless.

THEODOR HERZL
Excerpts from Theodor Herzl's Diaries

Israel's Declaration Of Independence

The Land of Israel was the birthplace of the Jewish people. Here their spiritual, religious and national identity was formed. Here they achieved independence and created a culture of national and universal significance. Here they wrote and gave the Bible to the world.

Exiled from the Land of Israel the Jewish people remained faithful to it in all the countries of their dispersion, never ceasing to pray and hope for their return and the restoration of their national freedom.

Impelled by this historic association, Jews strove throughout the centuries to go back to the land of their fathers and regain their statehood. In recent decades they returned in their masses. They reclaimed the wilderness, revived their language, built cities and villages, and established a vigorous and ever growing community, with its own economic and cultural life. They sought peace yet were prepared to defend themselves. They brought the blessings of progress to all inhabitants of the country and looked forward to sovereign independence.

In the year 1897 the First Zionist Congress, inspired by Theodor Herzl's vision of the Jewish State, proclaimed the right of the Jewish people to national revival in their own country.

This right was acknowledged by the Balfour Declaration of November 2, 1917, and reaffirmed by the

Mandate of the League of Nations, which gave explicit international recognition to the historic connection of the Jewish people with Palestine and their right to reconstitute their National Home.

The recent holocaust, which engulfed millions of Jews in Europe, proved anew the need to solve the problem of the homelessness and lack of independence of the Jewish people by means of the reestablishment of the Jewish State, which would open the gates to all Jews and endow the Jewish people with equality of status among the family of nations.

The survivors of the disastrous slaughter in Europe, and also Jews from other lands, have not desisted from their efforts to reach Eretz Yisrael, in face of difficulties, obstacles and perils; and have not ceased to urge their right to a life of dignity, freedom and honest toil in their ancestral land.

In the Second World War the Jewish people in Palestine made their full contribution to the struggle of the freedom-loving nations against the Nazi evil. The sacrifices of their soldiers and their war effort gained them the right to rank with the nations which founded the United Nations.

On November 29, 1947, the General Assembly of the United Nations adopted a resolution requiring the establishment of a Jewish State in Palestine. The General Assembly called upon the inhab-itants of the country to take all the necessary steps on their part to put the plan into effect. This recognition by the United Nations of the right of the Jewish people to establish their independent State is unassailable.

It is the natural right of the Jewish people to lead, as do all other nations an independent existence in its sovereign State.

Accordingly we, the members of the National Council, representing the Jewish people in Palestine and the World Zionist Movement, are met together in solemn assembly today, the day of termination of the British Mandate for Palestine; and by virtue of the natural and historic right of the Jewish people and the Resolution of the General Assembly of the United Nations.

We hereby proclaim the establishment of the Jewish State in Palestine, to be called *Medinat Yisrael* (The State of Israel).

We hereby declare that, as from the termination of the mandate at midnight, the 14th - 15th May, 1948, and pending the setting up of the duly elected bodies of the State in accordance with a Constitution, to be drawn up by the Constituent Assembly not later than the 1st October, 1948, the National Council shall act as the Provisional State Council, and that the National Administration shall constitute the Provisional Government of the Jewish State, which shall be known as Israel.

A Truly Jewish Commonwealth

The State of Israel will be open to the immigration of Jews from all countries of their dispersion ; will promote the development of the country for the benefit of all its inhabitants ; will be based on the principles of liberty, justice and peace as conceived by the Prophets of Israel ; will uphold the full social and political equality of all its citizens, without distinction of religion, race or sex ; will guarantee freedom of religion, conscience, education and culture ; will safeguard the Holy Places of all religions ; and will loyally uphold the principles of the United Nations Charter.

The State of Israel will be ready to cooperate with the organs and representatives of the United Nations in the implementation of the Resolution of the Assembly of November 29, 1947, and will take steps to bring about the Economic Union over the whole of Palestine.

We appeal to the United Nations to assist the Jewish people in the building of its State and to admit Israel into the family of nations.

In the midst of wanton aggression, we yet call upon the Arab inhabitants of the State of Israel to preserve the ways of peace and play their part in the development of the State, on the basis of full and equal citizenship and due representation in all its bodies and institutions — provisional and permanent.

We extend our hand in peace and neighborliness to all the neighboring states and their peoples and invite them to cooperate with the independent Jewish nation for the common good of all. The State of Israel is prepared to make its contribution to the progress of the Middle East as a whole.

Our call goes out to the Jewish people all over the world to rally to our side in the task of immigration and development and to stand by us in the great struggle for the fulfillment of the dream of generations for the redemption of Israel.

With trust in Almighty God, we set our hand to this Declaration, at this Session of the Provisional State Council, on the soil of the Homeland, in the city of Tel Aviv, on this Sabbath eve, the fifth of Iyar, 5708, the fourteenth day of May, 1948.

A Truly Jewish Commonwealth

It is not a commonwealth of Jews that should be established, but a truly Jewish Commonwealth. A truly Jewish commonwealth can be none other than one in which the precepts of Moses with regard to the equalization of property, the appeals of the Prophets for social justice, are translated into reality.

MARTIN BUBER,
Zion and Youth

Ud

In Daphne I met Ud. Daphne is a Jewish agricultural settlement in Upper Galilee; Ud is a baby. The queer monosyllable by which he is known was not bestowed cappriciously; nor is it a pet name. Ud is a Hebrew word which means " the last brand," the ember plucked from the burning.

The boy and girl who were the parents of Ud had escaped from the Warsaw ghetto, after taking part in its last stand. Together they reached Palestine and in that land their son was born. They named him Ud. When I saw him he was a jolly, chubby baby of ten months, and he gurgled as happily as any baby with a less tragic and significant name. But the sign was upon him. Perhaps as he grew older he would resent his parents' dramatic choice, as children always resent the peculiar or the passionate in regard to themselves. No doubt child psychologists would seriously question the wisdom of involving a young life from the outset in the catastrophe from which his parents had miraculously escaped. However that might be, there he was, and I wondered if his mother, as she caressingly called his name — " Ud, Ud " — was aware each time of its terrible meaning and history.

I thought of still another child, born seven years earlier, in the fall of 1938. His mother had been one of a group of Jews driven out of the Sudeten area in one of the first of such expulsions. Because the family had been unable to get admission into any border town, the child's birthplace was a ditch. His mother named him Niemand, the German for " nobody."

The incident made something of an impression at the time. This was before the Nazi slaughterhouses had, among their other victims, destroyed the capacity for fellow feeling. We could still sense the anguish of this nativity, the terror of this Jewish mother's annunciation that the man-child she had borne was No One. In the years that have passed, I have often wondered about the fate of Niemand. Did he live? Did he escape the gas chambers? It is un-likely. There were so many ways for him to die; at any rate, I have not read his name among the few rescued. But he is unforgettable, as Ud is unforgettable.

From the German Niemand to the Hebrew Ud — there is the core of the calamity that befell my people. The symbolically named babies stand at either end of the great carnage, framing it with an artistic complete-ness which suggests a considered plan rather than the accident of a mother's despair or hope; Niemand, the prophetic name presaging the immense annihilation, and Ud, the small remnant!

MARIE SYRKIN,
Blessed Is The Match

Palestine is not primarily a place of refuge for the Jews of Eastern Europe, but the embodiment of the re-awakening corporate spirit of the whole Jewish nation.

ALBERT EINSTEIN,
The World As I See It

Our Unique Destiny As A Nation

It is a moving experience for me to come before this committee* of the United Nations for the purpose of summarizing the view and sentiments of the Jewish people at this turning point of its fortunes.

My mind goes back a quarter of a century to the previous assembly of nations which solemnly endorsed our program for the reconstitution in Palestine of our National Home. I came from the council room in which the mandate was ratified with the feeling that the most cherished ideals of our own history had been sanctioned by the conscience of all mankind.

Our ancient civilization, which had enriched the thought and spirit of the world, was to be given a free abode in the very cradle of its birth. Our people were to find a home— not a refuge, not an asylum, not a mere shelter, but a home with which their past memory and future hope were inseparably bound up. The Jewish people was to fashion its own political and social institutions in the image of its own character and tradition, on a level of equality with all other nations in the human family.

I can testify here that the estab-lishment of the Jews as a nation among the nations of the world was the real purpose and motive of that international covenant endorsed by the League of Nations.

It is no coincidence that the statesmen who developed the idea of organized international cooperation were prominently identified with the struggle for Jewish national equality as well. Wilson and Balfour, Lloyd George, Smuts and Masaryk and Cecil as well as the leaders in the creation of the United Nations found time amid their universal preoccupations, to plan for the Jewish State. . . .

Despite some of the things that have been said in this debate, I retain my belief in the prospect of Arab-Jewish cooperation once a solution based on finality and equality has received the sanction of international consent. The Jewish State in Palestine may become a pilot plant for processes and examples which may have a constructive message for its neighbors as well.

CHAIM WEIZMANN,
Address, 1947

* The Ad Hoc Committee on the Palestine Question, October 18, 1947.

The smallness of the state will be no bar to its full intellectual achievement. Athens was only one small city and the whole world is still its debtor. . . .

Life in Palestine offers our people not only a refuge among their kinsmen but also a chance of contributing to the rebirth of a nation and the development of its institutions. In this way the immigrant achieves a unity between himself and the society in which he lives.

Our remnants in Europe, who have before their eyes their six million slaughtered kinsmen, cannot stand the thought of another dispersion. They do not throw themselves on the mercy of the world. They are not suppliant, they are not beggars. They wish to be citizens of a Jewish society in which their capacities and ideals will be fully at home. . . .

Therefore, in establishing Jewish equality and nationhood, the United Nations can both solve the problem of Palestine's political future and relieve the darkest human tragedy of our time.

When this committee comes to plan the creation of a Jewish State, it will be fulfilling a proud historic mission. Despite its small scope, this enterprise stands high in the esteem of liberal thought. So many considerations of justice and humanity are involved.

There is redress for a persecuted people; equality for the Jewish people among the nations; the redemption of desert soil by cultivation; the creation of a new economy and society; the embodiment of progressive social ideas in an area that has fallen behind the best standards of modern life; the revival of one of the oldest cultures of mankind. . . .

I cannot allow this statement of the Jewish case to conclude without a word of appeal at this great bar of the world's conscience. A world which does not hear us in this moment of our agony would be deaf to the voice of justice and human feeling which must be raised loud and clear if the moral foundations of our society are to survive.

If you follow the impartial judgment of your own qualified committee and admit us to your honored table, we shall enter your company with a sense of the spiritual and intellectual challenge which the idea of the United Nations makes to the conscience of man. In giving us this opportunity you will be faithful to the noblest ideals which have been conceived by our ancestors and transmitted by them to the common heritage of the world.

This country made us a people; our people made this country.

DAVID BEN GURION,
Address, 1946

An Incandescent Moment

The history of every people fixes its eye upon a particular moment in which its qualities and attributes shine forth with special radiance beyond the normal level of every day achievements. No one can doubt that it was just such an incandescent moment that has been kindled in the life of the Jewish people in our own day and age. Beyond our expectations and perhaps beyond our merits we belong for all time to the generation of Israel's founding fathers. What we do in this generation will set the norms and the standards of Israel's life throughout all the perspectives which lie along future horizons.

I think it would be true to say that never in all human history has any purpose been accomplished against heavier calculations of chance. All the circumstances of time and of place argued against our success. The place was fixed by history on the shores of the Eastern Mediterranean in an area of crucial strategic importance coveted by powerful influences throughout the world, in a region where violent nationalisms were beginning to arise, more disposed to claim freedom for themselves than concede it to others. The time was the sequel to the Second World War, which left the Jewish people battered and bleeding from millions of wounds.

Here was a people which had seen six million of its kinsmen butchered and slaughtered in Europe. The institutions of Jewish life and culture lay about them in ruin. The pride and repute of the Jewish people, the oldest family of the human race, had been dragged down in an odious conspiracy of degradation. Out of the darkest depths of man's nature there has sprung at the throats of the Jewish people the most violent hatred which has ever convulsed or distorted the spirit of man.

Any observer would have been forgiven for thinking that this must be the end of the tormented journey of the Jewish people across the face of history. How could any people under the impact of such a blow decimating its manpower and humiliating its spirit summon out the energy with which to survive, still less the special resilience required to exhort its life to new levels of achievement and of sacrifice.

This was the climax of agony in the entire history of the Jewish people. Yet within three years of that lowest point in Jewish fortunes, the whole Jewish commonwealth had been re-established after two thousand years, its flag fluttered in the great circle of banners which symbolized the freedom and equality of all peoples on earth. Warm waves or renewed pride and confidence flowed into every home throughout the length and the breadth of the world in which the traditions and associations of the Jewish people were still maintained and revered.

Jewish history in our lifetime will forever be dominated by this most fantastic transition from the depths of paralyzing despair to unexpected pinnacles of sovereignty, pride, and achievement. Never was this people stronger than in its moment of weakness, never more hopeful than in its hour of despair.

ABBA EBAN,
Address, 1952

Zionism's Answer To Anti-Semitism

Zionism is the most consistent retort to anti-Semitism. Zionism accepts anti-Semitism as a fact, and endeavors to make the fate of the Jews independent of the consent of the non-Jews. It calls upon the Jews to take their destiny into their own hands, and to shape it by means of the historical deed instead of preaching morals, reason and humanity to non-Jews. Zionism expresses itself by watering deserts, draining marshes, founding a Jewish State, becoming a power; by securing to all those Jews who will not bow to oppression, humiliation and persecution the alternative of a homeland and a soil.

COUNT HENRY COUDENHOVE-KALERGI,
Anti-Semitism Throughout The Ages

Is Zionism A Utopia?

I am told Zionism is a Utopia. I do not know; perhaps. But inasmuch as I see in this Utopia an unconquerable thirst for freedom, one for which the people will suffer, it is for me a reality. With all my heart I pray that the Jewish people, like the rest of humanity, may be given spiritual strength to labor for its dream and to establish it in flesh and blood.

MAXIM GORKY

A Rendezvous With Destiny

Israel represents a great tradition and a universal ideal. It cannot be measured by the yardstick of territory alone. It must be seen and appreciated against the background of four thousand years of history. Viewed in this light, the creation of the State of Israel is one of the great developments in the annals of mankind. And what's more, whoever looks back at the achievements of the Jewish people while it was struggling against tremendous odds, cannot but come to the conclusion that the future of that people will not be like that of all other nations and that somewhere in the higher reaches of the human spirit it has a rendezvous with Destiny. . . .

The new epoch inaugurated by the rebirth of the State of Israel is but the beginning of its greatness. The vision of redemption which sustained us thousands of years had as its goal the complete redemption of the Jewish people and not of the Jewish people alone. There can be no redemption for the Jewish people without the redemption of all mankind. We can go on with our great and difficult task only by remaining true to our great vision — the vision of the Jewish Prophets which will be realized in the days to come.

DAVID BEN GURION

An Immemorial One

I do not bring you a new idea but an immemorial one. Yes, it is a universal idea — and therein lies its strength — old as our people which never even in the days of its bitterest need ceased to nourish it. This idea is that of the foundation of the Jewish State. It is extraordinary that through the long night of our history we Jews continue to dream this regal dream. . . . We plan for our posterity even as our fathers preserved the tradition for us.

THEODOR HERZL,
The Jewish State

The facts about Jewish life in the Christian world that have made Israel a necessity leave little room for Christian pride and moralizing. The rise of Israel should drive Christians to penitence and humility and, I think, also to gratitude.

J. C. RYLAARSDAM,
The New York Times, March 29, 1950

Palestine Became A Destiny

The Jewish people had its rise and growth in Palestine ; and Palestine has become a Holy Land to two-thirds of mankind because of the part the Jews played there. The history which the Jewish people enacted in Palestine has been accepted by the followers of Christianity and Mohammedanism as proof of God's providence in the career of mankind. The Patriarchs, Kings, and Prophets of Israel stamped themselves upon the human imagination to a greater degree than the national heroes of any other people. During their stay in Palestine, the Jews produced a literature which has given a common consciousness to the greater part of the human family. A land which forms the very texture of a people's life and genius is not a mere geographical entity that may be easily surrendered, but becomes, as Palestine became to the Jew, an inexorable destiny.

If the Jewish people has earned its right to Palestine through its achievements there, it has doubly earned that land through its unswerving devotion to it after the exile. Its devotion and yearning for the land has had the compelling power of an obsession. The Jew never stood up in prayer, never rose from a meal, never celebrated a Sabbath or festival, never rejoiced at a wedding, never mourned the loss of a beloved, never drew comfort from his religion without invoking the hope of restoration to Zion. The Jews have not omitted a single significant occasion, nor one single day in all the centuries that they have been dispersed among the nations, to reaffirm their right to national existence in Palestine. By that token the Jews have not merely upheld a claim in the face of forcible eviction; they have helped even in their absence to keep that land *spiritually* fruitful. The steadfast hope in their ultimate return to Palestine enabled the Jews to survive as a people. It has engendered whatever spiritual and cultural potentialities they still possess.

MORDECAI M. KAPLAN,
Judaism as a Civilization

Israel's Spiritual Capacity

The Jewish intellect will be uplifted and the emotional faculty will experience a corresponding revival and reinvigoration. The practical heroism of founding and planting, building and perfecting will be accompanied by the awakening of the dormant love of God and the fruitful cognition of His ways. New songs will be created, breathing the love of God and echoing His mighty Word. New and bright domains of culture will be discovered, tilled and fructified. The old will be renewed and the new will be sanctified. . . .

This dynamic flow will appear when the congregation of Israel and its spirit are united with the land of Israel. . . .

Great is the capacity of Israel for things Divine.

ABRAHAM ISAAC KUK,
Quoted in *Banner of Jerusalem*

A Generation Of Youngsters

During two thousand years of our march through the wilderness the song of Israel has wallowed with us like the legendary well of Miriam — at times appearing, at times hiding ; it has scarcely refreshed our soul, it has never satiated our thirst. And still, be that poetry blessed ! It was the song of Israel which kept us in existence, which gave us vision and comfort.

Now a generation of youngsters jumps in with a new song in hand, and Israel, the gray old-aged, leans on his staff, bows his ear and listens with his heart palpitating to that far voice — the voice of the future. Their ideas and their way of speech do not always conform with his mind, but he is aware of their loyal allegiance, of their thorough Jewishness, and thinks:

" Heaven knows, maybe these youngsters carry in their hands the tonic, the juvenile vigor for their old aged people, maybe they will re-erect its stature and adorn its gray head with a crown of honor and splendor."

CHAIM NAHMAN BIALIK

Spiritually, The Jews Never Left Israel

Spiritually the Jews never left Eretz Israel. In the Diaspora they live according to its calendar, cele-brating the spring and the harvest when it is spring and harvest time in Eretz Israel. They toast the Sab-bath and the Holy Days with wine pressed from grapes of the Home-land and forego necessities to be able to afford the Ethrog, whose sweet aroma is to them synonymous with the air of the Holy Land. A little soil from Eretz Israel is among the most precious possessions of Jews who dread nothing more than being buried in foreign soil without the comfort of a bit of Eretz Israel earth under their heads. Even in the grave their faces are turned toward Zion.

The undying Jewish love and attachment to Eretz Israel is the most unique example of loyalty and devotion. From the time of the first exile in Babylon, through the long night of the Middle Ages, down to our own day, every worth while Jewish effort, every spark of Jewish creativeness, every Jewish joy and every Jewish sorrow have stemmed from and been inspired by Eretz Israel. This tiny land, which had been home to the Jewish people for less than one-third of their historical career thus far, has been and is enshrined in the heart of every Jew deserving the name. In all countries and under many skies, for twenty-five centuries, day by day, Jews have thrice daily prayed for the restor-ation of their ancient Homeland, shedding tears of woe while remem-bering the vanished glory of Zion.

TRUDE WEISS-ROSMARIN
Jewish Survival

There Is Always Room In Mother's House

A country is not built up purely out of physical factors. It is naïve to say : " Here is an empty country and here are people who need a country. I shall take these people and put them into this empty country, and see, a country will arise." No ! America was not built in this way. South Africa was not built in this way. Land is needed. People are needed. The right kind of people are needed. But there is also needed an underlying principle such as that on which the great countries of the world have built the foundations of their civilizations. Countries like your own commonwealth (the United States) were built up out of two great moral factors : people tried to escape persecution, and people hoped to build up a better life and a new start ; and this is an indispensable component in the founding of a new civilization.

And this — not the fertility of its land — is the secret of Palestine. The stones of Palestine are not fertile — they have been made fertile. The sands of Palestine are not fertile — they have been made fertile not only by the water which has been poured on them, but by the sweat and blood and enthusiasm and energy of all the generations of people who took upon themselves the burden and the honor of the upbuilding of a country. . . .

This religious fervor, call it what you will, call it nationalism or religious fervor — the name does not matter — is the driving force behind the building of Palestine. And if you will test the countries which are being found for Jewish refugees in the light of this criterion, you will logically be driven to one country only and this is Eretz Yisroel. The other countries will absorb refugees, and they will stay refugees. But Palestine will be their national home. And even tested in the light of the physical factors, this particular, peculiar appeal which Palestine makes to the Jews has played the decisive part in the absorptive capacity. To put it perhaps in simpler language : There is always room in mother's house.

The difference between little Palestine and bigger, richer countries is one and one only. In other countries there is room for a definite number of Jews. But ask any Jew in Palestine, " What do you lack ? " and the answer will be : " More immigration! More ! More ! More ! "

CHAIM WEIZMANN,
Address, 1940

Anti-Zionism : Timidity And Self-Distrust

That freedom, that independence which most people have prized beyond life itself, for which the Boers staggered humanity, as our own ancestors staggered the Greeks and the Romans — are these mere moonshine ? Has the whole human race been wrong, and are the Anti-Zionists alone sane ? No, anti-Zionism may disguise itself in philosophy, wrap itself in religion, but at bottom it is the Marrano habit in us that has become second nature ; it is the yellow badge we wore for ages that is still stamped on our souls ; it is the timidity and self-distrust born of centuries of persecution ; it is the prisoner hugging his chains. All organs that are not used atrophy and decay ; as mankind has lost the use of its toes from not climbing, so, from not governing ourselves, we have lost the political instinct, the love of independence ; we have grown blind like the fish that swim in the dark caves of Kentucky. Mark Twain tells of a prisoner who lived in a dungeon for twenty years. One day he had a bright idea — he opened the door and walked out. He could have done so any time during those twenty years, but the idea had not occurred to him. I actually knew a man who lived twenty years on his back, under the impression that he was paralyzed. He wrote poems about his mattress-grave, as the Jew writes lamentations of his exile. One day there was an earthquake, and the patient leaped to his feet. Now he is married and has a family.

If a Jew tells you that a Jewish State is impossible, listen to him, for there are, indeed, grave difficulties.

But if he says it is undesirable, then remember he is a poor sick patient, who should be treated in a sanatorium. He is suffering from hereditary Marranoism. If, in addition, he has cold shivers about "the Zionist peril," the case is desperate. More pious critics admit a Jewish State is desirable but say we must not force the hand of Providence. What a splendid excuse for keeping our own hands in our pockets ! In Essex we have a sect called the Peculiar People, which is much persecuted by the police, because it leaves its sick children to die without giving them medicine. Prayer is their only medicine. We have been too long a Peculiar People in this sense. The best form of prayer is work. If Palestine can never be ours until we are good enough for it, what better way of becoming good than by working for it ? But I prefer the old Jew, who wept every Fast of Ab for his country, instead of working for it, to the new Jew who says our mission is to be scattered. We were scattered by force after years of desperate fighting against the Romans, and if it was God's will to scatter us, then it was blasphemous of our forefathers to resist the Romans at all, and to die in Jerusalem.

ISRAEL ZANGWILL,
Speeches, Articles and Letters

Of haunted houses it is said that they yield peace of mind only to the descendants of the original owner. Even so the soil of Eretz Yisrael will yield its sustenance and its beauty only to the descendants of those who wrote the *Tehilim* and who bled at Masada.

SOLOMON GOLDMAN,
Undefeated

Testimony To The Human Spirit

Within a single lifetime we have passed from a world in which the existence of an independent Israel seemed inconceivable into a world which seems inconceivable without its existence. I know of few more tangible testimonies in history to the power of the human will to assert itself against material odds. This is, perhaps, the primary value of Israel's rebirth to all those who are concerned with the vindication of faith against the fatalistic or deterministic theories of history, which sees the human being not as the primary agent of historic processes but merely as their helpless subject matter. Thus, quite apart from its context in the annals of the Jewish people, the rebirth of modern Israel would earn its place in history as a crushing argument in the eternal discussion between the claims of faith, and the doctrines which deny the human will any central part in governing the world's destiny. Those materialistic doctrines would have an impossible task to perform to explain Israel's revival solely in material or economic terms.

Now this belief in the power of the human will is a recurrent theme in Israel's history. The most distinctive attribute of Israel's character, the source of some weakness but of greater strength, is this stubborn, tenacious refusal to recognize the distinction between imagination and reality. In the grammar of classical Hebrew there is none of the sharp differentiation possessed by modern languages between that which is and that which shall be. This deliberate confusion has been illustrated at many stages of our history. In 1918, Dr. Weizmann went up to Mount Scopus, overlooking Jerusalem, to perform the ceremony of opening a new university. In its outward forms this resembled similar ceremonies whereby universities have been opened and dedicated in many parts of the world : the same forms, the same oratory, the same profuse platitudes as have been repeated on countless such occasions. There was one circumstance which made this solemnity distinctive. This was the fact that the university being opened did not exist at all. It was unrepresented even by a cornerstone. There were no means for its erection, and indeed no rational certainty that those who aspired to its establishment would ever live in the country at all. Yet because the establishment of a university in Jerusalem was for us a matter of passionate and intense will, the absence of these physical conditions was not an adequate reason to abstain from all the acts and gestures which should mark its fulfillment. Then, surely enough, within a decade the university existed and the ceremony, even in retrospect, no longer seems quixotic.

This deliberate confusion between imagination and reality marks all our religion and folklore.

ABBA EBAN

God had always chosen small countries through which to convey His messages to humanity.

CHAIM WEIZMANN,
Trial and Error

Gettysberg And Israel

Some half score years ago, our brethren established on sacred ground a nation conceived in the ethical and moral tenets of our great religion and dedicated to the proposition that the remnants of a once great people oppressed and persecuted must have a haven, a land, a nation of their own. Now they are engaged in a great Cold War, testing whether that nation, or any nation so conceived and so dedicated can long endure.

We are met in a great Temple of that religion. We have come to dedicate our hearts, our thoughts, our substance that that nation might live. It is altogether fitting and proper that we should do this, but in a larger sense our dedication, our consecration, is a small contribution. The brave men, living and dead, who struggled there have contributed far above our poor power to add or detract.

The world will little note nor long remember what we say here, but it will never forget what they did there. It is for us rather to be dedicated here to the work which they who have fought and bled have thus far so nobly advanced.

It is rather for us to be here dedicated to the great task remaining that from the remembered dead we take increased devotion to that cause for which they gave the last full measure of devotion. That we here resolve that those dead shall not have died in vain : that a nation under God shall have the right to freedom and life and that a government of the oppressed, by the oppressed, and for the oppressed shall not perish from the earth.

JOSEPH MILLER, Address, 1957

16

The Destiny of the Jew

We are nobly born; fortunate those who know it; blessed those who remember.

ROBERT LOUIS STEVENSON

Let others be ashamed of what they did to us in exile. We have every reason to consider our exile past with heads proudly lifted.

HAYIM GREENBERG,
Jewish Culture and Education in the Diaspora

We are God's stake in human history. We are the dawn and the dusk, the challenge and the test. How strange to be a Jew and go astray on God's perilous errands.

ABRAHAM J. HESCHEL,
The Earth Is The Lord's

The Eternal Riddle

Israel, my people.
God's greatest riddle,
Will thy solution
Ever be told?

Fought — never conquered,
Bent — never broken,
Mortal — immortal,
Youthful, though old.

Egypt enslaved thee,
Babylon crushed thee,
Rome led thee captive,
Homeless thy head.

Where are those nations
Mighty and fearsome?
Thou hast survived them,
They are long dead.

Nations keep coming,
Nations keep going,
Passing like shadows,
Wiped off the earth.

Thou art eternal
Witness remainest,
Watching their burial,
Watching their birth.

Pray, who revealed thee
Heaven's great secret:
Death and destruction
Thus to defy?

Suffering torture,
Stake, inquisition —
Prithee, who taught thee
Never to die?

Aye, and who gave thee
Faith, deep as ocean,
Strong as the rock-hills,
Fierce as the sun?

Hated and hunted,
Ever thou wand'rest,
Bearing a message:
God is but one!

Pray, has thy saga
Likewise an ending,
As its beginning
Glorious of old?

Israel, my people,
God's greatest riddle,
Will thy solution
Ever be told?

PHILIP M. RASKIN,
Songs of a Wanderer

Noble Beyond Any Other

Queer people this! Downtrodden for thousands of years, weeping always, suffering always, abandoned always by its God, yet clinging to Him tenaciously, loyally, as no other under the sun. Oh, if martyrdom, patience and faith in despite of trial, can confer a patent of nobility, then this people is noble beyond many another.

HEINRICH HEINE,
Quoted in *Heinrich Heine*, by
A. Meissner

What Remained Was The Word

They bound it with phylacteries round heart and head ; they fastened it to their doors ; they opened and closed the day with it ; as sucklings they learned the Word, and they died with the Word on their lips. From the Word they drew the strength to endure the piled - up afflictions of their way. Pale and secretive they smiled over the might of Edom, over its fury and the madness of its past works and its future plans. All that would pass ; what remained was the Word.

LEON FEUCHTWANGER,
Power

Israel Bears Witness

The binding force of an ethical force based on purpose has been dramatically confirmed in the history of the Jews : its practical consummation in our time perhaps merits our special note. Scattered to the four corners of the earth, the Jews, during the long period of the Dispersion, still retained their faith in a divine promise : in the restoration of Jerusalem, in the advent of a Messiah, and finally, in the prophecy of Isaiah, of the coincident coming of a day when the nations will no longer war against one another, but join together in ways of peace.

All these purposes may well, at many grievous times during the last two millenniums, have seemed delusional projections : the reactions of desperate souls to unfortunate political and social conditions : reactions bearing every mark of a collective neurosis. By holding to these purposes, the Jews kept together as a people under conditions that would have ground any less hopeful nation out of existence: that itself would constitute a pragmatic justification of purpose. But these goal-seeking people have done more than hold together, while their conquerors and oppressors, given to ephemeral satisfactions and immediate aims, vanished. Today the Jews have performed the incredible feat of returning as a unified political group to their native home in Palestine. Thus a collective purpose, working over an almost cosmic stretch of time, has brought its own fulfilment. By that fact, every contributory ceremony and ritual and prayer, every hardship and sacrifice, has been retrospectively justified. The mere existence of Israel today is a testimonial to the dynamics of purposive development. If the Greeks had had such a vision of life, they might have left an even deeper impression upon modern man.

LEWIS MUMFORD,
The Conduct of Life

The history of Israel, from Moses downward, is not the history of an inspired book, or an inspired order, but of an inspired people.

ARTHUR P. STANLEY,
The History of the Jewish Church

What Strength! What Humility!

Whatever pride the Jews derived from the knowledge that they were the designated guardians of a precious and eternal truth was more than compensated for by the heavy price which they were prepared to pay and did pay for it in suffering and persecution. This is the reverse side of the medal. For it was more than a spiritual treasure which they had come to possess for their own private satisfaction. It was a hard challenge to live by their faith and to carry it to a hostile and intolerant world, and in the process to "be despised and rejected by men and to become acquainted with grief." Each succeeding age tells its own story of the price that was paid. Over and again the actual dread realities equaled or surpassed the earlier tragedies. In the middle of the seventeenth century, one-third of the Jews of Europe were massacred; in the middle of the twentieth, two-thirds. From the slave pens of the Pharaohs to the gas chambers of Hitler, the *via dolorosa* of this people of the immemorial crucifixion has stretched long and desolate through the weary centuries. Yet they remained faithful. "Look down from heaven and see," rises the anguished cry from its litany of prayer, "how we have become a scorn and a derision among the nations; we are accounted as sheep, brought to the slaughter, to be slain and destroyed, to be smitten and reproached. Yet, despite all this, we have not forgotten Thy Name! We beseech Thee forget us not." What a rare diadem of proud sorrow is here, what strength and what humility!

And what shall be said of a people which through long, dark centuries of exile, outrage, and indignity could chant the refrain of a prayer so triumphant, so defiant, and so overflowing with gratitude as this: "Happy are we. How goodly is our portion, how pleasant our lot, how beautiful our heritage! How happy are we that we are privileged to proclaim at sunrise and at sunset, "Hear, O Israel, the Lord our God, the Lord is One!""

ABBA HILLEL SILVER,
Where Judaism Differed

Believe Not Thy Foes

Believe not thy foes when they say thou are forsaken like a useless slave, an old outworn servant who is summarily driven out of the house. Do not believe it, Israel! Between thy God and thee there is an unsettled reckoning that will one day be settled in thy favor, when grace will have struck the balance.

FRANZ WERFEL

The Eternal Protestant

What is the lesson of Jewish survival, not only to the Jews themselves, but to the world at large?

The question is in a way preposterous for a Jew. For Jews must know that the great achievement of our ancestors was that, by their persistence, they preserved Judaism. But from a nonsectarian or even a rationalistic point of view, the persistence of the Jewish tradition has also had far-reaching importance. Throughout the ages, the Jew has influenced mankind by remaining always what may be called an Eternal Protestant. Confident of the validity of his own faith, he has consistently refused to believe as other men believed, however much opinion was against him. Led by the Maccabees, the Jews refused to succumb to the attempt at Hellenization in the second century B.C.E., and thus made possible not only the survival of Judaism, but also the emergence of Christianity and Islam. Their implacable stubbornness secured them exemption from the general compulsion to conform to the state religion of the Roman Empire. And in the Middle Ages, in Europe, they and they alone stood out against the attempt of church and state to impose uniformity of belief everywhere.

This nonconformity served to keep alive some degree of freedom of thought in the world. It made people of intelligence realize the possibility that there might be another point of view, and so prevented their own thought from becoming wholly canalized. . . .

Jewish contributions to Occidental civilization in every sphere — political, social, scientific — have been owing largely to the exercise of those critical faculties which the Jew, because his background thought, and beliefs have not been those of the majority of the population, has possessed to an eminent degree. By finding the weak spots in older systems, he has helped to build up the new. Even today, we can see how in Central and Eastern Europe this Jewish solvent seems to be at work exposing the weak spots in the new Communist totalitarianisms, as it was at work a generation ago exposing those in the capitalist society of the time.

What in the Middle Ages was to some extent the passive achievement of the Jewish group, simply by virtue of its existence, came to be from the

French Revolution onward the conscious work of individuals. Apart from religion, the Jew's greatest significance to mankind in the period we are considering perhaps lay in the fact that he was—as he should remain—the Eternal Protestant.

CECIL ROTH,
Great Ages of the Jewish People

Heroism Without Equal

Certainly the heroism of the defenders of every other creed fades into insignificance before this martyr people, who for thirteen centuries confronted all the evils that the fiercest fanaticism could devise, enduring obloquy and spoilation and the violation of the dearest ties, and the infliction of the most hideous sufferings, rather than abandon their faith.

WILLIAM H. LECKY,
The Spirit of Rationalism

The Unbroken Chain

There are older nations than Israel, but Israel is the only nation with an unbroken cultural tradition of uninterrupted creativeness for thirty-five centuries. The descendants of the ancient Babylonians and Egyptians, as well as those of the Greeks and the Romans can still be traced among the present day populations of Mesopotamia, Egypt, Greece and Italy—however, these physical survivors have no connections whatsoever with their ancestors. They do not speak the languages they spoke, and their religion and cultural ideals are altogether different. There is lacking the "chain of tradition," the cultural continuity that makes the modern Jew not only the physical but also the spiritual descendant of his ancestors. The Hebrew language of today is still the same as that spoken in ancient Palestine and in which the Bible is written. Where there is, for instance, a marked difference between Old English, Middle English and Modern English, no such distinctions in either spelling, grammar, syntax or semantics, exist in Hebrew. Of course, the Hebrew language has grown and has been enriched in the course of millennia. Its basic structure, however, has not undergone any change whatsoever, a circumstance which enables the Jew whose mother tongue is Hebrew to read the Bible, or any other Hebrew classic without any difficulty. An average Englishman will not be able to read *Beowulf* or *The Canterbury Tales*, written only some centuries ago, without special philological training. To the uninitiated the language of these early English classics does not seem English at all. Nor will a contemporary Greek be able to read Homer with no greater difficulty than he would read a modern book or magazine — to say nothing of the populations of Mesopotamia and Egypt who were altogether unaware of the fact that their ancestors created a voluminous literature in picturesque cuneiform symbols and hieroglyphics, until modern archaeologists and scholars exhumed those treasures.

It is consequently not the eternity of the "Wandering Jew" that should puzzle the world but his retention of the continuity of Jewish culture and his remaining the heir, in all respects, of all the Jewish generations that lived and created before him.

TRUDE WEISS-ROSMARIN,
Jewish Survival

The Jewish People Would Not Be Defeated

The endurance of the Jewish people is a continuous exertion of the will in the face of adversity, of creative ingenuity in the midst of change.

We need not speak of the courage it needed to die for one's faith at the stake, or to become for its sake a wanderer in a hostile world. More impressive in its way was the ability to stand up to the choreography and *décor* of humiliation which the Middle Ages added to their economic and physical maltreatment of the Jew : the ghetto, the yellow badge, the spitting ceremonials, the insults, the naked foot-races, the blood libels, the accusations of poisoning the wells. Hundreds of thousands of little people accepted the verdict of an ever-renewed malevolence without a thought of purchasing security and comfort by defection. And escape was so easy, so simple ! The " racial " rejection of the Jew was unknown in the Middle Ages. It was all a matter of belief. The Churchmen were eager to win souls ; the conversion of the Jews was an ideal ; and there were prelates of a genuine Christian disposition who, protecting the Jews in times of popular bloodthirstiness, made the offer of Christianity in a spirit that was particularly tempting. The answer of the faithful was No ! The Jewish people had a task to complete and would not quit in the middle.

MAURICE SAMUEL,
The Professor and The Fossil

The Bush That Was Not Consumed

In the declension and dregs of ages, people have been inflamed with a spirit of cruelty and barbarity against them (the Jews). They were accused of being the cause of all the calamities that happened and charged with a world of crimes, which they never thought of. A vast number of miracles were invented in order to convict them, or rather upon a pretense of religion, to trample upon and oppress them. We have made a collection of the laws, which the councils and princes have published against them, whereby a judgment may be made of the iniquity of the ones and the oppression of the others. People did not keep within the bounds of the edicts against them. For they were frequently exposed everywhere to military execution, popular commotions and massacres. Yet by a miracle of Providence, which ought to astonish all Christians, this nation, hated and persecuted in all places for so many ages, still subsists in all parts of the world. . . . The bush of Moses, surrounded by flames, has ever burned without being consumed. The Jews have been driven out of all the cities of the world and this has only served to spread them abroad in all cities. They still live in spite of the contempt and hatred which follow them everywhere, while the greatest monarchies have fallen and are known to us only by name.

JACQUES BASNAGE,
The History of the Jews from Jesus Christ to the Present Time

Though Empires Have Perished

Israel—a people who have been overthrown, crushed, scattered ; who have been ground, as it were, to very dust, and flung to the four winds of heaven ; yet who, though thrones have fallen, and empires have perished, and creeds have changed, and living tongues have become dead, still exist with a vitality seemingly unimpaired.

HENRY GEORGE

A Book Of Nobility

All Jewish religious literature accepts and preaches the famous Talmudic sentence : " Of those who are oppressed and do not oppress, who are reviled and who do not (in reply) revile, who act only from love (to God), and rejoice in their sufferings, the Scripture says, They who love Him are like the sun when it rises in its might." But the most touching chapter about love of the enemy is contained in the history of the religious community of Israel. Judaism can tell of unspeakable suffering, of agonizing tortures of its children. But no wrong, no physical violence, have availed to stifle the human love in their hearts, a love not drowned in the stream of innocent blood. It is just from the very worst times that love of man speaks to us most distinctly and most from the heart. We possess popular books from the time of the worst persecutions, books on ethics, the authors of which must have been convinced when they wrote them that nobody but their co-religionists would ever read them. The most intimate voices speak to us from these books. They all join in one refrain : Love thy neighbor, and be merciful even to thine enemy. Nathan the Wise, whose wife and seven sons had been all murdered on the same day, and whose heart even then did not grow hard, does not live merely in the dreamland of poetry. He has a real existence in the history of the Jewish communities. The crusaders killed the wife and child of Eleazar ben Jehuda of Worms, and he himself remained wounded almost to death upon the ground. When, in his old age, he recorded the experiences of his life, so that he might bequeath them to succeeding generations, not a single work of hatred against his enemies was wrung from him. He too acknowledged but the one truth; it is better to suffer wrong than to do wrong. It is necessary to have read these medieval writings, which have scarcely anything to compare with them either in their own or much later times, in order to appreciate Jewish teaching in the full power of its love and its humanity, in all its tenderness of moral feeling. They helped not a little to make the story of Judaism's sufferings a book of nobility.

LEO BAECK,
The Essence of Judaism

We Have Every Reason To Be Proud

Undoubtedly, a civilization without a soil of its own, without territorial bounds, is from many angles an abnormal phenomenon. But Jews were successful in sublimating this abnormality. T h e y brought something with them into exile which I might seek to compare, if I were a poet, to Father Jacob's visionary (yet still real) ladder, which requires no more space than a ladder needs for its support in order to reach heaven (" a ladder set up on the earth and the top of it reached to heaven "). And who can say today, looking backward, that the almost fantastic history of the Jew was without significance, or dull or fruitless ? Upon vast expanses of time and out of nothing more apparent than memories, strivings, and aspirations, our people created such grand structures as the Babylonian T a l m u d, the palaces of Kabbalah and Hasidism, the gardens of medieval philosophy and poetry, the self discipline and inspirational ritualism of the *Shulchan Aruch*, the color and aroma of Sabbaths and holidays. All these to a great extent are creations of the *galuth*, ex-territorial conquests, and however onerous was our isolation from the world we lived in, still it gave us a sense of aristocratic exclusiveness, of lineage, of superiority. We were without territory — yet possessed of clear and fixed boundaries that Jews devotedly guarded ; without armies — and yet so much heroism ; without a Temple — and yet so much sanctity ; without priesthood — and yet each Jew, in effect, a priest ; without kingship — and yet with such unexcelled spiritual " sovereignty." Should we be ashamed of the exile ? I am proud of it and if *galuth* was a calamity (who can pretend it was not ?), I am proud of what we were able to perform in that calamity. Let others be ashamed of what they did to us in exile. We have every reason to consider our exile past with heads proudly lifted. None of us would idealize a prison ; but let those be ashamed who torment in prisons the better representatives of mankind, not those captives who in the darkness of their prison cell were inspired to compose paeans to freedom and truth.

HAYIM GREENBERG,
Jewish Culture and Education in the Diaspora

If it be true, as it obviously is, that the Bible is a creation of the Jews, it is also true, though not so obvious, that the Jews are a creation of the Bible.

JOSEPH JACOBS,
Jewish Contribution to Civilization

Lord of the world, I beg of you to redeem Israel. And if you do not want to do that, then redeem the Gentiles.

ISRAEL OF KOZNITZ

Invocation To The Kaddish

Good morning to you, Lord of the world !
I, Levi Isaac, son of Sarah of Berditshev, am coming to you in a legal matter concerning your people of Israel.
What do you want of Israel ?
It is always : Command the children of Israel !
It is always : Speak unto the children of Israel !
Merciful Father ! How many peoples are there in the world ?

Persians, Babylonians, Edomites !
The Russians — what do they say ?
Our emperor is the emperor !
The Germans — what do they say ?
Our kingdom is the kingdom !
The English — what do they say ?
Our kingdom is the kingdom !
But I, Levi Isaac, son of Sarah of Berditshev, say :
" Glorified and sanctified be His great name ! "
And I, Levi Isaac, son of Sarah of Berditshev, say :

I shall not go hence, nor budge from
my place
Until there be a finish
Until there be an end of exile —
"Glorified and sanctified be His
great name!"

LEVI YITZHAK OF BERDITSHEV,
Quoted in "In Time and Eternity"

Jews have always constituted a
minority, and a minority is constantly compelled to think; that is
the blessing of their fate.

LEO BAECK,
The Essence of Judaism

A Quiet Heroism

Judaism knows its own heroism
well, a quiet heroism : death for
faith and truth, death for the sanctification of the Name : the heroism
of those Jews who, rather than
deliver up an innocent man from
their midst whom a mad mob
feigned to be the slayer of a Christian
child, went to the synagogue and all
chose death rather than unrighteousness ; the heroism of those children
of ten, the Nikolajewsky Soldaty
(Soldiers of Nicholas I) who during
the twenty-five years of their military slavery were tortured in body
and in soul in order to be induced
to accept an alien faith and were
steadfast — these Jewish children
who resisted both the lure of favors
and the blood-soaked whip, these
little ones these great martyrs whom
the entire Russian Empire could not
break. These are the Jewish soldiers
in a foreign army who are our
heroes. Or take those Jews of Kowno
who in the year 1915, placed before
the alternative of delivering up as
hostages the leaders of their community or mass expulsion, chose the
latter. Truly, the Jewish people
knows a heroism of its own — the
heroism of a little people that during
two thousand years has been steadfast against a world of foes.

JACOB KLATZKIN,
Krisis und Entscheidung

The Power Of The Book

They had no state, holding them
together, no country, no soil, no
king, no form of life in common. If,
in spite of this, they were one, more
one than all the other peoples of the
world, it was the Book that sweated
them into unity.

LEON FEUCHTWANGER,
Power

The Jewish Story Beggars Fiction

This perhaps is the ultimate wonder of Jewish history. The Jew, if he would not die, should have become the gipsy of the world, an outlaw in intent as he was in fact. His hand should have been raised against each man, as society's was raised against him. He should have degenerated into a beast concerned only for the food and security which the world sought to withhold. That on the contrary he remained an enlightened human being, that he maintained and transmitted a culture, and against such odds, this is a phenomenon that beggars fiction. The fact of the matter is that the Jew did not become outlaw, gipsy or beast. He was saved from that fate by the heritage he bore with him.

The traditional culture of the Jew is then a matter of prime significance, both in the determination of his survival and of the character he came to assume. For with the Jew in all his restless movement went not only quantities of tangible objects, but a large body of possessions invisible to the physical eye. Ideas and ideals, as well as things, had their share in the determination of the Jew. The persecutor might torture Jews, might rob and despoil them of every object they called their own, he could not take from them the rich tradition which was theirs by right of inheritance. Through all shifts of time and circumstance, this alone was constant; through incessant confiscations, this remained inexpropriable.

MILTON STEINBERG,
The Making of the Modern Jew

No stain adheres to our flag. Blood aplenty — but our own! On this flag is inscribed : " The Eternal is my banner ! "

LUDWIG HOLLANDER,
Address, 1914

We Alone Survived

Of the whole welter of ancient peoples we alone survived. . . . Dispersed, broken into fragments . . . multi-colored and diversified, black and yellow and white, occidental and oriental but withal one people.

We survived, I should like to believe, because we were inveterate optimists. No obstacle stopped us, no crisis dismayed us, no catastrophe crushed us. We swallowed the bitterness of life and pursued the sweet thereof. Aye, we loved life — this very thing of living. " Be fruitful and multiply," we urged unashamed, unapologetic . . . " Remember us unto life, O King, that delightest in life. . . ." Israel wanted life abundantly, clung to it and lived.

We survived because of Torah. We loved life and our sages knew that life needs direction, norms, discipline. We denied ourselves that we might live. . . . We placed ourselves under the yoke of the Torah and rejoiced that we had *Mitzvot*. . . . The Prophets, the Scribes, the Pharisees fashioned Torah — the blending of thought with resolution — thought that leads to action. The Torah is teaching and living. Our greatest intellects concerned themselves with "everyday things." Even the trifles that "man treads under his heel" were the concern of Hillel, an Akiba, a Rashi, or a Maimonides.

We survived because ours was a genuine democracy. No caste system was permitted to develop, no autocrat went unchallenged. The lowly and the mighty were the children of Abraham, Isaac and Jacob. Smiths, peddlers, shoemakers could become great teachers and be hearkened to by the whole people. The son of a carpenter could believe himself a Messiah and humble fishermen might become the founders of a new religion.

At the end of the eighteenth century it could be maintained in civilized England that "everyone but an idiot knows that the lower classes must be kept poor," and that it were folly to educate the poor for they might become "insolent to their superiors." In Israel it was hoped in the remotest past, "Would God that all the Lord's people become Prophets." We could say to every man, *Bishvilkha Nivra Ha-Olam*, for thy sake the world was created.

We survived, I believe, above all, because of the prophetic voices that broke out in Israel from time to time. We were blessed with men that never made peace with the foibles of the people or the whims of the rulers. We were compelled to listen to denunciations that "cried aloud like a trumpet." We could not allow ourselves to sink into the sweet lassitude of dissipation and degeneracy which led so many peoples to despair and death. We were shaken by a mighty hand and outstretched arm. Israel, we were warned, "Wash ye, make you clean . . . cease to do evil; learn to do well; seek judgment, relieve the oppressed, judge the fatherless, plead for the widow."

SOLOMON GOLDMAN,
Crisis and Decision

A Miracle

A court philosopher was once trying to impress upon his French king the truth of religion. Whereupon the king turned to him and said, "I challenge you to cite a single miracle."

The Philosopher answered simply, "Sire, the Jews."

The Barometer Of Civilization

Here is a people upon which all the forces of fear, ignorance, and brutality have fastened, decreeing its elimination. If it lives, it proves that these demoniacal forces cannot permanently triumph in human affairs. Not because of his individual virtues, but because of his position, the Jew has been aptly described as the barometer of civilization, or, more aptly still, as the defender of the front-line trenches in the battle for human ideals. If he be destroyed, the furies of hell will be let loose on all groups that dare to think for themselves or cherish their own traditions, that seek to worship God or abstain from worship, in accordance with their own conscience. No religious sect, no national group, no scientific or philosophical seeker after the truth would long be safe in a world where the Jew, the world's most striking minority, has been annihilated. The Jewish people has a duty to live, in order that man's inalienable right to freedom may not die. In the words of an ancient prayer, " If we perish, who will sanctify thy Name ? "

ROBERT GORDIS,
The Jew Faces a New World

Who Should Be Afraid ?

Is not the Gentile's now traditional abhorrence of the Jew to be explained to a large extent as in essence his abhorrence of himself in his treatment of the Jew ? For is it not a familiar fault of human nature to wreak vengeance most terribly not upon the one who has misused us but upon the one who we have ourselves misused in a desperate endeavor to transfer to another the burden of our offending ? However, this may be, the Jew is a living embodiment of all that is most grievous in Christian history. For a Gentile to come into the presence of a Jew is to feel himself embarrassed, stricken with shame, convicted of sin. In the face of the heritage of horror which the centuries bestow upon the Gentile from out of the years of oppressive relations with the Jew, I marvel that any Gentile can ever find anything in any Jew to blame. . . . It is the master and not the slave, the hater and not the hated, the persecutor and not the persecuted, who before God must be " afraid."

JOHN HAYNES HOLMES,
Through Gentile Eyes

Freedom For The Jew

The denial of freedom to the Jew denies it to the Gentile. Any impairment of justice for Israel impairs universal justice and ultimately corrupts and enslaves the nation guilty of the offense. . . .

S. PARKES CADMAN

The Classical People Of Martyrdom

Many today have little understanding for martyrdom. They fail to see that it represents the highest moral triumph of humanity — unwavering steadfastness to principle, even at the cost of life. They equally fail to see the lasting influence of such martyrdoms upon the life and character of the nation whose history they adorn ; that such nation is henceforth a stronger and more vital organism, endowed with new powers of the spirit, and above all with a heightened self-consciousness which nothing can daunt. In all human history, there is not a single noble cause, movement or achievement that did not call for sacrifice, nay sacrifice of life itself. Science, Liberty, Humanity, all took their toll of martyrs ; and so did and does Judaism. Israel is the classical people of martyrdom. No other people has made similar sacrifices for Truth, Conscience, Honor and Human Freedom.

JOSEPH H. HERTZ,
Daily Prayer Book

If There Are Ranks In Suffering

If there are ranks in suffering, Israel takes precedence of all the nations ; if the duration of sorrows and the patience with which they are borne ennoble, the Jews can challenge the aristocracy of every land ; if a literature is called rich in the possession of a few classic tragedies — what shall we say to a National Tragedy lasting for fifteen hundred years, in which the poets and the actors were also the heroes ?

LEOPOLD ZUNZ,
Synagogale Poesie

Fidelity To Creed

The Jews were the supreme example of fidelity to creed, notwithstanding the attempts of the different states to crush or entice them. Their steadfastness, combined with the influence of their own Scriptures, served as an example for the resolute Protestants, who declined to be forced into belief in the dominant creed. Religious liberty has been rightly described as the parent of political liberty ; but for the clashing of the sects, the forces of absolutism would have crushed out both political and religious liberty, as they did in France and Spain. And religious liberty is of even more spiritual consequence than political, since it keeps alive the principle that there are certain spiritual ideals without which life itself is not worth living. The Jews have been the supreme example of devotion to this ideal, and have been silent, though effective, martyr witnesses, not so much of their own truth, but of the supreme value of the ideal element in human nature and development.

JOSEPH JACOBS,
Jewish Contributions to Civilization

The Humanity Of The Jews

The Jew has suffered so much hurt, he has endured so many injustices, experienced so completely the misery of life, that pity for the poor and the humiliated has become second nature to him. And in his agonized wanderings, he has seen at close range so many men of all races, and of all countries, different everywhere and everywhere alike, that he has understood, he has felt in the flesh of his flesh, that Man is one as God is One. Thus was formed a people which may have the same vices and the same virtues as other peoples, but which is without doubt the most *human* of all peoples.

EDMUND FLEG,
Why I Am a Jew

As Eternal As Hope

In its journey through the desert of life, for eighteen centuries, the Jewish people carried along the Ark of the Covenant, which breathed into its heart ideal aspirations, and even illumined the badge of disgrace affixed to its garment with a saintly glory. The persecuted Jew felt a sublime, noble pride in being singled out to perpetuate and suffer for a religion which reflects eternity, by which the nations of the earth were gradually educated to a knowledge of God and Morality from which is to spring the salvation and redemption of the world. Such a people, which disdains its present but has the eye steadily fixed on its future, which lives as it were on hope, is on that very account eternal, like hope.

MOSES GASTER,
Sabbath and Festival Prayer Book

The Enlisted Army Of The Lord

The Jews regarded themselves as the chosen people not because of their racial qualities, but because of having been selected to be the servants of God to carry his moral law to the world. They looked upon themselves as a covenanted people, a kingdom, not of supermen, but of priests. This covenant with God was an act of will on both sides, a matter not of the fatalism of blood but of choice. Admission into this covenant was open to all men of all races at all times, also as a matter of choice. The Prophets of Israel constantly reminded the Jews of the non racial character of their especial relationship to Yahweh : " Are ye not as the children of the Ethiopians unto Me O children of Israel ? said the Lord. Have not I brought up Israel out of the land of Egypt and the Philistines from Caphtor, and Aram from Kir ? " (Amos 9 : 7) .

The Jews regarded themselves as the enlisted army of the Lord. They therefore submitted to an especially rigorous discipline of laws to insure their survival, as well as the effective prosecution of their mission. Their mission was not conquest or racial mastery or territorial "Lebensraum," but to be a "light unto the Gentiles." These laws were therefore not binding upon the non-Jews. The latter could acquire full merit and in all things be the equal of the most pious Jews simply by obeying, not the elaborate Mosaic code of laws, but the few elementary and universal laws of mankind — the so - called Seven Laws of the Noachidae. The gates of Paradise would be open to the righteous among the Gentiles, declared the Rabbis, equally with the righteous among the Jews who faithfully obeyed all the six hundred and thirteen positive and negative commandments.

Israel's God was the God of all nations. Israel's sole prerogative lay in carrying on an arduous and self-sacrificing moral and religious leadership.

ABBA HILLEL SILVER,
The World Crisis and Jewish Survival

For The Emancipation Of The Jews

In the infancy of civilization, when our island was as savage as New Guinea, when letters and arts were still unknown to Athens, when scarcely a thatched hut stood on what was afterward the site of Rome, this condemned people had their fenced cities and cedar palaces, their splendid Temple, their fleets of merchant ships, their schools of sacred learning, their great statesmen and soldiers, their natural philosophers, their historians, and their poets. What nation ever contended more manfully against over-whelming odds for its independence and religion ? What nation ever, in its last agonies, gave such signal proofs of what may be accomplished by a brave despair ? And if, in the course of many centuries, the op-pressed descendants of warriors and sages have degenerated from the qualities of their fathers . . . shall we consider this as a matter of reproach to them ? Shall we not rather con-sider it as a matter of shame and remorse to ourselves ? Let us do justice to them. Let us open to them the door of the House of Commons. Let us open to them every career in which ability and energy can be displayed. Until we have done this, let us not presume to say that there is no genius among the countrymen of Isaiah, no heroism among the descendants of the Maccabees.

LORD MACAULEY,
Address, 1853

Gifts

" O World-God, give me Wealth ! "
    the Egyptian cried.
His prayer was granted. High as
    heaven behold
Palace and pyramid ; the brimming
    tide
Of lavish Nile washed all his land
    with gold.
Armies of slaves toiled ant-wise at
    his feet,
World-circling traffic roared through
    mart and street,
His priests were gods, his spice-
    balmed kings enshrined,
Set death at naught in rock-ribbed
    charnels deep.
Seek Pharaoh's race today and ye
    shall find
Rust and the moth, silence and dusty
    sleep.

" O World-God give me Beauty ! "
    cried the Greek.
His prayer was granted. All the earth
    became

Plastic and vocal to his sense ; each
    peak,
Each grove, each stream, quick with
    Promethean flame,
Peopled the world with imaged grace
    and light,
The lyre was his, and his the breath-
    ing might
Of the immortal marble, his the play
Of diamond - pointed thought and
    golden tongue.
Go seek the sunshine race, ye find
    today
A broken column and a lute un-
    strung.

" O World--God, give me Power ! "
    the Roman cried.
His prayer was granted. The vast
    world was chained
A captive to the chariot of his pride.
The blood of myriad provinces was
    drained
To feed that fierce, insatiable red
    heart.

Invulnerably bulwarked every part
With serried legions and with close-
meshed code,
Within, the burrowing worm had
gnawed its home,
A roofless ruin stands where once
abode
The imperial race of everlasting
Rome.

"O Godhead, give me Truth," the
Hebrew cried.
His prayer was granted ; he became
the slave
Of the idea, a pilgrim far and wide,

Cursed, hated, spurned, and scourged
with none to save
The Pharaohs knew him, and when
Greece beheld,
His wisdom wore the hoary crown
of old.
Beauty he hath forsworn, and wealth
and power.
Seek him today, and find in every
land,
No fire consumes him, neither floods
devour ;
Immortal through the lamp within
his hand.

EMMA LAZARUS,
Anthology of Modern Jewish Poetry

"Es Vet Zein Gut"

There have been times when we
have been obviously threatened with
complete destruction. Somehow or
other we came through. It doesn't
mean that the Jewish people, as
such, is a very extraordinary moral
phenomenon. It means that there
seems to be incorporated in this
group an idea which is imperishable.
It is this notion of the ideal of the
unphysical triumphing over the
physical which — whenever I get
these temporary moods of depression and uneasiness — lifts me outside the temptation to speak sadly,
and sends me out again after a
momentary period of recovery, to
tell my fellow Jews, "Es vet zein
gut — it will be good."
It may take a long time, but if

we can't have this feeling, if we
can't have this faith, then the whole
business, all the miserable struggle,
the agonies, and all the self search-
ings don't mean a thing. And I am
not prepared to admit that the world
doesn't mean a thing. If I were, I'd
stop writing, I'd stop lecturing, I'd
just lie down and perish without a
Kaddish. I just do not believe that
the world doesn't mean a thing.
And the people, or the group, the
community which has longest and
most persistently repudiated the idea
that the universe doesn't mean a
thing is the one in whose employ I
am.

MAURICE SAMUEL,
The Grand Perspectives of Jewish
History

What Fiction Could Match This Reality?

The story of the Jews since the Dispersion is one of the epics of European history. Driven from their natural home by the Roman capture of Jerusalem (70 A.D.), and scattered by flight and trade among all the nations and to all the continents; persecuted and decimated by the adherents of the great religions — Christianity and Mohammedanism — which had been born of their scriptures and their memories; barred by the feudal system from owning land, and by the guilds from taking part in industry; shut up within congested ghettos and narrowing pursuits, mobbed by the people and robbed by the Kings; building with their finance and trade the towns and cities indispensable to civilization; outcast and excommunicated, insulted and injured; yet without any political structure, without any legal compulsion to social unity, without even a common language, this wonderful people has maintained itself in body and soul, has preserved its racial and cultural integrity, has guarded with jealous love its oldest rituals and traditions, has patiently and resolutely awaited the day of its deliverance, and has emerged greater in number than ever before, renowned in every field for the contributions of its geniuses, and triumphantly restored, after two thousand years of wandering, to its ancient and unforgotten home. What drama could rival the grandeur of these sufferings, the variety of these scenes, and the glory and justice of this fulfillment? What fiction could match the romance of this reality?

WILL DURANT,
The Story of Philosophy

Afraid Of Darkness?

I am no child, afraid of darkness.
God has led me through so many
    nights with a light of fire,
Surely no darkness is too dark —
    with Him.
When I walk with Him, even the
    night shineth as the day,
The darkness is as the light. . . .
Egypt, Babylon, Greece, Rome. . . .
Crusade, Black-Death, Exile, Crematorium,
Pharoah, Haman, Nero, Hitler. . . .

I have lived too long, experienced
    too much,
Known too many nights, not to see
That they are, like the day,
Only an aspect of eternity.
This night too shall pass,
And in the morning light
We shall behold Thy face, O Lord,
    in righteousness;
And in Thy light shall we see light.

ALBERT S. GOLDSTEIN,
Temple Bulletin

A Citizen Of The World

Not allowed to be a citizen in any land, the Jew became perforce a citizen of the world, and as a citizen of the world he performed an irreplaceable service. For one of his greatest and most characteristic functions throughout history has been his part as an intermediary — not only intellectual, but economic, social, and political as well. In addition to his role as the Eternal Protestant, he was also the " International Jew " — a title properly of pride not of obloquy. He always had the advantage of standing astride more than one civilization. He had personal connections and interests not hemmed in by political borders. He had a realization of lands and cultures lying far distant from those of his own environment. He had access to foreign languages. His kinsfolk were scattered in many lands, so that in every country there was some coreligionist who could act as his correspondent or his agent, or give him hospitality, or extend him credit. Hebrew could carry him, at a pinch, from one end of the world to another, and lay open to him the intellectual treasures of every age and every land.

CECIL ROTH,
Great Ages and Ideas of the Jewish People

The Heroic Dignity Of The Wandering Jew

At the threshold of these expulsions (from European countries), it was necessary for the Jew only to accept a formula in order to be saved the pangs of exile. The acceptance of a single drop of baptismal water was enough to entitle him to remain and enjoy his property, the scenes in which he had been brought up and the land where his fathers lay buried, and to avoid the hideous uncertainty of the future which lay before him. There were, of course, some Jews who chose that easier way. But they were a tiny minority. The ungainly figure of the Wandering Jew, clad in rags, footsore, weary, and penniless, snatching repose for a few moments until some new storm buffeted him on toward a new stage in his wanderings — that ungainly figure acquires a heroic dignity when one realizes that he could have thrown off his rags, and clad himself in scarlet, and enjoyed peace and quiet and affluence, by pronouncing one single word — a word which he did not pronounce.

LOUIS GOLDING,
The Jewish Problem

The Gold Of God

Our life is beset with difficulties, yet it is never devoid of meaning. The feeling of futility is absent from our souls. Our existence is not in vain. There is a Divine earnestness about our life. This is our dignity. To be invested with dignity means to represent something more than oneself. The gravest sin for a Jew is to forget what he represents.

We are God's stake in human history. We are the dawn and the dusk, the challenge and the test. How strange to be a Jew and to go astray on God's perilous errands. We have been offered as a pattern of worship and as a prey for scorn, but there is more still in our destiny. We carry the gold of God in our souls to forge the gate of the kingdom. The time for the kingdom may be far off, but the task is plain : to retain our share in God in spite of peril and contempt. There is a war to wage against the vulgar, against the glorification of the absurd, a war that is incessant, universal. Loyal to the presence of the ultimate in the common, we may be able to make it clear that man is more than man, that in doing the finite he may perceive the infinite.

ABRAHAM J. HESCHEL,
The Earth is the Lord's

The Prophetic Ferment

The Prophets dreamed great dreams for their people, not as military conquerors but as spiritual servants of mankind. They brought them the gift of suffering for great ideals. A covenant of destiny had been established between God and Israel at Sinai. Israel had been chosen by God, "betrothed unto Him in faithfulness." Alone among the idolatrous nations of the earth to recognize the true nature of God, Israel was bound by the very fact of that exclusive recognition to constancy and to an exceptional loyalty to God. By the same token it was subject to an exceptional retribution for any acts of disloyalty : "You only have I known of all the families of the earth, therefore will I visit upon you all your iniquities."

In post-exilic times this concept of election was still further deepened by the motif of mission. The Prophets put the mantle of their own destiny upon their people Israel. Israel was to be a prophetic people, not because the spirit of divine prophecy had now come to rest on Israel collectively, whereas previously it had been vouchsafed only to isolated individuals, but because the people, now widely scattered over a far-flung Diaspora, could become, even as the Prophets themselves were, the messengers of God, to bring His word and His truth to the Gentiles. Tried in the furnace of affliction and refined by suffering, Israel could become a witness to the peoples, a light to the nations.

Whether Israel has fulfilled this mission in history, whether it actually has been "in the midst of many peoples as dew from the Lord, as shower upon the grass," let the great social movements of mankind which felt the impact of Israel's dynamic spirit through the ages, surging and creative in living men and women, bear witness. Let the Cross and Crescent bear witness — for they kindled their torches at the sacred fires of Israel's altars. Let the Renaissance and the Reformation and the American Revolution bear witness — for they too felt the dynamic drive of the Hebraic spirit. Let all the mighty movements for reform and righteousness in our day bear witness. . . .

A nation, as a whole, is of course never "prophetic." But Israel fostered the great spiritual and humanitarian ideals of the Prophets unremittingly through the ages. In school, home and synagogue the spirit of each succeeding generation was nurtured on them. They were thus kept alive for the great conjunctures and the explosive moments in human history. From time to time, some gifted son of Israel recaptured some of their ancient power and impetuosity, and through him they swept forward again as a powerful and fructifying social movement over the face of the earth.

It is this prophetic ferment in the soul of the race, as real in the modern as in the ancient world, which the enemies of Israel and mankind most dread. It is also the testament of Israel's immortality!

ABBA HILLEL SILVER,
The World Crisis and Jewish Survival

Unshaken As The Continent

Pride and humiliation hand in hand
Walked with them through the
    world where'er they went ;

Trampled and beaten were they as
    the sand,
And yet unshaken as the continent.

HENRY W. LONGFELLOW,
Jewish Cemetery at Newport

The Great Deeds Of A Little People

'Tis a little people, but it has done great things. When in the land in which it first came to national consciousness, it created a conception

of the Highest Being of the universe, which has been adopted in essence by the foremost races of humanity. It had but a precarious hold on a few crags and highlands between the desert and the deep sea, yet its thinkers and sages with eagle vision took into their thought the destinies of all humanity, and rang out in clarion voice a message of hope to the down-trodden of all races. Claiming for themselves and their people the duty and obligations of a true aristocracy, they held forth to the peoples ideals of a true democracy founded on right and justice. Their voices have never ceased to re-echo around the world, and the greatest things that have been done to raise men's lot have been done always in the spirit, often in the name, of the Hebrew Prophets.

Nor did their beneficial activities cease when they were torn away from their own land by all-powerful Rome. For nearly two thousand years they have taken their share in all the movements that have made the modern European man. At times they have helped to spread culture from one nation to another; at others, they have helped to light it anew in a fresh land. On some occasions they have even been leaders in these movements, but mostly they have been content to take their share in the cultural development of their fellow-men, contributing to it by the qualities which their unique position among the nations had developed in them. In the intricate warp and woof of civilization Jewish threads have been at all times constituent parts of the pattern, and to attempt to remove or unravel them would destroy the whole design

JOSEPH JACOBS,
Jewish Contribution to Civilization

Kol Nidre

Kol Nidre — chant of ages,
Chant of Israel, chant of sorrow,
Measuring off the throbbing heart-
    beats
Of a people bowed in anguish,
Crushed by tyrants, thwarted,
    broken,
Wand'ring ever — homeless, weary.
Generations set your motif
Out of trials, hopes and yearnings,
Added each its variations
To your theme and to your cadence.
Diverse lands and diverse periods
Poured their soul into your music.

When we hearken with our hearts
    tuned,
We can hear the lamentations
Through time's corridor resounding;
We can see revealed before us
Heroes, martyrs, saints and scholars,
Loyal, steadfast sons of Israel
Sanctifying God, their Father.

Kol Nidre — chant of ages,
Chant of pain and chant of pathos,
Mingled with your notes of sorrow
Vibrant measures trill and quiver,
Rising to a great crescendo

With the Jew's undying spirit
As he raises 'loft his Torah,
Symbol of his faith and vigor.
Notes of joyous exultation
Crept into your dirgeful music
As with fortitude he cherished
All his fathers held most sacred.
While our hearts beat to your
   rhythm,
Stir us with new consecration
To our fathers' God, to serve Him
With our heart and soul and fervor.

Kol Nidre — chant of ages,
Chant of grief and chant of triumph,
Echoing, this night of mem'ries,
In the ears and heart of Israel,
Once again you draw together
All dispersed and all God's faithful
To return and humbly seek Him —

Suppliants for His grace and pardon.
Faced by grim, appalling forces
In these days of woeful living,
Do we plead before God's mercy
For His strength, His help, His
   guidance.
With your plaintive chant, Kol
   Nidre,
Rise our prayers to heaven ascend-
   ing,
For a surcease of man's sorrows,
For the dawn of peace and freedom,
When all hearts are purged of
   hatred,
Passions, lusts that rend asunder.
Then all men will stand together
To acknowledge God, their Father.

MORRIS SILVERMAN,
High Holiday Prayer Book

When Is A People Chosen ?

A people is chosen not because of any racial superiority ; there is no such thing. All men are the children of Adam ; all are created in God's image — Jew and Gentile, Hebrew, Ethiopian, Philistine or Aramaean. A people is chosen when it has the will to live in a way which would express God's spirit on earth. A people is chosen when it measures its growth by moral and spiritual and not by material and geographic standards. A people is chosen when it is held together by spirit and not by might. A people is chosen when its highest ideal is not to get as much as possible from the world but to contribute of its best to the world, when it endeavors to live as the "Servant of the Lord—a blessing unto the nations." Israel did not always live up to this position. But it is a historic fact that Israel, of all the peoples, always considered itself a candidate for such a position. When one is a candidate one is often elected ; when one is not a candidate, one can hardly be elected.

DAVID ARONSON,
The Jewish Way of Life

Next Year In Jerusalem

The Jew freed the world and the world enslaved the Jew. The Jew blessed the world with his own passion for that human liberty which for thousands of years the world denied the Jew. And still forever the chant of the Jew is, "Next year may we be in Jerusalem." Not that the Jews all together dream of returning to any earthly Jerusalem, but they have not given up their dream of bringing all mankind to the Jerusalem of human liberty for all the inhabitants of all the lands. That dream the Jew refuses to relinquish. A thousand Hitlers cannot rob Israel of a vision un-dimmed by his tears and his blood. The more cruelly the world seeks to shatter his dream, the more deeply the Jew remains under its spell. Whether the world shall yet choose to enter into the heritage of human freedom we do not know. But this Jewish history makes sure —that the Jew will never revise downward his eternal insistence upon every manner of freedom. Blessed they whose soul remains true to the ancient vision of their people ready to suffer and endure and strive that all men may be "in Jerusalem next year."

STEPHEN S. WISE,
As I See It

An Eternal People

The Sages were convinced that Israel could never be broken. They compared the hardihood and persistence of their people to the strength of the sapphire. For when "placed on the anvil and struck with the hammer, the sapphire remains intact, while the anvil is split and the hammer is broken. . . ." Thus is also the fate of the nations that attempt to crush Israel between the anvil and the hammer: the nations are broken and Israel lives on. The history of the Eternal People bears out the trust of the Rabbis that "whenever afflictions are visited upon Israel, the afflictions pass and Israel endures." And so, elaborating on the prophetic parable of Israel as an olive-tree, the Sages offered the homily that "just as the leaves of the olive-tree do not fall off, either in the summer or in the rainy season, so Israel will never disappear —neither in this world nor in the world-to-come."

TRUDE WEISS-ROSMARIN,
Jewish Survival

What Is A Jew?

What is a Jew? This question is not at all so odd as it seems. Let us see what kind of peculiar creature the Jew is, which all the rulers and all nations have together and separately abused and molested, oppressed and persecuted, trampled and butchered, burned and hanged —and in spite of all this is yet alive! What is a Jew, who has never allowed himself to be led astray by all the earthly possessions which his oppressors and persecutors constantly offered him in order that he should change his faith and forsake his own Jewish religion?

The Jew is that sacred being who has brought down from heaven the everlasting fire, and has illumined with it the entire world. He is the religious source, spring, and fountain out of which all the rest of the peoples have drawn their beliefs and their religions.

The Jew is the pioneer of liberty. Even in those olden days, when the people were divided into but two distinct classes, slaves and masters —even so long ago had the law of Moses prohibited the practice of keeping a person in bondage for more than six years.

The Jew is the pioneer of civilization. Ignorance was condemned in olden Palestine more even than it is today in civilized Europe. Moreover, in those wild and barbarous days, when neither life nor the death of any one counted for anything at all,

Rabbi Akiba did not refrain from expressing himself openly against capital punishment, a practice which is recognized today as a highly civilized way of punishment.

The Jew is the emblem of civil and religious toleration. "Love the stranger and the sojourner," Moses commands, "because you have been strangers in the land of Egypt." And this was said in those remote and savage times when the principal ambition of the races and nations consisted in crushing and enslaving one another. As concerns religious toleration, the Jewish faith is not only far from the missionary spirit of converting people of other denominations, but on the contrary the Talmud commands the Rabbis to inform and explain to every one who willingly comes to accept the Jewish religion, all the difficulties involved in its acceptance, and to point out to the would-be proselyte that the righteous of all nations have a share in immortality. Of such a lofty and ideal religious toleration not even the moralists of our present day can boast.

The Jew is the emblem of eternity. He whom neither slaughter nor torture of thousands of years could destroy, he whom neither fire nor sword nor inquisition was able to wipe off from the face of the earth, he who was the first to produce the oracles of God, he who has been for so long the guardian of prophecy, and who transmitted it to the rest of the world — such a nation cannot be destroyed. The Jew is everlasting as is eternity itself.   LEO TOLSTOY

Israel's Distinctive Note

While some fragments of its culture would doubtless survive the death of the Jewish people, its passing would mean the extinction of that indefinable quality men call the Jewish spirit. This spirit cannot be imprisoned in a definition, but it is unmistakably evident in all the diverse manifestations of the Jewish genius. We meet it in the tenderness of Deuteronomy, the passion of Amos, the world perspective of Isaiah, the wise understanding of human nature of Akiba, the intellectuality of Maimonides, the sympathy of the Besht, and even in the inexhaustible wells of Jewish humor which have been the saving grace of a people in agony. In all that is authentically Jewish, one finds the hallmark of the Jewish spirit, a deep compassion for human suffering, a hatred of oppression, an understanding of the sorrows of existence coupled with a brave love of life, an immortal blending of realism and idealism. The quintessence of the Jewish attitude to life is the realization that though strait and narrow is the gate, and charged with punishment the scroll, the gate leads to man's true kingdom, and the scroll ends on a note of consolation and rebirth. In all humility, Jews feel that the world desperately needs these precious qualities of heart and mind, if ever it is to awaken from its nightmare and see the light of a new dawn.

It is reasons such as these, obscurely felt and frequently unexpressed, that help to explain the desperate struggle for Jewish survival. The Jew finds encouragement in the fact that there is no imminent danger of his physical extinction. Increasingly, however, he wants more than the empty husk, and seeks the full richness of Jewish life.

Modern Jews wish to assure the future of their people, because they love life and refuse to die. And also because they seek to avoid the countless tragedies of the storm-tossed, homeless Jews who are torn from their moorings and find no peace and no dignity anywhere. Finally, because they believe that the survival of the Jew and the healthy functioning of his spirit enriches the wisdom and the nobility of civilization. In a word, the Jew has a high sense of the value of his people and its heritage to the world, however he may conceive of both.

In the great symphony of civilization, Israel has its own distinctive note. The Jew today seeks after a rich and meaningful Jewish life, not because he is insensible of his duty to his fellow-men, but rather because he seeks to perform it to the full. Bernard Lazare has said, "Being a Jew is the least difficult way of being truly human." We may go further.

For the Jew, there is virtually no other way.

ROBERT GORDIS,
The Jew Faces a New World

The Jews Had Something To Live For

No doubt, the "alien character" of the Jews, which was partly of their own making and partly forced upon them, contributed to keeping the group distinct and intact. Yet it is no satisfactory explanation of the "puzzle" of Jewish eternity. Negative factors are not sufficiently potent to keep a people alive and vigorously creative for over two thousand years, especially if all tangible vestiges of nationhood are absent. Moreover, the forces of hatred operating against the Jew in the past did not deny him the choice of ceasing to be a Jew. Until the rise of racial anti-Semitism, Jews could stop being Jews by embracing Christianity. The positions of honor some Jewish apostates attained in the medieval Church prove that baptism was indeed the key to equality for Jews who cared to use it. It is patently anachronistic, therefore, to assert that the Jews survived because they could not become extinct in the nations. Until the promulgation of the Nuremberg laws, Jews could stop being Jews — and multitudes did so.

The record proves that the Jews survived not because of negative reasons, but because they had something to live for. The negative factors, chief among them anti-Semitism, should be cited as a reason why many Jews deserted their people rather than as a prop of Jewish survival. Persecution and hatred were, after all, aimed at the "stubborn" Jews only, while those who yielded to persuasion were received with open arms. The Jewish masses made homeless by expulsions, of which the "Expulsion from Spain" was but one, could have kept their homes had they consented to baptism.

The notion that the Jews survived because of the force of hatred which held them together is a delusion of the philosophy of emancipation and assimilation, which argues that favorable conditions and relaxation of the outside pressure tend to wean Jews away from Judaism. But those Jews who wanted to escape from the ghetto did not have to wait for its official abolition; they could walk out triumphantly at the moment they stepped up to the baptismal font. The epidemic of baptism which gripped German Jewry in the first half of the nineteenth century was not a reaction to anti-Semitism ; it was not an escape from a burden. It was little more than a nonchalant gesture. There is an answer to the question why the children and grandchildren of the Jewish martyrs deserted their people and its faith without compunction : Ignorance of Judaism and the concomitants thereof — the loss of a Jewish *raison d'etre* and of the positive values of Jewish life, had made the emancipation-intoxicated and assimilation - dedicated Jews an easy prey for the negative forces tearing them away from their people.

It is not infrequently argued that conditions most favorable to the prosperity of the individual Jew are most injurious to the survival of the Jews as a religious community and as a nation. Here, too, confused thinking leads to mistaking the effect for the cause. Jewish history proves that the creative periods of Jewish self-assertion were times free from persecution. The Bible was created by a free people, living on its own soil. The Talmud and the Midrashim originated in a setting of relative freedom and toleration, only their codifications were hastened by the fear of impending disaster. Rashi's commentaries were written in a setting of freedom and tolerance, before the Crusaders made life unbearable for the Jews of the Franco-German territory. During the " Golden Age of Hebrew Literature " in Spain, the Jews enjoyed liberty and security in the Islam-dominated parts.

Virtually all the great Jewish classics, the works which in their sum total represent the Jewish heritage, originated in times of Jewish prosperity and freedom from persecution and oppression.

Jewish history and literature prove convincingly that it was for positive reasons that the Jews survived the most trying hardships. To aver that they survived because they were bitterly persecuted is about as logical as to state that Mr. X survived a severe illness because of the added complication of double-pneumonia. If Mr. X recovered from his sickness, aggravated by pneumonia, it was doubtless due to his physical fitness and the skill of his physician. Analogously, the Jews survived because of their almost miraculous fitness and their unique spiritual stamina.

Again, and over again, it must be stressed that the Jews survived because they had something to live for : the fostering and propagation of the national religious cultural heritage.

TRUDE WEISS-ROSMARIN,
Jewish Survival

In defeat we are victorious ; in death we are reborn.

SHOLOM ASCH,
Tales of My People

The Vindication Of Judaism

In all the pains which Israel has had to endure there is also contained some elevating element. Judaism has to suffer numerous attacks almost every day, new and yet old ; but do these attacks not betray something of a touching defence, a eulogy before the seat of the judge of truth ? For what have been for the most part the weapons used in the fight against Judaism in ancient or in modern times ? Some employed weapons of oppression, the deprivation of rights, and deeds of violence, others used the tools of misjudgement, of misrepresentation, and of falsehood. There is hardly an outrage which, committed against Judaism, did not appear as sovereign right ; hardly an invention which, planned against Judaism, was not made to assume the appearance of reality, hardly a halftruth which, used in judgement against Judaism, was not regarded as entire truth. How small must be the confidence of those who almost invariably employ such means, and what importance, what right, must that possess against which such weapons, almost exclusively, are employed !

The history of the nations contains the vindication of Judaism. Whereever truth was victorious, and justice was permitted to abide, Judaism found welfare, understanding and acknowledgment. Whereever a feeling for humanity and for righteousness began to stir, a Jewish community was able to breathe in peace. The degradation of the Jews was never an isolated phenomenon, but only one incident, though the saddest, in a general enslavement. In the same way, their emancipation has everywhere been only a part, though a very significant part, of a liberation of an entire people. Whether they willed it or not, the rulers, statesmen and nations who labored for true civilization were the defenders and benefactors of the Jews. Consciously or unconsciously, every one who stood for the progress of morality has stood up for them. If the Jews demand security for Judaism and its unrestricted existence, they need only ask for truth and straightforwardness in the land. There is no better vindication. To quote Ranke : " The greatest good fortune which can happen to any men is to defend the common cause in their own cause."

This may be some consolation in the fact of sad occurrences, and it brings new justification to Jewish hopes in the future. When the Jews are concerned, it is not the exclusive concern of the Jews. Their claims are the claims of conscience, of the commandment. They do not ask that they should be honored, but only that right and truth should be honored. They do not desire to be treated with special benevolence, but only that others should learn to know them, to know what they are, and why. Judaism is open to all ; so, too, are the religious treasures which it possesses, the religious goal which is its trust ; he who wishes to see is able to see. Jews acknowledge the treasures possessed by other religions, especially by those sprung from the Jewish midst and out of the Jewish spirit. He who holds convictions, respects convictions. Filled with reverence for the task which it contains, the Jews realize what their religion really means and is. They know that there can be applied to it the words of one of the old Jewish sages : " The beginning bears witness to the end, and the end will at long last bear witness to the beginning."

LEO BAECK,
The Essence of Judaism

A Warning To Would-Be Oppressors

The preservation of the Jews is really one of the most signal and illustrious acts of divine Providence. . . .

The Jews can go up higher than any other nation, they can even deduce their pedigree from the beginning of the world. They may not know from what particular tribe or family they are descended, but they know certainly that they all sprung from the stock of Abraham. And yet the contempt with which they have been treated and the hardships which they have undergone in almost all countries, should, one would think, have made them desirous to forget or renounce that original ; but they profess it, they glory in it : and after so many wars, massacres, and persecutions, they still subsist, they still are very numerous : and what but a supernatural power could have preserved them in such a manner as none other nation upon earth hath been preserved ?

Nor is the providence of God less remarkable in the destruction of their enemies, than in their preservation. . . . We see that the great empires, which in their turns subdued and oppressed the people of God, are all come to ruin ; because though they executed the purposes of God, yet that was more than they understood ; all that they intended was to satiate their own pride and ambition, their own cruelty and revenge. And if such hath been the fatal end of the enemies and oppressors of the Jews, let it serve as a warning to all those, who at any time or upon any occasion are for raising a clamor and persecution against them.

THOMAS NEWTON,
Dissertations on the Prophecies

The Acme Of National Heroism

Almost all peoples know how to die heroically in a crisis. But to resist step by step over a period of two hundred years, as the Jews did, without turning to the extreme of revolt, to resist now violence, now seduction, to let themselves neither be crushed by the threats of Caligula nor be tempted by the splendor of Herod, who sought to introduce into Judea the temples, circuses and arts of Greece, to have before their eyes the example of a whole world yielding, and yet themselves not yielding, that is the acme of national heroism !

SAMUEL USTAZADE SILVESTRE DE SACY,
Variétés Littéraires, Morale et Historiques

Going, Going . . .

As the modern world opens, Jewry and Judaism are still very much on the scene. A fascinating historical drama is revealed. The auctioneer is Time, the buyer, Oblivion. The peoples come up on the block, one after another, the hammer is lifted, the established formula is intoned : " Going ! Going ! Gone ! " But there is one people that appears on the block regularly, and over it the words " Going ! Going ! " have been repeated again and again : again and again it has looked like a sale — but the third word has never been pronounced over it.

MAURICE SAMUEL,
The Professor and The Fossil

17

I Shall Not Die

Israel has a divine and prophetic role to play in the concert of nations and in the progress of united humanity toward an era of universal justice and peace. The millennial vision abides eternally in the Torah and illumines the hope of all its children.

ABRAHAM A. NEUMAN,
Landmarks and Goals

And marked will be their seed among the nations and their offspring among the peoples. Everyone that will see them will point to them as a community blessed by the Lord.

Isaiah 61 : 9

Barring some unforeseen catastrophe that may overtake the whole human race, the Jew is here to stay.

ROBERT GORDIS,
Judaism For The Modern Age

The Promise Of Our Religious Genius

The three religious parties, Orthodox, Conservative, and Reform, constitute what has been felicitously called catholic Judaism. Wide as are some of their differences in belief and practice they are not separatist sects but differing members of one religion. They are united not only by kinship and history and the bonds of a common destiny but also by a deep abiding faith in religious principles which they hold to be immortal and which they cherish for the happiness of humanity.

Common to them all is the belief that Israel has a divine and prophetic role to play in the concert of nations and in the progress of united humanity toward an era of universal justice and peace. The millennial vision abides eternally in the Torah and illumines the hope of all its children. The creative religious genius which has produced the world's greatest Prophets and has given the greater part of mankind its religion and ethics still holds great promise for endless generations to come who will build the foundations of "a new heaven and a new earth." Whatever interpretations a religious party or individual may give to this Jewish Messianic faith, its essence is spiritually alive with optimistic faith in God and the future of mankind. Therein lies the strength and the unity of Judaism.

ABRAHAM A. NEUMAN,
Landmarks and Goals

What We Want From Judaism

1 We want Judaism to help us to overcome temptation, doubt and discouragement.

2 We want Judaism to imbue us with a sense of responsibility for the righteous use of the blessings wherewith God endows us.

3 We want the Jew so to be trusted that his yea will be taken as yea, and his nay as nay.

4 We want to learn how to utilize our leisure to best advantage physically, intellectually and spiritually.

5 We want the Jewish home to live up to its traditional standards of virtue and piety.

6 We want the Jewish upbringing of our children to further their moral and spiritual growth and to enable them to accept with joy their heritage as Jews.

7 We want the synagogue to enable us to worship God in sincerity and truth.

8 We want our religious traditions to be interpreted in terms of understandable experience and to be made relevant to our present-day needs.

9   We want Judaism to find rich, manifold, and ever new expression in philosophy, in letters, and in the arts.

10 We want all forms of Jewish organization to make for spiritual purpose and ethical endeavor.

11 We want the unity of Israel throughout the world to be fostered through mutual help in time of need, and through cooperation in the furtherance of Judaism at all times.

12 We want Judaism to function as a potent influence for justice, freedom and peace in the life of men and nations.

Reconstructionist Prayer-book

Brilliant With Light

In the Ryks Museum in Amsterdam the Dutch people treasure the masterpiece of Rembrandt called, incorrectly the Night Watch. Rembrandt painted this picture three centuries ago. It was placed in the great hall of the tavern in which the Arms Guild met, and in time came to be covered with smoke and soot. The colors grew so dark and somber that those who gazed upon the canvas thought it portrayed the guard marching out at night to meet the enemy. Then someone cleansed the canvas and restored it to its original colors. Now we see it is not a picture of the night but a picture of the day, filled with glorious hues and flooded with sunlight and glowing with noontide warmth and beauty—a picture reborn, the pride of Holland and one of the chief glories of the world of art.

We have allowed too many of our great ideals and visions to be covered with the smoke and grime of this Iron Age. We mistake them for pictures of darkness and despair when in reality they are brilliant with light and glorious with richness and power.

COMMISSION ON SOCIAL JUSTICE, *Central Conference of American Rabbis,* 1934

Vision For Our Day

I see in Palestine a Jewish Commonwealth where the homeless Jews of the world have found rest, where the Jewish spirit has been reborn, whence flow to the dispersion inspiration and the stuffs on which it feeds.

I see the Jewries of the world, each at ease and firmly rooted in the land of its residence, each unswervingly devoted to the polity and culture of that land and at the same time the bearer and transmitter of a living Hebraism, significant to itself, its environment and the world.

Most specifically, I see an American Jewry, emancipated along with all other Americans from the restraints of prejudice, secure against violence, free to fulfill itself without hindrance.

An American Jewry alight with a religious faith hallowed by antiquity and responsive to the mystery of all things, yet sanctioned by the best in modern thought and clean with reasonableness.

An American Jewry standing four square by Judaism's great moral ideals, sharpening them into the keenest contemporaneousness, applying them boldly, imaginatively — so that the name Jew is a synonym for the practice and advocacy of justice, compassion, freedom and peace.

An American Jewry literate in both its heritages, the American and the Hebraic, creative in both, cross-blending and fertilizing the two until all devotion to one shall connote blessing for the other as well.

An American Jewry whose household is set in order.

An American Jewry which, having labored that Zion be rebuilt, now draws waters in joy from the fountainhead of the Jewish spirit.

I see in sum a Jewry which in its inner life has made of Judaism what it is intended to be, what it is now in some measure, and what it can become in infinitely greater degree — that is to say, a source of blessing.

And I see all this set in a new, brave and free world which Jews, together with all men of good will, have helped to set free, laboring as individuals but also as Jews, as members of a fellowship consecrated from the womb to the ideal of a new, brave and free world. . . .

Shall not Jewish dreams and ideals, hands and hearts, blood and anguish have contributed to this end so long desired and prayed for ? Will it then be a little thing — will it not rather be accounted a very great thing — to have played a part, not the largest perhaps but not the meanest either, in the building of the Kingdom of God on earth ?

MILTON STEINBERG,
A Partisan Guide to the Jewish Problem

Marked Will Be Their Seed

He who feels the pulse of American Jewish life can detect . . . the beginnings of a Jewish renaissance, the budding forth of a new spirit. The Jews of America, as represented in their noblest and best . . . are fully alive to the future of their country as a center of Jewish culture. They build not only hospitals and infirmaries, but also libraries ; not only tradesmen and laborers, but also scholars and writers. Everywhere we perceive the evidence of a new life.

To be sure, we are only at the beginning. Gigantic and complicated tasks confront us in the future. The enormous stores of latent Jewish energy that are formlessly piled up in this country will have to be transformed into living power. The dead capital which we constantly draw from the Ghetto will have to be made into a working capital to produce new values. We first of all have to lay our foundation : to rescue the Jewish education of our future generations from the chaos in which it is now entangled. But we are on the right road. . . . The American Jews will work and live for a Judaism which will encompass all phases of Jewish life and thought ; which will not be a faint sickly hot-house plant, but as it was in the days of old, " a tree of life for those who hold it fast, bestowing happiness on those who cling to it. . . ."

When we try to penetrate the mist that encircles the horizon of the present, a vision unfolds itself before our mind's eye, presenting a picture of the future American Israel. We perceive a community great in numbers, mighty in power, enjoying life, liberty and the pursuit of happiness : true life, not mere breathing space ; full liberty, not mere elbow room ; real happiness, not that of pasture beasts ; actively participating in the civic, social and economic progress of the country,

fully sharing and increasing its spiritual possessions and acquisitions, doubling its joys, halving its sorrows ; yet deeply rooted in the soil of Judaism, clinging to its past, working for its future, true to its traditions, faithful to its aspirations, one in sentiment with their brethren wherever they are, attached to the land of their fathers as the cradle and resting place of the Jewish spirit ; men with straight backs and raised heads, with big hearts and strong minds, with no conviction crippled, with no emotion stifled, with souls harmoniously developed, self-centred and self-reliant ; receiving and resisting, not yielding like wax to every impress from the outside, but blending the best they possess with the best they encounter; not a horde of individuals, but a set of individualities, adding a new note to the richness of American life, leading a new current into the stream of American civilization ; not a formless crowd of taxpayers and voters, but a sharply marked community, distinct and distinguished, trusted for its loyalty, respected for its dignity, esteemed for its traditions, valued for its aspirations, a community such as the Prophet of the Exile saw it in his vision : " And marked will be their seed among the nations, and their offspring among the peoples. Everyone that will see them will point to them as a community blessed by the Lord."

ISRAEL FRIEDLANDER,
Past and Present

The Character Of Jewish Optimism
I Shall Not Die But Live

The memory of ancient disasters, stubbornly foiled by our ancestors, will bring the past generations to our aid. We, the Jews, have never believed that Utopia waits at the next turning of the road. Our Prophets did not envisage the perfection of society as the achievement of one day. They saw perfection at the end of days, after many cycles of progress and retrogression. It will come, but only from an accumulation of effort, from the sustained labor of the will. It will come not as a result of accident or miracle but through the travail of mankind. It is this profound conviction that society can become humane; it is this grand determination to make it humane that have made the Jews indestructible. They never spoke of *Untergang* but left that to the triumphant peoples. The Jew said, "I shall not die but I shall live." At the moment of the blackest defeat in our history, when the Temple was reduced to ashes, Jerusalem sacked, our sages and our young driven naked and barefoot along the stony road to Babylon, Jeremiah arose to preach hope: "Yet again will I build thee up and thou shalt be built. . . . Yet again shall thou adorn thine timbrels, and go forth in the dances of those that make merry. . . . He that scattereth Israel will gather him and keep him as a shepherd his flock."

The spirit which burned in him, burns in us.

SOLOMON GOLDMAN,
Undefeated

Reconstructing Jewish Life

The reconstruction of Jewish life and thought will thus have to consist in the pursuit of the following objectives:

1. The rebuilding Eretz Yisrael as the creative center of Judaism.
2. The creation of an adequate social structure for democratic Jewish communal life in the Diaspora.
3. The redirection of Jewish education to conform with the conception of Judaism as a religious civilization.
4. The revitalization of Jewish religion.
5. The stimulation of Jewish cultural creativity in literature and the arts.
6. The participation of Jewry in social movements that seek ampler freedom, stricter justice and better cooperation among men and nations.

MORDECAI M. KAPLAN,
The Future of the American Jew

Building For Tomorrow

The voluntary, organic Jewish community will not emerge tomorrow or the day after. The organizational problems are at present insuperable. But there is value in setting forth the fundamental *ten principles* upon which it will ultimately be built :

1. The unity of Israel as a people the world over, expressing itself in a common religious and cultural tradition.

2. The centrality of the Jewish religion as the heart of Jewish expression and of Jewish brotherhood.

3. The role of the land of Israel as offering not only a secure home for the large numbers of oppressed Jews in the world today, but also an all-Jewish environment to further Jewish creativity and thus enrich the lives of all Jews everywhere.

4. The survival of American Jewry as a vital and active element in the Jewish people, which will be able to make its creative contribution to Jewish life and thought.

5. Simultaneously, the position of American Jewry as an integral part or element of the American people, since group loyalties, morally conceived and culturally expressed, are not mutually exclusive.

6. The duty and destiny of the state of Israel, and of world Israel, as yet incompletely realized, to advance the messianic ideals of the One God and of the One Humanity, embodied in a world order of social justice, individual and group freedom, and universal peace.

7. The right of all Jews, affirmed by Jewish tradition, to fellowship in Israel, however far removed they may be at present from an acceptance of an affirmative attitude toward Jewish tradition.

8. The welcoming of participation, in one or another phase of Jewish life, by such individuals and groups as are unable to give their assent to Jewish religious practices and ideals, with the recognition of the proper role of their activities in the over all pattern of organic Jewish life.

9. The establishment of cooperative relations, wherever possible, between the organic Jewish community as here envisaged, and those elements of the Jewish people remaining outside of its scope.

10. The recognition that Jewish education, both for children and for adults, conceived in the broadest terms and based on the three pillars of faith, culture, and people, is the central concern and the basic enterprise of the organic Jewish community.

ROBERT GORDIS,
Judaism for the Modern Age

Eternal People

Though life's relentless waves will
flow
O'er many kingdoms blotted out
below,
The long eternity of future years
Will see a people that was nursed on
tears

Alive and strong; its ancient spirit
bright
Lighting the dark with an eternal
light.

MORDECAI ZEVI MANEH,
Eternal People

Hallmarks Of Jewish Maturity

We are the largest, the richest, the freest, the most influential secularly the most schooled Jewish community in history. We who stood with Moses at Mount Sinai and entered into an everlasting covenant with our God, also fought at Valley Forge, at Gettysburg, at Pearl Harbor. On the Liberty Bell that tolled the glad tidings of the birth of a new nation "conceived in liberty and dedicated to the proposition that all men are created free and equal," is the master text from *our* Bible; on the pedestal of the Statue of Liberty is a dedication written by one of our daughters. Surely, after resisting every tyrant through all these millennia since Moses, in a manner that has drawn the universal admiration of civilized men, and after three hundred years of mingling our prayers, our hopes, our sweat, our tears, our blood with the rest of the pilgrims and refugees that compose our American nation, we should — at this late date — be a mature American Jewry.

Mature Jewish people, living in freedom, will not exhaust themselves in self-doubt: *who* are we? *what* are we? *why* are we?

Phrasing this self-doubt in brilliant intellectual terms and the latest jargon does not invest it with maturity. Too many of our books and journals and lecture platforms are nothing more than intellectual bowling alleys; one sets up the pins, the other knocks them down. The brilliant are they who leave nothing standing.

Mature Jewish people, living in freedom, boasting of their equality, will not be fearful, leaping from one hole of concealment to another like scared rabbits, loudly proclaiming the brave American principle of the right to differ and at the same time, in practice, expunging every trace of difference from their thinking and their living. Mature, free men, worthy of their freedom, live in integrity of heart and mind and fear not.

Mature Jewish people, living in

freedom, will not formulate escape philosophies and cover their nakedness with a patch work of shibboleths; perverting noble — even sacred—words: Jews by *faith* and faith only, and reducing faith to a propaganda term cranked out on mimeograph machines, with no personal devotion, no *Mitzvot*, no *Kavanah*; or proclaiming *integration*, but meaning assimilation, or conformity. As Jews and as Americans we are the children of dissenters, not of conformists.

Mature Jewish people, enjoying full rights and liberties, bountiful opportunities such as no Jewish generation ever enjoyed, with their sons and daughters in the highest councils of the nation, free to leave this country at will, free to migrate to Israel at will, will not whine about being in *galuth* to second class citizens. . . .

Mature Jewish people will not develop high blood pressure over trends, tendencies, percentages of belief or disbelief in religious ceremonials; neither will they develop hardening of their spiritual arteries and freeze the yearnings, vagaries, restlessness of their adolescent years into a " classic" pattern. They will not spin like the weather vane with every breeze of public opinion. Rather, they will be like the needle in the compass, steady, whatever winds may blow sheaves of statistics in their faces, and move forward.

Once upon a time there were two brothers, both religious leaders of their people. One watched the latest trends, constantly taking the pulse of the people; the other communed with his God. Aaron gave us a golden calf: Moses, Ten Commandments.

Mature Jewish people will labor in uprightness, worship in sincerity, educate their children in honorable self - esteem, condition themselves and their children to appreciate the great reserves of heart and mind in the multitudes about us, and, like their fathers, gladly accept the yoke of the Kingdom of Heaven, praying and working for the day when the Kingdom of arrogance shall have passed away from the earth.

BERYL D. COHON,
Sermon, 1953

The Vision Of The Future

Jewish ethics is inspired with a great optimism. It is not optimistic in the sense that it proclaims that everything that is is good ; but in the sense that Browning makes Rabbi ben Ezra say : " Grow old along with me, the best is yet to be." The Jew's vision embraced a glorious future for the whole human race. Jewish ethics is pure idealism, not only in motive, but in hope. That is what is meant by the Jew's Messianic hope.

The Jew has never admitted that his ideals have as yet been completely realized by any man or by any society. He is in the world to witness to his own high ethical and spiritual ideals. The refrain of Jewish history and Jewish aspiration is that the Messianic age is still to come. Revere, as the Jew does, the past, he does not glorify it. He roots in it, but he spreads out, as a good, old strong, and beautiful tree must do, towards the sky. He looks to the rising sun of the future and beholds it, with healing on its wings, shining for all humanity. When man shall have completely learned the law of life, in justice and love, that was to come out of Zion, and shall have realized the ideal of the word as it was revealed in Jerusalem, indeed, when men and nations shall come to be taught of the Eternal so as to learn of His ways, then will be made manifest the effect of perfect righteousness. Then will swords be beaten into plough-shares and spears into pruning hooks, men will learn war no more, there will be peace. According to Jewish teaching, the culture of humanity will only then be complete and perfect, when the law of righteousness, to use the words of Jeremiah, comes to be written in human hearts, when men follow it instinctively, when as do the creative artists in their work, they carry out in their lives, with joy, what in thought they recognize as law and duty. Then will God's Kingdom be established. He will be acknowledged as One, with one united humanity worshipping Him and realizing the perfect ethical life, in the name of Him who said, "For I am the Lord, Who doth exercise mercy, justice and righteousness in the earth, for in these things I delight."

SAMUEL SCHULMAN,
Jewish Ethics

A Great Era Lies Before Us

Little could the early Jewish settlers in the colonial period or the Jewish patriots who fought in the War of Independence realize the ultimate world significance of the Judaism which they planted on this American continent. Nor was there a deeper appreciation of the destiny of American Judaism among the tens and hundreds of thousands that came to this country with increas-ing tempo in the nineteenth and twentieth centuries. Only now in the great tragedy that has befallen the world and the Jews can we trace the outline drawn by the invisible hand that fashioned the destiny of our great community. What the enemy destroyed over there we rebuild tenfold here. The agony and grief of our martyred brethren will not crush our faith but steel our determination to build a greater, richer and nobler Judaism in this land.

A flaming fire burns over the graves of our tortured martyrs. The bodies may be dead in the sodden earth but their souls hover over the soil saturated with their holy blood. Their souls will find no peace until their spirits find new life in the hearts of their living brethren. Even now one can hear these invisible spirits move in two columns. One is being wafted over the hills of Palestine in the dreams and hopes of the builders of Zion. Another column is advancing upon us in America to vivify and vitalize the greatest Jewry in the history of the Diaspora.

A great era lies before us. We are indeed on the eve of a mighty Jewish destiny. The rhythm of Jewish history is beating with irresistible force.

ABRAHAM A. NEUMAN,
Landmarks and Goals

I Shall Not Forsake Thee

Our ultimate purpose is to raise a generation of Jews in America whose " old men shall continue to see visions and whose young men will dream dreams." These dreams will give them no rest and may even cause them " to tremble and fear," as Jacob did, because of their own inadequacies and their realization of the awe-inspiring dimensions of the enterprise. But those who persevere in the task will, like Father Jacob, hear the reassuring divine promise, " I shall not forsake thee until I shall have fulfilled all that I promised unto thee." In that promise we shall never lose faith.

SIMON GREENBERG

Convinced Of The Ultimate Triumph

Eager to cooperate in every movement for the prevention of war, the real feeling of the Jew is, as it has always been, that for a permanent peace the paramount need is justice. As in the northern saga, the mighty ash tree, *Ygdrasill*, supports the whole universe, its roots extending into the dwelling of the gods, the abode of the giants, and into the regions of darkness and coldness, the Jew felt and still feels that only the tree of righteousness supports the whole universe, and that its roots must extend into all human relations, religious, social, and economic. He realizes that, as at the roots of the tree *Ygdrasill*, at its roots too the forces of darkness and selfishness are gnawing perpetually.

But reaching into the deepest depth of the human heart, this tree cannot be uprooted.

Convinced of the ultimate triumph of right, the Jew confidently looks forward to the Messianic age when the sun of righteousness will rise with healing in its wings and that healing will be Universal Peace.

JOSEPH S. KORNFELD,
Judaism and International Peace

I Do Not Know What Despair Is

I as a Jew do not know what despair is. Despair means utter futility, being utterly lost. I will never be lost. I know where I came from, I know where I am going. I am the son of Abraham. Despite all my imperfections, deficiencies, faults and sins, I remain a part of that Covenant that God made with Abraham ; we are going toward the Kingship of God and the Messianic era. This is the preciousness of being a Jew.

ABRAHAM J. HESCHEL,
Address

We Are The Children Of Destiny

Look back upon the panoramic view of Jewish history and behold our American community of over five million Jews. What does this mean to you ? Does it not mean that the time has come when American Jewry must take up the banner, even as every great Jewry did in former days ? Is not the hand of God upon us ? I am using the theological term very realistically. Is it not we who are now summoned in the roll call of Jewish destiny ? What other sense would this great phenomenon of American Jewry make ? Are we merely an accidental conglomeration of human beings who have been brought together without plan or design, by forces of blind historic impact, like sand that is scattered by the wind and shifted aimlessly from place to place ?

Ponder upon this amazing phenomenon of American Jewry and you will suddenly be liberated from the fears that beset and bewitch so many among us. You will then not be fearful or apologetic about our people in America. I, for one, do not feel that it is necessary for us to engage in counter - anti - Semitic polemics to show the world how good we are or, on the other hand, that we are not as bad as they think we are. I am willing without any apologia to assert and to defend the proposition that we are an honorable folk ; that we do our part fully ; that our people have played an important role in America ; that we have repaid America to the full for everything that America has given us in such rich abundance.

I am fully confident that the honor of our family life will stand up well against that of any other social group, measured by any standard. I believe that our sons and daughters who have been admitted to American colleges have done well by the opportunities afforded them. Our judges, lawyers, physicians, journalists, social workers, merchants, industrialists and philanthropists have, on the whole, made a very good record. But I sometimes lie awake at night and think and wonder : did it really require the extraordinary record of three thousand years of history, during which our community produced Prophets, poets, singers, psalmists, men of wisdom, martyrs, philosophers, ethical teachers, so that three thousand years later, out of them might be born a generation that would lead simple, decent, good lives — but uninspired by any great vision of destiny, unresponsive to any overtones of their collective life ?

There is a poetic concept in Jewish lore that on the Sabbath every person who observes the holiness of the day is granted an over-soul. Surely there must be such an over-soul of the Jewish people in that which alone can justify and validate our existence as a collective entity. This is a thread that makes our Jewish existence rational. We are children of destiny. We have been brought to this country of freedom and opportunity, and we have been vouchsafed riches, influence and power, not merely to accumulate personal fortunes ; nor even solely to help sustain our people in other lands with the surpluses that we have accumulated. American Jews have a higher role to play in the drama of Jewish history. How shall we determine that role ? As Jews always did : through their religion and their writings. Look at Jewish literature ; read its poetry ; study its philosophy, its ethical writings. These have been the instruments through which Jews made their contributions to civilisation. These have been the means through which they promoted their own spiritual development and enriched the nations of the world. By these high standards American Judaism is now to be counted, weighed and measured.

What will be the verdict of history ? We need not be apologetic about the past nor fearful of the future. We are a young community in America. Our history as a community of over a million souls is not older than half a century. In this short period, we have done much, but our accomplishments must be interpreted only as a promise for the future. And this future will be molded and recorded in the writings of our learned scholars ; above all, in the original creations of thought and spirit which American Jewry will add to the content of Judaism and the religion of mankind.

ABRAHAM A. NEUMAN,
Landmarks and Goals

My Utopia On Earth

The Western world has created two great epics of the next world — *The Divine Comedy* and *Paradise Lost*. Both Dante and Milton in describing Heaven slipped into the common error which I am discussing. Each of them portrayed it as a place where there are no problems, where existence is effortless. The result is that life in Heaven as they picture it is so much a bore that Hell seems inviting by contrast. Even the poets were bored with their notions of Heaven, otherwise why should both of them have written so much better verse in describing Hell ? For the fact is that Dante's *Inferno* is as literature better than his *Paradiso*, and Milton's *Paradise Lost* far outstrips his *Paradise Regained*.

The ancient rabbis may have been as naïve as Dante and Milton in their imaginings of the next world, but they were much wiser about human nature. They knew men too well to suppose that they would be happy doing nothing and being problem free.

No, in their description of eternal bliss, the souls of the blessed are described as being very busy, and as having plenty of problems. They contemplate and seek to compre-

hend the infinite mystery of God's being. They study Torah in adult classes. They perform the *Mitzvot* — at least the more spiritual *Mitzvot*. And they take an active interest in the still unfinished career of man on earth, in his struggle for goodness and truth.

This, say the rabbis, is really Heaven ; not to be without problems but to have all one's problems positive, inherently worth while, ends in themselves.

It is in this spirit, too, that I envisage my utopia on earth. When I look into the human future I see scientists still struggling with problems, but they are the problems of wresting the truth from nature, not of wasting time fighting for freedom of the intellect. I see artists still working day and night at their canvases and marble, but to incarnate their vision of beauty, not to keep the wolves from their doors. I see all men laboring not to ward off hunger, disease, and enslavement, but for self-fulfillment and mutual aid. I see each religion and culture exerting its fullest energies but for the purpose not of fighting off the assault of other faiths and traditions but so as to make the most of its own resources for its own sake and that of the world. I see each polity, each economy hard at work but with one problem only — to give to each person the maximum of freedom, the most generous access to the good things of living. I see each national state very very busy not in defending itself against its neighbors but in doing its best for its citizens and its sister national states.

This to me will be heaven on earth. This is the direction in which all of us must move — toward a Sabbath of Sabbaths which like this day is not problem free but which rather frees us for those problems which are inherently affirmative and precious, the problems in which life finds meaning.

MILTON STEINBERG,
A Believing Jew

AUTHOR INDEX